The Pluriverse of Human

The impasse currently affecting human rights as a language used to express struggles for dignity is, to a large extent, a reflection of the epistemological and political exhaustion which blights the global North. Since the global hegemony of human rights as a language for human dignity is nowadays incontrovertible, the question of whether it can be used in a counter-hegemonic sense remains open. Inspired by struggles from all corners of the world that reveal the potential but, above all, the limitations of human rights, this book offers a highly conditional response. The prevailing notion of human rights today, as the hegemonic language of human dignity, can only be resignified on the basis of answers to simple questions: why does so much unjust human suffering exist that is not considered a violation of human rights? Do other languages of human dignity exist in the world? Are these other languages compatible with the language of human rights? Obviously, we can only find satisfactory answers to these questions if we are able to envisage a radical transformation of what is nowadays known as human rights. Herein lies the challenge posed by the Epistemologies of the South: reconciling human rights with the different languages and forms of knowledge born out of struggles for human dignity.

Boaventura de Sousa Santos is Emeritus Professor of Sociology at the University of Coimbra (Portugal), and Distinguished Legal Scholar at the University of Wisconsin-Madison (USA). He has written extensively on globalization, sociology of law and the state, epistemology and social movements. One of his most recent publications *The End of the Cognitive Empire: The Coming of Age of Epistemologies of the South* (2018).

Bruno Sena Martins is a senior researcher at the Centre for Social Studies, University of Coimbra and co-coordinator of the Doctoral Program *Human Rights in Contemporary Societies*. He was Vice-President of CES/UC Scientific Board and Co-coordinator of the Democracy, Citizenship and Law Research Group (DECIDe). His research interests include racism, disability, human rights and colonialism.

Epistemologies of the South

The global North has faced growing difficulty in making sense of the broad changes sweeping the world, from the financialization and neo-liberalization of the world economy to the growth of inequality on an unknown scale in its persistence, extension and diversification of segregation, discrimination and violence. Uneasiness has been growing within the social sciences at the feeling of inadequacy and even irrelevance of current work and established theory in its attempt to get to grips with such a world.

The main idea underlying this series is that the experience of the world is much broader than the Eurocentric understanding, and what is known as the global South has been for centuries—and remains in contemporary times—an inexhaustible source of experiences, knowledges, political and social innovations, and celebrations of difference. Challenging the canonical and Eurocentric epistemological tradition, including the social sciences and humanities themselves, this series innovates through the encounter and dialogue with other epistemologies that have historically emerged in the South.

Series Editor: **Boaventura de Sousa Santos**, University of Coimbra (Portugal)

Epistemologies of the South
Justice Against Epistemicide
Boaventura de Sousa Santos

Knowledges Born in the Struggle
Constructing the Epistemologies of the Global South
Edited by Boaventura de Sousa Santos and Maria Paula Meneses

Demodiversity
Towards Post-Abyssal Democracies
Edited by Boaventura de Sousa Santos and Maria Paula Meneses

The Pluriverse of Human Rights
The Diversity of Struggles for Dignity
Edited by Boaventura de Sousa Santos and Bruno Sena Martins

The Pluriverse of Human Rights

The Diversity of Struggles for Dignity

Edited by Boaventura de Sousa Santos
and Bruno Sena Martins

Routledge
Taylor & Francis Group

NEW YORK AND LONDON

First published 2021
by Routledge
52 Vanderbilt Avenue, New York, NY 10017

and by Routledge
2 Park Square, Milton Park, Abingdon, Oxon, OX14 4RN

Routledge is an imprint of the Taylor & Francis Group, an informa business

© 2021 Taylor & Francis

The right of Boaventura de Sousa Santos and Bruno Sena Martins to be identified as the authors of the editorial material, and of the authors for their individual chapters, has been asserted in accordance with sections 77 and 78 of the Copyright, Designs and Patents Act 1988.

Library of Congress Cataloging-in-Publication Data
Names: Santos, Boaventura de Sousa, editor. |
Martins, Bruno Sena, editor.
Title: The pluriverse of human rights: the diversity of struggles for dignity/edited by Boaventura de Sousa Santos and Bruno Sena Martins.
Description: New York, NY: Routledge, 2021. |
Series: Epistemologies of the south
Identifiers: LCCN 2020055587 | ISBN 9781032012216 (hbk) |
ISBN 9781032012223 (pbk) | ISBN 9781003177722 (ebk)
Subjects: LCSH: Human rights. | Dignity. | Social change.
Classification: LCC JC571 .P575 2021 | DDC 323–dc23
LC record available at https://lccn.loc.gov/2020055587

ISBN: 978-1-032-01222-3 (hbk)
ISBN: 978-1-032-01221-6 (pbk)
ISBN: 978-1-003-17772-2 (ebk)

Typeset in Bembo
by Deanta Global Publishing Services, Chennai, India

Contents

Contributors

Khalid Anis Ansari is Senior Assistant Professor (Sociology) and Director of Dr. Ambedkar Centre for Exclusion Studies & Transformative Action (ACESTA) at Glocal University, India. He broadly works in the field of social and cultural theory and takes keen interest in both grassroots organizing and scholarly interventions to publicize the history of resistance movements, particularly the socio-political aspirations of subordinated caste Pasmanda Muslims. He was awarded the HIVOS PhD Fellowship—Pluralism Knowledge Programme (2010–2013) for his doctoral work on caste movements among Indian Muslims with the University of Humanistic Studies (UvH), Utrecht, the Netherlands.

Marta Araújo holds a PhD from the University of London (2003). She is Principal Researcher at the Centre for Social Studies (CES) since 2005, where she lectures in the PhD Programmes "Democracy in the 21st Century" and "Human Rights in Contemporary Societies". She is Guest Lecturer in the Black Europe Summer School (International Institute for Research and Education, Amsterdam). She has published internationally, and currently is a member of the Editorial Board of publications on sociology, race and education, in Brazil, Britain, Portugal and the United States. Her research interests centre on the (re)production and challenging of racism and Eurocentrism, with a particular interest in education.

Pratiksha Baxi is Associate Professor at the Centre for the Study of Law and Governance, Jawaharlal Nehru University, New Delhi, holds a doctoral degree from the Department of Sociology, Delhi School of Economics, University of Delhi. She has an abiding interest in researching the social life of law, violence and gender. She has published widely on rape, sexual harassment, "honour crimes", mass violence, medical jurisprudence, politics of judicial reform, access to justice, and feminism. She has authored *Public Secrets of Law: Rape Trials in India* (Delhi: OUP, 2014). This book is an ethnographic account of rape trials in Gujarat. Baxi initiated and continues to lead the Law and Social Sciences Research Network (LASSnet), anchored at the Centre for the Study of Law and Governance, Jawaharlal Nehru University. This interdisciplinary network has brought together more than five hundred scholars, researchers and lawyers from different parts of the world

Angeles Castaño Madroñal holds a PhD in Social Anthropology from the University of Seville and is Professor of Social Anthropology at the University of Seville, Spain. She is Coordinator of the group "Estudios para el Desarrollo ICoDeS Medi-África" of the University of Seville. She is currently working on interculturalism, racism and subalternities in Andalusia from the perspective of decolonial studies, with a focus on the Mediterranean context.

Cayetano Fernández is a junior researcher at the Centre for Social Studies (CES), currently integrated in the project POLITICS—The politics of anti-racism in Europe and Latin America: knowledge production, decision-making and collective struggles, particularly in the research stream "Cultures of Scholarship and State Universities: the study of racism and (post)colonialism in higher education". In collaboration with the University of Granada (Spain) and other entities, he has been working in several researches related to Roma in different fields. Currently, his research interest focuses on Racism in Academia, particularly, in the anti-gypsyism produced in the field of the so-called Romani Studies. He is also a founder-member of the Roma Decolonial organization Kale Amenge, a collective project which aims to link knowledge production and Roma advocacy.

Silvia R. Maeso holds a PhD in Political Sociology from the University of the Basque Country. Silvia is Principal Researcher at Centre for Social Studies (CES) and member of the Research Group on Democracy, Citizenship and Law (DECIDe). She lectures in the PhD Programmes: "Democracy in the 21st Century" (FEUC/CES) and "Human Rights in Contemporary Societies" (CES/IIIUC); and in the International Master "Roads to Democracy(ies)" (UC/University of Siegen). She was recently awarded a Consolidator Grant, funded by the European Research Council, with the project POLITICS—The politics of anti-racism in Europe and Latin America: knowledge production, decision-making and collective struggles.

Nelson Maldonado-Torres is Professor of Latino and Caribbean Studies, and of Comparative Literature at Rutgers University, New Brunswick. Director of the Rutgers Advanced Institute in Critical Caribbean Studies. Former President of the Caribbean Philosophical Association (2008–2013), and 2018–2019 Academy of Sciences of South Africa's Distinguished Visiting Scholar, his publications include *Against War: Views from the Underside of Modernity* (Duke UP, 2008), and the collection of essays *La descolonización y el giro decolonial*, compiled by the Universidad de la Tierra (Chiapas, Mexico) in 2011. He has published a numerous articles and book chapters, and has also guest edited two special issues on "mapping the decolonial turn" for the journal *Transmodernity*.

Bruno Sena Martins is a senior researcher at the Centre for Social Studies, University of Coimbra and co-coordinator of the Doctoral Program "Human Rights in Contemporary Societies". He was Vice-President of CES/UC Scientific Board and Co-coordinator of the research group "Democracy, Citizenship and Law Research Group (DECIDe)". His research interests include racism, disability, human rights and colonialism. He has undertaken ethnographic fieldwork in Portugal, India and Mozambique.

Maria Paula Meneses, a Mozambican scholar, is currently a principal researcher at the Centre for Social Studies, University of Coimbra. Previously she taught at Eduardo Mondlane University (Mozambique) and University of Seville (Spain). At the heart of her research interests are the relations between knowledge, power and societies, paying special attention to people who experienced the violence of the colonial encounter. Among the books she edited are *Law and Justice in a Multicultural Society: The Case of Mozambique* (with Boaventura de Sousa Santos and João Carlos Trindade, 2006); *Epistemologías del Sur* (Epistemologies of the South, with Boaventura de Sousa Santos, 2009); and *Mozambique on the Move. Challenges and Reflections* (with Sheila Khan and Bjorn Bertelsen, 2018).

João Arriscado Nunes is Professor of Sociology at the School of Economics and Senior Researcher at the Centre for Social Studies, University of Coimbra. Co-coordinator of the Doctoral Program "Governance, Knowledge and Innovation" and a member of the coordinating team of the project ALICE—Strange Mirrors, Unexpected Lessons, directed by Boaventura de Sousa Santos and funded by the European Research Council.

Boaventura de Sousa Santos is Emeritus Professor of Sociology and director of Centre for Social Studies, University of Coimbra (Portugal), and Distinguished Legal Scholar at the University of Wisconsin-Madison (USA). He has written and published widely on the issues of globalization, sociology of law and the state, epistemology and social movements. Among his most recent publications are *Cognitive Justice in a Global World: Prudent Knowledges for a Decent Life* (2007); *Epistemologies of the South: Justice against Epistemicide* (2014); *If God Were a Human Rights Activist, Stanford University Press* (2015); *Épistémologies du Sud* (2016); *Decolonising the University. The Challenge of Deep Cognitive Justice* (2017); *The End of the Cognitive Empire: The Coming of Age of Epistemologies of the South* (2018).

Cecília Macdowell Santos holds a PhD in Sociology from the University of California-Berkeley and a Master in Law from the University of São Paulo. She is Researcher at the Centre for Social Studies (CES) at the University of Coimbra and Professor of Sociology at the University of San Francisco (USF). At CES, she is a member of the Research Group on Democracy, Citizenship and Law (DECIDe), co-coordinates the PhD program on "Human Rights in

Contemporary Societies" and lectures in the PhD program "Law, Justice and Citizenship in the 21st Century". Her current research interests centre on two subject areas: discourses and practices on violence against women and legal mobilization of human rights at the local, national and transnational scales.

Julia Suárez-Krabbe is Associate Professor of Cultural Encounters at Roskilde University, Denmark, and Associate Researcher at the Centre for Social Studies, University of Coimbra, Portugal. She co-founded and coordinated the Decoloniality Europe network, and is also a founding member of Freedom of Movements, which works against racism, Islamophobia and coloniality in Denmark. Her research emphasizes questions of race and racism in relation to human rights, citizenship, development, antiracist social movements, "other" knowledges and decolonial social change. She is the author of *Race, Rights and Rebels: Alternatives to Human Rights and Development from the Global South* (2017), and, as part of the Freedom of Movements Research Collective, coordinated the study "Stop Killing Us Slowly. A Research Report on the Motivation Enhancement Measures and the Criminalization of Rejected Asylum Seekers in Denmark" (2018).

Preface

Boaventura de Sousa Santos and Bruno Sena Martins

The impasse currently affecting human rights as a language used to express struggles for dignity is, to a large extent, a reflection of the epistemological and political exhaustion which blights the global North. This impasse cannot be separated from the way in which imperialist agendas have weakened the credibility of human rights in the international arena, evident in the systematic use of double standards to justify wars over resources or tactical moves on the economic or geopolitical chessboard. The current situation is also the result of narrowing the scope of human rights, to the extent that it has become the lowest common denominator for rights, possibly mobilized to deal with the curtailment of certain civil and political rights or in emergency situations that call for humanitarian aid, but displaying little interest in struggles against the systemic oppression imposed on the world by capitalism, colonialism and patriarchy.

From the perspective of the epistemologies of the South, overcoming this impasse therefore involves confronting the epistemological and political exhaustion that pervades the critical thinking and emancipatory narratives of the global North. It is a matter of recognizing and overcoming the colonial prejudice which prevents the Eurocentric world from learning from the experiences of those who, in different parts of the world, are resisting the iniquities of a global context essentially founded on the universalist ambitions of Western modernity.

This book contains 18 texts which reflect the dialogue established by researchers from every continent, who present us with themes and social situations which, in different ways, invite us to consider the place of human rights within the epistemologies of the South. Together with the chapters it contains, it is the result of the exchanges and learning generated by the ALICE project.[1] It is the third volume in the "Epistemologies of the South" collection, which presents the results of research and debates that have taken place throughout the ALICE project and continue to fuel the "Epistemologies of the South" research programme hosted by the Centre for Social Studies at the University of Coimbra, coordinated by Boaventura de Sousa Santos.

Since all collective work is the product of shared knowledge, it is important to acknowledge all the people, movements and organizations who have made this project and the research programme focussing on the epistemologies of the South possible. Firstly, we would like to thank all the people and movements who agreed to take part in the various initiatives, ranging from the Popular Universities of Social Movements, the Conversations of the World, discussion forums and individual and group interviews. We also wish to thank the activists and academics from all over the world who have contributed to the various volumes in the Epistemologies of the South collection, responding to the challenge of an emancipatory science that can uphold dignity and restore hope.

Special reference should also be made to the Centre for Social Studies as the institutional host of the ALICE project and, above all, the generosity of its academic and administrative staff, who have contributed to the success of the project and its subsequent materialization as a research programme. In particular, we wish to acknowledge the dedication of Inês Elias and tireless work of Rita Kácia Oliveira, who devoted herself body and soul to the philosophy of the project. Finally, a word of thanks for the diligent work of Victor Ferreira in revising the texts and checking references, and to Sheena Caldwell and Scott Culp for the translations into English of texts written in other languages.

Note

1 *ALICE—Strange Mirrors, Unsuspected Lessons: Leading Europe to a new way of sharing world experience*, coordinated by Boaventura de Sousa Santos, financed by the European Research Council, hosted by the Centre for Social Studies, University of Coimbra, 2011–2016 (www.alice.ces.uc.pt).

Acknowledgements

This book was developed in the context of the research project ALICE—Strange Mirrors, Unsuspected Lessons—coordinated by Boaventura de Sousa Santos at the Centre for Social Studies of the University of Coimbra, Portugal, between 2011 and 2016. The project was funded by the European Research Council, 7th Framework Program of the European Union (Fp/2007–13)/ERC Grant Agreement n. [269807].

Introduction

Boaventura de Sousa Santos and Bruno Sena Martins

The hegemonic, North-centric concept of human rights has today reached an impasse as a language for emancipatory social change. The narrowness and selectiveness of its ideas are proving incapable of confronting systemic injustices and oppression caused by capitalism, colonialism and patriarchy. At the same time, believing itself to be the favoured custodian of an inviolable civilizational conquest, the abstract universality of human rights is hostile to any counter-hegemonic concepts emerging from insurgent, revolutionary or simply non-Eurocentric perspectives. Hegemonic or conventional human rights are thus, in our opinion, because of their Western, monocultural origins (although this poses no threat to their universal aspirations), the fact that they have served double standards and imperialist arguments within the geopolitical arena, and because nowadays they have established themselves as the minimum denominators of the law according to an individualist, neoliberal, colonial, North-centric world order. Moreover, they are based on a concept of human nature which considers it to be individual and qualitatively different from non-human nature, since they are founded on the idea that anything that counts as a violation of human rights is defined by international declarations, multilateral institutions and non-governmental organizations.

Since the global hegemony of human rights as a language for human dignity is nowadays incontrovertible, the question of whether it can be used in a counter-hegemonic sense remains open (Santos, 2015). Inspired by struggles from all corners of the world that reveal the potential but, above all, the limitations of human rights, this book offers a highly conditional response. Essentially, the prevailing notion of human rights today, as the hegemonic language of human dignity, can only be resignified on the basis of answers to simple questions: why does so much unjust human suffering exist that is not considered a violation of human rights? Do other languages of human dignity exist in the world? Are these other languages compatible with the language of human rights? Obviously, we can only find satisfactory answers to these questions if we are able to envisage a radical transformation of what is nowadays known as human rights.

Condemned to irrelevance or cynical exploitation, the most harmful consequence of the crystallization or acritical celebration of human rights is that it undervalues struggles and forms of knowledge which, in many regions of the world, offer resistance to present inequalities and past injustices. Concepts of human dignity are emerging, forged from these struggles and knowledge, which could be combined with the language of human rights if the latter could be conceived of as a key element in an intercultural and emancipatory ecology of ideas of human dignity. This is the paradox which we must examine. Potentially, human rights has a plasticity that could enable it to form part of the radical agendas for resistance in the context of counter-hegemonic struggles. However, it has been held hostage to a form of metonymic reasoning that chains it to an understanding of the world that is reduced to a Western understanding. In an attempt to overcome this metonymic reasoning in the search for counter-hegemonic narratives, we have adopted the epistemologies of the South. As formulated by Boaventura de Sousa Santos, this is a set of inquiries into the construction and validation of knowledge born in struggle, of ways of knowing developed by social groups as part of their resistance against the systematic injustices and oppressions caused by capitalism, colonialism, and patriarchy (Santos, 2014).

Envisaging human rights as a counter-hegemonic language implies understanding why unjust suffering and so many violations of human dignity are not recognized as violations of human rights. Not only is the vulnerability of life unequally distributed throughout the world, but there are certain enduring perspectives on empathy and recognition of humanity which still prevent certain lives and forms of suffering from qualifying as "grievable" (Butler, 2004). In the same sense, Njabulo Ndebele, referring to racism as the key defining element of borders in the context of South Africa, denounces what he describes as the "global sanctity of the white body" (2007: 137), a body attributed with an inviolable status, in inverse proportion to the vulnerability of the black body. This interpretation presents us with the need to confront the problematic relationship between the hegemonic language of human rights and the enduring hierarchies between humans, based on differences between their bodies, livelihoods, ancestry, gods, desires and passions, memories and the territories they inhabit. We must also address the way in which certain violations of human dignity are recognized and ranked within interpretative frameworks and plans of action determined by geopolitical realism and imperialism (Falk, 2009), the rationale for the intermittent presence of humanitarianism (Agier, 2010; Barnett, 2011) and the construction of vulnerable victims devoid of knowledge or agency (Das, 2007; Merry, 2007). These frameworks of understanding reveal how violations of human rights are registered (but not recognized as such) without sounding the rallying cry of "never again" to make any effective changes to the structures responsible for distributing precariousness within human dignity.

Envisaging human rights as part of a collective of languages of dignity would imply beginning with a profound understanding of the voices (the cries and murmurs), struggles (resistance and riots), memories (traumatic and triumphant) and bodies (wounded and insubmissive) of those subalternized by modern hierarchies based on capitalism, colonialism and patriarchy. It involves producing a sociology of absences (Santos, 2006, 2014), revealing the existence of the inhabitants of the "zones of non-being" (Fanon, 1952), zones that have been dispossessed, yet are capable of remarkable resurgence. Only then will it be possible to understand the grammars of dignity in terms of the different senses of the human that emerge from the contexts in which they are lived. Essentially, we are referring to the limitless experience of the world in which the "epistemologies of the South" are rooted (Santos, 2014), which brings us closer to the reality of those who are fighting for the right to be considered human (Baxi, 1986).

Since the South is most clearly defined by the fact that it has been silenced, listening carefully to these forms of resistance and resurgence presents a challenge that is more difficult than it may seem and it is highly likely that some of these silences have been reproduced in the pages of this book. The task which it proposes is precisely that of thinking critically about the absences, emergences and possible intercultural translations that can be used beyond conventional human rights. From this, we can advance with a provisional mapping of what we term post-abyssal human dignities, necessarily constructed upstream of what we consider to be the abyssal genealogy of human rights. In order to do so, it is important to begin by looking at the past and present of conventional human rights.

Hegemonic or Conventional Human Rights

The search for a counter-hegemonic concept of human rights must start with an understanding of the historical path by which it is has come to be conventionally understood and defended or, in other words, the current dominant concepts associated with its liberal, individualist and Western matrix and the prevailing first-generation liberties (civil and political rights). The global hegemony of human rights as a language of human dignity coexists alongside the disturbing realization most of the world's population is not the subject of human rights, but the object of its discourse. In this sense, the way in which the discourse of human rights has been consolidated, by separating subjects and objects, is aptly described by Makau Mutua (2001), who argues that a founding metaphor exists in the "savages, victims and saviours" triad, from which hegemonic practises and discourses have been established for human rights.

Many of the limitations that can be identified in the emancipatory potential of conventional human rights are linked to a triumphalist teleology which sees the notion of human dignity conveyed in human rights as the product solely of Western history and culture, which should be universalized as an unconditional human asset. It assumes that all other alternative grammars of human dignity which have competed with it throughout history are inherently inferior in ethical or political terms.

This "teleological illusion" (Santos, 2015) leads the temptation to draw up a linear narrative that establishes its own precursors. Thus, as Samuel Moyn observes, it is common to find historical narratives which define such diverse elements as the natural law of Aristotle, Christian universalism, natural law, the United States Declaration of Independence (1776), the Declaration of the Rights of Man and of the Citizen (France, 1789) and the Universal Declaration of Human Rights (1948) (Moyn, 2010) as the precursors of the current international system of human rights.

This linear narrative is the result of the bias which is introduced by reading history backwards, so that the past is constructed on the basis of the current hegemony of the Eurocentric concept of human rights. We have argued (Santos, 2015) that this linearity is implausible, given that at any point in history different ideas of human dignity would have been competing against each other and the triumph of one, in this case human rights, is a contingency that can be explained *a posteriori* but could not have been foreseen in any deterministic sense. Thus, the historical triumph of human rights has very often translated into a violent reconfiguration of history: the same acts which—viewed from the perspective of other concepts of human dignity—were acts of oppression or domination are reconfigured as acts of emancipation and liberation when carried out in the name of human rights. This reconfiguration is characteristic of a broader process inherent to Western modernity: on the one hand, it demands the unequivocal superiority of Western traditions, clearing them of associations with the colonial-racist matrix whilst, on the other hand, it masks the fact that the monocultural affirmation of the West is based on the continuing appropriation of traditions and knowledge from other continents and places in the world,[1] made possible by the colonial project. As Aníbal Quijano (2005) and Enrique Dussel (2000) have shown, the epistemological arrogance of Western modernity is the other face of the arrogance of the modern colonial conquest.

One good example of this construction of a linear narrative for human rights is the precedence that has been established for the declarations resulting from the independence of the United States of America, the French Revolution and the human rights system established after the Second World War.[2] In fact, had it not been for the Second World War and the impact of the Holocaust, there is nothing to suggest the emergence of human rights, firstly because the values on which they are based were not even minimally disseminated or incorporated into public opinion and, secondly, because human rights are the by-product of a traditional system of intergovernmental politics (Falk, 1999). The Universal Declaration of Human Rights was only ratified internationally due to a combination of bad conscience, indifference and cynicism on the part of heads of state, and the idealism of certain, less important, diplomats (Falk, 2000, 2009; Glendon, 2001; Moyn, 2010).

In fact, until the 1970s, human rights had a negligible impact on struggles for human dignity that was virtually limited to strategic denunciations exchanged between the United States and the Soviet Union during the Cold War. The consensus was that civil and political rights took precedence over economic and social rights. In the 1970s, however, human rights began to play an unforeseen leading role in the international arena when it was adopted as the only available emancipatory narrative in the face of the apparent failure of the socialist utopia and the crisis in the idea of the nation state (Moyn, 2010). The fact that human rights took root internationally within a liberal matrix which conceived of them as individual rights, thus prioritizing civil and political rights, cannot be separated from the way in which were imposed on the ruins of the socialist utopia.

In fact, as many other authors have noted, the emergence of human rights as a language of dignity from the 1970s onwards coincides with the indisputable hegemony of neoliberalism worldwide in the face of the collapse of the socialist regimes. Moreover, the terms of this historic convergence have been the subject of some interesting discussions, such as the debate between Susan Marks and Samuel Moyn. Focussing on the historical interpretation of human rights produced by Moyn in *The last utopia* (2010), Susan Marks (2013) accuses the author of failing to consider the extent to which the consolidation of the human rights movement from the 1970s onwards was instrumental in the establishment and spread of a neoliberal regime characterized by its promotion of privatization, deregulation and the dismantling of the Welfare State. She emphasizes, for example, the way in which this connection surfaces in the work of Naomi Klein (2007), who considers the emergence of the human rights movement a relevant condition for the consolidation of neoliberalism. The key question was, faced with escalating neoliberalism, how human rights could create a culture of denouncing the abuses of neoliberalism without confronting the structural conditions which make these abuses possible.

Moyn responded by repeating that the emergence of human rights and the consolidation of neoliberalism were historically contemporaneous and identified what he claimed were common negative conditions, namely the focus on post-colonial and developmentalist states, a commitment to prioritize the individual and individual liberties, and a lack of faith in the state, even when the success of both these projects depended on it (Moyn, 2014: 155, 156). However, for Moyn the relationship between neoliberalism and human rights ends with these shared negative conditions and the fact that the hegemonic establishment of both was contemporaneous, since he considered it excessive, on the basis of the existing data, to talk about any interdependence or synergy (conversely, Moyn considers that the interdependence between imperialism and human rights is stronger, although intermittent). Yet, even though he rejects the idea of any deep complicity or co-dependency with neoliberalism, Moyn recognizes that the discourse of human rights has been powerless to produce a systemic critique of socioeconomic relations that are increasingly defined by the unequal distribution of wealth. Instead of criticizing human rights, Moyn claims that the critics of neoliberalism should acknowledge its unsuitability, as an apolitical language, to contest economic, structural and systemic inequalities, implying that there is a need for other languages of dissent that would serve this purpose better.

Regardless of how both authors understand the relationship between human rights and neoliberalism, and despite the potential for human rights to form part of systemic and anti-capitalist struggles, this debate is sufficiently illustrative of the urgent need for a hermeneutics of suspicion to be applied to what we have termed conventional human rights. Teleological triumphalism is thus unsustainable, due to the arbitrary nature of its definition of the precursors of human rights, the evident kaleidoscope of manufactured linearities, and its celebration of an impassive present. In fact, it is not possible to conceive of, or celebrate, an emancipatory path without boldly confronting the systematic "dignity takings" (Atuahene, 2014) organized by capitalism, colonialism and patriarchy.

The second problem with triumphalist teleology in our view is that it does not give sufficient consideration to the different concepts of humanness represented in what is claimed to be the historical genealogy of human rights. Obviously, this is an opportunity to cite Aristotle's defence of natural slavery or the many supporters of the revolutions that took place at the end of the eighteenth century, who would sing the praises of the inalienable rights of man without ever considering that they could apply to slaves or women. However, focussing only on the emergence of the international human rights system in the previous century, Balakrishnan Rajagopal (2009) states that it was created with a "birth defect" due to the fact that it was constituted with a blatant lack of input from certain non-Western cultures and communities. Equally, Boaventura de Sousa Santos (1999) has argued that an intercultural script is needed for human rights. To this day, Rajgopal affirms, human rights has never recovered from this birth defect, mainly due to its failure to respond to colonialism, the most important political question of the twentieth century—a vast narrative in which the Cold War was only one of the many storylines. Here too, the anti-systemic weaknesses of the international human rights system are evident.

In fact, the deliberate lack of any reference in the Universal Declaration of Human Rights (UDHR) to the self-determination of peoples at a time when half the world was under the yoke of colonialism must be considered significant, nor can we ignore the irrelevance, until late on, of the language of human rights, to the majority of anti-colonial struggles. In this sense, the "Declaration of the Colonial Peoples of the World" (1973), delivered by Kwanme Nkrumah in 1945 at the end of the Pan-African Congress in Manchester, clearly prefigures the omission that was a defining feature of the UDHR, approved three years later. However, the point is not to denounce how far the human, which is the basis of conventional human rights, ostensibly excluded a significant section of humanity until very recently. This allegation may even be countered by the claim that its progressive openness should be celebrated. What should be understood is how human rights are based on a value system which is fundamentally anti-humanist in terms of how it establishes hierarchies and forms of sub-humanity. In other words, human rights have an abyssal genealogy (Santos, 2015). Some of the key processes which structure inequalities in the contemporary world (such as racism, sexism or oppression of the disabled) and the founding violence of Eurocentric modernity (such as political-military colonialism, slavery and genocide of indigenous peoples) are related in various ways to ontological policies which naturalize bodies and essentialize hierarchies within an unequal distribution of human prerogatives.

Human Rights and Abyssal Thinking

A critical reading of conventional human rights cannot fail to recognize that its potential is circumscribed within the paradigmatic framework of modern Western thinking. To a certain extent, as we have argued (Santos, 1995), it is possible to see Western modernity as a paradigm founded on the tension between social regulation and emancipation. However, this tension fails to consider the situation of those who are considered less human and whose existence is also defined by the dichotomy of appropriation/violence. The point is that modern Western thinking is based on an invisible distinction between metropolitan societies and colonial territories (Santos, 2007, 2014). Moreover, the regulation/emancipation dichotomy only applies to metropolitan societies: it would be unthinkable to apply it to colonial territories, since they lie on the other side of the line. Modern Western thinking is therefore abyssal thinking, profoundly determined by the creation of two separate universes: the universe "on this side of the line" and the universe "on the other side of the line". Although it is invisible, this division is so consistent that "the other side of the line" disappears as a reality. The appropriation/violence dichotomy has always operated in colonial societies, although the force exerting the tension can remain invisible precisely because it takes place on the other side of the line, in a space made non-existent and therefore incapable of compromising Western claims for the universality of the regulation/emancipation dichotomy or, in other words, claims for the universality of the emancipatory potential of human rights.

As an emancipatory discourse, human rights were historically designed to operate on this side of the abyssal line, in metropolitan societies. This is because the idea that humanity comprises a shared project, namely universal human rights, lies at the centre of the modernist imagination. This humanist imagination was incapable of understanding that, once combined with colonialism, capitalism would be unable to abandon the concept of the sub-human as an integral part of humanity. Within the colonial-racist nexus there is a close link between epistemology and ontology, clearly emphasized by Nelson Maldonado-Torres (2007), who proposed the concept of the coloniality of being, alongside the coloniality of knowledge and power. This awareness of abyssal exclusions should emphasize the way in which, throughout history, women have faced an accumulation of patriarchal and heterosexual oppression together with exclusion based on racialization and colonial hierarchy (Spivak, 1999; Lugones, 2007).

The colonial zone is therefore the social territory of modernity, created and most efficiently preserved by a violent system, yet at the same time sufficiently demarcated by abyssal lines to ensure that the violence deployed there is structurally invisible or irrelevant in the metropolitan zone. The abyssal lines of modernity enable us to conceive of abysses which, even today, leave vast populations in the global South exposed to colonialism, its legacies and the asymmetries of the modern world system, defined on the basis of the oceanic expansionism of the Iberian peoples at the end of the fifteenth century. However, given their power to separate realities and people, abyssal lines operate not only in terms of geopolitical borders and the seas and walls that divide up worlds but also in the interstices, subtly separating adjacent realities, sometimes in the same street and city.

In fact, if we consider, for example, the "little Europes" which, in various places throughout the world, defined the privilege of the settlers in colonial territories, or the significant presence of enslaved African subjects in colonial Europe from the fifteenth century onwards, we find a centuries-old, racially policed proximity in openly "familiar" areas between the metropolitan and the colonial.[3] Having inherited the legacy of the many colonial experiences in the world, including internal colonialism, and aware of the flows of economic globalization and migrations characteristic of the present day, we have to understand the abyssal line on the basis of our capacity to recognize it both in the "imperial South" and in the experience of the immigrant with no papers working clandestinely in the cities of the global North. Thus, the colonial as constituted by the abyssal lines of modernity emerges as a metaphor for those who see their life experiences as taking place on the other side of the line.

To a great extent the abyssal lines of modernity are best characterized, in the words of Boaventura de Sousa Santos, by their power to create non-existence:

> The division is such that "the other side of the line" vanishes as reality becomes non-existent and is indeed produced as non-existent. Non-existent means not existing in any relevant or comprehensible way of being.
> (Santos, 2007: 45)

The ontological limit of conventional human rights, as part of Western modernity, is the impossibility of recognizing the full humanity of subjects who are abyssally excluded. This is because being understood in any relevant or comprehensible way means, above all, having the power to represent the world as one's own, on one's own terms. The Western understanding of the universality of human rights cannot conceive of the existence of different principles of human dignity and social justice. Therefore, we must face the fact that human beings who are not acknowledged by human rights are never going to see them as belonging to them, thus establishing their irrelevance as a counter-hegemonic or post-abyssal language for a large part of the world. Herein lies the epistemo-logical challenge of reconciling human rights with the different languages and forms of knowledge born out of struggles for human dignity. This is why the abyssal line is such a central idea to the epistemologies of the South.

Post-Abyssal Dignities and the Epistemologies of the South

Although the legacy of conventional human rights shows how limited its emancipatory possibilities have been, this does not, in our view, prevent it from being resignified on the basis of other forms of knowledge and loci of enuncia-tion. It is therefore important to recognize that human rights can be a language of power or resistance, and of hegemony or counter-hegemony (Santos, 1995, 1999). Acknowledging the many struggles in which human rights has pursued emancipatory agendas and not wishing to waste this experience, we are seeking to broaden its horizons and infiltrate the narrow certainties it encompasses, in an attempt to determine the extent to which it can be challenged and mobilized in the name of post-abyssal dignities based on the epistemologies of the South.

From this perspective, human rights need to be reinvented, in dialogue with other grammars of dignity, to overcome the abyssal exclusions established by the monocultural arrogance of the modern Western paradigm which created it. This implies focussing on the distinction between abyssal and non-abyssal exclusions and giving priority to the latter. In the epistemologies of the South, the priority given to abyssal exclusions and the struggles which oppose them is due to the fact that the epistemicide caused by the modern Eurocentric sciences is far more destructive on the other side of the abyssal line. It is also because the epistemologies of the North—even at the heart of critical perspectives inspired by emancipatory ideas, such as those frequently expressed in terms of conven-tional human rights—are unaware of the massive universe of extermination, knowledge and struggle that has been placed on the other side of the line. However, establishing this priority does not mean that non-abyssal exclusions are not important: the global fight against modern domination will never be successful if it does not include them. We certainly aim to criticize modern sci-ence and Eurocentric law for hiding the fact that the humanity governed by the tension between regulation and emancipation (metropolitan socialization) is only possible in capitalist, colonial and patriarchal societies because of the per-sistent reproduction of the dehumanized, the group of racialized and gendered bodies governed by the tension between appropriation and violence (colonial socialization). The ideal behind the pluriverse of the human which this book aims to explore is to defeat the abyssal lines of modernity.

Among the procedures in the epistemologies of the South that urge us to expand the present and contract the future, we would define the "ecology of knowledges" and "intercultural translation" (Santos, 2007, 2014) as funda-mental to a post-abyssal displacement of human rights. The ecology of knowl-edges sets out a perspective on human rights constructed on the basis of the epistemologies of the South which is essentially founded on a categorical rejection of the universalist claims of modern Western science and law. However, in arguing that the criteria for validating knowledge cannot be external to the knowledge they validate, the epistemologies of the South also reject ahistorical, neutral and absolutist relativism which does not allow for perspectives anchored in a situated reality.[4] Thus, in the fight against oppression and the search for alternatives, knowledge must be validated in terms of its usefulness in maximizing the possibility of success for struggles against oppression. Therefore, human rights do not take precedence over other forms of knowledge and narratives of dignity, nor should they be subject to *a priori* invalidation. Even knowing that human rights finds it difficult to confront abyssal exclusion, that it often takes the form of civilizational arrogance, and that in its present form it is humanitarian and palliative by nature, it is not appropriate to immediately invalidate the struggles in which it may prove useful.

Stripped of the universal arrogance that brought it into existence, human rights could become part of an ecology of knowledges dedicated to the struggle against oppression and the affirmation of various narratives of human dignity. This ecology of knowledges must first be linked to a "sociology of absences" (Santos, 2014), which can make visible and amplify violations of human dignity which are not known and recognized as a such in the epistemological, ontological, empathetic, historical and media frameworks produced by the global consciousness of the Western matrix. Moreover, since the ecology of knowledges is fuelled by a "sociology of emergences" (Santos, 2014) from which a future with concrete possibilities can be planned, this will involve recognizing struggles which give life and meaning to human rights and vernacularize them in practice.

Our second proposal is intercultural translation, returning to the idea that the emancipatory possibilities for rights essentially depend on their intercultural reinvention (Santos, 1999). Rajagopal states that "languages of emancipation are multiple and have a contradictory and sometimes uneasy relationship with what we call 'international human rights'" (2009: 59). Through intercultural translation, human rights are drawn into dialogue with cultures, theologies and political agendas which displace them, bringing them closer to the South and the struggles for existence, and reconstitute them through emerging notions of humanity that aim to dislodge the commonplaces of narratives of social emancipation and reconstruct their horizons. The proposal to move towards the South to resignify the borders of humanity, as constituted by conventional human rights, is not merely a matter of decentring to create more inclusive concepts. It involves the challenge of making global social justice dependent on global cognitive justice and acknowledging the obvious shrinking of Europe due to its evident political exhaustion, which at present does not enable it to produce any alternative ideas (Santos, 2017). It is also justified by the fact that events and global conflicts in the South very often anticipate those which occur later in the North, as argued by Jean Comaroff and John Comaroff (2012), amongst others. The issue therefore is how the effects of the global capitalist vortex are first felt in the global South, where they prefigure the oppression and struggles that will come to affect the global North.

In our view, a counter-hegemonic concept of human rights will always have to be intercultural, given that it is produced from translations of different political ontologies (Mol, 1999, 2002) which redefine and expand the grammars of human dignity in each place and time within the contingencies of struggles. We draw on Ian Hacking's understanding of ontology, associated with the process of "dynamic nominalism" (2002: 26), to affirm that what is made to exist is the result of the historical dynamics of naming and the subsequent use made of names. In this sense, the notion of human dignity is definitively constructed within the historical struggles that name and claim it. The emerging notions of humanity which must confront Western human rights and engage it in dialogue are not emergent because they are new—in fact many maintain vital links with their ancestry. As James Clifford observed with regard to the resurgence of indigenous identity in the Americas, "cultural endurance is a process of becoming" (2013: 7) or, in other words, cultural resilience very often produces an ontology of being within the struggle that gives it meaning, thus creating and recreating it. Therefore, it is these long-postponed dialogues that will have to be new. In this sense, it is important to foster mutual understanding among struggles which aim to eliminate or reduce unequal power relations and transform them into relations based on shared authority through discourses and practices that develop connections directed towards a "subaltern cosmopolitanism" (Santos, 2018). This ongoing task of translating from concrete struggles for dignity is certainly more post-abyssal than any illustrious general theory on what human dignity might be.

At a time when democratic, economic and ecological challenges call for renewed politics of existence and grammars of good living, the vitality of anti-colonial, anti-patriarchal and anti-capitalist struggles nowadays offers Western modernity the only opportunity to reinvent itself, ironically on the basis of forms of humanity which it has so eagerly subjugated.

The ALICE Pluriverse

This book and the texts which it contains are to a large extent the result of exchanges and learning generated by the ALICE project.[5] In addition to the case studies which come from the project, we have included the work of researchers who are tracking the struggles and resistance of those reinventing the grammars of dignity on a daily basis throughout the world.

A pluriverse of languages, geographies and bodies engaged in struggle emerge from the texts in this book: populations subjected to humanitarian interventions throughout the world, displaced by the right to development, the embodied memories of the survivors of the Bhopal disaster, populations on the peripheries of Brazilian cities, members of the Pasmanda Muslim movement in India, the forgotten histories of women in Mozambique during the colonial period, the struggles against sexual violence in India, migrants and refugees confronted with the Mediterranean border, the feminist campaigns in the Inter-American Court of Human Rights, institutional racism in academia in Portugal, the centuries-old internal colonization of the Roma people in Europe, and refugees in internment camps in Denmark.

The first, more theoretical, section entitled "Human Frontiers" contains chapters dedicated to exploring how the idea of humanity essentially depends on frontiers which, although contingently defined, become significant due to the way in which they define the terms of the different struggles for dignity. The three chapters focus on the historical, religious and teleological systems that establish hierarchies for humans, define the criteria for belonging to humanity or sub-humanity, and establish relations between the human, the divine and nature.

The second section, "Struggles and Emergences", contains nine chapters whose reflections are based on the concrete empirical reality of struggles for human dignity.

Part I—Human Frontiers

In Chapter 1, "Human Rights, Democracy and Development", Boaventura de Sousa Santos analyzes the tensions and imbalances which human rights must consider in order to establish itself as an effective counter-hegemonic grammar. The text analyzes, in particular, the need for intercultural translation between Western values and non-Western principles of human dignity. This involves addressing different worldviews in order to resignify the human as part of biodiversity, and nature as a necessary condition for a plurality of ontologies expressed through enchanted and ancestral worldviews far removed from the modern Western visions, in which it materializes as an object. The author engages in a critical dialogue with the cosmologies, emerging non-human rights and struggles (of indigenous, Afro-descendent and peasant populations) which expose the massive violations of dignities resulting from extractivist capitalism, as well as the way in which the right to development has overlapped, in the global North and the imperial South, with the urgent need to reverse ecological destruction.

In Chapter 2, "'A Being Who is Not Made to Suffer': On the Difference of the Human and on the Differences of Humans", drawing on a genealogy of humanitarianism, João Arriscado Nunes analyzes the ways in which Western security and humanitarian policies are put into practice in "emergency humanitarian situations" and the forms of resistance which challenge them. This approach is the starting point for examining how human borders and attributes are expressed in different concepts of human dignity, as well as the differences between humans, including the denial and qualified attribution of humanness. Drawing on the epistemologies of the South, the author proposes a view of suffering that considers it a condition of human existence, but also the result of specific and mutually constructed forms of oppression which are differently named and recognized. The way in which humanitarian emergencies, mobilized by the struggle against particular forms of suffering and threats to life, very often produce a local and temporary suspension of the demarcation between human being and non-being, is illustrative of this argument.

In Chapter 3, "On the Coloniality of Human Rights", Nelson Maldonado-Torres explores the implications of a modern Western and colonial hegemonic concept of the human. In this decolonial reading, the human rights discourse is understood in relation to the "chain of being" which defined the Western understanding of human beings and their relationship with god. The eighteenth-century affirmation of the "rights of man", although apparently expressing the emergence and expansion of secularism, preserves a link with the Western theological concept of the human defined by Eurocentric coloniality. In the author's opinion, this genealogy defines the inhumanity of Eurocentric humanism and, on this basis, how the colonial line and hierarchies between human beings are defined.

Part II—Struggles and Emergences

In Chapter 4, "Revisiting The Bhopal Disaster: Times of Violence and Latitudes of Memory", Bruno Sena Martins explores the vivid memories of the survivors of the biggest industrial disaster in history, based on fieldwork carried out in the city of Bhopal, India. This approach draws on interpretations of time, violence and demarcations of humanity which define the social memory. In particular, it examines the processes by which some lives are disproportionately exposed to violence and fail to receive fair compensation, as well as the mechanisms used to eliminate certain kinds of suffering from the Western social memory. We are presented with "abyssal exclusions" created by a colonial-capitalist nexus whose power, in combination with the hierarchies of religion and caste which reject Muslims and Dalits, is revealed in the denial of the value of the lives of the Bhopal survivors. Finally, he analyzes how the biographical and corporeal vulnerability imposed by the disaster has created spaces for expression, narratives of resistance and "post abyssal memory" communities.

In Chapter 5, "Pluralism and the Post-Minority Condition: Reflections on the 'Pasmanda Muslim' Discourse in North India", Khalid Anis Ansari considers the breakthroughs created by the Pasmanda movement among minority groups in India. The author shows how the Pasmanda movement is involved both in the broader context of the struggles of the subordinate castes and also in the defence of the most important minority religious group in India, the Muslim community. From a caste perspective, the movement has shaken up the majority–minority (Hindu–Muslim) duopoly and destabilized the related conceptual associations. The author therefore reveals how this movement represents an important challenge for the current minority imagination and for its discursive field of secularism, rights and cultural reform.

In Chapter 6, "Picturing Law, Reform and Sexual Violence: Notes on the Delhi Protests of 2012–2013", Pratiksha Baxi analyzes the representations, struggles and sociolegal dynamics following the brutal gang rape of a 23-year-old woman on Delhi bus on 16 December, resulting in her death. In particular, the author examines the legal and discursive impact of the significant, unprecedented public protests calling for justice in the face of the "public secret" of rape. One of the aspects discussed concerns the media coverage of the protests and how it repeatedly isolated and highlighted India as a den of sexual violence, in an obvious cultural alterization and racialization of rape and sexual abuse. In addition, the author analyzes the nuances of the different feminist anti-rape discourses, the emergence of a thirst for revenge calling for the death penalty, lynching and castration, and the lingering phallocentric and colonial attitudes evident in the different representations of the rape and the protests which followed.

In Chapter 7, "Women and Mass Violence in Mozambique During the Late Colonial Period", taking Mozambique as a case study Maria Paula Meneses addresses the silencing of the experiences of many African women during the colonial period, as victims of the combined oppression of capitalism, colonialism and patriarchy. She explores, on the one hand, the need for fair recognition of how women experienced particular forms of suffering and violence under colonialism and, on the other hand, their narratives of resistance. Given the lengthy armed conflict (1964–1974) between the Portuguese army and the Mozambican nationalists, the context in Mozambique very clearly reveals the centrality of women's suffering and struggles. The author identifies a radical disjunction in Mozambique between the way in which women mobilized and sacrificed themselves in the front lines of the anti-colonial struggle and the scant recognition they have received in the post-colonial period for the role they played in the nationalist struggle. The position of women in the fight for national liberation, as the victims of massacres or as guerrillas and key figures providing essential logistical support for guerrilla campaigns, calls for changes to the patriarchal rationale embedded in society and clearly evident in androcentric nationalist histories.

Chapter 8, "Women's Human Rights, Legal Mobilization and Epistemologies of The South", by Cecília MacDowell Santos, is based on research into cases of violation of women's rights presented against Brazil at the Inter-American Court of Human Rights by human rights NGOs, social movement activists and victims. The author analyzes the strategies and discourses formulated by the plaintiffs and the local impact of these international legal mobilization strategies. With reference to concrete cases, the different types of knowledge deployed to mobilize transnational justice are identified: legal knowledge of human rights, feminist legal activism, popular feminist knowledge, and what is termed corporeal knowledge by the author.

In Chapter 9, "The Power of Racism in Academia: Knowledge Production and Political Disputes", Marta Araújo and Silvia R. Maeso question the dominant concept of racism that circulates within academia and political debates and, at the same time, enshrines a specific set of power relations. The authors examine how proposals for an in-depth, systemic analysis of racism have not been accepted, thus evading any effective confrontation with the legacy of a racial governmentality rooted in imperial European projects and institutionalized in contemporary democracies. Examining international debates in relation to the Portuguese situation, they show how the hegemony of a particular concept of racism—closely connected with political and academic concerns over fascism and anti-semitism and with little interest in considering structural racism—has become complicit in protecting and reproducing racial privilege in academia. Considering the fundamental divergences affecting anti-racism as a political field, they support an interpretation which recognizes racism as a political phenomenon linked to the notion of institutional racism, in which prejudice and attitudes should be considered merely as the tip of the iceberg.

In Chapter 10, "The Roma Collective Memory and the Epistemological Limits of Western Historiography", Cayetano Fernández analyzes how the history that has been created about the Roma people is a white construct which has primarily produced an ontological search for, and legitimation of, white identity. Problematizing the history that has been built around the Roma, the author examines how the epistemological foundations of history as a discipline are influenced by the system of domination underlying European modernity and its civilizational ambitions. In Fernández's reading, objectivity and faith in "the facts" of history constitute an "epistemological naivety" which evades any critical examination of coloniality, the abyssal lines of modernity and the implications of situated knowledge.

In Chapter 11, "Rights, Confinement and Liberation: Rearguard Theory and Freedom of Movement", Julia Suárez-Krabbe argues that hegemonic globalization reproduces the rationale of the colonial era and that racism is a globalized system of oppression closely linked to capitalism. The author begins with the specific case of asylum seekers in the Sjælsmark Deportation Centre north of Copenhagen, in Denmark. Analyzing the legal structures that apply to the individuals detained in the camp, the author identifies what she describes as the outlines of a "death project" carried out by the global elites, which is materializing in Europe and targeting immigrant populations. In a dialogue with Achile Mebembe's concept of necropolitics and the work of Boaventura de Sousa Santos on the sociology of law, she argues that unequal access to legal power reveals abyssal lines and the urgent need to dismantle a system of differentiated jurisdictions structured by racism.

In Chapter 12, "The Mediterranean as the EU Human Rights Boundary", Angeles Castaño Madroñal discusses the persistence, in the twentieth century, of "coloniality" and "abyssal thinking" with regard to European space. She analyzes in particular how the border established in the Mediterranean, a dividing line which is both symbolic and physical, has come to represent a mass grave in recent history, which should be seen as part of the genocidal violence perpetrated by Europe. The examination of the terms for the constitution of the single European area reveals that the Mediterranean periphery has been constructed as a southern border in the face of migration, flows and traffic crossing the global South. In this interpretation, focussing on the problem of migration and European politics, the author presents us with the solidity of "colonial abyssal lines" and the enduring links between racialized ways of constructing borders and the terms of internal colonialism in Europe. Deploying the imagery of the comic strip, she reveals the similarities between a certain "People's Europe" and the contingents of Inhumans involved in interplanetary traffic in the dystopian world of Marvel Comics.

Notes

1 See, for example, Bernal (1987).
2 See, for example, Hunt (2007).
3 See, for example, Stoler (2002).
4 See the discussion developed by Abdullahi A. An-Na'im (1987), amongst others.
5 ALICE—Strange Mirrors, Unsuspected Lessons: Leading Europe to a new way of sharing world experiences, financed by the 7th Framework Programme of the European Union (FP/2007–2013)/ERC Grant Agreement no. 269807.

References

Agier, Michel (2010), "Humanity as an Identity and Its Political Effects (A Note on Camps and Humanitarian Government)", *Humanity*, 1(1), 29–45. doi: 10.1353/hum.2010.0005

An-Na'im, Abdullahi A. (1987), "Religious Minorities under Islamic Law and the Limits of Cultural Relativism", *Human Rights Quarterly*, 9(1), 1–18. doi: 10.2307/761944

Atuahene, Bernadette (2014), *We Want What's Ours: Learning from South Africa's Land Restitution Program*. Oxford: Oxford University Press.

Barnett, Michael N. (2011), *Empire of Humanity: A History of Humanitarianism*. Ithaca, NY: Cornell University Press.

Baxi, Upendra (1986), "From Human Rights to the Right to Be Human: Some Heresies", *India International Centre Quarterly*, 13(3/4), 185–200.

Bernal, Martin (1987), *Black Athena*. London: Vintage.

Butler, Judith (2004), *Precarious Life: The Powers of Mourning and Violence*. London: Verso.

Comaroff, Jean; Comaroff, John (2012), *Theory from the South: or, How Euro-America is Evolving toward Africa*. Boulder, CO: Paradigm Publications.

Clifford, James (2013), *Returns: becoming indigenous in the twenty-first century*. Cambridge, MA: Harvard University Press.

Das, Veena (2007), *Life and Words: Violence and the Descent into the Ordinary*. Berkeley, CA: University of California Press.

Dussel, Enrique (2000), "Europe, Modernity and Eurocentrism", *Nepantla: Views from South*, 1(3), 465–478. Available at https://muse.jhu.edu/article/23901/summary

Falk, Richard (1999), *Predatory Globalization: A Critique*. Cambridge: Polity Press.

Falk, Richard A. (2000), *Human Rights Horizons: The Pursuit of Justice in a Globalizing World*. London: Routledge.

Falk, Richard A. (2009), *Achieving Human Rights*. New York: Routledge.

Fanon, Frantz (1952), *Peau noire, masques blancs.* Paris: Seuil.

Glendon, Mary Ann (2001), *A World Made New: Eleanor Roosevelt and the Universal Declaration of Human Rights.* New York: Random House.

Hacking, Ian (2002), *Historical Ontology.* Cambridge, MA: Harvard University Press.

Hunt, Lynn (2007), *Inventing Human Rights: A History.* New York: W.W. Norton.

Klein, Naomi (2007), *The Shock Doctrine: The Rise of Disaster Capitalism.* New York: Metropolitan Books/Henry Holt.

Lugones, María (2007), "Heterosexualism and the Colonial/Modern Gender System", *Hypatia*, 22(1), 186–209.

Maldonado-Torres, Nelson (2007), "On the Coloniality of Being: Contributions to the Development of a Concept", *Cultural Studies*, 21(2–3), 240–270. doi: 10.1080/09502380601162548

Marks, Susan (2013), "Four Human Rights Myths", in David Kinley, Wojciech Sadurski, and Kevin Walton (eds.), *Human Rights: Old Problems, New Possibilities.* Cheltenham: Edward Elgar, 217–235.

Merry, Sally Engle (2007), "Introduction: Conditions of Vulnerability", in Mark Goodale and Sally Engle Merry (eds.), *The Practice of Human Rights: Tracking Law between the Global and the Local.* Cambridge: Cambridge University Press, 1–38.

Mol, Annemarie (1999), "Ontological Politics: A Word and Some Questions", in John Law and John Hassard (eds.), *Actor Network Theory and After.* Boston, MA: Blackwell, 74–89.

Mol, Annemarie (2002), *The Body Multiple: Ontology in Medical Practice.* Durham, NC: Duke University Press.

Moyn, Samuel (2010), *The Last Utopia: Human Rights in History.* Cambridge, MA: Belknap Press of Harvard University Press.

Moyn, Samuel (2014), "A Powerless Companion: Human Rights in the Age of Neoliberalism", *Law and Contemporary Problems*, 77(4), 147–169.

Mutua, Makau (2001), "Savages, Victims, and Saviours: The Metaphor of Human Rights", *Harvard International Law Journal*, 42, 202–245.

Ndebele, Njabulo S. (2007), *Fine Lines from the Box: Further Thoughts about Our Country.* Roggebaai: Umuzi.

Nkrumah, Kwame (1973), "Declaration to the Colonial Peoples of the World", in Kwame Nkrumah (ed.), *Revolutionary Path.* New York: International Publishers, 125-134.

Quijano, Aníbal (2005), *Colonialidade do poder, Eurocentrismo e América Latina.* Buenos Aires: CLACSO.

Rajagopal, Balakrishnan (2009), "The International Human Rights Movement Today", *Maryland Journal of International Law*, 24(1), 56–62.

Santos, Boaventura de Sousa (1995), *Toward a New Common Sense: Law, Science and Politics in the Paradigmatic Transition.* New York: Routledge.

Santos, Boaventura de Sousa (1999), "Toward a Multicultural Conception of Human Rights", in Scott Lash and Mike Featherstone (eds.), *Spaces of Culture: City, Nation, World.* London: SAGE, 214–229. doi: 10.4135/9781446218723.n12

Santos, Boaventura de Sousa (2006), *A gramática do tempo: para uma nova cultura política.* Porto: Afrontamento.

Santos, Boaventura de Sousa (2007), "Beyond Abyssal Thinking: From Global Lines to Ecologies of Knowledges", *Review (Fernand Braudel Center)*, 30(1), 45–89.

Santos, Boaventura de Sousa (2014), *Epistemologies of the South: Justice against Epistemicide.* Boulder, CO: Paradigm Publications.

Santos, Boaventura de Sousa (2015), *If God Were a Human Rights Activist*. Stanford, CA: Stanford University Press.

Santos, Boaventura de Sousa (2017), "Una Nueva Visión de Europa: Aprender del Sur Global", in Boaventura de Sousa Santos and José Manuel Mendes (eds.), *Demodiversidad. Imaginar Nuevas Posibilidades Democráticas*. Madrid: Akal, 59–92.

Santos, Boaventura de Sousa (2018), *The End of a Cognitive Empire: The Coming of Age of Epistemologies of the South*. Durham, NC: Duke University Press.

Spivak, Gayatri Chakravorty (1999), *A Critique of Postcolonial Reason: Toward a History of the Vanishing Present*. Cambridge, MA: Harvard University Press.

Stoler, Ann Laura (2002), *Carnal Knowledge and Imperial Power: Race and the Intimate in Colonial Rule*. Berkeley, CA: University of California Press.

Part I

Human Frontiers

Chapter 1

Human Rights, Democracy and Development

Boaventura de Sousa Santos

Introduction

The constellation of human rights is nowadays in turmoil. This state of affairs is emerging primarily as an impasse, revealing the limitations of conventional human rights, a language of dignity whose hegemony is nowadays indisputable. Since I reject any monolithic vision of human rights, recognizing the different power relations and bodies that mobilize them, it is necessary to explain what I have in mind when I refer to the hegemonic or conventional version of human rights. I consider that any conventional understanding of human rights has the following characteristics: rights are universally valid regardless of the social, political and cultural context in which they operate and the different human rights systems that exist in different parts of the world; they are based on a concept of human nature which sees it as individual, self-sustaining and qualitatively different from non-human nature; violations of human rights are defined by universal declarations, multilateral institutions (courts and commissions) and non-governmental organizations (which are mainly based in the North); the recurring phenomenon of the double standards deployed to assess the observance of human rights does not in any way compromise the universal validity of human rights; respect for human rights is much more problematic in the global South than in the global North (Santos, 2015).

This current turmoil within the constellation of human rights also enables us to discern promising horizons for emancipatory agendas which aim to transcend conventional understandings of human rights. These horizons, which are being defined in various regions of the world, point towards effective recognition for the limitless experiences of the world in the light of the epistemologies of the South, in the belief that any understanding of the world far exceeds a Western understanding of the world. As I have formulated them, the epistemologies of the South are a set of inquiries into the construction and validation of knowledge that has emerged out of the struggles of those who have resisted the systematic oppression of capitalism, colonialism and patriarchy (Santos, 2014). Hence I have argued for an intercultural conceptualization, in the light of which human rights can, and should, be reformulated on the basis of experiences which confront us with a pluriverse, composed of world views which permeate and extend beyond the borders of modern Western thinking (Santos, 1999).

As Arturo Escobar clearly notes (2016: 13), in taking the limitless experiences of the world as its premise, the epistemologies of the South lay claim to a distinct ontological dimension. Hence, I believe that activists and thinkers who still acknowledge the emancipatory possibilities of human rights should consider the challenge presented by the social struggles, epistemologies and political ontologies through which different populations and collectives have been reclaiming the world in which they live. Many of the appropriations of human dignity which nowadays shape the most promising emancipatory plans for a subaltern cosmopolitan legality (Santos and Rodríguez-Garavito, 2005) are associated with non-European concepts which, combined with ancestral world views and intercultural political ontologies, reveal the close bond between post-abyssal humanity and non-human nature.

I would identify three tensions which are constitutive of the current turmoil and, at the same time, represent a challenge for any emancipatory resignification of human rights in the light of the epistemologies of the South. The first refers to the tension between the right to development and the ceaseless destruction of the environment. The second refers to the tension between the collective aspirations of indigenous and peasant communities of Africa, Latin America and Asia, and the individualism that defines the original human rights canon. The third refers to the tension that results from the inadequacy of the language of rights, in particular human rights, in terms of recognizing the existence of non-human subjects.

These three tensions reveal the abyssal genealogy of human rights—as discussed in the introduction to this book—which are the product of an itinerary characterized by the precedence and universalist ambitions of the liberal world views that have become hegemonic in Western modernity. As previously noted, the dominant versions of Western modernity are constructed on the basis of abyssal thinking, which divides the world abyssally into metropolitan and colonial societies (Santos, 2007, 2014). It has divided it in such a way that the realities and practices on the other side of the line, in the colonies, pose no threat to the universality of the theories and practices that prevail in the metropole, on this side of the line. As an emancipatory discourse, human rights was historically designed to apply only on this side of the abyssal line, in metropolitan societies. I have argued that, far from having been eradicated at the end of the colonial period, this abyssal line, which produces radical exclusions, continues in other forms (neocolonialism, racism, xenophobia, the permanent state of exception regarding terrorists, undocumented immigrant workers, asylum seekers or even ordinary citizens who are the victims of austerity measures dictated by financial capital). International law and conventional human rights doctrines have been used to ensure this continuity. Hence, it is crucial to distinguish between what are nowadays conventional human rights and the possibility, identified in this text, of establishing human rights as part of an ecology of post-abyssal dignities.

The Right to Development *versus* Environmental Degradation

In most countries the history of the different types of human rights is contingent, uneven and full of discontinuities, advances and retreats. Nevertheless, it is clear that in establishing different types of human rights, different political processes are set in motion. Civil and political rights were always at the heart of liberal theory, constituting rights won from the state in order to restrict state authoritarianism. In other words, human rights originated in an anti-state initiative which has contained contradictory political meanings over the last two hundred years. Unlike civil and political rights, economic and social rights consist of benefits provided by the state, assuming the active cooperation of the latter, and are based on a political struggle for the social appropriation of the surpluses amassed by the state through taxes and other sources of revenue. The realization of these human rights depends entirely on the state and therefore implies a change in the political nature of state activity. This transformation occurred with the transition from the liberal or constitutional state to the welfare constitutional state in the global North, and the developmentalist or neo-developmentalist state in the global South. These are very different political processes, although it may be said that, in general, whilst the democratic conservative camp maintained an anti-state position and favoured a liberal concept of human rights, focussing in particular on civil and political rights, the progressive camp of the anti-neocolonial nationalisms or the various democratic lefts has defended the central role of the state as crucial to building social cohesion and has tended to favour the social-democratic or Marxist concept of human rights, paying greater attention to economic and social rights. Over the years, the idea of the indivisibility of human rights has been gaining (more theoretical than practical) acceptance and, consequently, the idea that only recognition of the different types of human rights ensures respect for any individual right.

The collective right to development, claimed in particular by African countries, was only recognized much later and even then only very selectively. The first steps towards establishing the right to development came with the Declaration on Social Progress and Development (1969) and the African Charter on Human and Peoples' Rights (1981) and came to the fore following the United Nations Declaration on the Right to Development (1986) and the various UN World Conferences held during the 1990s. The right to development was based on ideas similar to those that would later be enshrined in dependency theory. The philosophy of the Non-Aligned Movement would come to fruition in the demands made by countries of the then Third World for international guarantees to ensure the essential conditions for their development, which basically involved contesting the unequal trading conditions on the international market. One example of this inequality was the fact that Third World countries were condemned to exporting raw materials at prices fixed by the countries that needed them, rather than by the countries that were exporting them. However, it also emerged out of the Cold War. The right to development in the context of the Cold War meant that it was possible to choose between capitalism, enmeshed in a process of globalization, or the always latent socialist alternative for development. In the mid-1970s this demand evolved into the New International Economic Order movement, which the developed countries, led by the US, firmly and steadfastly opposed. The response of the global North, which intensified after the collapse of the Soviet Bloc, was neo-liberalism, through which the right to development became the obligation to develop. Having neutralized any potential for development that was not governed by the norms of the Washington Consensus, with compliance ensured by the International Monetary Fund, World Bank and later the World Trade Organisation, capitalist development was imposed as a cast-iron condition.

Within the ambivalent central position which the state has always occupied as a threat and guarantee of human rights, notwithstanding the accepted liberal and progressive versions, I believe it is important to emphasize how development, whether as a celebration of the civilization of the global North or an anti-imperialist aspiration of the global South, remains, even in the twenty-first century, the unchanging hallmark of state political projects, even those in the global South that claim to pursue social justice in the face of colonial and imperialist legacies. In fact, one of the most enduring legacies of colonialism, clearly reflecting a genealogy based on Western concepts, is precisely the representation of Asia, Africa and Latin America as underdeveloped Third World continents and the creation of developmentalism as a structural discursive field for the social reality and politics of the post-war world (Escobar, 1995).

The ubiquity of developmentalism is evident in the way in which, at the beginning of the twenty-first century, progressive governments which embraced developmentalism came to power in many states in the global South, particularly in Latin America, seeing the boom in natural resources as a great opportunity to give them the freedom to introduce social policies and redistribute income. This model, which some have called neo-developmentalism or neo-extractivism,[1] has without doubt enabled important policies based on redistribution and fighting poverty to be implemented. However, despite its more nationalist, statist profile, since this is a model based on neo-extractivism, it reflects a neo-liberal rationale which does nothing to contest the global argument for capitalist accumulation. The weaknesses of this model as a political proposal are easily exposed by the economic difficulties which are the immediate result of international fluctuations associated with natural resources.

The neo-developmentalist model is part of a concept of progress in which one of the deadliest consequences is environmental destruction. The driving forces behind mining, oil, natural gas and agricultural frontiers are becoming increasingly powerful, and anything that stands in their way and blocks their path tends to be destroyed as an obstacle to development. These highly attractive forces excel in transforming the increasingly disturbing signs of the immense environmental and social debt they create into the inevitable cost of "progress". It is difficult to produce any political assessment of this model because its relationship to human rights is complex and easily suggests that we are faced with incompatible, rather than indivisible, human rights. In other words, according to the frequently cited argument, we cannot aspire to improve social and economic rights, the right to food security for the majority of the population or the right to education without inevitably accepting violations of the right to health and the environmental and ancestral rights of indigenous and Afro-descendant peoples to their territories. It would only be possible to show that the said incompatibility masks a mismanagement of indivisibility through different time scales, which is virtually impossible given the urgent short-time demands. Under these conditions, it becomes difficult to activate precautionary principles or long-term arguments. And when will the boom in natural resources come to an end? When will it become clear that the investment in natural resources has not been duly offset by investment in human resources? When there is no money for generous compensation schemes and subtle impoverishment creates resentment that is difficult to manage in a democracy? When the levels of environmentally related diseases are unacceptable and overburden the public health systems until they become unsustainable? When water contamination, impoverishment of the land and destruction of the forests become irreversible? When indigenous populations and Afro-descendant and river-dwelling peoples who have been expelled from their land wander through the outskirts of cities, demanding the right to the city that will always be denied to them?

In an age in which the fight against global warming and environmental destruction, which is disproportionately affecting populations in the global South, is imposing itself as an agenda that forces us to question the system of capitalist accumulation (see, for example, Klein, 2014), it appears to make little sense to defend the sacrificial narrative that characterizes the ideology of progress. In fact, modern Eurocentric thinking is based on the idea that progress demands reasonable sacrifices in the interests of a future that will, as a result, be able to offer greater benefits. The issue here is that the fairness of these sacrifices has been justified by the existence of an abyssal line which ensures that the benefits produced in metropolitan societies and social interaction are recognized, whilst minimizing the sacrifices made in colonial societies and social interaction, where the present losses have never been offset by future benefits. Hence there are two faces to the ideology of progress: the one which shows a relative symmetry between sacrifice and benefits, and one showing the incommensurability of sacrifice and benefits. The abyssal line has prevented both from seeing each other in the mirror.

The Western capitalist and colonialist concept of humanity is unthinkable without the concept of subhumanity. Once those displaced by environmental disasters, megaprojects, mining and deforestation and those who are victims of agribusiness and pesticides are considered fully human and their lives, knowledge and respect for non-human nature are recognized, we will be able to confront the unsustainability of developmentalism and review the incommensurability of the benefits and sacrifices imposed by the abyssal lines of modernity. At a time in which there is a growing consensus on the catastrophic consequences of global warming and the plundering of the earth's resources, the social and environmental costs of development are becoming increasingly clear. The current development model is reaching the limits of planet Earth's capacity. The voices of dissent continue to propose alternative development concepts, but the truth is that development has become more antisocial, more closely linked than ever before to growth, increasingly dominated by financial speculation and increasingly predatory on the natural environment.

For the first time in history, capitalist development is seriously threatening nature's capacity to restore its life cycles, reaching ecological limits that are recognized by independent and United Nations experts and various committees as red lines beyond which damage becomes irreversible, putting life on earth at risk. In 2020, the hottest year ever registered, various climate hazard records were broken in the US, India and the Arctic and extreme weather events are becoming more and more frequent and serious. We face drought, flooding, food crises, speculation involving agricultural produce, increasing shortages of drinking water, agricultural land turned over to biofuels and deforestation. Gradually, we are realizing that the crisis factors are increasingly linked and are ultimately manifestations of the same crisis which, given its dimensions, is a crisis of civilization. Everything is connected: the food crisis, environmental crisis, energy crisis, financial speculation in commodities and natural resources, land grabbing, unregulated expansion of agricultural borders, voracious profiteering from natural resources, scarcity of drinking water and privatization of water, violence in rural areas, expulsion of peoples from their ancestral lands to pave the way for major infrastructures and megaprojects, diseases created by damage to the environment that are shockingly exposed in the higher incidences of cancer in certain rural areas in comparison to urban zones, genetically modified organisms, consumption of pesticides, etc.

The Rio+20 Earth Summit (2012), together with the Paris Agreement (2015), proved a complete failure due to the barely concealed collusion between the elites of the global North and the emerging countries to prioritize the profits made by their businesses at the expense of the future of humanity. The current threat clearly reflects how the frameworks for social action in our societies are divided between two extreme time frames—one for urgency and the other for a paradigm shift—with the former calling for immediate action before it is too late and the latter demanding changes in production and consumption, social relations and concepts of nature that will probably take generations to realize. As neither of these time frames coincides with the one which governs democratic political action (the electoral cycle) and, given that capitalist extractivism is now greedier than ever before for natural resources, the destruction of nature seems equally unstoppable and is trivialized by public cynicism, denial or pseudo-remedies such as green capitalism.

Collective World Views *versus* Individual Rights

The link between neo-liberalism, progress and development requires us to search for a subaltern cosmopolitanism, constructed from the bottom up by exchanging experiences and linking the struggles of the movements and organizations of the excluded and their allies in various parts of the world. Eurocentric modernity, including many of its critical traditions, is based on the "monoculture of linear time" (Santos, 2006), the idea that history has a single recognized meaning and direction. This meaning and direction has been formulated in various different ways in the last two hundred years as progress, revolution, modernization, development, growth and globalization. Common to all these formulations is the idea that time is linear, with the core countries in the world system at the forefront, together with the knowledge, institutions and forms of social interaction that prevail within them. This argument produces non-existence by declaring that, in terms of the temporal norm, anything that is asymmetrical in relation to what is defined as advanced, is backward. It is through this logic that Western modernity produces the non-contemporaneity of the contemporary, the idea that simultaneity hides the asymmetries of the historical times that converge within it.

The idea of linear time disqualifies forms of existence that are seen as backward or outside the accepted (modern) time and renders them invisible, thus marginalizing the cultures and ontologies that are most convincingly opposed to development or alternative development and moving closer to the imperative to accept alternatives to development, as the following examples show.

In October 2012, in a cry of despair, the Guarani-Kaiowá community in Pyelito Kue/Mbarakay-Iguatemi-Mato Grosso do Sul (MS) sent a letter to the government and Ministry of Justice in Brazil in response to an eviction order issued by the Federal Court of Navirai (MS). After describing a cruel list of threats, deaths, expulsions and gunmen, "in an indigenous community surrounded by soy, sugar cane and hate", as Egon Heck, coordinator of the CIMI (*Conselho Indigenista Missionário*—Indigenous Missionary Council), reported, they stated that:

> we want to be killed and buried with our ancestors right here, where we are today, and we therefore ask the government and the Federal Court not to issue the order for our eviction/expulsion but instead to decree our collective death and bury us all here. We ask, once and for all, for them to order our decimation and complete extinction and for tractors to be sent to dig a large hole for our bodies to be thrown in and buried. This is our request to the federal judges. We await the decision of the Federal Court. Decree the collective death of the Guarani and Kaiowá of Pyelito Kue/

Mbarakay and bury us here, since we have all decided not to leave, alive or dead.[2]

When I read this letter, it took me back 15 years to the time when the U'wa people of Colombia threatened to commit mass suicide if the project to drill for oil on their sacred land went ahead. At the time, I was doing research in Colombia and followed the case at close quarters. Although fighting for land with one's life—which was the message of the Guarani-Kaiowá—is not the same as contemplating mass suicide, it is impossible not to make the connection, since the U'wa were also fighting to save their territory from being contaminated by Western greed.[3] The U'wa people won national and international support to stop the drilling under the terms in which it had been proposed. The fate of these and other indigenous and Afro-descendant peoples and peasants fighting to defend their collective rights is firmly linked to the planet as a whole, and calls on us to see these populations as key voices for thinking about alternatives in the contemporary world.

The question we should address is that of determining to what extent human rights constitutes a language capable of giving due recognition to long-established voices and existences that have been forced into the margins of modernity. The limitations of hegemonic human rights are evident here too, in some of the most decisive challenges of our time. The United Nations Universal Declaration of Human Rights, the first major universal declaration of the last century, which was followed by several others, only contemplates two subjects in law: the individual and the state. Peoples are only recognized insofar as they are transformed into states. It is important to note that in 1948, when the Declaration was adopted, there were many new peoples, nations and communities that did not have a state. From the perspective of the epistemologies of the South, the Declaration still cannot be considered as anything other than colonialist (Burke, 2010; Moyn, 2010; Terretta, 2012). In referring to equality in the eyes of the law, it should be recognized that, at the time when the Declaration was written, individuals in large parts of the world were not equal because they were subjected to collective domination, and individual rights offer no protection to those under collective subjugation. This was not contemplated in the Declaration, which emerged at a high point in bourgeois individualism, at a time when sexism was part of common sense, sexual orientation was taboo, class domination was an internal matter for each country and colonialism still had power as a historical agent, albeit significantly undermined by Indian independence. With the passing of time, sexism,[4] colonialism[5] and other, cruder forms of class domination have also been recognized as giving rise to violations of human rights. From the 1960s, anticolonial struggles became part of the United Nations agenda.[6] However, self-determination as it was understood at the time only referred to peoples subjected to European colonialism. The exercise of self-determination on this basis relegated many peoples to the status of the internally colonized: indigenous peoples in various continents are a good example of this. It would take 30 more years before the right of indigenous peoples to self-determination was recognized with the United Nations Declaration on the Rights of Indigenous Peoples, approved by the United Nations General Assembly in 2007. Prior to this, lengthy negotiations were required before the International Labour Organisation would approve Convention 169 on indigenous and tribal peoples, in 1989.

Since collective rights do not feature in the original canon of human rights, the tension between individual and collective rights emerges from the historical struggle of social groups subjected to exclusion or discrimination who could not therefore receive adequate protection through individual human rights. The struggles of women, indigenous peoples, Afro-descendant peoples, groups who are the victims of racism, gays and lesbians to achieve recognition for collective rights have shaped the last 50 years, in a process that has always been extremely contentious and always faced reversal. There is not necessarily a contradiction between individual and collective rights, except for the fact that there are many types of collective rights. It is possible to distinguish between two types of collective rights, namely primary and derived rights. We refer to derived collective rights when, for example, workers organize themselves into trade unions and give the latter the right to represent them in negotiations with employers. However, when a community of individuals is entitled to rights irrespective of their organization or decisions made by its members to renounce their individual rights in order to assert the right of the community, this is an instance of primary collective rights.

Collective rights exist to lessen or eliminate the insecurity and injustice experienced by collectives of individuals who face discrimination and systematic oppression because of who they are, not what they do. Very slowly, collective rights have begun to be included in both national and international political agendas. Nevertheless, the contradiction or tension with regard to the more individualist concepts of human rights is always present. Recently, the recognition of the collective rights of indigenous and Afro-descendant peoples has had a particularly visible political presence, above all in Latin America, and has become controversial whenever it translates into affirmative action in the form of extensive reviews of national history, education and health systems, administrative autonomy and collective rights to land and territory (see, for example, Rodríguez-Garavito, 2015).

The hegemony of a universal concept of human dignity underlying human rights, and based on Western presuppositions, reduces the world to the Western understanding of it, thus ignoring or trivializing crucial cultural and political experiences in countries in the global South. This is the case with movements that resist oppression, marginalization and exclusion which have emerged in recent decades and whose ideological bases have little or nothing to do with the Western cultural and political references which prevailed throughout the twentieth century. These movements do not formulate their demands in terms of human rights: on the contrary, they are frequently formulated in accordance with principles which contradict the dominant principles of human rights. The roots of these movements often lie in historical identities, as is the case with the indigenous and Afro-descendant peoples' movements, particularly in Latin America, and the peasant movements in Africa and Asia. Despite the enormous differences between them, these movements share the fact that they have emerged from non-Western political references and were established, to a large extent, as resistance to Western domination. Conventional thinking on human rights lacks the theoretical and analytical tools that would enable it to position itself with some measure of credibility in relation to these movements and, even worse, does not consider it important that it should do so. It tends to apply the same abstract, generic prescription for human rights, hoping that the nature of the alternative ideologies and symbolic universes can be reduced to specifically local phenomena that will have no impact on the universal canon of human rights.

Human Rights *versus* the Rights of Nature

Abyssal cartography is inherent to modern knowledge and within it the colonial zone is the universe *par excellence* of incomprehensible beliefs and behaviour that can never be considered knowledge and is therefore beyond true and false. The disqualification of non-metropolitan realities and knowledge might lead us to suppose that there is no real knowledge on the other side of the line, only beliefs, opinions, magic, idolatry and intuitive or subjective understandings which, at best, could serve as the objects or raw material for scientific research. The utter strangeness of such knowledge and practices led to the actual denial of the human nature of its agents. The social contract theories of the seventeenth and eighteenth centuries stated that modern individuals or, in other words, metropolitan men, entered into the social contract by abandoning the state of nature in order to create civil society. The state of nature is therefore understood as the primordial state, in relation to which modern legality is constituted: it is both universal and also instrumentalized as a colonial zone, rendered invisible by the abyssal line, in which concepts of rights and legality do not apply. On the basis of these abyssal concepts of epistemology and legality, the universal tension between regulation and emancipation applied on this side of the line does not clash with the tension between appropriation and violence applied on the other side of the line.

In order to perceive the bond of meaning between emerging humanities, post-abyssal humanities and non-human nature, it is necessary to understand that the universal aspect of human rights has always coexisted with the idea of a primordial "deficiency" in humankind, namely the idea that not all beings with a human phenotype are fully human and therefore should not enjoy the status and dignity conferred on humanity. Without this, we would be incapable of understanding Voltaire's ambiguity with regard to the issue of slavery or the fact that John Locke, the great theorist of modern human rights, made a fortune in the slave trade. It is possible to defend both the liberty and equality of all citizens and, at the same time, slavery because of the said abyssal line underlying human rights, which makes it possible to define who is truly human and therefore benefits from human rights and who is not and therefore does not enjoy these rights. The latter situation is a reversal of human rights, as brilliantly analyzed by Franz Hinkelammert (2004): the supposedly primordial nature of human rights is based on the denial of humanity imposed on certain groups of human beings. As clearly demonstrated within the limited scope of the declarations issued at the end of the eighteenth century announcing the inalienable rights of all men (see, for example, Hunt, 2007), the exclusion of humans underlies the modern concept of humanity. The Western patriarchal, capitalist and colonialist concept of humanity is unthinkable without the concept of subhumanity—both in the past and now, albeit in different ways.

From this selective attribution of humanness, which is a structural feature of Western human rights, the limits defined for expansion also emerge: even when conventional human rights imagined including all human beings, it never envisaged anything more than humans. The modern subjects of rights are exclusively human. In contrast, in other grammars of dignity humans are incorporated into much broader entities—the cosmic order, nature—on the understanding that the protection offered to humans is of little value if the former are not also protected. This is discussed by Marisol de la Cadena (2015) in her analysis of the rich and complex interdependent relationship established in Andean cosmology and ecology with non-human entities, the "earth beings".

The perspective which sees the Western idea of nature as a "globalised localism"[7] (Santos, 2001: 71) reveals the singular nature of the prevailing concept of the human in Eurocentric modernity, which is constructed from an extraordinary dissociation between the meaning of human existence and the cosmic and natural order.[8] In fact, Western Cartesian ideas about nature are as dominant as they are exceptional. All the cultures which European colonial expansion encountered from the sixteenth century onwards had a concept of nature that was closer to that of Baruch Spinoza (1632–1677), in which nature is seen as a living being (*natura naturans,* in Latin, as opposed to *natura naturata*) which we belong to and whose wellbeing is a condition of our own wellbeing: nature does not belong to us, we belong to nature. Spinoza's vision, in which God and nature are coextensive (*Deus sive Natura*), was examined by the Inquisition due to allegations of pantheism. The prevailing concept for Eurocentric modernity was that of Descartes: nature as *res extensa,* a nature-object defined by Cartesian dualism and devoid of subjectivity and spiritual meaning. Since Western modernity was not monolithic in terms of ontologies, the colonial conquest had the effect of reducing or even eliminating its internal diversity. Any concepts within Western modernity that did not serve the conquest were abandoned or eradicated: it was for this reason that Pascal, Montaigne and Spinoza were discarded, being of no benefit either to missionaries or to the conquest. Thus it is not surprising that the concept of human rights which claimed to be universal was, in fact, very specific—and this became very clear when it was confronted with other concepts of dignity and nature. Hence, it is necessary to perceive the cultural differences in how different populations conceive of relations with nature, time and the transcendent in terms that are close to the "political ontologies" (see, for example, Blaser, 2013; Cadena, 2015; Escobar, 2016) used to analyze "political strategies to defend or re-create worlds that retain important relational and communal dimensions, particularly from the perspective of the many present-day territorial struggles" (Escobar, 2017: 1616–1620).

The Western nature–society dichotomy conceals a hierarchy in which everything that is natural or closer to nature is considered inferior and flawed in terms of culture and valid knowledge. However, recent reality persists in showing us that we can only save the planet and preserve the dignity of life if we are willing to learn from the knowledge that has been excluded and oppressed. Thanks to the struggles of the populations most excluded by capitalist development (indigenous peoples, Afro-descendant peoples, women, peasants), a new generation of human rights is emerging, based on the idea that non-human beings essential to human life have human rights of their own, with a specific logic and broader scope than those of human beings, whether individual or collective. Due to its scope, Article 71 of the 2008 Constitution of the Republic of Ecuador, which is linked to the indigenous peoples' philosophy of nature, may be considered pioneering in this respect. For the Andean peoples, far from being a natural resource that is available and can be appropriated on an unconditional basis, nature is the earth mother (*pachamama* in Quechua), the source and foundation of life and therefore the centre of the ethics of care. Article 71 states:

> Nature, or Pacha Mama, where life is reproduced and occurs, has the right to integral respect for its existence and for the maintenance and regeneration of its life cycles, structure, functions and evolutionary processes. All persons, communities, peoples and nations can call upon public authorities to enforce the rights of nature. To enforce and interpret these rights, the principles set forth in the Constitution shall be observed. The state shall give incentives to natural persons and legal entities and to communities to protect nature and to promote respect for all the elements comprising an ecosystem.[9]

The Constitution of the Republic of Ecuador also includes the concept of *sumak kawsay*, a Quechua expression which corresponds to the Spanish term *buena vida* (good life). The same is true of the 2009 Constitution of Bolivia, which includes *pachamama* concepts and, in Article 8, refers to *suma qamaña* (an Aymara word which corresponds to the Spanish *vivir bien*, or good living).[10]

This is a major example of what I have termed the "sociology of emergences" (Santos, 2006). It is known that this constitutional precept has been systematically disrespected in the past decade for the usual reason (which has existed since the seventeenth century): the imperatives of capitalist development. Nevertheless, it is a legal and constitutional innovation that forms part of the struggle of humanity, since it reflects the insurgent, anticapitalist, anticolonial and antipatriarchal spirit of the times which is emerging in the margins of the dominant ideas and policies and is also flourishing in other places and contexts.

The most recent and famous case concerns the granting of human rights to the River Whanganui (also known as Te Awa Tupua), a sacred river for the indigenous Maori peoples of New Zealand because it is considered their ancestor. After 140 years of negotiations, the river has been recognized by the state as a living entity that must be protected to ensure the continuity of existence to the greatest possible extent. When they were completed, the minister in charge of the negotiations, which were "the longest in the history of New Zealand", stated that "Te Awa Tupua will have its own legal identity with all the corresponding rights, duties and liabilities of a legal person".

Recognizing this juridical and political innovation, the minister added: "The approach of granting a legal personality to a river is unique [...] it responds to the view of the iwi of the Whanganui river which has long recognized Te Awa Tupua through its traditions, customs and practice". This acknowledgement of legal pluralism and the need for intercultural translation between the various concepts of law and the living being entitled to rights is not an empty statement, as Article 71 of the Constitution of the Republic of Ecuador proved to be, to some extent. In this case, the agreements include compensation for the Maori people for damage to the river amounting to 80,000,000 New Zealand dollars, and 1,000,000 dollars to establish the legal framework for the river. As has been noted, the decision to attribute a legal personality to the River Whanganui acknowledges the injustices in the colonial history of New Zealand, establishes legal pluralism in the face of the legacy of colonial law and may prove a valuable instrument in the environmental challenges that result from the exploitation of resources (Charpleix, 2017; Rodgers, 2017). Moreover, it exposes how

> the ontological foundations of Western approaches to law, society and geography are generally based on a nature/culture hierarchy in which humans have assumed supremacy and the natural environment is viewed through utilitarian, resourcist and economic lenses.
>
> (Charpleix, 2017: 27)

A few months later, using the same arguments, New Zealand granted a legal personality and autonomous human rights to the Taranaki Mountain. Under the terms of the law,

> Eight local Māori tribes and the government will share guardianship of the sacred mountain [...] in a long-awaited acknowledgement of the

indigenous people's relationship to the mountain, who view it as an ancestor and whanau, or family member.

The new status of the mountain means that if someone abuses or harms it, it is the same legally as harming the tribe.[11]

Far from remaining a New Zealand idiosyncrasy, legal struggles are emerging in India[12] (see, for example, O'Donnell, 2017) and other places with the aim of conferring the status of living being and the entitlement to human rights on non-human entities which are considered part of the natural world by Western culture,[13] or *Res extensa*, in Descartes' terms.

The innovation of intercultural legality could not fail to be met with resistance from conservative politicians and jurists. One opposition politician sarcastically asked the New Zealand Prime Minister whether it was not absurd to attribute a legal personality and human rights to something which had no head, limbs or gender. The reply was unexpected: "and does a company or a corporation have a head, limbs and gender?" However, this resistance does not only stem from conventional conceptions of law and nature. The new post-human generation of human rights is completely changing the terms and amounts of compensation for damage caused to the wellbeing of these living beings which are now independent holders of rights. For example, the compensation that a company which contaminated a river is liable to pay cannot be restricted to the value of the fish which can no longer be caught because the river has died. It must include the recovery of all the ecosystems linked to the river and its banks and therefore the amount rises exponentially. In 1944, in his book *The Great Transformation*, Karl Polanyi (2012) had already demonstrated that if capitalist companies which caused irreparable damage to nature were made to pay adequate compensation, they would go bankrupt.

As a whole, these innovations point to a project for society that follows far more diverse paths than those adopted by capitalist, dependent and extractivist economies. These world views favour a social economy model (Acosta, 2009: 20; León, 2009: 65) based on harmonious relations with nature. In Gudynas' argument (2009: 39), nature ceases to be natural capital when it becomes natural heritage. This perspective does not rule out the acceptance of a capitalist economy but is opposed to the idea that global capitalist relations determine the logic and pace of change. The complexity of these new rights lies in the fact that they not only mobilize different cultural and cosmogonic identities but also new political economies that are firmly anchored in controlling natural resources.

Conclusion

The link between the different factors in the present crisis should, as soon as possible, lead to links between the social movements engaged in fighting them.

It is a slow process in which the weight of the history of each movement counts more than it should, although there is already evidence of links between the struggles for human rights and food sovereignty, against pesticides, genetically modified food, unpunished violence in rural areas, financial speculation in food products, and in favour of agricultural reform, the rights of nature, environmental rights, the rights of indigenous peoples and quilombola communities, the right to the city, the right to health, the solidarity economy, agroecology, taxation of international financial transactions, popular education, community health, the regulation of financial markets, etc.

Conferring human rights on a river or establishing constitutional recognition for the rights of nature are ways of raising the profile of peoples and struggles whose knowledge represents an external critique of the modern Eurocentric values underpinning conventional human rights, addressing post-abyssal dignities based on relations with nature and the cosmos. In the context of resistance to colonial and neo-liberal extractivist developmentalism, they also constitute a perceptive dialogue with the central focus that the language of rights has acquired in Eurocentric grammars of dignity. In fact, taking the constitutional emergences in Latin America as an example, the idea of the rights of nature/*pachamama* is, in itself, an intercultural concept. In the indigenous world view, *pachamama* is the provider and protector of life and it therefore makes as little sense to talk of the rights of nature as the rights of God in the Christian world view. "Rights of nature" is a hybrid that combines Eurocentric concepts of rights with the indigenous concept of nature. It is, in my view, a contribution towards addressing the loss of meaningful critical thinking in Eurocentric theory which I have discussed in my previous work (Santos, 2014: 33–34).

In the early decades of the twenty-first century the recognition of rights for non-human nature is one of the most instructive examples of two procedures which form the basis of the epistemologies of the South, namely the ecology of knowledges and intercultural translation. The ecology of knowledges is based on the idea that different forms of knowledge are incomplete in different ways and that creating awareness of this reciprocal incompleteness is a precondition for achieving cognitive justice. Intercultural translation is an alternative both to the abstract universalism underpinning general Eurocentric theories and the idea of the incommensurability of cultures. Translation can take place between hegemonic and non-hegemonic forms of knowledge or between different forms of non-hegemonic knowledge. The importance of the latter lies in the fact that it is only through reciprocal intelligibility and the subsequent possibility of combining non-hegemonic forms of knowledge that it is possible to construct a counter-hegemony. Intercultural translation presupposes the existence of different cultures, but not the polarity of pristine, uncontaminated entities. The fact that indigenous concepts, world views or philosophies may be recognized in a hypermodern document (the political constitution of a country) is in itself an intercultural translation between oral ancestral knowledge and written Eurocentric knowledge. We are contemplating hybrid forms that create new phenomena which cannot be reduced to their constituent parts. This pragmatic, non-essentialist perspective which aims to strengthen social struggles opens up new possibilities for intercultural translation involving struggles and movements in different parts of the world. The possibility emerges of a paradigm shift that will enable us to move beyond an anthropocentric vision to a biocentric concept of human rights, in the light of colonized ontologies and world views that have been disqualified for so long. Nothing could make better sense, given that we are living in a world that presents us with modern problems for which there are no modern solutions. Drawing on concepts of humanity that are as much emerging as ancestral, we can grasp some indications of the future of the urgent intercultural and post-abyssal reconstruction of human rights.

Notes

1 According to Alberto Acosta, "extractivism is a mode of accumulation that started to be established on a massive scale five hundred years ago [...] We will use the term extractivism to refer to those activities which remove large quantities of natural resources that are not processed (or processed only to a limited degree), especially for export. Extractivism is not limited to minerals or oil. Extractivism is also present in farming, forestry and even fishing" (2013: 62).

2 The full text of the letter is available in the Articulação dos Povos Indígenas do Brasil (APIB) blog: <http://blogapib.blogspot.pt/2012/10/carta-da-comunidade-guarani-kaiowa-de.html>.

3 See Beatriz Eugenia Sánchez (2001: 5–142).

4 In 1979, the United Nations General Assembly adopted the Convention on the Elimination of All Forms of Discrimination against Women (CEDAW) in order to legally implement the Declaration on the Elimination of Discrimination against Women. Described as the Magna Carta of women's rights, it came into force on 3 September 1981. The Convention defines "discrimination against women" (Article 1) as "any distinction, exclusion or restriction made on the basis of sex which has the effect or purpose of impairing or nullifying the recognition, enjoyment or exercise by women, irrespective of their marital status, on a basis of equality of men and women, of human rights and fundamental freedoms in the political, economic, social, cultural, civil or any other field". The Resolution "Human rights, sexual orientation and gender identity" was approved by the United Nations Human Rights Council on 14 June 2011. The proposed Declaration includes a condemnation of violence, harassment, discrimination, exclusion, stigmatization and prejudice on the basis of sexual orientation and gender identity.

5 The United Nations Declaration on the Elimination of All Forms of Racial Discrimination (1963), states: "Considering that the United Nations has condemned colonialism and all practices of segregation and discrimination associated therewith, and that the Declaration on the Granting of Independence to Colonial Countries and Peoples proclaims in particular the necessity of bringing colonialism to a speedy and unconditional end".

6 Hoping to speed up the process of decolonization, in 1960 the United Nations General Assembly adopted Resolution 1514, also known as the "Declaration on the Granting of Independence to Colonial Countries and Peoples" or simply the "Declaration on

Decolonisation". It stated that all peoples had the right to self-determination, solemnly proclaiming the need to bring colonialism in all its forms and manifestations to a speedy and unconditional end. The Special Committee on Decolonisation (also known as the Committee of the 24 for Decolonisation, Committee of 24 or simply the Decolonisation Committee) was created in 1961 by the UN General Assembly for the purpose of monitoring the implementation of the Declaration and making recommendations on its application.

7 Globalized localism "is the process by which a particular phenomenon is successfully globalized, whether it be the worldwide activities of the multinational, the transformation of the English language into a lingua franca, the globalisation of American fast food or popular music or the worldwide adoption of the same laws of intellectual property, patents or telecommunications aggressively promoted by the USA. In this mode of production of globalisation, what is globalised is the winner in a struggle for the appropriation or valuation of resources or the recognition of difference. This victory translates into the capacity to dictate the terms of integration, competition and inclusion. In the case of the recognition of difference, the globalised localism implies the conversion of the triumphant difference into a universal condition and the consequent exclusion or subordinate inclusion of alternative differences" (Santos, 2001: 71).

8 The actual notion of a "biological individual" can be problematized in modern Western science itself in the light of the vital symbiotic relationships involving plants and animals, and the infinite number of microorganisms that are essential for metabolic processes and physiological functions (see, for example, Gilbert et al., 2012).

9 Available at: <www.asambleanacional.gob.ec/sites/default/files/documents/old/con stitucion_de_bolsillo.pdf>.

10 A vast bibliography is available nowadays on the concept of *sumak kawsay*. See, amongst other works, Chancosa (2010), Gudynas (2011: 441–447), Walsh (2010: 15–21), Tortosa (2011), Acosta (2013: 61–86; 2014: 93–122), Giraldo (2014), Hidalgo Capitán et al. (2010: 17–21), Unceta (2014: 59–92) and Waldmüller (2014).

11 *The Guardian*, 22 December 2017. Available at: <www.theguardian.com/world/2017 /dec/22/new-zealand-gives-mount-taranaki-same-legal-rights-as-a-person>.

12 This legal opening in India, in the meantime reversed by the Supreme Court, is the result of a decision by the High Court of Uttarakhand dating from March 2017 which granted legal rights to the Ganges and Yamuna rivers and the Gangotri and Yamunotri glaciers. In the light of this decision, the status of legal minor should be granted to the said rivers and glaciers, whilst their guardianship would be attributed to various individuals in the State of Uttarakhand.

13 It is also worth considering how, in the context of southern Africa, Godfrey Museka and Manasa Madondo (2012) describe the power of an environmental pedagogy anchored in the Shona/Ndebele cosmology and the values found in Ubuntu philosophy.

References

Acosta, Alberto (2009), "Siempre más democracia, nunca menos", in Alberto Acosta and Esperanza Martínez (eds.), *El Buen Vivir una vía para el desarrollo*. Quito: Abya-Yala, 19–30. Available at http://base.socioeco.org/docs/acosta-martinez-el_buen_vivir.pdf

Acosta, Alberto (2013), "Extractivism and Neoextractism: Two Sides of the Same Curse", in Miriam Lang and Dunia Mokrani (eds.), *Beyond Development. Alternative Visions from Latin America*. Quito: Fundación Rosa Luxemburg, 61–86. Available at https://www.tni .org/files/download/beyonddevelopment_complete.pdf

Acosta, Alberto (2014), "Post-crecimiento y post-extractivismo: dos caras de la misma transformación cultural", in Gustavo Endara (ed.), *Post–Crecimiento y Buen Vivir. Propuestas globales para la construcción de sociedades equitativas y sustentables.* Quito: Friedrich Ebert Stiftung (FES-ILDIS), 93–122.

Blaser, Mario (2013), "Ontological Conflicts and the Stories of Peoples in Spite of Europe: Towards a Conversation on Political Ontology", *Current Anthropology*, 54(5), 547–568. doi: 10.1086/672270

Burke, Roland (2010), *Decolonization and the Evolution of International Human Rights.* Philadelphia, PA: University of Pennsylvania Press.

de la Cadena, Marisol (2015), *Earth Beings: Ecologies of Practice across Andean Worlds.* Durham, NC: Duke University Press.

Chancosa, Blanca (2010), "Sumak Kawsay desde la visión de la mujer", in Antonio Hidalgo-Capitán, Alejandro Guillén and Nancy Deleg (eds.), *Sumak Kawsay Yuyay: Antología del Pensamiento Indigenista Ecuatoriano sobre Sumak Kawsay.* Huelva y Cuenca: FIUCUHU, 221–227. Available at http://dspace.ucuenca.edu.ec/bitstream/123456789/21745/1/Libro%20Sumak%20Kawsay%20Yuyay.pdf

Charpleix, Liz (2017), "The Whanganui River as Te Awa Tupua: Place-Based Law in a Legally Pluralistic Society", *The Geographical Journal*, 184(1), 19–30. doi: 10.1111/geoj.12238

Escobar, Arturo (1995), *Encountering Development: The Making and Unmaking of the Third World.* Princeton, NJ: Princeton University Press.

Escobar, Arturo (2016), "Thinking-Feeling with the Earth: Territorial Struggles and the Ontological Dimension of the Epistemologies of the South", *Revista de Antropología Iberoamericana*, 11(1), 11–32. doi: 10.11156/aibr.110102

Escobar, Arturo (2017), *Designs for the Pluriverse: Radical Interdependence, Autonomy, and the Making of Worlds (New Ecologies for the Twenty-First Century).* Durham, NC: Duke University Press [Kindle version].

Gilbert, Scott F.; Sapp, Jan; Tauber, Alfred I. (2012), "A Symbiotic View of Life: We Have Never Been Individuals," *Quarterly Review of Biology*, 87(4), 325–341. doi: 10.1086/668166

Giraldo, Omar (2014), *Utopías en la era de la supervivencia. Una interpretación del buen vivir.* México, DF: Editorial Ítaca; Universidad Autónoma Chapingo.

Gudynas, Eduardo (2009), *El mandato ecológico. Derechos de la Naturaleza y políticas ambientales en la nueva Constitución.* Quito: Abya Yala.

Gudynas, Eduardo (2011), "Buen Vivir: Today's Tomorrow", *Development*, 54(4), 441–447. doi: 10.1057/dev.2011.86

Hidalgo-Capitán, Antonio; Guillén, Alejandro; Deleg, Nancy (2010), "El indigenismo ecuatoriano y el *Sumak Kawsay*: entre el buen salvaje y la paja del páramo", in Antonio Hidalgo-Capitán, Alejandro Guillén and Nancy Deleg (eds.), *Sumak Kawsay Yuyay: Antología del Pensamiento Indigenista Ecuatoriano sobre Sumak Kawsay.* Huelva y Cuenca: FIUCUHU, 17–21. Available at http://dspace.ucuenca.edu.ec/bitstream/123456789/21745/1/Libro%20Sumak%20Kawsay%20Yuyay.pdf

Hinkelammert, Franz (2004), *Crítica de la Razón Utópica.* Bilbao: Desclée de Brouwer.

Hunt, Lynn (2007), *Inventing Human Rights: A History.* New York: W.W. Norton.

Klein, Naomi (2014), *This Changes Everything: Capitalism vs. the Climate.* Toronto, ON: Alfred A. Knopf Canada.

León, Irene (ed.) (2009), *Sumak Kawsay/Buen Vivir y cambios civilizatorios.* Quito: FEDAEPS.

Moyn, Samuel (2010), *The Last Utopia: Human Rights in History*. Cambridge, MA: Belknap Press of Harvard University Press.

Museka, Godfrey; Madondo, Manasa Munashe (2012), "The Quest for a Relevant Environmental Pedagogy in the African Context: Insights from unhu/ubuntu Philosophy", *Journal of Ecology and the Natural Environment*, 4(10), 258–265.

O'Donnell, Erin L. (2017), "At the Intersection of the Sacred and the Legal: Rights for Nature in Uttarakhand, India", *Journal of Environmental Law*, 30(1), 135–144. doi: 10.1093/jel/eqx026

Polanyi, Karl Paul (2012), *A Grande Transformação: as origens políticas e económicas do nosso tempo*. Lisbon: Edições 70.

Rodgers, Christopher (2017), "A New Approach to Protecting Ecosystems: The Te Awa Tupua (Whanganui River Claims Settlement) Act 2017", *Environmental Law Review*, 19(4), 266–279. doi: 10.1177/1461452917744909

Rodríguez-Garavito, César (ed.), (2015), *Human Rights in Minefields Extractive Economies, Environmental Conflicts, and Social Justice in the Global South*. Bogotá: Dejusticia.

Sánchez, Beatriz Eugenia (2001), "El reto del Multiculturalismo jurídico. La justicia de la sociedad mayor y la justicia indígena", in Boaventura de Sousa Santos and Mauricio Garcia Villegas (eds.), *El Caleidoscopio de las Justicias en Colombia, Tomo II*. Bogotá: Ediciones Uniandes, 5–142.

Santos, Boaventura de Sousa (1999), "Toward a Multicultural Conception of Human Rights", in Scott Lash and Mike Featherstone (eds.), *Spaces of Culture: City, Nation, World*. London: SAGE, 214–229. doi: 10.4135/9781446218723.n12

Santos, Boaventura de Sousa (2001), "Os Processos de Globalização: Introdução", in Boaventura de Sousa Santos (ed.), *Globalização: Fatalidade ou Utopia?* Porto: Afrontamento, 31–106.

Santos, Boaventura de Sousa (2006), *A gramática do tempo: para uma nova cultura política*. Porto: Afrontamento.

Santos, Boaventura de Sousa (2007), "Beyond Abyssal Thinking: From Global Lines to Ecologies of Knowledges", *Review (Fernand Braudel Center)*, 30(1), 45–89. http://www.jstor.org/stable/40241677

Santos, Boaventura de Sousa (2014), *Epistemologies of the South: Justice against Epistemicide*. Boulder, CO: Paradigm Publications.

Santos, Boaventura de Sousa (2015), *If God Were a Human Rights Activist*. Stanford, CA: Stanford University Press.

Santos, Boaventura de Sousa; Rodríguez-Garavito, César (2005), "Law, Politics, and the Subaltern in Counter-Hegemonic Globalization", in Boaventura de Sousa Santos and César Rodríguez-Garavito (eds.), *Law and Globalization from Below: Towards a Cosmopolitan Legality*. Cambridge: Cambridge University Press, 1–26.

Terretta, Meredith (2012), "'We Had Been Fooled into Thinking that the UN Watches Over the Entire World': Human Rights, UN Trust Territories, and Africa's Decolonization", *Human Rights Quarterly*, 34(2), 329–360. doi: 10.1353/hrq.2012.0022

Tortosa, José (2011), *Maldesarrollo y mal vivir: pobreza y violencia a escala mundial*. Quito: Abya-Yala.

Unceta, Koldo (2014), "Post crecimiento y desmercantilización. Propuestas para el Buen vivir", in Gustavo Endara (ed.), *Post-Crecimiento y Buen Vivir Propuestas globales para la construcción de sociedades equitativas y sustentables*. Quito: Friedrich Ebert Stiftung (FES-ILDIS), 59–92.

Waldmüller, Johannes (2014), "Buen Vivir, Sumak Kawsay, 'Good Living': An Introduction and Overview", *Alternautas*, 1(1), 17–28. Accessed on 5.12.2017, at http://www.alte rnautas.net/blog/2014/5/14/buen-vivir-sumak-kawsay-good-living-an-introduction-a nd-overview

Walsh, Catherine (2010), "Development as *Buen Vivir*: Institutional Arrangements and (De)colonial Entanglements", *Development*, 53(1), 15–21. doi: 10.1057/dev.2009.93

Chapter 2

"A Being Who is Not Made to Suffer"

On the Difference of the Human and on the Differences of Humans

João Arriscado Nunes

> *Hegemonic domination lies in the naturalization of human suffering as a fatality or necessity.*
>
> Boaventura de Sousa Santos (2014: 225)

Introduction

At the beginning of the 21st century, the tension between the affirmation of a common humanity as a protagonist of human rights and the recurring creation of new forms of discrimination and exclusions which negate this sense of a common belonging to humanity continue to mark the debates on the conceptions of human dignity and what it means to be human, reiterating, in different versions, the problem of how to affirm, simultaneously, one's equality and the recognition of difference (Santos, 2004). Human dignity is pronounced and affirmed in different idioms and grammars that are not recognized in the language of rights as shaped by Western society's sense of human rights or presented as particular modulations of such. One of these languages is humanitarianism.

This chapter, in taking up the observation made by Françoise Vergès (2001), will first examine present-day humanitarianism and identify the traces of the legacy derived from the 19th-century movements that fought for the abolition of slavery and which had strong ties to various religions or religious currents. This legacy aids in elucidating how humanitarianism, in the various forms that it has assumed over its history, is characterized by the forms of producing differences amongst human beings which corresponds to a distribution of attributes of humanity based on the assertion of a common experience of suffering. In its recent versions, medicine's delegation of the task of responding to identifiable suffering with the threat to the integrity and life of the body defines a grammar of the attributions of humanity legitimated by a certain form of knowledge and practice—medicine—and establishing a "hierarchy of suffering" which defines urgencies and priorities (Farmer, 2005: 29–30), a secularized version of the humanitarian orientations inherited from the 19th century or rooted in the different theological conceptions of suffering and care (Santos, 2014). Based on this exploration, we propose a perspective on suffering, one that is based on the epistemologies of the South, and with due respect paid to Fanon, who is fully cognizant of this common experience as well as the variety of ways that one can suffer, not through fatality or necessity but as the result of distinct and mutually constituted forms of oppression, and given that they are named, narrated and confronted, they encounter "unjust human suffering together with the pathos of the will to resist against it" (Santos, 2014: 225).

Within the European cosmovision, which served as the foundation for human rights in the 18th century, all men are created free and equal. Human beings who are born free and endowed with reason are recognized as having been duly afforded these rights. However, what is notable about this precept is the extent to which a significant sector of humanity has been excluded from any enjoyment of human rights. Women, children, enslaved, colonized peoples, and the disabled have either seen their birth right restricted or deprived. The 20th century witnessed an increased recognition of humanity for many persons, groups and communities who had suffered from exclusion, even succeeding in sparking discussions on the extension of certain human rights to non-human creatures, although this acknowledgement was the result of long- and hard-fought struggles.

Beginning in the 1970s, and also with its origins in the West, a grammar of common humanity gained visibility and relevance. This grammar is founded on the matrix idea of a humanity defined by the sense of belonging to a common species, united by a shared experience which is the suffering inscribed upon the bodies. Violations of human rights and human dignity become expressed as threats to life or to the integrity of bodies subjected to unnecessary violence or suffering. The answer is the intervention directed at saving lives and relieving one's suffering, suspending the reference to differences and inequalities to treat each human being as a being who is vulnerable to suffering and threatened by violence, be it the consequence of human action or a calamity caused by nature. Its exemplary manifestations are the operations carried out by organizations dedicated to humanitarian emergency medicine, configuring a regime of private care based on an explicit distinction between the sufferer and the carer and, more recently, on the distinction between the innocent victims of unnecessary suffering and the perpetrators of the situations of violation of human dignity centred on that which threatens one's physical integrity and deprives one of the basic conditions for survival. In these operations, the baseline seems to be momentarily placed in suspension, within a demarcated space, whose *exemplary/archetypal* manifestation is the refugee camp.

If, as Boaventura de Sousa Santos notes, the trivialization of suffering is tied to a "declassifying and disorganizing of the body" that separates the "soul from the body" and devalues the "visceral dimension of suffering, its visible mark of experience lived in the flesh" (Santos, 2015: 71), humanitarian medicine then seems to rescue this lived dimension of experience that is incorporated into suffering. But this is now mediated by the knowledge and practices of medicine and thus subject to the limitation of an access to suffering "made of epistemological (subject/object), categorial, and professional distances" (Santos, 2015: 71). One of its effects is, through these interventions, to create or recreate divisions and separations that redistribute attributes and abilities, tracing new lines that are visible—in the spatial and material organization of the interventions and in the spaces that they create—and invisible—for example, through the suspension of reference to existential experience and forms of sociability of those who are the object of assistance—instituting and reproducing the separations and exclusions which perpetuate the abyssal divide between metropolitan and colonial sociabilities, and between the subjects and objects of human rights (Santos, 2014).

How Do Humans Suffer? A Genealogy of Humanitarianism

"A being who is not made to suffer": Rony Brauman, one of the historic leaders of *Médecins Sans Frontières* affirmed in an interview the reason underlying the organization's commitment and the form of humanitarianism that it spearheads which is to alleviate "unnecessary suffering" (Brauman, 1996, 2004). In this statement, humanity as a species appears exposed to forms of suffering that demand a response via intervention in situations where the lives or the physical integrity of human beings is in imminent danger. Humanitarian intervention, thus, requires choices between the suffering which at any given moment deserves a response and that which is excluded from said response. Some situations of suffering merit urgent responses. Others require responses in the medium or long term. Still others are reduced to a secondary or invisible state, often the result of the difficulty or incapacity encountered in responding to them. Some of these situations, as Bruno Sena Martins notes (Chapter 4) in his reference to the Bhopal disaster and its consequences, serve to concentrate extreme and durable forms of suffering caused by the confluence of capitalist, colonial and patriarchal oppression that have persisted for generations. But humanitarian intervention is frequently the other side of the coin of military intervention, which is also carried out in the name of defending human dignity, although it generates more suffering and brings about the death of human beings (James, 2010). Humanity "that is not made to suffer" includes, in fact, many humanities, different in the definition of what counts as the suffering that merits urgent intervention. As Paul Farmer underscores, "the capacity to suffer is, clearly, part of being human. But not all suffering is equal" (2005: 50). And not all lives confronted with suffering are treated with the same dignity and recognition, even in death (Butler, 2004, 2010).

Manifest here are the tensions with which the genealogy of humanitarianism is fraught. They are inseparable from that which Maldonado Torres describes (Chapter 3) as being the process of secularization that moulds the modern Western conception of human rights. These tensions refer to those which also marked the 19th-century initiatives and campaigns that advocated for the abolition of slavery as well as entered the discussion on the differences between "civilised people" and "savages", the origins of the human species, and the differences amongst the races which fed what would later be called "scientific racism" in the final decades of the 19th century. For those who defended abolition, suffering was considered a mark of humanity and dignity for those persons who fell under the yoke of slavery. But in question was not just any suffering. As would happen with the issue of poverty, those who suffered might well be deemed as either deserving or undeserving of the attention and care doled out by these movements. The violent and outraged slave—such as those who would unilaterally declare the abolition of slavery in Haiti (then the French colony of Saint-Domingue), rallying in the late 18th century, appropriating the principles proclaimed by the French Revolution, and later declaring the first independent nation to be governed by slaves and the descendants of former slaves—was a figure compared with that of the peace-loving and praiseworthy image of the opponents of Uncle Tom, himself the embodiment of suffering that would be viewed as "deserving" or "legitimising" of the attentions of abolitionists (Vergès, 2001; Desmond and Moore, 2009).

Charles Darwin, in *The Descent of Man*—the book published in 1871 in which he examined the implications of his concept of natural selection to explain the origin and evolution of the human species—presented one of the first discussions based on the exhaustive review of what had been previously on the topic of the merits of comparing the monocentric and polycentric theses on the origins of human beings and their differences expressed as characteristics of the various human races.

Basing his statements on the scientific knowledge of his time, Darwin vigorously defended the idea that all human beings were of one single species, indeed, one of the branches in the lineage of the great primates and in fact distinguished from other closely related species which had gone on their own evolutionary path. The second part of *The Descent of Man* was dedicated to the discussion of that which Darwin named sexual selection, a third form of selection that coexisted alongside natural selection and artificial selection. Both themes were the focus of intense controversy in Victorian society, and Darwin's positions would continue to carry considerable weight in later decades, coming relatively soon after the polemics which initially pitted evolutionists against creationists.

The first topic opened a decades-long debate on the existence of different subspecies of humans corresponding to distinct races with differentiated characteristics and abilities which could be placed on a hierarchy characterized by specific moments in an evolutionary process of the savage state to the civilized state, a process that culminates in the affirmation of the superiority of the Caucasian race. Darwin's work constituted one of the first moments of systematic criticism to what would later be called scientific racism. In the positions presented and discussed at length by Darwin in the first part of his work *The Descent of Man*, the reader notes his conviction that all human beings were members of the same species, unquestionably, without exception, and independent of any those differences inscribed as phenotypes which lead one to identify and distinguish the races. It is this conviction that we also find associated with Darwin's opposition to slavery and his support of the abolitionist cause. But it is important to note that the existence of the races was, at that time, accepted by those who proclaimed the oneness of the species and the equal capacities of all human beings. The Haitian intellectual and politician Anténor Firmin (1850–1911), writing in 1885 on the "equality of the races", defined anthropology as "the study of Man in his physical, intellectual, and moral dimensions as he is found *in any of the different races which constitute the human species*" (Firmin, 1885: 15; emphasis added). The differences amongst the races were considered at the time to be the result of evolutionary and historical processes.

The discussion of difference and sexual selection sparked other types of debate, welcomed by feminist and suffragist movements in the United States as a demonstration that, as the Theory of Evolution postulated, women would not be relegated to positions and societal roles determined by immutable nature or by the divine imposition of the Creator (Hamlin, 2014). In Victorian England, in contrast, Darwin's work appeared as a durable contribution to the affirmation and consolidation of inequalities between the sexes and the legitimation of patriarchal domination as well as the persistence of hetero-patriarchal stereotypes in the field of biology (Roughgarden, 2005).

A question taken up by Darwin in the same work has been rarely the object of comment, although it is of particular interest for the present theme. Chapter 4 of Book 1 is dedicated to the "moral sense" of the human species and to its "origin and nature". According to Darwin's vision, this corresponds to what is revealed by the examination of "the early and undeveloped condition of this faculty in mankind" (2004: 141). The virtues considered most important are recognised amongst men [sic] or a rude existence when they seek to associate,

> but are practised almost exclusively in relation to the men of the same tribe; and their opposites are not regarded as crimes in relation to the men of other tribes. No tribe could hold together if murder, robbery, treachery, &c., were common; consequently such crimes within the limits of the same tribe 'are branded with everlasting infamy', but excite no such sentiment beyond these limits.
>
> (Darwin, 2004: 141)

Darwin next cites a set of practices from different regions around the world considered acceptable, or even encouraged and celebrated, by their populations such as the North-American Indians' scalping of enemies, the practice of decapitation amongst the Dayaks (a population on the Island of Borneo), the common practice of infanticide, or finally suicide viewed as an act of courage (and not as a crime) or an act deemed as honourable when confronted with an enemy attack.

Slavery has long been debated, defined as a "great crime" even though it was not considered as such in the past "even by the most civilised nations" and may have been "in some ways beneficial during ancient times" (Darwin, 2004: 141–142). The explanation lies in the holding of slaves who in general are of different races from their masters. He goes on to add, "As barbarians do not regard the opinion of their women, wives are commonly treated like slaves".

The majority of "savages", including Negroes, North-American Indians and other "primitives", would be indifferent to the sufferings of strangers, "or would even delight in witnessing them", an observation corroborated by the observation that "the women and children of the North-American Indians aided in torturing their enemies", adding that, "Some savages take a horrid pleasure in cruelty to animals, and humanity is an unknown virtue" (Darwin, 2004: 142).

However, despite these manifestations of indifference to suffering and the pleasure associated with cruelty,

> besides the family affections, kindness is common, especially during sickness, between the members of the same tribe, and is sometimes extended beyond these limits. Mungo Park's touching account of the kindness of the negro women of the interior to him is well known. Many instances could be given of the noble fidelity of savages towards each other, but not to strangers; common experience justifies the maxim of the Spaniard, 'Never, never trust an Indian.' There cannot be fidelity without truth; and this fundamental virtue is not rare between the members of the same tribe: thus Mungo Park heard the negro women teaching their young children to love the truth. This, again, is one of the virtues which becomes so deeply rooted in the mind, that it is sometimes practised by savages, even at a high cost, towards strangers; but to lie to your enemy has rarely been thought a sin, as the history of modern diplomacy too plainly shews. As soon as a tribe has a recognised leader, disobedience becomes a crime, and even abject submission is looked at as a sacred virtue.
>
> (Darwin, 2004: 142)

For Darwin, in essence, suffering that is accepted voluntarily to benefit the well-being of the tribe or group can be associated with a virtue of great esteem, such as courage or one's capacity for sacrifice, even when Darwin refers to the Fakirs of India driven by "foolish religious motive" (Darwin, 2004: 143).

Darwin concludes that

> actions are regarded by savages, and were probably so regarded by primeval man, as good or bad, solely as they obviously affect the welfare of the tribe—not that of the species, nor that of an individual member of the tribe. This conclusion agrees well with the belief that the so-called moral

sense is aboriginally derived from the social instincts, for both relate at first exclusively to the community.

(Darwin, 2004: 143)

Or, as he goes on to state, they confine sympathy to members of the same tribe.

Even considering, therefore, the existence of a single human species, differences seem to arise in the relationship with suffering, so often experienced as an act inflicted upon another, and with the capacity to feel sympathy for those who do not belong to what Darwin calls a "tribe". Negro women, according to accounts from the time, were said to show the greatest kindness in teaching their children such virtues as the value of truth.

However, the relationship with suffering, and in particular the ability or inability to recognize the suffering of others outside one's tribe, as well as the capacity to inflict cruel suffering on enemies, strangers and animals is explicitly acknowledged as a line which separates the "savages" from the "civilised".

It is worth contrasting Darwin's position with that of his contemporary, Anténor Firmin, in the latter's already cited work on the equality of the races (1885). Firmin refers to the idea—only to immediately rule it out—that some people will defend the notion that

> the Negro's so-called insensitivity is another special characteristic that distinguishes him from individuals of the White race in terms of their nervous system. This has never been ascertained. Such a conclusion was based on the observation of Blacks who had been stupefied by their infernal treatment and desensitized by numerous whippings. In some cases, this apparent insensitivity was a manifestation of courage on the part of individuals who would proudly and stoically suffer in silence rather than pass for a coward. Such cases would often involve fanaticism of some sort.
>
> (Firmin, 1885: 92)

Firmin (1885: 93–94) comments on these cases with examples from history and mythology, as in those of the Christian martyrs, or cases of Negro men who would refuse anaesthesia during surgery, thus desiring to demonstrate tolerance to suffering and pain apart from the differences of race. But this affirmation of a common insensitivity to pain seems to have been tempered, in the case of Negro men, by their need to assume such courage and stoicism as a challenge to their being made inferior:

> I know many Black men who have shown astounding courage during a surgical operation which they underwent without anesthesia. They stoically supported the horrific pain in order to avoid passing for a coward. When the surgeon asked them whether they could undergo surgery without anesthesia, these believed they would lose face if they declined. It is a stupid sort of bravery, but it shows the natural pride and courage of the

Black Ethiopian, a man who is always ready to face any trial in order to deserve the respect and admiration of others

(Firmin, 1885: 94)

The question of the differences that may exist amongst human beings tends to gravitate, here, towards the moral dimension, interfering with explanations based on biological difference, itself understood by Darwin and his intellectual descendants as difference within the same species. However, the emphasis on the moral sense and on intellectual capacities has served to create a new landscape on which, throughout the 20th century, an alternative way of affirming differences as hierarchy was built. In these differences, suffering has occupied a very special place.

The abolitionist movement, as has already been noted, would inflect another sense into the relationship with suffering. It is in the movement's actions that the notion of "morally legitimate suffering" will come to assume a central place in the humanitarian policies of the late 20th century.

The "New" Humanitarianism and Human Suffering

Humanitarianism, initially inspired by the founding of the Red Cross in the 19th century, adopted a new profile and took on a new face, beginning in the 1970s through a position which did not yield to the sovereignty of nations when responding to recognizable crises, the threat to life and the physical integrity of populations or groups whose situation demanded some form of intervention to alleviate human suffering and save lives in danger. This form of action found its legitimacy in its emphasis on human rights, if even at times indirectly. Some protagonists of this new humanitarianism, such as Bernard Kouchner, one of the founders of the *Médecins Sans Frontières* (an organization we will discuss later), would introduce the idea of a "right to intervene", implying the desire to go beyond humanitarian assistance based on strict neutrality with respect to the parties involved in the given situations (especially those of armed conflict) as defended by the Red Cross, thus problematizing one of the oldest and most problematic principles on which humanitarianism was founded.

A contentious aspect in the history of the new humanitarianism, especially following the Cold War, was its close connection with military interventions allegedly launched in the interest of protecting populations or communities under threat and of guaranteeing the safeguarding of human rights. Humanitarian intervention thus served as either justification for or warning against military actions, as the case of NATO's 1999 intervention in Kosovo demonstrates (Fassin, 2010: 281). However, the moral allegations of the humanitarian interventions would later be put to the test in other situations, generally associated with the great displacement of populations affected by war, natural disasters or persecution.

A closer look at the practice of humanitarian intervention shows that, beyond its differences in relation to actions explicitly aimed at condemning human rights violations, humanitarianism operates in the name of defending "dignity" (Redfield, 2013). As Fassin observes (2010: 277), the differences between these ways of understanding human dignity tend to be less marked on the ground, especially when the humanitarian intervention includes a testimony of the violations of the lives and integrity of peoples, groups, communities or populations affected by the crisis situation that had justified said intervention. These convergences become clearer when the relationship between humanitarianism and human rights, today constituted in normative bodies and inspiring distinct modes of intervention, is considered under the point of view of their common kinship in a genealogy that has endeavoured to make the dignity of all human beings as members of a common humanity compatible with the alleged differences at the core of a common humanity, which would justify any condition of inferiority and deny the recognition of one's full humanity. Women, children, colonized peoples, "savages" and the insane were thus placed under suspicion as to whether they were indeed fully human. In recent versions of humanitarianism, another form of establishing and legitimizing differences amongst human beings has come to occupy a growing space.

The organization *Médecins Sans Frontières* (MSF) became the exemplary manifestation of this new humanitarianism, sustained from the outset by the criticism of "third-world-ism" and the ensuing political, social and ethical impasses, and by the adoption of a human rights discourse aimed at totalitarianism. Emergency medical intervention in situations threatening the life and integrity of those individuals at risk of falling victim to natural disasters, armed conflict or persecution has allowed for the identification of violations of human dignity with respect to the threats to bodily safety that they suffer. Whereas other organizations and movements which defended human rights understood health as access to one's rights, as well as the conditions for assuring them via universal health care, organizations providing humanitarian medical services have sought to protect human lives in peril, wherever and whenever they are being threatened. The philosophical justification of this difference can be found in the recuperation of an Aristotelian distinction made by Hannah Arendt (and later by Giorgio Agamben) between the "bare life" (zoe) and "qualified life" (bios), with the former being exposed to risk in emergency situations, and beyond the distinctions of history, class, race, ethnicity, gender, sexual orientation, age or religion (Redfield, 2013). Situations of emergency would thus become revelatory of the common condition of a humanity exposed to suffering, configuring a mode of intervention in terms of its particular scale and temporality, incompatible with the long-term involvement that used to characterize the initiatives of promoting access to health care as a right.

A mark of the "new" humanitarianism is its focus on interventions that have mobilized medical knowledge and practices; more precisely, those that allow for addressing situations of emergency, life or death or those that threaten one's bodily integrity, thus bestowing the decisive role of the protagonist chiefly upon the doctors and organizations that they will come to establish, as in MSF and *Médicins du Monde* (Redfield, 2013; Fox, 2014). The objective was not the general defence of human rights or the attempt to contribute to the betterment of the human condition in situations that are an affront to human dignity, but instead to alleviate suffering wherever and whenever it occurs, as well as save lives via emergency interventions (Ticktin, 2011: 17). The victims of human rights violations are thus converted into the sick as they have been affected by some form of physical damage, with their condition as human beings who are suffering or whose lives or physical integrity are at risk representing the criterion for providing aid. The "universal truth of humanity" is thus inscribed upon the bodies that suffer (Ticktin, 2011: 15), a "new humanity" that is recognized by the noticeable violence or damage inflicted upon the body. The mapping of post-abyssal human dignities, proposed in the introduction of this book, must address the volatile ontology of the human unveiled by the apparatus of humanitarian emergencies.

A more precise observation of humanitarian practices indicates that terms such as "dignity"—frequently used in humanitarian medicine—allow for a convergence with the discourses and practices that come to the defence of human rights and report any violation. In the field, as was previously mentioned, there is less of a marked distinction, especially when humanitarian interventions include witnesses to the violation of human rights and the physical integrity of human beings (Fassin, 2010: 277).

The practice of humanitarian emergency medicine, however, faces dilemmas and problematic situations that incite certain tensions, not only with other forms of intervention made legitimate by their reference to human rights but with conceptions of human dignity and human suffering which do not fit within the boundaries of their policy. These tensions fuel the critical dynamics within some humanitarian medicine organizations, with special reference to MSF (Rambaud, 2015). An example of this discussion appears in a report from MSF-Holland with respect to the response to the 2001 Ebola outbreak in Uganda:

> The public health response was probably being dealt with in the traditional (local) way by shutting people away in the barn and not feeding them or looking after them. Such a response traditionally would probably have broken the epidemic as quickly as anything we did, but the motivation for MSF was the alleviation of individual suffering. Alleviation of suffering and dying with dignity was enormously important. We know we saved very few lives.

The objective was to show the central concern of the organization in alleviating the suffering of those afflicted with the disease, contrasting it with the "traditional" public health measures. Equally affirmed is the importance afforded to guaranteeing a dignified death to those whose lives could not be saved.

Well known are the conflicts and tensions which emerge, pitting the need to guarantee the viability of the organization's emergency interventions, whose explicit objective is to save lives, against those public health responses that strive to preserve the collective conditions for survival and their eventual expansion and consolidation, as happens with some human-rights-oriented health care interventions. Taking up the principles of Liberation Theology, Paul Farmer (2005) has sought to show the possibilities for and the obligation to find a compatible middle ground for these two positions in emergency situations through what he identifies as the call to pragmatic solidarity. Although this may only mean saving few lives, it is viewed as an ethical imperative associated with alleviating suffering and ascribing value to all human life and always considering those conditions beyond the emergency situation. It is not surprising, then, that support of pragmatic solidarity has often been criticized as being an exercise that may cause perverse effects, discrediting public health interventions given that the desire to save lives may well end up falling short, having been carried out partially or in a limited fashion, generating unreal expectations with respect to the humanitarian actors' capacity for intervention.

In case of the emergency interventions of organizations such as the MSF, as well as those of organizations or projects dedicated to pragmatic solidarity within the framework of a broader commitment to the development and consolidation of public health structures, a common point of reference is found with regard to human life, particularly when the lives of specific human beings in a situation of emergency are under threat and when the question of the dignity of human beings is raised, even when this dignity is respected in the way or conditions in which suffering individuals die.

The similarity extends to the tensions which emerge with respect to emergency interventions and the promotion of public health. In the case of MSF, as Redfield (2015) comments, we can find an expression of this tension when an organization's judgement is withheld in terms of how rigorously local practices are performed and how to recognize the "possibility of iatrogenic harm, a somber possibility that extended beyond care itself" (Redfield, 2015: 39). Redfield continues, citing the discussion at the General Assembly of MSF-France in 2005, on the organization's approach to the outbreak of the Marburg virus which had just occurred in Angola. During this discussion, there was mention of the need to change the established modes of intervention in medical emergencies which, as will be seen later, can aid in eroding how individuals impart respect for the dignity of human beings who suffer and who MSF is committed to assist. One participant went so far as to say that the organization was being reduced to "health police", and another lamented the "remote, paranoiac attitude of the majority of caregivers", thus widening the already large gap that exists between doctors and patients.

Most ultimately agreed that the *brutality of the operation was regrettable*, and concluded that in future anthropologists and psychologists should be involved to a greater degree in such circumstances, since *caregivers' actions consist here in particular of supporting the patients and their loved ones through the dying process*.

(*apud* Redfield, 2015 39; emphasis added)

Redfield adds the following enlightening commentary: "In later operations, MSF would attempt to some degree to recognize the humanity of its patients" (Redfield, 2015 39, emphasis added).

In other words, there is still lingering doubt as to whether the interventions, whose goal is to respond to suffering in a medical emergency, would recognize what transforms bodies that suffer into human beings who merit a type of treatment that acknowledges and relates to them as human beings. But where can one find this humanity? Might the very practice of emergency medicine contribute to the erosion of the primary goal of saving lives and alleviating suffering? Once again, Redfield makes a pertinent comment, this time during the post-Ebola outbreak period in 2014:

When the virus unexpectedly appeared in West Africa, humanity took a backseat to security. The breach in the larger social membrane, however, ran deeper and wider than any gap in protective clothing.

(Redfield, 2015: 39)

Attempting to propose a moral for the Ebola outbreak, Redfield seems to associate himself with Farmer by saying "there is no packaged substitute for an effective health care system" (Redfield, 2015: 41).

Fanon: The Body That Suffers and the Criticism of Neo-Hippocratism

In 1952, Fanon published his first, remarkable book, *Black Skin, White Masks*. This was also the year in which a series of articles were published that discussed the condition of immigrants from North Africa who were treated in health care units in France. Fanon was a psychiatrist, and having learned much from the innovative ideas of François Tosquelles and other pioneers of institutional psychiatry, he displayed an interest (which he would later pursue in his work in Algeria and Tunisia) in the diversity of experiences relating to human suffering, particularly those associated with racism and colonialism (Fanon, 2011, 2015: 135–446). Contrary to the majority of his French colleagues, Fanon was sympathetic to how colonial violence was imposed, despite those practices whose specific goal was to deal with suffering and to bring relief and healing. Fanon's contributions in the following years took up such themes as the elucidation of the conditions and determinations of different types of psychopathology associated with the various fundamental forms of violence found in colonial domination—ones affecting, albeit in different ways, the colonized, the colonizers and the agents of colonization—such as the effects (just as much for the sake of domination as for liberation) of radio programmes and "the voices on the radio" (Fanon, 2011: 322ff.).

Fanon's interests—in the diversity of the experiences and the languages of suffering in the colonial context and the struggle for liberation, in the way that both the colonized and the colonizers were affected by the violence of colonialism, and in violence itself and the response to it—allow us to recognize not only his humanity but also that which separated these interests, requiring distinct understandings of how different individuals suffered and shared this suffering. The debate over attributing moral legitimacy to certain forms of violence that sought to respond to colonial violence did not deter Fanon from pursuing his identification and understanding of the forms of suffering that the violence generated by colonialism and by the response to it were creating amongst those suffering from them, and in certain conditions, amongst those who perpetrated said violence upon the colonized and who shared colonialism as a point in common.

Fanon described the ailments of North African patients in French hospitals as "pain without lesion [...] illness distributed in and over the whole body [...] continuous suffering" and how their complaints led the doctors to the "easiest" (diagnostic) attitude: "the negation of any type of morbidity" (Fanon, 2011: 694). This negation of "real" suffering confronting the doctors would thus be the expected result of what Fanon describes as a particular "medical orientation" he calls "neo-Hippocratism"; in other words, they are concerned less with making a "diagnosis of an organ" than with making a "diagnosis of a function", still far from becoming predominant in the study of pathology. Fanon labels this orientation "a flaw in the practitioner's thinking", a "very dangerous flaw" (2011: 695). This is based on the presuppositions of medical thinking which proceed from the symptom to the lesion, given that "every symptom requires its lesion". Yet in certain patients, something seems to go wrong: they display symptoms but not the lesions to which the symptoms should be pointing. The patient is thus seen as "indocile, undisciplined", someone who does not know "the rules of the game" (2011: 696–697). In the absence of a lesion, the diagnosis will be [...] "North African syndrome!" (2011: 697):

> The medical staff discovers the existence of a North African syndrome. Not experimentally, but on the basis of an oral tradition. The North African takes his place in this asymptomatic syndrome and it automatically put down as undisciplined (cf. medical discipline), inconsequential (with reference to the law according to which every symptom implies a lesion) and insincere (he says he is suffering when we know there are no *reasons* for suffering).
>
> (Fanon, 2011: 697 emphasis in the original)

Here we are faced with a conception of "real" or "legitimate" suffering sanctioned by medical science. We shall encounter it in renewed versions in humanitarian medicine: it is that which allows for the convergence of the symptom and the lesion, marked on the body in an identifiable way by diagnostic procedures and which define the threat that must be treated via clinical intervention. The body that suffers (legitimately) is the body that is damaged or whose integrity is threatened by a lesion, which must be identified through symptoms compatible with the biomedical definition that establishes the link between a symptom or symptoms and the lesion. It should therefore not be surprising that humanitarian medicine, and in particular its more powerful and visible version—emergency medicine—should find itself outside its own territory when it encounters forms of suffering that do not fit neatly into the relationship between symptoms and lesions. We can thus better understand the resistance which marked certain moments in the history of organizations dedicated primarily to humanitarian emergency medicine to expand their intervention to problems associated with mental health, and with the expression of what is described in their jargon as "trauma". One of the consequences of this difficulty is that, in certain situations, frequent manifestations of suffering associated with forms of violence that are not directly inscribed on the body via lesions or diagnosable deficiencies may encounter resistance to their being recognized as "real" or "legitimate" suffering in the way that humanitarian intervention defines it as a feature common to all humanity.

Refusing concessions to neo-Hippocratism and its criteria for identifying "real" suffering, Fanon follows the course begun by the pioneers in psychosomatic medicine via the "situational diagnosis". This includes the inquiry into the immediate environment of the sick person, the individual's "occupations and preoccupations", sexuality, "inner tension", the feeling of security or insecurity, threats, evolution and history of his life (Fanon, 2011: 697–702). Fanon would come to appreciate the limits of this approach during his experience in Algeria in the form of intense contact with the conditions of colonialism and cultural differences. Thus it became possible to denounce the dehumanizing force of racism and the power of the stigma associated with "Arab", recognizing the forms through which suffering is expressed and seeks out the appropriate paths for attending to this suffering. In this process, both common humanity and the differences in which it is manifested through diverse ways of naming and allowing suffering to be expressed are brought to the centre.

In the final part of the chapter from *The Wretched of the Earth*, which examines mental illness and the colonial war, Fanon (2011: 660–672) discusses the colonialist theories that depict North Africans as constitutionally prone to crime and violence and likely to react to pressured situations by inflicting violence onto others. According to one of these theories (2011: 659), one of the traits of the North African would allegedly be his scarce or non-existent "emotivity" or, according to another commentator, his state of being "born lobotomized"—which would explain their indifference to the suffering of others.

Fanon shows that specific and severe disturbances identified as psychosomatic appear in conditions of extreme vulnerability such as war, persecution, torture, physical violence, forced displacement, being deprived of the basic conditions to support life […] He describes certain disturbances as being "cortico-visceral", relating them to the effects of war even in the absence of direct exposure to combat or acts of violence inflicted directly on those persons presenting these disturbances (Fanon, 2011: 657–659). He also raises the question of the possible existence of common types of experiences as generating mental disturbances associated with being exposed to violence and armed conflict in the colonial setting.

The disturbances which Fanon ascribes to one of the groups of his classifications (group g) leads him to consider this group as the only one which can be specifically associated with the situation of colonial domination and anticolonial strife in Algeria. It is interesting to note that, in Fanon's commentaries, the suggestion emerges that there might common types of experience and that the manifestation of disturbances that arise in permanent "states of emergency" associated with what Boaventura de Sousa Santos calls "the abyssal condition" (Santos, 2014).

Fanon voices harsh criticism of the colonialist conception of these health conditions and types of suffering as a "congenital stigma of the 'native'" allegedly stemming from the "predominant extrapyramidal system in the colonized", which, according to the eminent authorities in psychiatry at the time, would be proof of a neurological state characteristic of colonized peoples and consequently a natural condition of inferiority that would thus be unsurmountable or unalterable. These descriptions were common long before the start of the Algerian Revolution and the war for independence (Fanon, 2011: 658–659).

Fanon's work had a significant influence on both ethno-psychiatry and on the approaches that it mobilized whose intent was to open spaces that would enable people who had life experiences and who came from distinct social and cultural backgrounds to meet in a cultural and social territory where it was unfamiliar for them to express how they suffer in such terms and language (Beneduce, 2007). This demanded intense work be done with the themes explored by Fanon, such as culture and memory, and, for the field of critical ethno-psychiatry, the legacy of Fanon's work has been crucial for dealing with the dynamics of suffering understood as the result of mutual intersections and conditioning of what he termed the phylogenetic, ontogenetic and sociogenic. This includes not only the ample forces of the making and unmaking of care-related connections and relationships which mould the singularity of being. The partial suspension of the reference to the sociogenic dimension is common in approaches to suffering that are today proposed by humanitarian emergency medicine (and frequently the object of criticism in internal discussions at humanitarian organizations) and are a condition to their viability. Fanon thus invites us to consider the structural and historical conditions of suffering associated with the different forms of oppression which converge as much in the colonial setting as in the post-colonial. This consideration withstands the operation of objectivation under the form of "determinants", described and identified as discrete influences that affect the causal trajectories that lead to violence, oppression and suffering. The processes of determination appear, rather, in their mutual construction and expression incorporated as violence and suffering, to be a disorder or disease, without their being confused with or reduced to a translation of biomedical categories (including those in psychiatry) of disease, disturbance or trauma (Farmer, 1993; Kleinman et al., 1997; Das et al., 2000, 2001; Lovell et al., 2014; Das, 2015; Nunes and Siqueira-Silva, 2016). Fanon is not only aware of the diversity of experiences incorporated into suffering but also connects them to the then available forms of care. His descriptions seem to anticipate the formulations that we will encounter later in social epidemiology and Latin-American Collective Health in which health, disease and care are interwoven into a single process.

Ticktin (2011) and Giordano (2014) have shown how an approach that is influenced by Fanon's work can offer an important point of entry for dealing with the condition of immigrants and refugees in Europe (in France and Italy, in this case). It becomes possible to conceive of an approach that is different from the official forms of triage based on the medical and moral assessment of suffering and trauma as a justification for asylum or residency requests. As Fassin and Rechtman (2011), among others, have shown, these modes of assessment have also become routine for humanitarian interventions in the Global South and have often contributed to reaffirming the idea of how the populations, communities, people and groups associated with the Global South, including immigrants and refugees, are incapable of defence and lack the capacity to act, thus turning them into objects in the humanitarian and human rights discourse.

What is at stake is the understanding of those expressions and languages through which suffering shows itself and speaks that have not found space in the nosological categories of biomedicine (and psychiatry in particular). Only thus can we recognize the limits of any approach to suffering and care that does not consider the need to expand the space where the intersections of the processes that put constraints on health, disease and care occur. This is a necessary condition so that the struggle for human dignity and human rights can be taken beyond the emergency humanitarian response to "life in crisis", and into the direction that a human being is a being that is "more than a body" (Fanon, 2011: 703), but always preserving at the core the affirmation of dignity that is inscribed upon vulnerable bodies, made of relationships with other bodies along the collective process of transformation of a human existence that is relational and procedural.

The De-Naturalization of Human Suffering

The construction of an existential phenomenology in the scope of the epistemologies of the South cannot be reduced to the expressions which frame it in the renewed versions of a neo-Hippocratism already criticized by Fanon, neither in the proliferation of the notion of trauma as a way to place suffering in the space where it "belongs" to the knowledge and practices of biomedicine and the biomedicalization of health. This phenomenology will have to consider suffering as the meeting place of the oppressions of capitalism, colonialism and the (hetero)patriarchy. It must seek out, as Gordon (2015) suggests, the dimensions which evade the conventional reductions of Eurocentric versions of experience and the ways that it becomes aware. It must find root in the recognition of the types of suffering as the expression of a characteristic condition of this convergence of oppressions in its lived out and situated experience, which is also the condition of liberation from unjust forms of suffering. But the distribution of the types of suffering is also marked by the drawing of the abyssal line which demarcates the zones of being and non-being, of existence and non-existence (Santos 2014, 2015). The distribution, however, seems to cross this line at multiple points in which situations of humanitarian emergency arise, those in which a local and temporary suspension of the demarcation between being and non-being occurs, one which does not abolish the demarcation but creates in the zones of non-being spaces of recognition of a humanity which is defined by its condition of threat to life and to the integrity of the bodies which suffer. This form of recognition lasts as long as the emergency, and it is generally confined to the spaces that are organized and managed to respond to the emergency. Its most visible manifestation is the camp, planned and governed according to the needs of the emergency medical intervention, but also with an existence that is restricted by dynamics beyond the control of the organizations involved. This space is also a temporary suspension of history, relationships, forms of sociability, experience and memory of those men and women for whom survival means explicit adherence to the discipline of the field (Agier, 2008, 2010; Redfield, 2013). Human beings treated in the camp will manifest the legitimacy of their suffering through submission to their discipline, yet their existential condition continues to be marked by an experience lived out beyond their passing through the camp. The camp therefore assumes the liminal condition of a space in which the possibility of a future existence depends on the acceptance of a temporary situation of suspension of being beyond the being-body whose suffering is a mark of humanity recognizable through the knowledge and practices of emergency medicine. It is not surprising, then, that organizations of humanitarian medicine are repeatedly beset by debates and deliberations of a political and ethical nature as to how to recognize the humanity of those men and women with whom they work. But, for those who live in the camps, in situations in which the emergency has become a permanent condition, suffering will increasingly define them as beings whose humanity has been seized by the conditionality of accepting their condition of being victims unable to guarantee the care that others will have to bring from "the other side" of the abyssal line.

For Boaventura de Sousa Santos, the discourses on human rights—and as we have seen, the positions and policies that humanitarianism invokes—converge with the progressive political theologies with respect to denouncing unjust suffering and the liberation of the oppressed from this suffering. Different versions of liberation theologies, according to Santos, favour different forms of suffering in different situations, moments and phases of its history. These forms of suffering—affirming the dignity of those men and women who suffer, both as persons and as collectives, peoples, communities or groups who share characteristics that turn them into targets for various types of oppression and violence—recognize the diversity and the configurations that the forms assume, as well as the very bodies that suffer, as places where the different forms of oppression and violence are inscribed (Santos, 2014: 106–172). When suffering manifests itself in its bodily dimension as "declassifying and disorganizing of the body" (Santos 2015: 71), humanitarian policy and the types of emergency intervention that give it form tend to favour the identification of common humanity as a vulnerability that is manifest in situations of crisis, in which alleviating suffering and saving lives via medical intervention appears as a moment of salvation for the power of modern Western medicine and the need for a reaffirmation of the line that separates those who suffer and those who, recognizing this suffering, possess the knowledge, capabilities and means to alleviate it. Humanitarianism and its policies have thus found—in their simultaneous affirmation of the commitment to alleviate suffering and save lives and neutrality in terms of the causes of this suffering and the danger that these lives face—the legitimization of a form of intervention that did not take long before it provoked crises and tensions that still persist at the heart of certain organizations which, with undeniable courage, generosity and abnegation, have sought to respond to the precarious existences of human beings who, either as persons or collectively, are victims of extreme forms of oppression and violence. James Orbinski, when receiving the Nobel Peace Prize awarded to MSF in 1999, defined the humanitarian act in this way: "to seek to relieve suffering, to seek to restore autonomy, to witness to the truth of injustice, and to insist on political responsibility".[1] This partial problematization of neutrality as the brand of humanitarianism, however, does not serve to explicitly identify the capitalist, colonial and patriarchal oppression which feeds this unnecessary and unjust suffering.

Human suffering is that which is "common among the various forms of discrimination and oppression" (Santos, 2014: 90). The insurgent cosmopolitanism on which the struggle for human dignity is founded, whether spoken in the language of human rights or in other languages, is founded on the "global and multidimensional character of human suffering", and on "the destabilizing image of multiform suffering caused by human initiative" which is "as overwhelming as it is unnecessary" (2014: 90–91) a type of suffering viewed as "a fatality or necessity" (2014: 225). However, this conclusion should take us further than humanitarian politics postulates, beyond the task (and without a shadow of a doubt) of saving lives and alleviating the suffering that affects bodies, of affirming common humanity defined by one's belonging to a common species, since "it is not human nature but human initiative that unites us" (2014: 91). If a decades-long experience has allowed organizations founded on the premises of humanitarianism to internally open discussion on suffering and human dignity beyond the space defined by the neo-Hippocratic inheritance and by the capture of those who have caused suffering, it is the historical and persistent experience of discrimination and oppression to which peoples, communities, social groups and individuals have been subjected and which underlies the demand for confronting and eliminating unjust forms of suffering, those which are the result of episodes of discrimination, oppression and violence which is multiple, named, narrated, denounced and fought by those who have suffered them, of the "contradiction between the life experiences of the oppressed and the idea of a decent life" (Santos, 2014: 225).

Confronting unjust suffering, if one follows the path of progressive theologies, is based on the articulation "of the visceral engagement in a succoring gesture or unconditioned care, and the political struggle against the causes of suffering as part of the unfinished task of divinity" (Santos, 2015: 72) through a struggle for cognitive, social and historical justice and through human dignity rooted in the knowledge and experiences of those who suffer oppression and injustice.

Note

1 Available at: www.nobelprize.org/nobel_prizes/peace/laureates/1999/msf-lecture.html.

References

Agier, Michel (2008), *Gérer les indésirables. Des camps de réfugiés au gouvernement humanitaire.* Paris: Flammarion. doi: 10.1353/hum.2010.0005

Agier, Michel (2010), "Humanity as an Identity and Its Political Effects (A Note on Camps and Humanitarian Government)", *Humanity: An International Journal of Human Rights, Humanitarianism, and Development*, 1(1), 29–45.

Beneduce, Roberto (2007), *Etnopsichiatria. Sofferenza mentale e alterità fra Storia, dominio e cultura.* Roma: Carocci Editore.

Brauman, Rony (1996), *Humanitaire, le dilemme.* Paris: Editions Textuel.

Brauman, Rony (2004), "From Philanthropy to Humanitarianism: Remarks and an Interview", *South Atlantic Quarterly*, 103(2–3), 397–417. doi: 10.1215/00382876-103-2-3-397

Butler, Judith (2004), *Precarious Life: The Powers of Mourning and Violence.* London: Verso.

Buttler, Judith (2010), *Frames of War: When is Life Grievable?* London: Verso.

Darwin, Charles (2004[1871]), *The Descent of Man, and Selection in Relation to Sex.* 2nd ed. London: Penguin.

Das, Veena (2015), *Affliction: Health, Disease, Poverty.* New York: Fordham University Press. doi: 10.5422/fordham/9780823261802.001.0001

Das, Veena et al. (eds.) (2000), *Violence and Subjectivity.* Berkeley, CA: University of California Press.

Das, Veena et al. (eds.) (2001), *Remaking a World. Violence, Social Suffering and Recovery.* Berkeley, CA: University of California Press.

Desmond, Adrian; Moore, James (2009), *Darwin's Sacred Cause. How a Hatred of Slavery Shaped Darwin's Views on Human Evolution*. New York: Houghton Mifflin Harcourt.

Fanon, Frantz (2011), *Œuvres*. Paris: Éditions La Découverte.

Fanon, Frantz (2015), *Écrits sur l'aliénation et la liberté*. Paris: Éditions La Découverte.

Farmer, Paul (1993), *AIDS and Accusation: Haiti and the Geography of Blame*. Berkeley, CA: University of California Press.

Farmer, Paul (2005), *Pathologies of Power: Health, Human Rights, and the New War on the Poor*. Berkeley, CA: University of California Press.

Fassin, Didier (2010), "Heart of Humaneness: The Moral Economy of Humanitarian Intervention", in Didier Fassin and Mariella Pandolfi (eds.), *Contemporary States of Emergency. The Politics of Military and Humanitarian Interventions*. New York: Zone Books, 269–293.

Fassin, Didier; Rechtman, Richard (2011), *L'empire du traumatisme. Enquête sur la condition de victime*. Paris: Flammarion.

Firmin, Joseph-Anténor (1885), *De l'égalité des races humaines (Anthropologie Positive)*. Paris: Librairie Cotillon.

Fox, Renée C. (2014), *Doctors without Borders: Humanitarian Quests, Impossible Dreams of Médecins Sans Frontières*. Baltimore, MD: Johns Hopkins University Press.

Giordano, Cristiana (2014), *Migrants in Translation. Caring and the Logics of Difference in Contemporary Italy*. Berkeley, CA: University of California Press.

Gordon, Lewis R. (2015), *What Fanon Said. A Philosophical Introduction to His Thought*. London: Hurst.

Hamlin, Kimberley A. (2014), *From Eve to Evolution. Darwin, Science, and Women's Rights in Gilded Age America*. Chicago, IL: University of Chicago Press. doi: 10.7208/chicago/9780226134758.001.0001

James, Erica Capla (2010), *Democratic Insecurities. Violence, Trauma, and Intervention in Haiti*. Berkeley, CA: University of California Press.

Kleinman, Arthur; Das, Veena; Lock, Margaret (eds.) (1997), *Social Suffering*. Berkeley, CA: University of California Press.

Lovell, Anne M.; Pandolfo, Stefania; Das, Veena; Laugier, Sandra (2014), *Face aux désastres. Une conversation à quatre voix sur la folie, le care et les grandes détresses collectives*. Montreuil-sous-Bois: Ithaque.

Nunes, João Arriscado; Siqueira-Silva, Raquel (2016), "Dos 'abismos do inconsciente' às razões da diferença: criação estética e descolonização da desrazão na Reforma Psiquiátrica Brasileira", *Sociologias*, 18(43), 208–237. doi: 10.1590/15174522-018004308

Rambaud, Elsa (2015), *Médecins sans frontières, sociologie d'une institution critique*. Paris: Dalloz.

Redfield, Peter (2013), *Life in Crisis: The Ethical Journey of Doctors without Borders*. Berkeley, CA: University of California Press.

Redfield, Peter (2015), "Where There is No Kit", *Limn*, 5, 36–41. Available at http://limn.it/medical-vulnerability-or-where-there-is-no-kit/

Roughgarden, Joan (2005), *Evolution's Rainbow. Diversity, Gender, and Sexuality in Nature and People*. Berkeley, CA: University of California Press.

Santos, Boaventura de Sousa (ed.) (2004), *Reconhecer para Libertar*. Porto: Afrontamento.

Santos, Boaventura de Sousa (2014), *Epistemologies of the South. Justice against Epistemicide*. Boulder, CO: Paradigm Publications.

Santos, Boaventura de Sousa (2015), *If God Were a Human Rights Activist*. Stanford, CA: Stanford University Press.

Ticktin, Miriam (2011), *Casualties of Care. Immigration and the Politics of Humanitarianism in France*. Berkeley, CA: University of California Press. doi: 10.1525/california/978052 0269040.001.0001

Vergès, Françoise (2001), *Abolir l'esclavage: une utopie coloniale. Les ambiguités d'une politique humanitaire*. Paris: Éditions Albin Michel.

Chapter 3

On the Coloniality of Human Rights

Nelson Maldonado-Torres

Introduction

Human rights are generally considered to be one of the fundamental contributions of the Western world to global politics. They are meant to be protectors of individuality and sovereignty. As useful as they have or can be, there is, however, a fundamental limit to what they can achieve: they presuppose, rather than establish or prove, the humanity of those who are supposed to be covered by them. Therefore, at best, they can only aspire to work effectively within a context that not only grants humanity to everyone but does so evenly. However, the very Western modernity that has generated the hegemonic discourse of the "Rights of Man" is also the global episteme that generated the view of colonial ontological differences among human beings. These differences not only make some human beings appear as more human than others but also establish hierarchical relations of power among them.

The hierarchical character of the ontological relations that become central in Western modernity tend to have a colonial structure in the sense that they firmly divide populations and sectors within populations in terms that acquired legitimacy and an apparent aura of normalcy in modern colonial ventures. Discovery, conquest, colonization, rape and slavery become some of the predominant practices that acquire a new meaning or form in this context and that are taken to be largely normal, especially when those on the receiving end are not regarded as white or Europeans. I use the term coloniality to refer to the normalization of colonial ontological relations as well as to the practices, institutions, and cultural, social and epistemological formations to which they give rise.[1]

It would be easy to think that the notions of human rights and coloniality are simply in a direct and simple opposition to each other, demonstrating how complex and plural Western modernity is. Some may be tempted to consider coloniality the venom that human rights came to cure. However, some differences can be more superficial than they appear, and their very opposition can be functional to a larger goal. Identifying this requires a radical examination, in the sense of excavating and examining the roots of an issue. Here, I attempt a radical exploration of some basic linkages between human rights and coloniality.

My central argument is that human rights discourse, as typically known, plays a key part in a shift in the Western understanding of human beings and their relation with God, with each other, and with nature from a "chain of being" with God at its head to a "system of nature" and a heavily Eurocentric and dehumanizing humanism. This shift involves the displacement of the centrality of the notion of a vertical relation between God and human beings while it increases and strengthens the idea of vertical differences among those clearly understood as human beings and many others whose humanity would be in question. Human rights discourse sought to anchor equality among those who were recognized as fully human. If the notion of a vertical relation between God and human beings was expressed in the concept of the "chain of being", the ontologically vertical relations among human beings could be identified as coloniality. Human rights discourse plays an important role in the challenge to the order of the world reflected in the notion of the chain of being and, in spite of appearances to the contrary, advances the one sustained on coloniality.

I first start with contextualizing the emergence of declarations of the "Rights of Man" in the late eighteenth century within a contingent historical process that led to the formation of a secular line in the modern West. This secular line, together with a colonial ontological line, provides the basis for a reconceptualization of the meaning of humanity in modernity. The declarations of the "Rights of Man" are a crucial part of this redefinition and they aim to secure some level of equality among those considered to be at the top of the ontologically and naturalistically defined human species. With the shift from the "Rights of Man" to human rights in the twentieth century, one can more clearly observe the extent to which those rights serve as ways to call for assimilation to Western ideas of the human and socio-political formations, as well as substitutes for engaging in decolonization. Like other Western concepts that have been used to thematize the living conditions and freedoms of those at the top of the ontological hierarchy, human rights have also been claimed by the dehumanized and the decolonized, particularly in contexts where the dominant institutions that have a bearing on a situation are liberal in character and where revolutionary struggles are next to practically impossible. But the more substantial struggle for decolonization often involves a challenge to the framework of the broad secular and ontological lines of Western modernity rather than the assimilation into them through appeals to concepts such as human rights. This leads to a vision of transcending Western modernity/coloniality rather than of being included into it (or into its institutions) through appeals to specific rights or recognition of the importance of diversity.

The "Rights of Man" and the Secular Line: A Genealogical Overview

The "Rights of Man" that are declared in the late eighteenth century can be understood as part of a revolt against hereditary monarchy, nobility and medieval hierarchies. This revolt did not start in the Enlightenment, just like capitalism and other institutions and ideas of modernity did not start in the Enlightenment either (Wallerstein, 1991). At its bottom, this political and theoretical struggle was part of a larger debate in the long sixteenth century regarding the position of human beings (*humanitas*) in relation with the divine (*divinitas*) that could be traced back at least to the European Renaissance. What happened in the context of the Enlightenment was not the creation but the more widespread acceptance of certain formal distinctions between God, Man and the animal world. It was establishing these formal distinctions, more than advancing "politically relevant rights such as freedom of speech or the right to participate in politics" that were at stake in the English and French conceptions of human rights and the Rights of Man in the eighteenth century (Hunt, 2007: 23).

In short, the philosophical exploration of the "Rights of Man" is part of the larger humanistic, and increasingly secular, project of creating clear lines of demarcation and distinction between the divine, the human and the animal world. I have referred to this in another context as the production of the secular line in Western modernity (Maldonado-Torres, 2015). It is worth examining the production of this line with more attention.

While one of the characteristic features of the Western medieval world consisted in the attempt to differentiate Christianity as the one true religion from other perceived religious formations as false religions, to which I have referred to as theological difference, the humanistic revolution of the European Renaissance concentrated its attention in creating lines of differentiation between the divine (*divinitas*), humanity (*humanitas*) and the so-called natural and animal world (Maldonado-Torres, 2014, 2015). This other set of lines belongs to the order of secular difference, where "Man" is the central referent.

The difference between God, human beings and animals was generally understood in the Christian medieval world and in the Renaissance in terms of a "great chain of being", a concept present in the work of Aristotle and of Neoplatonists such as Plotinus, who influenced Christian theology. In Aristotle's work, the chain of being served the role of a regulative principle or logic that indicated that all beings in the universe could be classified in terms of gradual links that went from the highest to the lowest. In Plotinus's work, the notion of a hierarchy of being is even more developed and served to provide a justification for the existence of evil in spite of the absolute goodness of God. Plotinus believes that the "goodness" of the universe consisted in its fullness, and fullness includes a maximum diversity of elements which means that the best universe had to contain both a multiplicity of good and a multiplicity of evil.

Christians widely adopted the notion of the chain of being, considering the Christian God as the highest and most perfect being, followed by celestial beings and human beings down to animals and inorganic material. Human beings played a major role in the narrative of salvation, and they were considered to be not only the highest form of organic life but also those for the sake of whom God sacrificed himself. Humans were the highest form of creation in the world, but their greatness was intrinsically tied to the grace of the Supreme Being itself. Everything human therefore obtained value in relation to this connection with the divine. Also, the social, political, and economic order was linked together and meant to mirror the chain of being itself. So, just like there was a God on top of creation, there was a King on top of kingdoms, and so on. The conception of the edifice of the cosmos served as the blueprint for the construction of the social, political and economic order.

There was never a full consensus about the specific conception of the chain of being, but the chain of being became an overwhelming metaphor in the medieval Christian world to understand the nature of creation and the order of the world. Support for it was found in "ancient" philosophy and the scriptures, while it was propagated by theology, the teachings of the Church, along with rituals, laws and daily practices, among various other ways. The assertion of the "Rights of Man" in the eighteenth century testifies to a long process of debate about the characterization of the chain of being and the place of "Man" in it. It is a debate that can be traced back to artistic and literary works from the twelfth to the sixteenth century, which started to express the notion that there was something inherently valuable in human activity and human production. If similar works had been created in the past, it was now that they were collectively making, or appropriated to make, an impact on what was later going to become "Western" consciousness.

Perhaps the clearest text that went in the direction of finding an alternative conception of "Man" was Pico della Mirandola's "Oration on the Dignity of Man" (Pico della Mirandola, 1956, originally published in 1486 as *Oratio de hominis dignitate*), which is often depicted as a manifesto of the European Renaissance. In the "Oration", della Mirandola tells the Christian story of the creation of the world in a way that positions "Man" between God and animals. "Man" appears as a being endowed with an open-ended set of possibilities in comparison to nature and animals, which are prescribed one meaning or function by the Creator. The "Oration" is an essay with philosophical content but not a traditional philosophical treatise per se. It uses literary devices such as storytelling to convey a concept and an image with the view of "Man" that Renaissance artists, scientists and philosophers were also putting forward.

It is very illuminating that while one finds the most direct and influential initial assertion of the dignity of "Man" in an "Oration", the most explicit and perhaps enduring claims of the "Rights of Man" will be found in "Declarations". These are two different genres with different presuppositions and implications. The Latin word "Oratio" means discourse as well as prayer, and the text concludes with a prayer: "let us now, with the prayer the outcome may be fortunate and favorable, as to the sound of the trumpets, joint battle" (Pico della Mirandola, 1956: 69). The assertion of the dignity of Man is a discourse as well as a prayer simultaneously directed to peers as well as to someone who is beyond the limits of one's horizons. The prayer is, rhetorically at least, a humble recognition of something beyond. This is different from a "declaration", in which there is the sense of the creation of a new beginning or at least the assumption of a status already enjoyed but not fully understood or adopted. It is as if, with the pronouncement of the Rights of Man, at least some dimension of the sense of dignity that was initially expressed as a prayer is then vigorously asserted as a "declaration". This new assumption in the form of a "declaration" serves as a basis not only to claim the independence of a territory from a European empire in the case of the United States of America but also, and more crucially, to assert a more complete acceptance of the independence of "Man" from divine *autoritas* and from existing traditions that limit the expression of a secular political order. This secular political order was to be grounded not on God, but on "we the people". "The Rights of Man" refer to the rights of the individuals who are conceived to be part of such a "we".

As much as philosophy and political theory may have paved the way for the political revolutions and declarations of the late eighteenth century and their assertion of the "Rights of Man", the idea of the "Rights of Man" would have probably failed to advance without that which helped to make della Mirandola's *Oration* so influential, the power of storytelling and literature. Lynn Hunt highlights the role of literary work in the eighteenth century's advancement of the idea of the "Rights of Man". At that moment, literature became a device that helped develop a sense of "empathy" with other people. This empathy provided an emotional layer that was crucial to conceive or imagine of a human community on the basis of shared humanity instead of on the basis of shared divine origin or creation. According to Hunt,

> In the eighteenth century, readers of novels learned to extend their purview of empathy. In reading, they empathized across traditional social boundaries between nobles and commoners, masters and servants, men and women, perhaps even adults and children. As a consequence, they came to see others—people they did not know personally—as like them, as having the same kinds of inner emotions. Without this learning process, "equality" could have no deep meaning and in particular no political consequence. The equality of souls in heaven is not the same thing as equal rights here on earth. Before the eighteenth century, Christians readily accepted the former without granting the latter.
>
> (Hunt, 2007: 40)

Hunt highlights the role of the novel, and particularly novels of psychological identification in the eighteenth century. The three greatest of such novels, "Richardson's *Pamela* (1740) and *Clarissa* (1747–48) and Rousseau's *Julie* (1761) were all published in the period that immediately preceded the appearance of the concept of 'the rights of man'" (Hunt, 2007: 39). These epistolary novels and accounts of torture had, according to Hunt, "physical effects that translated into brain changes and came back out as new concepts about the organization of social and political life" (Hunt, 2007: 33).

As important as literature was to produce a sense of empathy that helped to establish the emotive basis for equality and of imagining a commonly shared humanity, this form of empathy and equality confronted two serious challenges. The first one had to do with gender, colonialism and slavery. Would the idea and feeling of equality extend to women, colonized and enslaved peoples? And if so, what would be the consequences of that and what would be needed for it to happen? The second challenge had to do with the very dialectical development of the notion of the "Rights of Man" as tied to the idea of the nation-state and the citizen. While the "Rights of Man" displaced (or renewed in different terms) the notion of the privileges of nobility and helped to create a socio-political organization anchored in the idea of the citizen, the very idea of citizenship in a nation-state delimited or modified the feeling of empathy. At the end, one was called to be, concretely, the citizen of a nation-state with a particular language, religion, customs, etc. Thus, one's immediate duties and responsibilities were extended to other citizens within the nation-state, but not necessarily outside it. I see these two challenges not only as practical difficulties faced by the unfolding of the secular line and of its basic forms of differentiation but as indications of the existence of yet another line, also constitutive of Western modernity. This is not a theological line that distinguishes one religion from another, or a secular line that differentiates the secular space from religious ones, but a line that distinguishes different forms of being, different essences, as it were, and that can take the form of a Manichean divide between an essentially defined good and an essentially defined evil. This is an ontological line that defines and delimits the space of authentic humanity and separates it from lesser forms of humanity. The Renaissance humanist revolution, the eighteenth-century psychological literature and the declarations of independence and the "Rights of Man" have to be understood not only in relation to the emergence and expansion of secularism but also in relation to this ontological line and coloniality. This contextualization and explanation of the ontological line will lead to the identification of the coloniality of human rights.

Towards a Critique of the Order of Man: The Secular and the Ontological Colonial Line or Line of Damnation

As we have seen, it is possible to consider the European Renaissance as a humanist revolt that sought to proclaim the dignity of Man vis-à-vis God and the animal world. These are terms of the debate that Lynn Hunt highlights when discussing the invention of the "Rights of Man" in the eighteenth century. I have located this invention in the larger scope of what I have referred to as the production of the secular line in modernity. However, the challenges faced by the emerging notions of the Rights of Man and the literature of empathy that one can relate to it point to a more complex picture of the European Renaissance and of modern European humanist revolts. For European modernity involves not only the production of a secular line but also a colonial one, which is a central referent to properly understand the depth of the challenges faced by the Rights of Man and the connections between declarations of human rights and coloniality. The colonial line is crucial for the particular modalities of gender and racial differentiations in Western modernity (challenge one), and highly informs the concept of the nation and of the nation-state (challenge two).

The colonial line is the most basic and primary expression of coloniality, understood as the production of ontological differences hierarchically organized in colonial forms as part of the modern civilizational order. In this sense, the colonial line can also be referred to as the modern/colonial line. The modern/colonial line is responsible for dividing the world in lighter zones, closer to civilization, and darker zones, closer to context defined by early death and torture—torture being worse than death itself. In that sense, both the European Renaissance and the Enlightenment, which are typically identified with civilization, also had what Walter Mignolo has called their "darker side", which puts in question the very definition of civilization (Mignolo, 2003).

For Mignolo, the "darker side" of modernity is produced by what he refers to as the "colonial difference" (Mignolo, 2000). For him, colonial difference is a physical and imaginary space or location where "two kinds of local histories", one increasingly global and imperial, and the other colonial, confront each other (Mignolo, 2000: ix). Colonial difference can be understood, in the terms that I am using here, as the outcome of lines of demarcation of spaces and histories, but also of knowledges and experiences. In that sense, one can refer to various forms of colonial difference, epistemic and ontological among them, as Mignolo does (Mignolo, 2011: 88). My genealogical argument here is that the transition from a Christian worldview that conceived the world through theological difference to one increasingly ordered through principles of secular difference took place in a context that replaced the centrality of belief with ontological distinctions and, therefore, theology with modernity/coloniality. That is, in Western modernity, what matters most for the purpose of the classification of peoples is not what they believe but what kind of beings they are. The classification is crucial for determining the possibility of claiming or enjoying the perceived privileges of modern civilization or not.

The modern/colonial ontological line has been theorized in multiple ways. It of course relates to Anibal Quijano and Immanuel Wallerstein's concept of coloniality (Quijano and Wallerstein, 1992), to Quijano's coloniality of power (Quijano, 2000), to Mignolo's "darker side" and modernity/coloniality (Mignolo, 2000, 2003), to Lugones's coloniality of gender (Lugones, 2007), to Sylvia Wynter's genealogy of humanism and blackness (Wynter, 1984, 1991), as well as to what Boaventura de Sousa Santos has referred to as the abyssal line— an abyss that ruptures the chain of being, one might say (Santos, 2007). I join Sylvia Wynter and Lewis Gordon in following Frantz Fanon's lead to explore ontological colonial difference in terms of damnation and then examine its relation with decolonization, all of which helps to determine with more precision the coloniality of human rights (Wynter, 2001; Gordon, 2005; Gordon, 2015).

Crucial for understanding the emergence of colonial ontological difference is that part of the European Renaissance coincided with the "discovery" and invention of the "New World", which led to new sets of questions that shifted the ways in which human dignity was affirmed. In that context, the challenge for European humanists became not only that of asserting the dignity of Man in relative autonomy to God, but also explaining and justifying the perceived hierarchical difference between Europeans, on the one hand, and the apparently discovered peoples and, soon enough, the black African people that they took as slaves, on the other. This means that Western modernity involved not only the creation of a secular line to give more autonomy to Man from God, but that there was also simultaneously a line of dehumanization demarcating the difference between Man and new creatures of modernity: those who were looked upon as if they were there in order to be raped, enslaved and colonized. In a context where modernity posits itself in terms of a secular narrative of salvation, the colonized cannot but appear as condemned.

The condemned are those below the modern/colonial ontological line. They are beings whose ontological status is considered to be uncertain at best. While their ontological status can be uncertain, the same does not happen necessarily with the certainty about that uncertainty. That is, the way in which ontological uncertainty is identified is typically straightforward and clear as it is guided by the presence of sensory data, particularly visual. This is the reason why colour becomes so pronounced as a means of identifying ontological uncertainty or ontological inferiority in modernity. From here, it follows that the colonial line has also been identified as a colour line (Du Bois, 1999). What is called race is one of the most systematic attempts, although by no means the only attempt, to bring immediacy and certainty to the identification of damnation: that is, to identify how far from embodying the idea of Man certain beings are.

Damnation is a form of ontological differentiation that includes racial difference but is more fundamental than that. The ontological colonial line or line of damnation creates two zones: a zone of salvation where the world and its resources are perceived as being there "for our sake" (*propter nos*; see Wynter, 1991), and another that is populated by entities whose very existence is regarded as problematic and dangerous. Since the world is perceived to be best without them, ideally, they would disappear after their bodies are used to build civilization and to satisfy the needs of the civilized. In the worst-case scenario, the condemned remain living and have to be managed as to remain outside of the zone of civilization or to only have limited access to it. The task of managing the modern/colonial line so as to determine how and at what speed subjects marked as condemned can have access to which area of civilization is what today is meant with diversity (at the level of civil society and the nation-state) and development (at the geopolitical level).

The condemned or, to follow Fanon more closely, *damné* can be understood as an ontologically inferior being or mode of subjectivity that is created by modern colonialism, which entailed naturalized slavery. The *damnés* of the earth are those who are trapped in the hellish existence of the plantation or colony and of other forms of modern surveillance, control, exploitation, violence and annihilation. To be condemned is to live in conditions where, first, one faces not simply lack of inclusion and indifference, but more exactly expropriation, extermination, various modalities of death and conditions that can be considered, in certain cases, worse than death, such as rape and torture; and, second, where one cannot change the situation because either one is never fully admitted into the zone of civilization or because any degree of admission into it is predicated on the affirmation of the difference between the world of Man and that of the condemned. That is, the colour line and other forms of the modern/colonial line are not lines of exclusion, but lines of damnation, which means that it is a categorical mistake to try to counter coloniality with inclusion. In fact, to ask for inclusion in modern institutions and projects in a context marked by the colonial line (contexts where race and other forms of discrimination have become systematic) not only perpetuates coloniality but also seeks to increase the active involvement of the *damnés* in the structure that reproduces their own damnation. Diversity, inclusion and development are key terms in the gospel of modernity/coloniality, particularly in its liberal and neoliberal expressions. They focus on assimilation into the modern idea of civilization, and on selective and limited inclusion in spheres other than the modern dehumanizing exploitation of labour and the "darker" elements of modernity that are necessary for the apparently selected few to enjoy the goods of salvation.

The *damnés* are not Man, but not innocent animality either. Existentially speaking, they live in a zone of damnation below the zones of being (facticity) and nonbeing (freedom), where humanity is typically defined and Man is anchored. In that sense, as Fanon would put it, the *damné* is not Man. If Man, for Jean-Paul Sartre, is "condemned to be free" (Sartre, 1966: 186), the *damnés* are condemned to remain narcissistically sequestered in a condition where the imposed image of themselves is one that is premised on their inferiority, which makes them look at whiteness for salvation. In this condition, hell is not, like in Sartre, "other people" (see Sartre's play *No Exit*, in Sartre, 1989), but one's very own self and the sociogenically generated zone of damnation. Those who are considered to embody full humanity, or those in the zone of salvation, can become authentic individuals in the encounter with death (Heidegger) or in the realization of absolute freedom (Sartre). But the zone of damnation is a zone where individuality is banned as subjects are considered to be one with their past and with the collective to which they are said to belong (Fanon, 2008). Also, the encounter with the possibility of their death is not an extraordinary event but rather part of their day-to-day experience.

Given the nature of coloniality and anti-blackness, this situation is particularly dramatic in black colonial subjects, which is why Fanon dedicates his first book to study black people (Fanon, 2008). In it, Fanon notes that the white is not simply another, but a master, and that his gaze is already part of the very concept and lived experience of blackness. No matter what their perceived social and economic status is, black subjects are therefore in the zone of damnation, which is a zone of paralysis where wearing white masks constantly takes the place of what is supposed to be a dialectic between being and nonbeing out of which, as he puts it, authenticity can emerge. This means that, in Western modernity, even the dialectic between being and nonbeing is displaced and, as it were, colonized by a form of negrophobia that typically finds expression in the divide between black and white. This is part of the coloniality of being in modernity, in which being itself seems to be overdetermined from without. The black's modality of existence takes place below the dialectic between being and nonbeing, where the only destiny for the black is not authentic existence, but whiteness.

Authenticity fails in responding to the crisis—that is, the call for a decision—of the modern/colonial age in that it does not properly recognize or respond to the production of a zone of damnation. The production of this new zone is no less than a metaphysical catastrophe, rupturing a human reality defined by being and nonbeing and constructing one that takes the shape of a Manichean structure where notions of absolute good and absolute evil displace the power of the division between being and nonbeing. Modern civilization, in this sense, is to be understood not as the unfolding of the ontological distinctions between being and nonbeing but by the catastrophic creation of a Manichean world divided between essential good and essential evil. The modern/colonial ontological line is a Manichean one: it elevates goodness and evil from the realm of ethics to that of ontology, where they take the character of unbridgeable essences. This Manichean relation serves as the main reference to define reality, displaces and redefines the role of being and nonbeing, and freezes any sense of dialectic.

Given this state of affairs, calls for diversity and inclusion, progress and development, authenticity and empathy to address this situation are at best naïve, and at worst used to further strengthen coloniality. In either form, they serve to counter the one action that alone can challenge this order: decoloniality. Decoloniality is far from just a matter of political revolution or a call for independence; it is rather a form of metaphysical insurrection that seeks to end coloniality's metaphysical catastrophe. This metaphysical insurrection has to do with the emergence of a call for a good beyond the Manichean good of the modern/colonial system. This good shatters through the colonization of being and nonbeing by Manicheism and can have, as a result, the start of a dialectic that is from then on not seen as final or self-sufficient. That is, if coloniality ontologized good and evil, decoloniality deontologizes and decolonizes them turning them back to the sphere of human existence and praxis with ethical, political and metaphysical implications. Decoloniality is, in short, an ethic-political, epistemic and symbolic struggle to create a reality of human inter-relationality beyond the word and world of Man.

Decoloniality challenges the verticality of the ontological colonial line. This is different from empathy, which takes place within the space of horizontal differences among those who can claim to be Man. In face of the coloniality of being, understood as the production of a sphere of existence below the zones of being and nonbeing, empathy is limited to those who are in the zone of full humanity, and it is extended to those in the zone of damnation in a partial, selective and temporary manner and only to the extent that they show indubitable signs of not only respecting, but also incorporating, the word and criteria for legitimate action that is normative in the world of Man. This kind of empathy reinforces the divide between Man and the *damnés* as it merely expresses an impulse for inclusion, which cannot be but an implicit imperative of assimilation. This is a vicious circle that perpetuates the reality and sense of being-damned.

Declarations of the "Rights of Man" and calls for empathy among those recognized as Man presuppose a skewed account of modernity, based on limited views that only focus on certain aspects of the secular line. The declarations obscure the relevance of the colonial line and of its entanglement with the secular line. Overwhelmingly, the *damnés* were killed, raped and enslaved in the colonies, while God, at least the Christian God, was pushed from the public to the private realm in the heart of the European empires. The "Rights of Man" are in large measure the Rights of Man to engage in both processes: differentiating and securing the order of Man from pretensions of divine authority in any political structure, and keeping the *damnés* in their place, whether this place is the plantation, the colony or the periphery, in urban, suburban and rural areas of the nation-state, or domestic spaces, especially violent ones.

Coloniality would continue to unfold through the eighteenth and nineteenth centuries. During that period, if the secularity of human rights contributed to imagining Man as distinct and autonomous from God, the coloniality of human rights—that is, the denial of humanity or the expectation of assimilation into the narrative of Western civilization by appeals to human rights—legitimized the difference between the order of Man and the zone of damnation. It would not take much time, however, for coloniality to directly affect those in the zone of salvation. Twentieth-century fascism, and particularly Nazism, would take imperialism and ethnic cleansing to a level where Europeans could no longer evade their recognition as problems: the imperial aggression of Germany in the very European continent and the systematic elimination of Jews, Gypsies, Slavs and various other groups considered as either undesirable or as threatening, backed up by science. Fascism introduced and further developed ideas and practices from the zone of damnation to the zone of modern salvation. This would lead to a renewed engagement with human rights and, indeed, to a new declaration. The question is whether the new formulation of human rights preserved broke away or continued in a different form the coloniality of the eighteenth- and nineteenth-century "Rights of Man".

The Coloniality of Twentieth-Century Human Rights

The opposition to the hubris of national socialism—a hubris already anticipated in the heightening of imperialism and racism in the nineteenth century that led to over 60,000,000 deaths in the Second World War—led to a resurgence of human rights discourse and to their enshrinement in a new declaration: the Universal Declaration of Human Rights. As Lynn Hunt points out, this declaration expanded the number of inalienable rights typically recognized in uses of human rights, it

> prohibited slavery and provided for universal and equal suffrage by secret ballot. In addition, it called for freedom of movement, the right to a nationality, the right to marry, and more controversially, the right to social security; the right to work, with equal pay for equal work at a life-sustaining wage; the right to rest and leisure; and the right to education, which should be free at the elementary levels.
>
> (Hunt, 2007: 204)

For Hunt, this represented a triumphant comeback of human rights discourse, now anchored institutionally in the nation-state as well as above and beyond the nation-state in the United Nations and in international courts of justice.

Hunt concludes her book on the invention of human rights with the idea that

> the human rights framework, with its international bodies, international courts, and international conventions, might be exasperating in its slowness to respond or repeated inability to achieve its ultimate goals, but there is no better structure available for confronting these issues.
>
> (Hunt, 2007: 213)

As she notes, one particularity of the Universal Declaration of Human Rights is that it focuses primarily on issues to be addressed and not in the more general goal of asserting the particularity of Man vis-à-vis the divine and the animal world, like it was to some extent the case in the previous declarations. In my view, this is partly because, by the middle of the twentieth century, the particularity of Man and the ability of Man to build a government based on the idea of his rights and the rights of the citizen had already been accomplished. Monarchies and the view ordered by the "chain of being" were no longer a challenge to the more secular organization of the social world. The secular space of the nation-state had already been created and the theological lines between a presumably true religion and false religions resituated within the normative codes of the nation-state. In most cases, what was defined as religion came to be seen as part of the character of nation-states. At the same time, religious differences, inside a state and between states, were merged with national characteristics and racial differences, giving new dimensions to religious conflicts. The Nazis, like other empires throughout the nineteenth century, mobilized both science and religion in their racial understanding of the world.

Twentieth-century human rights discourse sought to respond to a number of conveniently defined problems that Western modernity itself had created. These problems were manifested in the elimination of millions of people and in the internal devastation of Europe. The question was whether this response was the result of a deep realization of the common humanity of all beyond what the idea of the citizen and the structure of the nation-state had permitted, or was it an opposition to the hubris of imperialism and colonialism in the face of the scandalous nature of Nazism, but not an opposition to imperialism and colonialism themselves. That is, to what extent were Europeans and others reacting against the excess of imperialism and racism, understood as the production of mass genocide and the creation of death camps, as well as the decimation of Europe and the deaths of millions of Europeans, but not opposing imperialism and racism as such and in their various manifestations? Put differently, to what extent did human rights discourse emerge to protect the order of Man from chaos while providing little to no consideration to the zone of damnation and the project of decolonization?

Before declaring the apparent triumphant return of human rights discourse into the mainstream of modern political consciousness and theory and before celebrating its achievements, as Hunt does, it is necessary to explore more in depth what were precisely the problems that human rights discourse came to help address and what was the understanding of such problems in the middle of the twentieth century. Shortly after the publication of the Universal Declaration of Human Rights, the Martiniquean intellectual, poet and political thinker Aimé Césaire conducted an incisive analysis of Nazism and the turn to human rights. For Césaire, the turn to human rights was a limited response to an inadequately formulated problem. The problem at the moment was conceived in terms of Nazism and anti-semitism and not of colonialism and racism more amply. And when Europeans were pushed to consider the problem of colonialism, the response that Césaire found was that colonialism was different from Nazism because colonialism was a means of civilizing the colonized. This led Césaire to conclude that if "the very humanistic, very Christian bourgeois of the twentieth century" railed against Hitler he was being inconsistent and that, at bottom, what he could not

> forgive Hitler for is not *crime* in itself, *the crime against man*, it is not *the humiliation of man as such*, it is the crime against the white man, the humiliation of the white man, and the fact that he applied to Europe colonialist

procedures which until then had been reserved exclusively for the Arabs of
Algeria, the coolies of India, and the blacks of Africa.

(Césaire, 2000: 36)

Césaire considered this form of thinking a trait of what he referred to as
"pseudo-humanism", a form of humanism that "for too long it has diminished
the rights of man, that its concept of those rights has been—and still is—narrow and fragmentary, incomplete and biased and, all things considered, sordidly
racist" (Césaire, 2000: 37).

Where Hunt sees the *International Declaration of Human Rights* as a return to
a discourse of equality after the nationalist hubris of Nazism, Césaire suggests
that it is in continuity with a long tradition of pseudo-humanism that was
"sordidly racist". In fact, where Hunt and others understand the emergence
of human rights in 1948 as an opposition to Nazism, Césaire points out that
Nazism remains hidden inside the liberal European bourgeoisie, or, as he puts
it, that without his being aware of it, "the very distinguished, very humanistic, very Christian bourgeois of the twentieth century [...] has a Hitler inside
him, that Hitler *inhabits* him, that Hitler is his *demon*" (Césaire, 2000: 36). The
idea of a close relationship between liberalism and Hitlerian national socialism supports the idea that, contrary to what Hunt indicates, post-Enlightened
Western liberalism and ethno-nationalism were not really too far apart, which
leads one to consider whether liberalism can be defined as a less intense form of
fascism—low-intensity fascism—or fascism an intense form of liberalism. I am
inclined for the first, but, however one puts it, the linkages between liberalism
and fascism are undeniable from a Césairean perspective. Césaire suggests not
only that the close proximity between liberalism and fascism is preserved in
the face of the Hitlerian version of nationalism, but also that something akin to
Hitlerism undergirds the consciousness and projects of the "very humanistic"
(with and without strong liberal tendencies) and "very Christian" (with and
without strong nationalist and conservative tendencies) bourgeoisie.

If liberalism and nationalism are not too far apart, Césaire suggests, it might
well be because underneath them there is the racist and colonialist bourgeoisie.
We simply misdiagnose the problems and the issues when we take liberalism
and nationalism as two separate ideologies, the dialectic of which leads to a
more superior form of thinking in the notion of international human rights.
It was this racist and colonialist bourgeoisie that claimed victory in the US
American and French Revolutions, as well as the privileged subject position
that declared the "Rights of Man" in the name of "we the people" and the
citizen. The declarations might have been part of the pseudo-humanism of
the racist and colonialist bourgeoisie. Continued calls for decolonization from
indigenous movements and "black" youth, among other sectors, might seem
to indicate that it is the same racist, colonialist—albeit to a little degree probably more multicultural in nature and "inclusive of diversity"—and patriarchal
bourgeoisie that is largely defining the nationalist and global corporate projects

today. But it is not only the bourgeoisie, it is also the classes and subjects who aspire to bourgeois status, as well as the very nationalist and conservative groups that would rather see the world organized across the ethno-centric and, for the most part, Christian-centric lines of differentiation and demarcation that have existed for the longest time in the modern/colonial age. The most serious challenge for human rights discourse then is not how it addresses the violent excesses of nation-states, but how they advance the movements for decolonization. Decolonization refers to the insurgency of those in the zone of damnation to destroy the ontological colonial lines that render them less than human.

Contrary to the *Declaration for the Rights of Man and Citizen*, the *International Declaration for Human Rights* was not primarily based on metaphysical claims about the nature of "Man". It was first and foremost the expression of an international accord about a minimum of standards for a kind of conviviality that would avoid the excesses that were experienced in the Second World War. What is often forgotten in this context is that while European powers, the United States and a few other countries were involved in the fight with or against Hitler, there were other territories, colonies, that were fighting for decolonization. European countries that had been major imperial powers in the nineteenth century were then assailed from the inside through Hitlerism and from the outside of Europe in the colonies. European powers were of course interested in doing everything possible to establish a limit of sorts to the kind of violence that could result in a destabilization of European and Western supremacy. The nation-state form had to be overseen and controlled to avoid the excesses of Nazism. And yet, the colonialist interests and racist perspectives of the European nation-states were so deeply entrenched that they "had to be prodded and pushed to put human rights on the agenda" when they sought out to build the United Nations (Hunt, 2007: 202). For example, Hunt notes that

> Great Britain and the Soviet Union had both rejected proposals to include human rights in the charter of the United Nations. [...] In addition, the United States had initially opposed China's suggestion that the charter include a statement on the equality of all races.
>
> (Hunt, 2007: 202)

Western powers, including the Soviet Union, feared something in the concept of human rights and the statement about the equality of races that could pose challenges to their interests. However, they could use the very concept of human rights to their advantage. While colonized peoples could use the notion of human rights to denounce colonialism—albeit typically within a framework that committed them to having the nation-state as their goal—Western colonial powers could use the same terminology to shift the conversation from decolonization to compliance with human rights. This is, in fact, where Samuel Moyn locates one of the main interests from Western powers in declaring international human rights. For Moyn, more significant for understanding the character of twentieth-century human rights discourse than the presumed eighteenth-century antecedents

> was that human rights were introduced in the midst of World War II as a replacement for the liberation from empire of which most around the world dreamed—as a kind of consolation prize, that was therefore spurned. At the end of the conflict, much of the world remained colonized, but many took empire to be at an end. Yet not only did human rights not imply the end of empire (indeed the imperial powers were their most significant proponents); many thought the Allies in their Atlantic Charter had promised decolonization, then took that promise back even as talk about "human rights" began.
>
> (Moyn, 2014: 138–139)

For Moyn, a crucial difference between the earlier declaration of the "Rights of Man" and the *Universal Declaration of Human Rights* is that, while the earlier rights were part of revolutionary struggles, the latter served to quell them. This was a tendency already shown earlier in response to the Haitian Revolution. It seemed that the revolutionary character of the "Rights of Man" stopped when not only the economic interests of the bourgeoisie were at stake, but, more fundamentally, when racialized subjects claimed revolutionary agency and any substantial sense of agency for that matter. Therefore, it is not strange that, as Moyn indicates, "twentieth century anticolonialism [...] most often eschewed the language of human rights, even [in the context when] the Universal Declaration had only just been propounded" (Moyn, 2014: 19). The commitment with colonialism and racism that Césaire had identified in the humanist and Christian bourgeoisie clearly continued in the twentieth century to the extent of recruiting human rights discourse to change the conversation away from revolutionary struggle and the radical questioning of capitalism and socialism to a matter of avoiding excesses of violence in nation-states, particularly when this happened in Europe or could be recognized as legitimate by Europe.

The "Rights of Man" were limited by their over-reliance on an abstract conception of human beings that was overdetermined, at the concrete level, by views about the qualitative difference between one set of human beings, increasingly understood as white, civilized and of European provenance, and another as uncivilized, savaged or inferior. This overdetermination continued affecting international human rights and found expression in the difference between what was portrayed as the absolute evil of the Second World War and the holocaust, on the one hand, and the supposedly lesser forms of violence that sought to civilize and not to eliminate populations, such as, allegedly, colonialism, on the other.

In the face of colonialism and the legacy of racial slavery, colonizers only considered the Second World War and the holocaust as significant. To the idea of Europe as the climax of civilization that already existed in the nineteenth century, the twentieth century saw the addition of the idea of Europe as the site of the climax of evil. In this context, colonialism will come to be regarded, not as an evil that must be confronted, but as a human, all too human production which, no matter how negative it was, needed to be seen as a vehicle to transmit civilization. Europe monopolizes the good of nurturing and spreading civilization as well as the use of the category of evil, now linked to the fascist holocaust. Human rights serve as a product of the good of European civilization to avoid fascist evils that menace the integrity of the "developed" nation-states. This understanding of good and evil sought to hide or render irrelevant the Manichean structure of the modern/colonial world, making human rights another vehicle of coloniality.

The coloniality of the new terms of the good of colonialism and fascist evil played itself out in the following way. On the one hand, if one accepted the premise of colonialism as a vehicle of civilization, then the future of the colonies had to be defined by a perpetual attempt to adopt European standards of civilization. That is, the colonies would be in route of rejecting colonialism and continue embracing European civilization. On the other hand, if one was not inclined to see anything particularly good in colonialism, the new terms led one to posit the fascist holocaust and the death camps as the one true evil with which one should not dare to compare anything else. That is in part why the notion of the "death camps" continues to inspire European philosophy and political theory in Europe while colonization is typically considered an affair of post-colonial studies and decolonial thinking. By appealing to this interpretation of the holocaust, Europeans could disentangle themselves more efficiently from colonialism and seek to provide what they perceived as radical critiques of modernity or the Enlightenment without having to consider colonialism seriously. As the theoreticians of what they consider to be the most radical expressions of evil, they also position themselves as leaders. While they do not have to seriously engage colonialism, everyone else is supposed to follow their theoretical lead in the assessment of the modernity and the holocaust. There is also the fact that, since the holocaust occurred in European lands and affected European peoples, Europe and European peoples can maintain in this way historical and theoretical centrality. In this view, the politics of Europe as the place with a maximum civilization join the politics of Europe as the place where the maximum suffering occurred. There is nothing then to look for out of Europe.

It is key that in this context it became important for Europeans to reject anti-Semitism and every kind of vulgar and explicit expression of racism, while at the same time, rhetorically at least by some important circles, embracing Jews into the fold of whiteness. The emergence of the state of Israel and the increasing whitening of certain Jews in the United States are part of a religious–secular narrative of redemption that shows the continued relationship between Christianity and the secular nation-state. Anti-semitism hardly disappears with this. Behind the white Christian embrace of the Jew, there is always the notion of the Jew as inferior or less in tune with the nation-state than the white Christian. Support for the state of Israel is both a question of geopolitical strategy for the benefit of Western countries as well as a matter of Christian destiny. The secular and the theological lines enter into strategic alliance operating in a field largely defined by ontological colonial lines.

In this process, the demand for decolonization acquires less and less weight and legitimacy, while human rights become each time more abstract and distant, serving only to mark the boundaries of violence in the new world order. This world order is a modern/racist, patriarchal and capitalist one, among other such features, which means that there will be a differentiation between several forms of violence. The violence that threatens this order will be considered excessive and require prompt action, while the violence and suffering that is an intended or unintended result of efforts to maximize the efficiency or to advance the major goals of the system will appear as necessary or non-substantial. One could interpret this response in Leibnizean fashion: one kind of suffering is part of the necessary evil that is a component of the best of all possible worlds, and the other is a form of excessive evil that can and must be addressed. Human rights thus becomes part of what Lewis Gordon referred to as the theodicy of the modern/colonial world (Gordon, 2013). This is yet another aspect of the coloniality of human rights.

Not only the identification of violence is selective and serves a purpose in the maintenance of order, but also the determination of suffering. Put bluntly, instead of universal empathy, one finds that the suffering of white Europeans and their descendants is perceived as more grievable than the suffering of other populations. At the same time, black and indigenous suffering typically remain in the lower scale of detectability, so much so that the identification of blackness or indigeneity in any context would lead to its determination as more natural or less problematic than otherwise. There is what could be referred to as a modern hermeneutics of suffering that is part of the coloniality of human rights which is necessary to always investigate carefully. This is not just about lack of empathy, but about a certain engineering of empathy, feeling and particular forms of reasoning that are functional to a system that is, to name only some of its key features, capitalist, racist and patriarchal at its core. This is the "demon" that Césaire identified in the "very humanistic, very Christian bourgeoisie" and that he believed kept justifying colonialism after the Second World War.

In this context, international human rights remain severely disconnected from the demand for decolonization and can actually be used against decolonial struggles. Another example of this is when appeals for individual rights are inflated and take primacy over struggles to change institutions and structures. In this and various other ways, international human rights can easily work in an environment that is not only capitalist but also colonialist, sexist and racist. This is also a version of international human rights that is made to the measure of the nation-state, even as the nation-state typically limits full rights to what it recognizes as its citizens and normative populations. At most, human rights serve to target some of the most explicit expressions of violence and, as I discussed above, even the interpretation of that violence is typically interpreted through Western colonialist and racist lenses.

Conclusion

Both the "Rights of Man" and international human rights have been largely functional to a modern/colonial framework. From here a question emerges: can human rights be decolonized? Would it make sense to refer to the decoloniality of human rights and, if so, what would that mean exactly? I have focused here on human rights within the conceptual economy of the modern/ colonial world for the purpose of examining the coloniality of human rights. One would have to explore how human rights discourses have been employed by others in struggles for decolonization. My sense is that any use of it is limited, as Moyn indicates, as well as strategic. Human rights can be considered a zone of struggle where the coloniality of human rights is sometimes met with a decolonial attitude that seeks to use them as an opportunity to challenge the order of Man (Maldonado-Torres, 2015). It is this larger challenge to metaphysical catastrophe and the colonial line, rather than an effort to comply with the imperatives and views of the secular line, that is the focus of decolonial struggles. This challenge takes place most radically when it is part of a comprehensive decolonization movement rather than as part of a discreet engagement with human rights.

Note

1 For related definitions of coloniality, see Quijano and Wallerstein (1992), Mignolo (2000), Quijano (2000), Wynter (2003).

References

Césaire, Aimé (2000), *Discourse on Colonialism*. New York: Monthly Review Press. Translated by Joan Pinkham.
Du Bois, W.E.B. (1999), *The Souls of Black Folk. Authoritative Text. Contexts. Criticism.* Edited by Henry Louis Gates Jr. and Terri Hume Oliver. New York: W. W. Norton.
Fanon, Frantz (2008), *Black Skin, White Masks*. New York: Grove Press [Kindle Edition]. Translated by Richard Wilcox.
Gordon, Lewis R. (2005), "Through the Zone of Nonbeing: A Reading of *Black Skin, White Masks* in Celebration of Fanon's Eightieth Birthday", *The C.L.R. James Journal*, 11(1), 1–43. doi: 10.5840/clrjames20051111
Gordon, Lewis R. (2013), "Race, Theodicy, and the Normative Emancipatory Challenges of Blackness", *South Atlantic Quarterly*, 112(4), 725–736. doi: 10.1215/00382876-2345252
Gordon, Lewis R. (2015), *What Fanon Said: A Philosophical Introduction to His Life and Thought*. New York: Fordham University Press.
Hunt, Lynn (2007), *Inventing Human Rights: A History*. New York: W. W. Norton.
Lugones, María (2007), "Heterosexualism and the Colonial/Modern Gender System", *Hypatia*, 22(1), 186–219. doi: 10.1111/j.1527-2001.2007.tb01156.x

Maldonado-Torres, Nelson (2014), "Religion, Conquest, and Race in the Foundations of the Modern/Colonial World", *Journal of the American Academy of Religion*, 82(3), 636–665. doi: 10.1093/jaarel/lfu054

Maldonado-Torres, Nelson (2015), "Transdisciplinariedad y decolonialidad", *Quaderna*, 3. Available at http://quaderna.org/transdisciplinariedad-y-decolonialidad

Mignolo, Walter (2000), *Local Histories/Global Designs: Coloniality, Subaltern Knowledges, and Border Thinking*. Princeton, NJ: Princeton University Press.

Mignolo, Walter (2003), *The Darker Side of the Renaissance: Literacy, Territoriality, and Colonization*. Ann Arbor, MI: University of Michigan Press [2nd ed.].

Mignolo, Walter (2011), *The Darker Side of Western Modernity: Global Futures, Decolonial Options*. Durham, NC: Duke University Press. doi: 10.1215/9780822394501

Moyn, Samuel (2014), *Human Rights and the Uses of History*. London: Verso.

Pico della Mirandola, Giovanni (1956), *Oration on the Dignity of Man*. Chicago, IL: Gateway Editions.

Quijano, Aníbal (2000), "Coloniality of Power, Eurocentrism, and Latin America", *Nepantla: Views from South*, 1(3), 533–580. Available at http://isites.harvard.edu/fs/docs/icb.topic203438.files/Anibal_Quijano.Coloniality.pdf

Quijano, Aníbal; Immanuel Wallerstein (1992), "Americanity as a Concept, or the Americas in the Modern World-System", *International Social Science Journal*, 44, 549–557. Available at http://www.javeriana.edu.co/blogs/syie/files/Quijano-and-Wallerstein-Americanity -as-a-Concept.pdf

Santos, Boaventura de Sousa (2007), "Beyond Abyssal Thinking: From Global Lines to Ecologies of Knowledges", *Review*, 30(1), 45–89. Available at https://www.jstor.org/stable/40241677

Sartre, Jean-Paul (1966), *Being and Nothingness: A Phenomenological Essay on Ontology*. New York: Washington Square Press, Pocket Books. Translation and Introduction by Hazel E. Barnes.

Sartre, Jean-Paul (1989), *No Exit and Three Other Plays: Dirty Hands, The Flies, The Respectful Prostitute*. New York: Vintage Books.

Wallerstein, Immanuel (1991), *Unthinking Social Science: The Limits of Nineteenth-Century Paradigms*. Cambridge: Polity Press.

Wynter, Sylvia (1984), "The Ceremony Must Be Found: After Humanism", *Boundary 2*, 12(3), 19–70. doi: 10.2307/302808

Wynter, Sylvia (1991), "Columbus and the Poetics of the *Propter Nos*", *Annals of Scholarship*, 8(2), 251–286.

Wynter, Sylvia (2001), "Towards the Sociogenic Principle: Fanon, Identity, the Puzzle of Conscious Experience, and What it is Like to Be 'Black'", in Mercedes F. Durán-Cogan and Antonio Gómez-Moriana (eds.), *National Identities and Sociopolitical Changes in Latin America*. New York: Routledge, 30–66.

Wynter, Sylvia (2003), "Unsettling the Coloniality of Being/Power/Truth/Freedom: Towards the Human, After Man, Its Overrepresentation—An Argument", *The New Centennial Review*, 3(3), 257–337. doi: 10.1353/ncr.2004.0015

Part II

Struggles and Emergences

Chapter 4

Revisiting the Bhopal Disaster
Times of Violence and Latitudes of Memory

Bruno Sena Martins

Introduction

An accident at a factory based in Bhopal, India, owned by Union Carbide India Limited (UCIL),[1] a subsidiary of the North American Union Carbide Corporation (UCC), led to the biggest industrial disaster in history. Estimates indicate that thousands of people died that night and in the weeks immediately after the accident, 25,000 more in the years which followed, and that today over 100,000 individuals suffer major, permanent after-effects (BMA & BGIA, 2012). Given the scale of the accident and the magnitude of the consequences, the low profile of the Bhopal disaster within the memory of the global North is surprising. It is, I believe, indicative of the radically different processes by which the idea of the human being and of suffering worthy of struggle and revolt are constituted. This reflection is linked, on the one hand, to a broad-based grammar of historical, cultural and politically engendered distinctions through which differences in the value of human life have been established and given meaning. As Judith Butler states,

> The human is understood differentially depending on its race, the legibility of that race, its morphology, the recognizability of that morphology, its sex, the perceptual verifiability of that sex, its ethnicity, the categorical understanding of that ethnicity.
>
> (Butler, 2004a: 2)

The argument that there are subjects and groups who have to fight for the right to be seen as human beings (Baxi, 1986; Fanon, 2004), thus exposing the hierarchy involved in the definition of human life, demonstrates not only the inequalities in ontological status produced in all societies but also the asymmetries established on a global level:

> lives are supported and maintained differentially, that there are radically different ways in which human physical vulnerability is distributed across the globe. Certain lives will be highly protected, and the abrogation of

their claims to sanctity will be sufficient to mobilize the forces of war. Other lives will not find such fast and furious support and will not even qualify as "grievable".

(Butler, 2004b: 32)

From the opening of the Bhopal factory in 1969 to the negligence that still affects the victims of the disaster nowadays, a web of events has unfolded which, as this chapter aims to show, offers evidence of a thriving colonial-capitalist nexus whose power is revealed in its disregard for the value of the lives of the Bhopal survivors.

In the dialogue I aim to develop in this text, engaging with the survivors of the Bhopal disaster and their experiences requires an analytical effort to overcome two forms of silencing. Firstly, there is the silencing that results from hierarchies which naturalize the subalternity of the survivors' experiences and ontological reflections, thus defining the terms of an essentially silenced voice; secondly, there is the silencing that results from the difficulty in understanding an industrial disaster over an extended period of time. In the latter case, I am referring to the way in which the decades following the disaster had to contend with a "slow violence" (Nixon, 2011) which continued to invade the everyday existence of those who survived the morning of 3 December 1984.

Bhopal: The Presence of Distant Places

This text is the result of ethnographic work carried out between December 2013 and February 2014 in the city of Bhopal, in close collaboration with the Sambhavna Trust (ST), a non-governmental organization (NGO) whose clinic, situated in the vicinity of the factory where the disaster took place, still provides health care for the survivors of Bhopal's disaster. During the time I lived in Bhopal, I stayed at the ST clinic where, from Monday to Saturday, 180 survivors received medical care (administered by practitioners of both conventional and Ayurvedic medicine). I was received by the ST as an academic interested in researching the Bhopal disaster and was offered the same conditions as those provided for volunteers from all over the world who wanted to be involved in the work of the organization, as well as support from a research assistant for my visits outside the clinic. Living in close proximity to the aftermath of the disaster—I woke every morning to the sound of the loudspeaker calling patients for their appointments—I was able to understand the long term in which the after-effects of the Bhopal disaster are inscribed: the constant suffering etched into people's bodies; the struggle for compensation and health care; the daily exposure to the effects of contamination; and the impact of congenital disorders affecting new generations. During my stay in Bhopal, I visited homes in the communities in the surrounding areas most severely affected by the disaster and was able to establish dialogues and interview survivors, activists, medical staff and journalists. In addition to the many conversations I had as part of my everyday life, I carried out a total of 35 more formal interviews, based on a semi-structured set of questions usually interwoven with information about the life stories of interlocutors (audio recordings were made of the interviews), always with the informed consent of the interviewees. I had the support of an interpreter for these interviews whenever the language barrier between Hindi and English proved difficult. I also carried out a documentary analysis at the ST library, which contains the most complete documentary and bibliographical archives on the Bhopal disaster and the campaigns which followed.

For a Portuguese researcher born six years before the disaster and, by luck and privilege, spared the harsher realities of life, engaging with the reality of the Bhopal survivors involved crossing a number of complex and challenging paths: linguistic, geographical, cultural, memorial and subjective.

The decades that now separate us from the Bhopal disaster mean that the central challenge is to gain an understanding of the extended period of time in which the implications of the disaster were experienced unremittingly by the Bhopal survivors. It is therefore necessary

> to account for how the temporal dispersion of slow violence affects the way we perceive and respond to a variety of social afflictions—from domestic abuse to posttraumatic stress and, in particular, environmental calamities. A major challenge is representational: how to devise arresting stories, images, and symbols adequate to the pervasive but elusive violence of delayed effects.
>
> (Nixon, 2011: 3)

In a study in which the present is still marked by the early hours of 3 December 1984—"that night", as everyone in Bhopal calls it, the night when family members, neighbours and other loved ones were lost and a life of physical pain, illness and traumatic memories began for so many—I recognized that it was necessary to immerse myself in the "local worlds of suffering". As Arthur Kleinman notes:

> For an ethnography of experience, the challenge is to describe the processual elaboration of the undergoing, the enduring, the bearing of pain (or loss or other tribulation) in the vital flow of intersubjective engagements in a particular local world.
>
> (Kleinman, 1992: 191)

Kleinman argues that whilst eminently biomedical interpretations of suffering falter when they come up against the teleological and existential issues which it poses, the more "culturalist" interpretations tend to confine themselves to a strictly intellectualist understanding of the subject. This is due, above all, to the fact that, in the wake of Max Weber, approaches to suffering have centred on the production of discourses that assume clear answers from coherent narratives of existence (Kleinman, 1992: 189–190). The idea that suffering is an itinerary which subjects seek to resist by producing perspectives of meaning that are culturally informed by specific local worlds, which necessarily coexist with chaos, the inexpressible and lack of meaning, reconciles us with an interpretation in which the body, cultural values and self-reflection, created within the vagaries of biography, can be addressed without contradiction or angst.

From this perspective, I endeavoured to produce a form of research that reflects two separate but complementary lines. On the one hand, this involved pursuing the meaning ascribed by subjects to destabilizing events that are sometimes so deeply inscribed in an incommunicable wounded subjectivity that they struggle to find words to express it. In this sense, I draw on what Boaventura de Sousa Santos has termed the "sociology of absences", whose aim "is to transform impossible into possible objects, absent into present objects" (Santos, 2014: 172). On the other hand, it was important to understand how "new languages" emerge from the fight against hardships, as narratives of resistance which, between wounded subjectivity and shared insurgence, produce proposals for justice and social change. I therefore subscribe to a "sociology of emergences", whose double aim is, "on the one hand, to know better the conditions of the possibility of hope; on the other, to define principles of action to promote the fulfilment of those conditions" (Santos, 2014: 184). Veena Das speaks of "embodiment of events or violence" (2010: 144) to refer to the embodied witnesses whose lives have endured an extreme violence. In this sense, the incorporation of violence takes the form of resistance and grieving, a statement of what may be the inviolable force of memory in the "local worlds" of existence.

"That Night": History and Histories

Bhopal is the capital of the state of Madhya Pradesh (literally, "the central province"). It is situated in central India and, according to the 2011 Census, has 1,798,218 inhabitants. The modern city of Bhopal was founded in the 18th century by Dost Mohammad Khan, an Afghan soldier, and became a semi-autonomous principality in the Mogul empire (a form of political organization in which the leader was known as the *Nawab*, if male, or *Begum* if female). Under British colonial rule, the state of Madhya Pradesh acquired the status of a *princely state*, which in practice meant that it became a protectorate governed by the local monarchs, descendants of the Mogul dynasty, through a *subsidiary alliance*, which involved agreeing to conditions imposed by the British colonial power. Unusually, Madhya Pradesh was governed by four women (*Begums*) from 1819 to 1926, and only ceased to be a *princely state* in 1949, when it joined the Indian Union following Indian independence in 1947. This meant that the state of Madhya Pradesh was the second-largest Indian state to be governed by Muslim monarchs up to the 20th century and explains why, in a predominantly Hindu country, a significant percentage of the population of the district of Bhopal is still Muslim today (in 2001, 73.05% of the population was Hindu and

22.8% Muslim, whereas in India as a whole the figures are 80.5% and 13.4%, respectively).[2]

Under Begum rule the state of Madhya Pradesh had begun to develop rail links with the rest of India and this, combined with its central geographical location, helped to establish Bhopal as an important rail hub during the first half of the 20th century. When the leaders of independent India decided to back growth in the domestic industrial sector, the excellent rail links with the rest of the territory were crucial in making Bhopal a suitable location for setting up industries, together with the tax incentives resulting from the fact that the state of Madhya Pradesh had been classified as a low development area.

However, the establishment of a UCIL factory in the city in 1969 cannot be separated from the changes imposed by what was known at the time as the "Green Revolution". In the first half of the 20th century, and in particular in the 1920s, India experienced severe famine and food shortages. When the same situation arose again in the 1950s, the Indian government launched the Green Revolution, an extensive programme designed to create self-sufficient food supplies through the use of agricultural technology. The measures adopted included the use of agricultural machinery, the expansion of irrigation infrastructures, the introduction of high-yield seeds and—a crucial factor for this analysis—an exponential increase in the use of pesticides in agricultural production (D'Silva, 2006: 29–34). In terms of pesticides, India increased its domestic production from 50,000 to 65,000 tonnes between 1966 and 1979 (D'Silva, 2006).

This was the context within which the decision was made to set up a factory in Bhopal that would be capable of producing carbaryl, a pesticide in the carbamate family patented by UCC and sold under the brand name Sevin. The factory opened in 1969. Initially, it was planned that operations at the factory would be limited to diluting compounds which came from the plant that produced them in the United States of America (USA), using inert local substances. However, for economic reasons it was later decided that the Bhopal factory should produce carbaryl locally by mixing methyl isocyanate (MIC) with alfa-naphtol (local production of MIC began in 1980). The factory was opened in the northern zone of Bhopal, 3 km away from the Hamidia hospital and 1.5 km from Bhopal railway station. It was built in an area full of substandard housing, thus creating a residential ring around the factory perimeter, which became more densely populated during the years the factory was in operation. The most underprivileged and marginalized members of society, who were Muslims and low-caste Hindus, lived in these houses and worked in the informal sector (and also in the plant itself and on the railways).

After midnight on 3 December 1984, a reaction in one of the (E-610) tanks where the MIC was stored led to the release of a cloud of toxic gases which spread to the surrounding areas, borne by the wind. The residents in the affected areas, sensing something in the air similar to pepper which made their eyes burn and caused serious breathing difficulties, began to flee in panic, seeking refuge from the invisible gas cloud and hoping to reach the hospital: it was a scenario of frantic, half-dressed people who had just woken up and families calling for each other and getting lost in the midst of the confusion. Dawn broke on 3 December to an apocalyptic scene of people temporarily blinded, vomiting, coughing and breathing in agony, masses of people and animals trampled underfoot on the streets and others seeking treatment at the Hamidia hospital, as well as steadily mounting piles of corpses.

On the night of the disaster, Gangaram was living a few hundred metres away from the plant, near the Oriya Basti Colony. He recalls the night of the disaster:

We were sleeping around 00:30, in the house. At that time, we heard a sound and everyone started shouting: "run away! run away! run away!" And then we came out of my house. And then we didn't go to my house, inside. We were four people in the family: me, my wife, and my two sons. We were unable to see clearly. Everyone comes out of their houses; all the community. On the other side of the railway track there was a yard of the railway, a big ground and everyone was running to there and we also followed. And we entered the railway and we saw eight or nine members of the family that were not dead, but fainted. We went inside but we saw the other guys, the families from the houses who had also fainted. So, my elder spoke at that time, he said to me: "Papa, run away! Papa, run away, because I am not feeling good". And I agreed with my son, with what he had said, and we went to Bhairpur,[3] very far away.

(Personal Interview [PI])

Gangaram headed for Bhairpur with his family and a neighbour. On the way, they found some water which they used to bathe his wife's eyes, as she had been blinded. When they reached Bhairpur, he said they found around 2,000 families who had also escaped the gas leak. There were no deaths amongst the escapees and the most immediate complaints were sore eyes and loss of sight. Two children were born that night in the midst of all the chaos. Hardly anyone was able to see. Later that day medical staff appeared with the police asking everyone to go to the hospital in Bhopal, but they were too afraid to return. Blindness was gradually giving way to blurred vision and then, on 4 December, the police returned to tell them that it was safe to go back to Bhopal. On his return, Gangaram went to the hospital where he was given drops for his eyes. This is his description of the scene he found when he got back to Bhopal:

Everyone was dead. After a few hours [...] second day, 4th December. We saw, at the time, the plants had no leaves; and the fruits had busted. And no plants had leaves. And then we continued and we saw on the left-side and right-side, everywhere, dead animals, dead bodies, people around dead bodies. Everywhere: dead bodies. Cats, dogs, people, cattle... everywhere. I was disturbed. And no one was there to take them. [...] And then the military start taking all of the dead bodies by truck to Hamidia Hospital. And we couldn't say who was Hindu who was Muslim.

(PI)

At the Hamidia hospital, some of the bodies that had been recovered were identified by family members so that the funeral rites could take place, in accordance with their respective faiths: Hindus were cremated and Muslims buried. However, as Gangaram stated, in addition to the distress, the confusion and difficulty in distinguishing between Muslims and Hindus[4] meant that many of the deceased did not receive the correct funeral rites or, in other words, that many Muslims were cremated and Hindus buried.

Due to exposure to the gas, Gangaram's wife, who was six months pregnant at the time of the disaster, suffered a spontaneous abortion; just one more consequence of the disaster for Gangaram's family. For Gangaram, the traumatic memories of the panic and deaths he had witnessed remained, together with chronic health problems, mainly respiratory complications, which affected the whole family.[5] After the disaster, Gangaram returned to his home near the factory. Like almost everyone else affected by the disaster, Gangaram continued to live next to the UCIL plant, in an area severely affected by the disaster. He did so because he had no alternative, but also because of a strong sense of belonging to the community.

The horror and chaos which Gangaram described to me were recounted in different ways by all the survivors of that night old enough to remember it. Confronting successive accounts of loss and resilience, almost invariably wrenched from memories that were hard to relive, accompanied by inadvertent tears and silences that could not be shared, only emphasized the immense wave of pain underlying the stories of so many of the inhabitants of Bhopal, usually the poorest families who still live in the slums surrounding the ruins of the pesticide plant.

Noor Jahan was still a girl when she moved with her parents and grandparents to Bhopal, more specifically to the Jai Prakach Nagar Colony, one of the residential areas most severely affected by the cloud of gas due to its proximity to the plant and the direction of the prevailing wind (north–west to south–east). In the early hours of 3 December, Noor, who was 12 years old, woke to the sound of her uncle screaming that there was a fire at the plant, before the news reached them that there had been a gas leak. Then Noor's family tried to flee:

I was sleeping with my uncle and aunt and they woke up and everyone felt like someone had burnt a red chilli. After a few minutes, the neighbours said there was a fire in the factory and we come out of the home and stay on the roadside. So, people come to the roadside and saw the cloud of smoke from the factory, and some people said: "This is the fog". People also said there was a blast in the gas tank and people run away by truck or by other vehicles; and we hadn't any type of vehicle, so we stayed there for two hours. After two hours, my uncle said that we should leave the place, and recollect all the family members. I picked up my uncle's daughter—she was one and a half-year-old. And then my uncle, my aunt and me we run, from the J.P. Nagar some three or four kilometres out of it, just walking. My uncle had forgotten to lock the door, so we came back home and then slept under the blankets.

(PI)

Luckily, in returning home, Noor and her aunt and uncle were adopting one of the strategies that could protect people from gas leaks:[6] staying indoors, trying to insulate the house to prevent air entering from outside, and putting damp towels over faces, if possible. However, the panic and total lack of information about the danger meant that the reaction of the overwhelming majority of local people was to leave their homes, often running, which increased inhalation of the toxic gases, principally MIC. Noor's family, like many others who lived near the plant, did not even know that it produced pesticides—many were simply unaware of this, or else thought that it manufactured batteries, the product for which UCIL was famous in India.

However, Noor's journey was to continue. When her uncle woke up, the family went to the platform by the railway station where many people were gathering, since they felt safer there. When her uncle and aunt decided to move on, Noor said she was unable to move anywhere, and was eventually found in a lorry that was carrying corpses:

So, I said to my aunt: "I don't want to go anywhere; I will stay here and I want to die here". […] I was unable to breath, and my body was not supporting me, my organs neither, and I couldn't walk, so I fell down under the railway truck, because of the weakness. So I had fell down and the municipal police vehicle came there and what they did was that they picked the bodies […] I don't know what they would do, maybe they would pick the bodies to take them to the hospital or to dump them somewhere. But, when they picked me and put me in the truck, my sister's husband recognised me and said: "she's our family member". And then they picked me and took me to the hospital, where they gave me some injection and tablets.

(PI)

Stories like Noor's, of people waking up alive beneath corpses that were being prepared for cremation or burial, are not unusual, a reflection of the chaos that reigned. Noor was only reunited with her parents and siblings ten days later, when she thought they were dead and they believed she had met the same fate. Many families never saw each other again. Noor told me that the 200 rupees per month she receives in compensation is not sufficient to cover the costs of visits to the doctor and that, whenever she can, she tries to find some extra money so that she can go to a private doctor and receive better care. In addition to her ongoing health problems, which have severely reduced her capacity to work, she explained the stigma that is attached to those known to have been affected by the gas. In her account and those of many other witnesses, this form of social inferiority is crucial in terms of marriage:

> I got married two and a half years after the disaster, but it was difficult because people didn't want to marry with those exposed to the gas. I also had difficulties, because after my marriage, after two years of marriage, my children got skin diseases. That is correct, because people, normal people, think that if you marry your girl or son to a gas-affected family, their children would also be gas-affected.
>
> (PI)

It is therefore very common for people affected by the gas leak to marry others in the same situation. In a society in which choosing a groom represents a major family commitment, defined by caste and socioeconomic status, those affected by the gas leak are restricted to a kind of endogamy in the face of widespread suspicion that the gas which entered their bodies may be passed on to future generations.

As I was saying goodbye, and before switching off the recorder, Noor, realizing that I had forgotten to ask about the fate of her companions on the night she fled from the disaster, called me and told me:

> The girl, that girl, my uncle's girl, she died one month after the disaster and my uncle died within three years, and my auntie also died within three years after the disaster—the three died. And my other uncle and aunt died also, in few years, because of the conditions of the diseases.
>
> (PI)

Obviously, the immediate impact of the disaster on families was very varied and depended, above all, on the area where they lived and the strategies they chose to protect themselves in the face of a danger whose nature and implications were unknown. However, few would have been as badly affected as the family of Sanjay Verma. Born in 1984, Sanjay has no personal memories of the disaster, but knew of its repercussions from his older sister and brother (aged 9 and 19, respectively, at the time) and his involvement as an activist working with the survivors: "But, after that night, my brother Sunil, my older sister Manta and I, we were the only three survivors; three sisters, two brothers and my parents died that night". Sanjay survived thanks to his sister, who told him the story years later:

> My sister wrapped me in a blanket and, since I was a baby, she wrapped me in a blanket and my sister, my brother and I—my sister had me in her

arms—they ran together; and then my brother had to go pee, when they were running—that's when they got separated—but still, somehow, my sister survived; since she had me in her arms I survived as well, and then we met our brother perhaps the morning after or something.

(PI)

Besides telling of the impact of the disaster that night, Sanjay's story is illustrative of its after-effects. The fact that Sanjay has no memories of the family he lost enabled him to have a relatively happy childhood in the orphanage where he lived with his sister. Things were different for his brother, Sunil. Although Sunil channelled his outrage at the event into his work as a leading activist in the years following the disaster, he eventually succumbed to the pain in a series of psychological disturbances that are very common amongst survivors (BMA & BGIA, 2012: 121), which led him to commit suicide in 2006. As Sanjay told me, it was through mourning his brother that he finally managed to reach a closer understanding of the subjective impact of the disaster on the survivors. It is a form of "knowledge" acquired by confronting the death of people one has been close to in the context of a collective disaster, part of an experience which, as can be seen in the interviews collected here, affects the overwhelming majority of those who survived. At this point, Sanjay understood the amount of pain his brother and sister had had to bear, having woken up on 4 December to the loss of seven members of their immediate family.

Engaging with these testimonies of the Bhopal disaster, collected over 30 years later, shows how memories are always profoundly individual. They involve recounting experiences that draw on a mass of feelings and traumas belonging to individual lives. In addition, there is the heavy burden of illnesses, chronic pain and disabilities that disproportionately affects the Bhopal survivors, which relates not only to the centrality of living bodily experience (Merleau-Ponty, 1999; Csordas, 1990) but also the incommunicability of physical pain and the existential anguish of the body made vulnerable (Martins, 2008; Das, 1997). Moreover, recalling these narratives, which are full of painful and potentially disturbing stories, involved, as I realized in the organization and aftermath of the interviews, a clear concern for self-preservation: an assessment of emotional readiness to undertake a difficult exercise in memory, the choice of a respectful and sympathetic audience, and a consideration of the suitability of their destination.

Analyzing the Bhopal disaster, Veena Das (1995: 138–174) examines how the experience of the victims was mobilized by professional discourses—administrative, bureaucratic, medical, legal—in such a way that the pain and suffering tend to be elided within narratives that legitimated the social order and modern institutions. As Shiv Visvanathan said shortly after the disaster: "the bureaucratization of the catastrophe has brought with it the reign of the Certificate. Only a governmental certificate determines what is real. The government decrees of compensation have become doles, transforming the victims into beggars"

(1986: 149). Thus, rather than an analysis immersed in the theodicy which Max Weber and—following in his footsteps—Clifford Geertz (1973) rightly examined in order to highlight the role of religious cosmologies in explaining suffering and the dissolution of the meaning of life, interpretations in the aftermath of the Bhopal disaster cannot be separated from a critical perspective on the mechanisms used by subjects and communities damaged by the disaster to resist devices which seek to reinscribe them as "docile bodies":

> Pain and suffering, however, are not simply individual experiences which arise out of the contingency of life and threaten to disrupt a known world. They may also be experiences which are actively created and distributed by the social order itself. Located in individual bodies, they yet bear the stamp of the authority of society upon the docile bodies of its members. Thus we need to examine the social mechanisms by which the manufacture of pain on the one hand, and the theologies of suffering on the other, become the means of legitimating the social order rather than being threats to this order.
>
> (Das, 1995: 138)

Veena Das considers that the sequel to the Bhopal disaster—which was understood from the outset as a collective event and therefore clearly distanced from the force of strictly individual interpretations of suffering—was therefore the negation of subjective and intersubjective dimensions of pain. This was due, in her opinion, to the power of the multinational chemical industry, the victims' lack of resources, and the use of bureaucratic arguments to define illness, in proceedings which turned suffering into a discourse, or verbal trope, that ultimately dissolved the existential reality of the survivors (Das, 1995: 138–174).

Whilst they are individual, the memories of Bhopal are, as can be seen, also heavily dependent, if not on a collective memory, then at least on shared histories which rewrite the past but also inscribe the subjects in the successive presents in which they speak. Kirmayer notes perceptively that

> Trauma shared by a whole community creates a potential public space for retelling. If a community agrees traumatic events occurred and weaves this fact into its identity, then collective memory survives and individual memory can find a place (albeit transformed) within that landscape. If a family or a community agrees that a trauma did not happen, then it vanishes from collective memory and the possibility for individual memory is severely strained.
>
> (Kirmayer, 1996: 189–190)

However, the situation in Bhopal and the statements I was able to collect have less to do with validating individual experience or creating space for expression—important as this may be—and more to do with an avowed fight for justice and a better life. This is particularly strong in Bhopal, given the injustice and insecurity that have been ostensibly and incessantly reproduced since 1984, and relates to what many local organizations call "the second Bhopal disaster".

The Subjects of "Slow Violence"

The list of events and decisions that culminated in the disaster of 3 December 1984 reveals a massive disregard for the lives of the residents in the slums north of the city of Bhopal. Firstly, there was the actual decision to open a pesticide plant in an already densely populated area without, over the years, taking any measures to prevent new building projects in the surrounding areas or produce a safety plan that included basic information for local residents on the dangers to which they were subjected, and also without drawing up any evacuation plans.

Secondly, the technology used to produce carbaryl in Bhopal was essentially unproven, due to its potential inability to adapt to specific features of local soils and climate; the adoption of a reaction method that was cheaper but involved greater risks; the existing restrictions on importing technology under protectionist Indian legislation; and the lax attitudes in general that resulted in the use of obsolete technology, thus establishing a wide gulf between the technologies and safety standards used in Bhopal and those in its parent company in the USA.[7]

Thirdly, increasing disinvestment had serious implications for safety, as the profitability of the Bhopal plant became an issue. Efforts, first to maximize profits and then, from 1981 onwards, to reduce losses were the result of various factors: technical difficulties in producing alfa-naphthol locally, a project that never came to fruition; the negative effects of years of drought on the demand for pesticides; and the introduction of new pesticides in India which were more efficient and cheaper than carbaryl (D'Silva, 2006: 66–67). This meant that by 1984, the year of the disaster, serious consideration was being given to the idea of dismantling the plant and reinstalling it in separate units in Indonesia and Brazil (ibid.: 88). Successive cuts to operations and staff meant that sensitive procedures were carried out by inexperienced personnel, repair and maintenance work came to an end and costs were reduced in crucial areas. To give a more precise idea of the impact of these cuts, it should be noted that the cooling system for the tanks which stored the MIC (where the initial reaction that triggered the disaster took place), whose function was to prevent endothermic reactions, had been switched off (2006: 90). Moreover, the gas-burning tower, designed to destroy gases in the event of a MIC leak, was not working on the night of the accident (ibid.).

According to the challenge launched in the introduction of this book, envisaging human rights as part of a collective of languages of dignity implies rescuing the voices, struggles, bodies and memories of those deemed subhuman. The way in which the lives of the residents of Bhopal were disregarded in the chain of events that led to the Bhopal disaster reveals a meticulous process of subalternization that allows the subhuman category to be reproduced. This category is embedded, on a local level, by the way in which the economic and cultural destitution of the slum dwellers reflects the racist and religious classifications in a country in which Muslims and low-caste Hindus are amongst the most excluded members of society. From a broader perspective, it is due to the fact that India still belongs to an area defined by the logic of the global inequalities of the world system, forged by the division between colonies and metropoles. India belonged to colonial space, a non-European exteriority still crystallized in the Western mind due to a lingering colonial-racist nexus created through European overseas expansion from the end of the 15th century onwards (Bethencourt, 2013). In this sense, the colonies or, to be more precise, former colonial territories, correspond to what Frantz Fanon's anti-colonial sensibility has termed "zones of non-being" (Fanon, 1967). In these demarcations of humanity, it can be seen, as Boaventura de Sousa Santos states, that "in western modernity there is no humanity without sub-humanities" (Santos, 2018: 20).

Given the ludicrous sums paid in compensation, the inadequate structures for providing medical care, and the pollution which still scars the area surrounding the site of the UCC/UCIL plant (BMA & BGIA, 2012; Elliot, 2014), it may be said that the three decades which followed the disaster are a remarkable illustration of the neglect to which the population affected by the impact of the Bhopal disaster has been subjected. The lives that were lost in Bhopal, as well as those of the survivors, therefore emerge as proverbial representations of ungrievable lives:

> Ungrievable lives are those that cannot be lost, and cannot be destroyed. Because they already inhabit a lost and destroyed zone; they are, onto-logically, and from the start, already lost and destroyed, which means that when they are destroyed in war, nothing is destroyed.
>
> (Butler, 2010: xix)

This explains why, after the disaster, no outcry on behalf of the dead or acknowledgement of the suffering endured by the living found amongst the wreckage of the disaster inspired any effective sense of justice on the part of the Indian state, the UCC in the USA or international institutions. Moreover, it is reflected in the hardships which followed in the wake of the disaster.

Firstly, the struggle for compensation by the survivors of Bhopal came up against an agreement signed, under the auspices of the Supreme Court of India, by the Indian government and the UCC. Under this agreement, the UCC paid 470 million to the Indian government, who received the sum on behalf of the victims—without ever having consulted them. This agreement invalidated any other civil or criminal proceedings against the UCC/UCIL. On the basis of the known damages at the time, it established an insignificant sum which enabled the UCC to continue its operations without further losses. The Indian government redistributed the money to the victims in a way that ensured that approximately 94% of them received less than 500 dollars, paid out over the years in monthly instalments of 200 rupees, a clearly inadequate amount to cover the most basic health problems affecting the survivors. In opting for such an unfavourable agreement, it is clear that the Indian government's main concern was not to antagonize international investors. Boaventura de Sousa Santos notes that states operate on the basis of three strategies: accumulation, hegemony and trust (2000: 279) and, in this case, given the agreement that was established, it would seem legitimate to conclude that the Indian state clearly prioritized accumulation over the trust of the citizens it purported to represent.

Secondly, it took a long time to determine criminal liability and this was dealt with lightly, exposing a framework of impunity. In 1991, responding to an appeal, the Supreme Court of India revoked the cessation of criminal accusations. However, Warren Anderson, the CEO of the UCC (who died in 2014) never appeared in India to answer charges of culpable homicide and the request for extradition, which was only issued in 2003, was constantly rejected by the USA. In 2010, eight senior Indian officials of the Indian subsidiary of the UCC (UCCIL) were charged and given fines and prison sentences of up to two years, leading to a public outcry over the court decision in the face of the disaster.

Thirdly, since the day of the disaster, the factory site and surrounding area have remained heavily contaminated. In particular, the soil and the underground water supply used in recent decades for domestic consumption by residents in the surrounding areas contains high levels of toxic substances. This was even proved in a study carried out by Greenpeace in 1999:

> In total, the survey conducted by Greenpeace International has demonstrated substantial and, in some locations, severe contamination of land and drinking water supplies with heavy metals and persistent organic contaminants both within and surrounding the former UCIL pesticide formulation plant.
>
> (Greenpeace, 1999: 4)

Given this, the demand to clean up the contaminated area (including reserves of compounds still stored hazardously in the former pesticide production area) became established as a crucial phase in the campaigns by activists and survivors (BMA & BGIA, 2012: 136–137). In 2001, the UCC was bought up by Dow Chemical, which inherited the pending UCC liabilities. Despite constant appeals by the Bhopal activists, to the present day, Dow Chemical still refuses to assume responsibility for cleaning up the contaminated area.

As victims of an ongoing disaster added to the 1984 event, the Bhopal survivors find themselves in circumstances marked by chronic illnesses that reduce their quality of life and capacity to work, receiving compensation that does not even provide for decent medical care. Moreover, without ever having seen anyone made accountable for the magnitude of the disaster which affected their lives, the next generations are suffering from congenital disorders and illness as a result of consuming contaminated water.

Over 30 years later, the opportunity to make contact with the community affected by the disaster brought me face-to-face with the descriptive force of what Rob Nixon has termed "slow violence"[8] (Nixon, 2009, 2011), which he considers to be "a violence that occurs gradually and out of sight, a violence of delayed destruction that is dispersed across time and space, an attritional violence that is typically not viewed as violence at all" (Nixon, 2011: 2).

It is therefore a form of violence which evades current interpretations and calls for a revised critical sensibility:

> Violence is customarily conceived as an event or action that is immediate in time, explosive and spectacular in space, and as erupting into instant sensational visibility. We need, I believe, to engage a different kind of violence, a violence that is neither spectacular nor instantaneous, but rather incremental and accretive, its calamitous repercussions playing out across a range of temporal scales.
>
> (Nixon, 2011: 2)

In fact, both the insidious nature of slow violence and the invisibility promoted by hierarchical regimes which collude in the social exclusion of those who were, and are, the victims of Bhopal contribute towards creating a framework in which the "rights of power" prevail over the "power of rights" (Falk, 2009: 25). This conclusion, reflecting a thriving imbalance of power which tends to perpetuate the destitution of the survivors, fails to value the gains and learning produced by stories of struggle and insurgency. It is in this sense that I believe it is important to consider the stories of Bhopal from the perspective of the "epistemologies of the South" (Santos, 2014).

"Epistemologies of the South": Resistance and Learning

In reflections established in close connection with the concepts of the "sociology of absences", "sociology of emergences", "ecology of knowledges" and "intercultural translation" (Santos, 2014; 2018), Boaventura de Sousa Santos defines the epistemologies of the South as

> a set of inquiries into the construction and validation of knowledge born in struggle, of ways of knowing developed by social groups as part of their resistance against the systematic injustices and oppressions caused by capitalism, colonialism, and patriarchy.
>
> (Santos, 2014: x)

In fact, from a perspective that responds to the forms of resistance generated after the Bhopal disaster, it is also possible to detect a counter-paradigmatic impetus by which the powers of colonialism,[9] capitalism and patriarchy have been challenged by the survivors. Without resources or political influence, the history of the struggle by the Bhopal survivors deserves to be recognized, and may be divided into three key forms of action. Firstly, there are the public demonstrations, namely demonstrations in the street, marches, hunger strikes and vigils, whether to put specific claims on the agenda or contest the decisions of the authorities or the courts, or to mark the anniversary of the Bhopal disaster or other relevant dates. In this context, it is important to highlight the important *padyartas*—long protest marches on foot—whose significance and visibility are crucial to the history of the struggle. The first *padyarta* took place in 1989 and was decisive in launching a culture of resistance: 75 women accompanied by 30 children (their own sons and daughters) walked more than 700 km to New Delhi to meet the Prime Minister. The second *padyarta*, also from Bhopal to Delhi, was in 2008. The fast carried out by five female survivors in Delhi in November 2014 should also be noted.

The second dimension of this resistance involves the use of the law, the courts and examination of public documents. Whether by instigating legal proceedings and lodging appeals or by using the right to information, activism in Bhopal has developed at a frenetic pace and has explored all the emancipatory possibilities of the law and engaged in close scrutiny of political decisions on different levels. The capacity of the Bhopal organizations to intervene, in addition to the commitment of the survivors, has benefited crucially from the presence of activists from more privileged areas and backgrounds who have dedicated their academic and social capital to the Bhopal cause.[10]

Finally, the support work of the NGOs mobilized to provide services to the survivors should be stressed, particularly the role played by the ST and the Chingari Rehabilitation Centre, the latter ensuring education and rehabilitation for children of the survivors born with congenital disorders and other disabilities. Both organizations are located near the empty factory and visit the local communities.

In addition to alleviating many of the desperate situations affecting the survivors and their families, these combined efforts have played a decisive role in some of the campaigns against the structural injustice that affects the Bhopal victims. It is worth noting some victories: the revocation, in 1991, of the ban on criminal proceedings against the heads of UCC/UCIL; the expedition of the Warren Anderson extradition request; the studies that were undertaken to assess the impact of the disaster on health and environmental pollution; the order issued by the Supreme Court to provide uncontaminated water for the local population (only implemented in 2014, after a great deal of pressure); the allocation, from 2010 onwards, of interest rates for victims linked to the compensation paid in 1989 by the UCC; the acceptance by the government, in November 2014, of the review of the medical categories used to attribute underestimated compensation payments.

The struggle by the Bhopal survivors was also instrumental in creating an immense spirit of solidarity amongst the communities affected, which is clearly evident in, for example, the way in which the identity of the survivor, a struggle in itself, removed any potential divisions between Hindus and Muslims, even those fuelled from outside.

The leading role played, from the outset, by women, as protagonists in the fight for the rights of the survivors should also be noted. It has a long history, dating back to the first *padyarta* in 1989, which was composed exclusively of women.[11] Champa Devi Shukla (a survivor who is now the trustee of the Chingari Rehabilitation Centre) explains the reasons for this:

> [we women] had to leave the house, to make money for our families, but at the same time we had to deal with all the suffering of the family, which caused immense anger, because none of it was our fault. We used to go to see the mentally disabled, and the babies who were born dead, was part of the support given to the victims. My granddaughter was born with a disability, a cleft palate. [...] Yes, we were all victims of the gas disaster. I saw my husband suffer, my children suffer. After seeing all this suffering, I had to work to take care of all my relatives. Suffering, this is what we feel. Last year I lost a son, who left a son and a daughter. Therefore, I feel that I have to overcome all my sorrows and have the strength to fight for the life of my grandchildren and my daughter-in-law.
>
> (PI)

As became evident throughout the fieldwork, Champa Devi Shukla's response reflects two dimensions that are crucial to the central role women assumed in the activism of the survivors. Firstly, there is the role which women play as the custodians of family wellbeing. The stories recounted earlier of Noor Johan and Mamta, Sanjay's sister, are examples of this. They contain one very significant detail, which also features in other narratives: on the night of the disaster, it was almost invariably the women who carried the children. As in other contexts, this social role played by women that is closely associated with family care (Shiva, 1988) means that, in the years following the disaster, women have emerged as representatives of a suffering that is not theirs alone: it is the suffering of their sons and daughters, their husbands and those who died. Moreover, in forcing them to assume a greater role in public life, the disaster transformed the traditional role of women. Although prior to the disaster many women, particularly Muslim women, were restricted to working in the home (doing the housework or rolling *beedis*[12] for sale outside), remarkable changes took place afterwards. A social restructuring took place, based on the destructuring caused by the disaster: in this new context, women had to supplement or replace their husbands' role as breadwinners, and also appear in the public arenas for intervention and protest as a means of actively alleviating the difficulties experienced in personal and family life. Thus, the struggle of the Bhopal survivors, in addition to being anti-colonial, anti-racist and anti-capitalist, also contained an interesting feminist narrative.

Learning from the memory of other places whose hardships are less well-known offers the possibility of reconstituting a social memory that does not conform to the boundaries of the "human" or the borders that previously defined what could be exploited, namely the colonial spaces. These memories are also vital lessons to the extent that they make it possible to realize how, very often, in a crucial way, "memory is not at the level of representation but at the level of a particular gesture with which you inhabit the world" (Das, 2010).

Conclusion

Just as it deprovincializes the narration of modernity (Chakrabarty, 2000), releasing histories of resistance emerging from such desperate situations as Bhopal may, ironically, be a way of releasing hope in places where sometimes there is still so much despair. The memory of injustice and violence—lengthily inscribed in bodies and testimonies—is crucial to establishing the need for alternatives to the way in which modernity has produced the categories of human and subhuman. The struggle for the survival of memory is inseparable from the struggle of the survivors, who are now inventing grammars of dignity and recognition.

I believe that, almost 40 years later, the lives and the voices of the Bhopal survivors may offer emancipatory temporalities. This is due firstly to the extent to which these voices confront the Eurocentric views on development, namely the way in which their narratives challenge the celebration of inexorable progress, clearly reflected in, for example, the modernist ideology underlying the "Green revolution"[13] or the necessary climate of entrepreneurial non-accountability upheld to ensure that international capital, seen as the driving force for the future, can operate without restrictions.

Secondly, these voices are raised to establish a place in the collective memory for a disaster which, despite its violent and dramatic nature, happened in a part of the world where the time frame for forgetting human suffering tends to run faster. Keeping alive the memory of a disaster that happened over 30 years ago in India adjusts the distance in time, synchronizing the memory of the human disaster in different latitudes.

Thirdly, the voices of Bhopal reinvent time by putting slow violence into a language that can be understood by the speed of media-based news. I refer here to the public protests, which are highly likely to be reported by the media, either because they feature codified sacrificial experiences in the case of the fasts or *padyartas*, or because demonstrations and commemorations are more cinematic and photogenic than slow, interior, invisible forms of suffering and resistance.

Drawing on what Boaventura de Sousa Santos defines as abyssal thinking (2014: 118–135), I believe it may be said that the lives of Bhopal contain the force of a post-abyssal memory in terms of their emancipatory and counter-hegemonic potential. This post-abyssal memory, I would argue, is one which identifies the abyssal memory as a second wave of colonial violence. The post-abyssal memory of violence must encompass the broad latitudes of modern experience, the vast Souths, bearing the bodies and acts of violence, the dead and the survivors, and acknowledging, as the promise of new forms of knowledge, the temporalities witnessed by those most familiar with the ruins of modernity.

Notes

1 UCIL was founded in 1934. Although Indian investors, including the Indian state itself, held shares in the company from 1956 onwards, the subsidiary was always majority-owned by UCC.
2 According to: <www.icssr.org/Baseline%20Survey%20of%20Bhopal%20District.pdf>.
3 Approximately 16 km away from Bhopal.
4 This affected men more, since the women's clothing, in particular the Hindu saris, often made it possible to identify which faith they belonged to.
5 The pesticide plant left the population affected by the gas leak with a legacy of permanent chronic illnesses, primarily pulmonary, ophthalmological, gynaecological and mental problems, muscular pains and headaches. This is confirmed on a daily basis by the doctors working at the ST clinic and by clinical studies (cf., for example, Eckerman, 2005: 107–117; Cullinan et al., 1996).
6 An emergency plan that would have minimised damage in the event of a disaster would include the following measures: an alarm bell; covering the face with a wet cloth; staying indoors if it was possible to insulate the building; walking instead of running; choosing a route that avoided the prevailing wind (Eckerman, 2005: 103).
7 Ingrid Eckerman (2005: 28–29) provides an exhaustive list of the deficiencies in technology and planning at the Bhopal factory.
8 It is no coincidence that the Bhopal disaster, via Indra Sinha's novel *Animal's People*, was one of the cases used by Rob Nixon to develop and substantiate the concept of 'slow violence'.
9 Understood here as the colonial legacy, in a sense similar to the "coloniality of power" (Quijano, 2000) or "imperial formations" (Stoler, 2008).
10 The most outstanding case is that of Ratinath Sarangi (Sathyu), a metallurgical engineer who, together with many other volunteers, hurried to Bhopal in the days after the disaster. He became so committed to the struggle of the survivors that he has lived in Bhopal since 1984. He is a trustee of the ST and leader of the Bhopal Group for Information and Action.
11 On the importance of women in the early years of the survivors' campaign, see Kim Fortun (2001, 217–250)
12 A type of cigarette that is very popular in India.
13 The Green Revolution in India and its close links to the Bhopal disaster clearly reflects how societies are increasingly forced to confront the risks generated by human actions, an idea famously summed up by Ulrick Beck (1992) as the "risk society".

References

Baxi, Upendra (1986), 'From Human Rights to the Right to be Human: Some Heresies', *India International Centre Quarterly*, 13(3/4): 185–200. Available at http://www.jstor.org /stable/23001445
Beck, Ulrich (1992), *The Risk Society. Towards a New Modernity*. London: SAGE.

Bethencourt, Francisco (2013), *Racisms: From the Crusades to the Twentieth Century*. Princeton, NJ: Princeton University Press.

BMA; BGIA — Bhopal Medical Appeal; Bhopal Group for Information and Action (2012), *The Bhopal Marathon*. Brighton: Bhopal Medical Appeal. Retrieved from http://www.bhopalmarathon.org/cryforbhopal/files/12.html

Butler, Judith (2004a), *Undoing Gender*. New York: Routledge.

Butler, Judith (2004b), *Precarious Life: The Powers of Mourning and Violence*. London: Verso.

Butler, Judith (2010), *Frames of War: When is Life Grievable?* London: Verso.

Chakrabarty, Dipesh (2000), *Provincializing Europe: Postcolonial Thought and Historical Difference*. Princeton, NJ: Princeton University Press.

Csordas, Thomas (1990), 'Embodiment as a Paradigm for Anthropology', *Ethos*, 18(1): 5–47. doi: 10.1525/eth.1990.18.1.02a00010

Cullinan, P.; Acquilla, S. D.; Dhara, V. R. (1996), 'Long Term Morbidity in Survivors of the 1984 Bhopal Gas Leak', *National Medical Journal of India*, 9(1): 5–10. Available at http://archive.nmji.in/approval/archive/Volume-9/issue-1/original-articles-1.pdf

Das, Veena (1995), *Critical Events: An Anthropological Perspective on Contemporary India*. Delhi: Oxford University Press.

Das, Veena (1997), 'Language and Body: Transactions in the Construction of Pain', in Arthur Kleinman, Veena Das et al. (eds.), *Social Suffering*. Berkeley, CA: University of California Press.

Das, Veena; DiFruscia, Kim T. (2010), 'Listening to Voices: An Interview with Veena Das', *Altérités*, 7(1), 136–145. Available at http://www.alterites.ca/vol7no1/pdf/71_Turcot DiFruscia_Das_2010.pdf

D'Silva, Themistocles (2006), *The Black Box of Bhopal: A Closer Look at the World's Deadliest Industrial Disaster*. Victoria, BC: Trafford.

Eckerman, Ingrid (2005), *The Bhopal Saga: Causes and Consequences of the World's Largest Industrial Disaster*. Hyderabad: Universities Press.

Elliott, J. (2014), 'India: After 30 Years, Bhopal is Still Simmering', *Newsweek*, January 12. Retrieved from http://www.newsweek.com/india-after-30-years-bhopal-still-simmering-288144

Falk, Richard (2009), *Achieving Human Rights*. New York: Routledge.

Fanon, Frantz (1967), *Black Skin, White Masks*. New York: Grove Press.

Fanon, Frantz (2004), *The Wretched of the Earth*. New York: Grove Press.

Fortun, Kim (2001), *Advocacy after Bhopal: Environmentalism, Disaster, New Global Orders*. Chicago, IL: University of Chicago Press.

Geertz, Clifford (1973), *The Interpretation of Cultures: Selected Essays*. New York: Basic Books.

Greenpeace (1999), *The Bhopal Legacy*. Retrieved on 21.10.2014, from http://www.greenpeace.org/international/Global/international/planet-2/report/1999/10/the-bhopal-legacy-toxic-cont.pdf

Kirmayer, Laurence (1996), 'Landscapes of Memory: Trauma, Narrative, and Dissociation', in Paul Antze and Michael Lambek (eds.), *Tense Past: Cultural Essays in Trauma and Memory*. New York: Routledge.

Kleinman, Arthur (1992), 'Pain and Resistance: The Delegitimation and Relegitimation of Local Worlds', in Mary-Jo Good, Paul Brodwin et al. (eds), *Pain as Human Experience: Anthropological Perspective*. Berkeley, CA: University of California Press.

Martins, Bruno Sena (2008), 'The Suffering Body in the Cultural Representations of Disability: The Anguish of Corporal Transgression', in Thomas Campbell, Fernando

Fontes, Armineh Soorenian and Chris Till (eds.), *Disability Studies: Emerging Insights and Perspectives*. Leeds: Disability Press.

Merleau-Ponty, Maurice (1999), *Fenomenologia da Percepção*. São Paulo: Martins Fontes.

Nixon, Rob (2009), 'Neoliberalism, Slow Violence, and the Environmental Picaresque', *Modern Fiction Studies*, 55(3): 443–467. doi: 10.1353/mfs.0.1631

Nixon, Rob (2011), *Slow Violence and the Environmentalism of the Poor*. Cambridge, MA: Harvard University Press.

Quijano, Anibal (2000), 'Colonialidad del poder y clasificación social', *Journal of World-Systems Research*, 6(2): 342–386. doi: 10.5195/JWSR.2000.228

Santos, Boaventura de Sousa (2000), *Crítica da Razão Indolente: Contra o Desperdício da Experiência*. Porto: Afrontamento.

Santos, Boaventura de Sousa (2014), *Epistemologies of the South: Justice against Epistemicide*. Boulder, CO: Paradigm Publications.

Santos, Boaventura de Sousa (2018), *The End of a Cognitive Empire: The Coming of Age of Epistemologies of the South*. Durham, NC: Duke University Press.

Shiv, Visvanathan (1986), 'II. Bhopal: The Imagination of a Disaster', *Alternatives*, XI(1): 147–165. doi: 10.1177/030437548601100106

Shiva, Vandana (1988), *Staying Alive: Women, Ecology, and Development*. London: Zed Books.

Stoler, Ann Laura (2008), 'Imperial Debris: Reflections on Ruins and Ruination', *Cultural Anthropology*, 23(2): 191–219. doi: 10.1111/j.1548-1360.2008.00007.x

Chapter 5

Pluralism and the Post-Minority Condition

Reflections on the "Pasmanda Muslim"
Discourse in North India*

Khalid Anis Ansari

Introduction

The modernist imagination of nation and democracy—along with the associated teleological aspiration of a territorial and homogenized political community—has been increasingly problematized in the era of late capitalism where
the social confronts enormous drives towards pluralization. In fact, compelled
by the empirical situation of ethnic nationalist movements in Eastern Europe
and various anxieties related to immigrant populations generally in the West,
the period from the 1990s onwards saw an immense interest in ideas of citizenship, multiculturalism and minority rights, especially in Western political
theory scholarship. At the heart of this "liberal-communitarian debate" rests
the interrogation of the liberal post-war orthodoxy that focussed squarely on
individual entitlements and rights in the conceptualization of citizenship in
a context where group-based subjectivities were ascendant. Obviously, fresh
questions were being posed on the nature of political community and solidarity
within the nation-state in an era where increasing international flows of capital,
labour and cultural products were threatening extant borders.[1]

In this context, "questions of ethnicity and minority rights" have been
addressed "with increasing gusto, even heatedness" and "the particular locus
of much of this discussion has centred on the merits, or otherwise, of multiculturalism as public (state) policy" (May, Modood and Squires, 2004: 3).
Historically, while the category "majority" has been by default occupied by the
most dominant cultural collectivity within the national territory, the notion of
"minority" has carried connotations of alterity, injury, subordination or disadvantage. The culture of the majority—which often masquerades as national
culture or secularism—frequently defines the centre through which other
cultures are evaluated and addressed (Connolly, 1996), thereby invoking fear

* I thank Prof. Sitharamam Kakarala and Dr. Caroline Suransky for being the constant inspiration in
  my work and for their sustained guidance. The conversations with Mohd Sayeed have been invalu-
  able in giving the argument some shape, however incomplete.

of cultural assimilationism or economic subjugation in the officially defined minorities. In the case of India, too, there has been a rich debate on minority rights along these lines in recent decades.[2]

However, while the discussion on minority rights has acquired centre stage, what is further striking is that, with the deepening of pluralism and democracy, new subterranean political subjectivities have emerged that are putting severe strains on official minority discourses (Eisenberg and Spinner-Halev, 2005). Some of these internal minorities that are now struggling to inscribe themselves onto the registers of justice may cut through the majority–minority dichotomy and find it to be deeply inhibitive in addressing their concerns. Are we therefore reaching the limits of dominant minority discourses? Is the minority space really capable of addressing the emerging questions around justice, difference and inequality that internal minorities bring to the table? While gender has dominated the discussions on internal minorities in India so far, this chapter reflects on the discursive ruptures in minority space in India instantiated by the pasmanda movement, which is a movement of subordinated castes within the largest religious minority, the Muslims. Employing caste analytics, the movement has complicated the majority–minority (Hindu–Muslim) duopoly and destabilized other related conceptual assemblages. I argue on the one hand that the symbolic destabilization inaugurated by the pasmanda movement poses a tremendous challenge to the extant imagination of the minority space and its discursive field of secularism, cultural rights and reforms. On the other hand, I take issues with the semantics of the term "minority within minorities" itself. Breaking away from the political templates of community articulations, the movement, rather than claiming the space of "minority within minority", calls forth new assemblages of political solidarities, discursive ruptures, symbolic inversions and social critiques. The emerging social and political conditions that inform the democratic striving of the pasmanda movement may tentatively be termed as "post-minority" in my view.

The Topography of "Minority" in India

Most contemporary categories of governance emerged with the advent of modernity and the related reconfigurations of sociality in various jurisdictions. While in the dominant imagination the putative Western model of a linear transition from tradition to modernity holds sway, thereby framing other experiences with modernity in terms of lack/difference, Sudipta Kaviraj takes objection to this view and suggests that "we should expect modernity not to be homogeneous, not to result in the same kind of social process and reconstitution of institutions in all historical and cultural contexts" (Kaviraj, 2010: 15). Especially, in understanding post-colonial contexts like India, "the specificities of colonialism need to be given prominence [...] precisely because the colonial project entailed the construction of very particular types of state institutions, political alliances, and forms of knowledge" (Witsoe, 2011: 621). Consequently, the theoretical liberal view of modernization that entailed, in the main, the transition from ascriptive collectivities to preference maximizing individualization, from traditional associationalism to depersonalized bureaucratization, and from faith to secularization, was complicated by at least three key trajectories that were installed during the colonial regime in India.

Firstly, the colonial regime privileged "numbers" and "community" over the individual in negotiating power and governance (Cohn, 2009). Particularly, colonial modernity and the operations of the decennial Census introduced a novel formulation of community by its efforts at enumeration and classification of subject population.

> The new 'communities' were now often territorially more diffuse than before, less tied to small locality, less parochial, on account of changes in communications, politics and society more generally. They were at the same time historically more self-conscious, and very much more aware of the differences between themselves and others, the distinctions between 'Us' and 'Them'. The new 'community', or 'enumerated community' [...] also became increasingly a part of a rationalist discourse—centrally concerned with numerical strength, well-defined boundaries, exclusive 'rights' and, not least, the community's ability to mount purposive actions in defense of those rights.
>
> (Pandey, 1997: 305–306)

Hence, the colonial knowledge system craftily laid out "ethnographic plots" which also quite often "encouraged the census takers to transfer the authority of self-classification from their subjects to themselves" (Viswanathan, 1998: 161). Secondly, the process of reform was informed by the agency of native elite interlocutors, primarily higher castes, and this gave rise to a distinguished version of colonial civil society and associationalism where membership was not universal, but rather segmentary (Kaviraj, 2010: 27–29). In this context, the approach to state policy and legislation was not primarily to satisfy the choices of individual subjects, but rather as "strategies" to achieve identity-based interests circumscribed by the colonial efforts at consolidating the regime through divide-and-rule. In a political economy mired by uneven development this led to social differentiation and intense competition for scarce resources (Sarkar, 2005: 55). Thirdly, there was ambiguity in the approach to secularization of social life or state. While there was a small section that favoured secularization after the modernist ideal type, the dominant opinion contrasted the materialistic, secularized and individualized West with the spiritual and communitarian East as a means to negotiate the charge of cultural inferiority levelled against the latter. In this sense, while it was acknowledged that faith traditions required reform, there was a sense that religion provided the resources and cultural depth that can scarcely be discounted and which the West lacked (Chatterjee, 1998a). While "Western societies were significantly secularized", in Indian society, as a contrast "religion provided the basis of primary and all-consuming group identities" (Kaviraj, 2010: 22). Consequently, in the context of the state, the

Indian variant of secularism was creatively defined not in terms of opposition to religion *per se*, but as the symmetrical treatment of all religions by the state and public policy (Bhargava, 2000). It is within this contaminated exchange between tradition and modernity that the post-colonial exceptionalism to liberal norms may be precisely located.

In the case of India, therefore, the techniques of governmentality had already classified/enumerated native populations and set up the key categories of governance much before the formation of the independent nation. One of the most pervasive effects of colonial ethnographic efforts was in homogenizing and systematizing social identities: especially religion and caste (Dirks, 2001: 7).[3] Even in pre-colonial times, allegiance to particular communities was considered valuable, but these communities were fuzzier, ambiguous and fluid. The systematization of identities and a differential patronage regime set up a series of tensions that later played out variously in the articulation of hegemonic secular nationalism or the religious/caste sub-nationalisms. The extension of separate electorates (1909) and reservations in employment for Muslims (1925) by the colonial regime was chiefly instrumental in fuelling forces of competitive religious nationalisms, both of Hindu and Muslim variety, which eventually led to the Partition holocaust due to the ill-conceived transfer of populations in the creation of the separate "Muslim" state of Pakistan in 1947 (Aloysius, 1997; Anderson, 2012). The fact that the distance between secular nationalism and Hindu majoritarianism was not as great as was imagined made the situation only worse (Upadhyaya, 1992).

In fact, in the backdrop of this colonial legacy of competitive antagonisms, one of the most urgent tasks that confronted the policy makers of the nascent Indian nation-state was the management of enormous diversity of the Indian social scene and incorporation of various minority demands for recognition within the citizenship regime.[4] While universal and equal citizenship was upheld as the constitutional ideal, exceptions were made in order to accommodate minorities—especially religious, linguistic, caste and indigenous tribal groups. Interestingly, in India, the minority rights framework was adopted by the Constitution in 1947, much before discussions on multiculturalism became vogue in Western academies (Kaviraj, 2010: 36–37). As a matter of fact, minorities were subdivided into sections that were granted "cultural rights" (referring to religious and linguistic groups) and "political rights" (referring to caste and indigenous tribal groups) (Robinson, 2012: 9–10). Hence, social policy in post-colonial India largely conceived religious identity, which also became a suspect category due to the Partition, in cultural terms and recommended protection for the same. In this sense, minority religions, like Islam or Christianity, were constituted as permanent minorities and became a subject of "minority rights".[5] Caste and indigenous tribal groups, on the other hand, were conceptualized in terms of hierarchy, disadvantage or stigma and therefore necessitated annihilation. Hence, castes and tribes became the subject of "social justice" and beneficiaries of positive discrimination policies (reservations or quotas) in parliamentary institutions, employment and education (Mahajan, 2002: 42–43;

Z. Hasan, 2009). The Constitution therefore constructed the official categories of Scheduled Castes (SCs), Scheduled Tribes (STs), Other Socially and Educationally Backward Classes (OBCs) and Minorities (religious and linguistic) to capture this complex reality for policy purposes. However, while SCs referred to the Dalits (formerly untouchables), STs to the indigenous tribes, and Minorities to the religious and linguistic collectivities, the OBC category was interestingly left ambiguous without any clear referents (de Zwart, 2000: 35–36).

Broadly, two important points need to be emphasized here. One, while all faith traditions in India are deeply divided internally on the basis of caste, sect, language and so on, the majority and minority categories were defined subsequently in terms of religion and cumulatively produced over time as bounded and undifferentiated categories through the intervention of law and state policy. Religion was re-signified as the master and overarching category through the repression of caste and other internal differentiations. Two, the majority–minority framework, or the ideology of secularism, though articulated as constitutional mechanisms to guarantee safeguards and assurance to Muslims who chose to stay back in India after Partition, may have kept intact the broad discursive territory from where "communalism"—understood as inter-faith violence or competitive segmentary political demands—as an ideology draws its force. Empirically, post-colonial India continues to be plagued by internecine discursive and violent clashes between the majority and a range of minorities,[6] so much so that "Muslims and minorities" have become "almost synonymous in political discourses" (Robinson, 2012: 32; emphasis in the original). In this sense, minority is not only an official state category but rather a political category in its own right.

It is within the aforementioned conceptual trajectory that the key elements of the majoritarian–minoritarian discourses are constituted and performed on a quotidian basis. Muslim (minority) discourse has been mostly arranged around emotive religio-cultural aspects at the expense of issues related to equity. The majority community is often charged with cultural imperialism, stereotyping and stigmatization. Apart from the perennial presence of episodes of communal violence and a profound feeling of persecution, controversies around language (Urdu), minority educational institutions (Aligarh Muslim University) or personal laws have usually gained public attention (A. Alam, 2003). In the last decade or so, Islamophobic attacks and the alleged arrests of innocent Muslim youth in terror cases have also been emphasized (Hashmi, 2011). The aforementioned elements of minority discourse may be sharply contrasted by a counter-majoritarian discourse by Hindu revivalists (Hindutva) that often raise the question of appeasement of Muslims by the state. The Muslims are framed as potential fifth-columnists and mocked for their alleged role in bringing about the tragedy of Partition. In the Hindutva discourse there are also demographic anxieties related to practices of conversions and proselytization carried out by Muslim and Christian missionaries, the demand for the removal of article 370, prohibition of cow slaughter and enactment of Uniform Civil Code (Robinson, 2012: 18–21). Such mutual discursive contestations and accommodation between majority–minority communities have dominated the political landscape in India since Independence, thereby ushering in a deep discontent among other marginalized constituencies that consequently experience their own justice claims or political arrival to be perpetually displaced and deferred.

Ruptures: The Emergence of "Pasmanda Muslim" Discourse

The policy consensus—religion as *difference*, caste as *inequality*—condensed in the politics of "minority rights" and "social justice", respectively, began to be seriously undermined by new social mobilizations and significant events of the 1990s—mainly, the demolition of the Babri Mosque, the acceptance of Mandal Commission Report and neoliberal economic reforms. These critical events produced dislocationary effects in the Indian social imaginary and the key elements in the official Indian ideology, especially the articulation of minority rights (and secularism), social justice (quota politics) and state socialism were destabilized (Menon and Nigam, 2007). In the discourse-theoretical framework advanced by Laclau and Mouffe, dislocationary events create a certain symbolic disorder where it becomes increasingly difficult for the existing discourses to confer a stabilized sense of identity to social subjects.

As far as the minority space is concerned, the emergence of the *pasmanda* movement was critical as it activated the repressed caste-based segmentations within Indian Muslims and challenged the key motifs of minority discourse. "Pasmanda", a Persian term meaning "those who have fallen behind", refers to Muslims belonging to the subordinated caste groups which constitute about 80 per cent of Indian Muslim population in demographic terms. The *pasmanda* identity was enacted by the All India Pasmanda Muslim Mahaz (henceforth Mahaz) led by Ali Anwar in 1998 in the Indian state of Bihar (Ghosh, 2007). Ali Anwar also forwarded the first major articulation of pasmanda politics in his book *Masavaat Ki Jung* (The Battle for Equality) (Anwar, 2001). Broadly, three kinds of Muslim status groups can be identified: One, those who trace their origin to foreign lands and the converts from Hindu higher castes (*ashraf*); two, the converts from clean occupational castes (*ajlaf*); and three, the converts from the formerly untouchable (Dalit) castes (*arzal*). Moreover,

> The *Ashraf* constitute the highest stratum within this structure. Their position and rank within the Muslim caste system is almost identical with that which the Brahman and Kshatriya grouped together are granted in the Hindu caste hierarchy. Thus both the Sayyad and Shaikh, as competent religious pedagogues and priests, are almost identical with the Brahman; whereas both the Mughal and Pathan, being famous for their chivalry, appear to be equal to the Kshatriya.
>
> (G. Ansari, 1960: 40)

The *ashrafs*, *ajlafs* and *arzals* are further internally differentiated into various ranked, occupational and endogamous groups like *julahas* (weavers), *mansooris* (cotton carders), *telis* (oil pressers), *saifis* (carpenters), *bakhos* (gypsies) and so on. Muslims usually use the term *zaat* or *biradari* for referring to caste and there are about 705 such groups according to the "People of India" Project (Jairath, 2011: 20). The Mahaz attempted to mobilize the "dalit-backward" Muslims by enacting the pasmanda as an oppositional identity to that of the hegemonic higher-caste ashraf Muslims, and instilled a radical negativity within the field of minority politics by employing caste analytics.[7]

It will be useful to note in passing that the availability of caste as a category for conducting politics by the pasmanda Muslims may be explained within the wider ethos of anti-caste movements and democratization in India generally. At least since the late nineteenth century onwards, the caste collectivities have stressed their social, economic and political claims. This "politics of numeric" witnessed both coalescence and differentiation in caste blocs; it was both "aggregative and dis-aggregative" (Kothari, 1997: 62). However, the overall evidence suggests that the number of castes had progressively declined in the country: smaller castes had merged to form larger units (Shah, 2002: 393). This process of interaction of caste with electoral politics has been seen as the democratization of caste (Jodhka, 2010). However, while the history of caste-based associations and movements within Muslims can be traced back to the early decades of the twentieth century (Ghosh, 2010), the recent impetus was offered by the recognition of about 80 Muslim subordinated caste groups by the Mandal Report as OBCs for granting quotas in public employment. This policy move was chiefly instrumental in the politicization of Muslim caste and resulted in what has been referred to as "mandalisation" of Muslim politics (Upadhyay, 2012). In the dominant imagination, it was widely held that while the hierarchical institution of caste was normatively sanctioned by Hinduism, the putative egalitarian religions like Islam or Christianity had no purchase with that. While at the normative/theological level the argument had some force, the sociological/empirical evidence suggested the contrary. In many recent works, caste emerged as a mode of social stratification (or system of social exclusion and power) in South Asia exceeding the category of culture/religion (Ahmad, 1978; Fuller, 1996; Sharma, 1999). Thus, despite different interpretative glosses on the stamp of caste within religions like Islam, Christianity or Sikhism, it was increasingly becoming difficult to invisibilize the caste question within these faith traditions.[8]

In pasmanda narratives, minority politics was revealed as a regime that secured the interests of the microscopic ashraf elite at the expense of the vast majority of Muslims. The pasmanda counter-hegemonic discourse challenged the dominant perception that Islam was an egalitarian religion and Indian Muslims on the whole constituted a marginalized community. In terms of theological hermeneutics, Masood Alam Falahi's work *Hindustan mein Zaat Paat aur Musalman* persuasively demonstrated how the notion of kufu (rules about possible marriage relations between groups) was read through the lens of caste by the casteist ulema and how a parallel system of graded inequality[9] was put into place in Indian Islam (Falahi, 2007). As far as the socio-political sphere was concerned, Ali Anwar's Masawat documented caste-based disenfranchisement of pasmanda Muslims at the hands of self-styled ashraf leaders in community organizations like madrasas, personal law boards, representative institutions (Parliament and State Assemblies) and departments, ministries and institutions that claim to work for Muslims (minority affairs, waqf boards, Urdu academies, AMU, Jamia Millia Islamia, etc.) (K. Ansari, 2013). Anwar also underlines stories of humiliation, discrimination and violence on caste grounds that various pasmanda communities have to undergo on a daily basis (Anwar, 2001).

Overall, the pasmanda discourse has attempted to destabilize the monolithic image of Indian Muslim community constructed from colonial phase onwards by revealing the internal differentiations in terms of caste and power. Consequently, the field of minority politics which has been quite content in raising symbolic and emotional issues so far has been interrogated for having failed to address the bread-and-butter concerns of the pasmanda Muslims, who come primarily from occupational and service biradaris and may be said to constitute the majority within minority in demographic terms. The caste movement among Indian Muslims is now consolidating with various organizations springing up in various jurisdictions.

Pasmanda Counter-Hegemonic Strategies

Pasmanda as a Political Subject: Reconfiguring Identity and Solidarity

The social constructivists have generally emphasized on the contingent and relational nature of identities (Gilroy, 1987; Giroux, 1992; Hall, 1992). As far as political identities are concerned, Mouffe suggests that "there can only be an identity when it is constructed as a difference, and that any social objectivity is constituted through acts of power" (Mouffe, 2013: 4). In this view, there are no naturalized identities and all political identities are affectively constituted in struggle with significant *others* and in a field criss-crossed by social antagonism. In the context of asymmetrical social relationships, domination is usually maintained by reproducing servility and denying authenticity to marginalized subjects. The identity of a subject depends as much on external ascription as on internal definition. Guru remarks "that a person who lacks self-respect, and does not aspire to attain it, cannot be humiliated" and "the struggle for humiliation and its contestation becomes more acute under the modern conditions" (Guru, 2009: 10). The making of the pasmanda as a political subject could similarly be located in its attempt to re-signify its marginal self *vis-à-vis* the ashraf *other* within the hegemonic discursive space of minority.

The pasmanda narratives foreground instances of discrimination and oppression meted out to lower-caste Muslims at the hands of the upper-caste counterparts. Most of the pasmanda communities are subjected to a complex culture of humiliation through circulation of several stories and jokes by the upper castes where even the titles of their castes are used in derogatory terms and often as curse-words.[10] Usman Halakhor, formerly Vice President of the Mahaz, recalls an incident in which some Muslim sweepers from Gorakhpur had visited Delhi to meet a Muslim cabinet minister and discuss their concerns. The minister replied, "*kya makhmal mein taat ka paiband lagana hai?*"[11] Halalkhor remarks that it reflects the perverse and hierarchical mentality of present-day ashraf Muslim leaders (Halalkhor, 2004). Another recurrent theme is the existence of separate graveyards for Muslims of various castes (especially higher) and the clashes that have followed the attempts at burial of low-caste Muslims (Anwar, 2003). In various locations lower-caste Muslims are not allowed to occupy the front rows in the mosques during prayers (Anwar, 2001: 64–68). The Muslims who converted from Dalit castes in historical time continue to face instances of untouchability in their everyday lives from both the higher Muslim and Hindu castes (Deshpande and Bapna, 2008). There is also evidence of social boycott, caste atrocity and extravagant revenge extracted by higher-caste Muslims (K. Ansari, 2009). It is this culture of shaming and humiliation that the disenfranchised Muslim caste groups have attempted to overcome by crafting a new identity that may become a vehicle for publicizing experiences of misrecognition and enabling resistance against it.

Hence, confinement within vertical solidarity on the basis of religion is sought to be critiqued in favour of horizontal solidarity between similar placed caste groups across religions. The pasmanda slogan "*Dalit-pichda ek saman, Hindu ho ya musalman*" (All Dalit-backward are alike, whether they be Hindu or Muslim) captures this radical notion of solidarity succinctly. Broadly, the movement has emphasized that the pasmanda Muslims are a majority within minority. Will this desire to be a majority lead to the constitution of a new orthodoxy? It looks less likely as the principle of graded inequality that anti-caste politics embodies acts against the formation of solidary identities in a phase of acute democratic differentiation. For instance, the "dalit Muslims" have expressed anxieties about being dominated by the "backward Muslims" within the space of the pasmanda movement itself (Azad and Ansari, 2011). However, even when expressing reservations about internal cleavages, Azad is optimistic and says:

> We brought a significant change in the perceptions of Muslim identity. Previously, the question was whether or not they were Muslim, but now the question is whether or not they are pasmanda Muslim. With this new identity we were able to address the problems specific to the lower caste Muslims.
> (Azad and Ansari, 2011)

The Question of Community Reform

The pasmanda movement has since its inception taken the question of social reform seriously and advanced a number of critiques with respect to casteist social practices, interpretative technologies related to religious texts, *maslaqi* (sectarian) conflicts and even patriarchal practices. In these critiques the gulf between normative Islam and actual social practice is often highlighted.

> There have not been many changes in the Muslim society even as we are on the verge of the twenty-first century [...]. There has not been even one percent incidence of inter-caste marriages though sanctioned by religion [...]. When in Islam and the Holy Quran there is no caste based discrimination, its presence in practice is even more dangerous. Who is to blame for the ills in the Muslim society? How to bring this to end? Instead of having a detailed discussion on the issue the tendency to gloat over is prevalent among the Muslims. This avoidance of healthy debate has only deepened the malaise.
>
> (Anwar, 2005a: 9)

Again, "the false pride about there being no discrimination in the Muslim society on the grounds of caste [...] and there being no untouchability, prevented efforts at the religious and non-governmental level with respect to social reform (islah muasshrah)" (Anwar, 2001: 23). Falahi has, in particular, attempted to historicize Indian Islam and offers an early interrogation of the supposed egalitarianism of textual Islam in India. His work is a rich compendium of fatwas (religious opinions) and positions of the ulema (religious scholars) of various schools of Islam and reveals the caste bias in their interpretative efforts.

Also, the entangled nature of caste, gender and faith emerges quite clearly in various entries in pasmanda literature. In Masawat, the author dedicates an entire chapter "Pyar Nikah par Zaat ki Pahredaari" (Caste Surveillance on Love Marriage) that foregrounds the issues of caste patriarchy, honour and surveillance through various reports/cases of tensions around love marriages within the Muslim community (Anwar, 2001: 159–166). Pasmanda Awaaz, the journal of the Mahaz, has raised questions related to dowry, the condition of pasmanda women in India and the gulf between the theory and practice of Muslim representative bodies such as the All India Muslim Personal Law Board (AIMPLB) on the issues of Muslim women. In a letter to the editor, Kahkashan Ahmad Hawari, hailing from the dhobi (laundry person) caste, recalls her experience in the madrasa where the teacher openly expressed his dislike for her friendship to another girl student belonging to higher sheikh caste when she was studying in fifth class (Hawari, 2004). Another letter by Shabana Azmi hits hard at the practice of veiling that according to her is an obstacle for girls in pursuing higher education (Azmi, 2005). While there are entries that strongly contest caste-based endogamy and restrictions on commensality within Muslims (M. Alam, 2005), there are recurrent critiques of the discriminatory practice of "triple talaq" (divorce in one sitting) and especially the All India Muslim Personal Law Board that legitimizes it (Nadwi, 2005; M. Sultana, 2005). Jamila Bano

in fact argues in favour of the formation of a separate Pasmanda Personal Law
Board altogether:

> This four-forked split in AIMPLB on the basis of sect and gender, if one
> were to look at the social location of their leadership closely, it is apparent
> that all of them come from *ashraf* sections. There is no representation of
> men-women from pasmanda communities. It is well-nigh probable that in
> future the men-women of the pasmanda communities would have to cre-
> ate another personal law board for themselves.
>
> (Bano, 2005: 7)

There is also anxiety over *maslaq*-based (loosely translated as "sects") antagonisms within Indian Islam (Shia–Sunni, Deobandi–Barelvi, etc.). These clashes
are often seen to be fomented by the elite Muslims to jeopardize the efforts
of lower-caste Muslims to organize and improve their situation. Shaheen
Sultana reports about the over-representation of upper castes in all *maslaqs* and
comments:

> The sectarian clashes are being deliberately manufactured to dissuade the
> mind of the people away from the movement of [...] pasmanda muslims
> in the country today [...]. These ulema divide the people in the name of
> various sects but join ranks for political bargaining. [...] They are all one
> when it comes to cornering tickets for the superior castes.
>
> (S. Sultana, 2005: 14)

Suheil Waheed also comments: Actually, the issue is not that of Shia–Sunni
or Barelvi–Deobandi. The issue is only of caste and that of 'high' and 'low'"
(Waheed, 2005: 18). Noor Hasan Azad on being asked whether Urdu was the
mother-tongue of Muslims says:

> "You talked about Urdu. I will ask whether Urdu is an issue of dalit
> muslims [...] Of course not! The mother tongue (s) for dalit muslims is
> region-based. I went to Darbangha, a district of Bihar. All the conversa-
> tions happened in Maithili, despite the fact that they know that I speak
> Urdu. Similarly, people speak Bhojpuri or Bangla in different regions. It
> is a false claim that Urdu is mother tongue of Muslims. Neither Urdu,
> nor Hindi is their mother tongue. *Unki matra bhasha to kshetriya hai* (their
> mother tongue is regional)
>
> (Azad and Ansari, 2011)

In the light of the discussion above, one may suggest that the recent discussions
generated within the Muslim community due to the challenge of the pasmanda
movement offer an aperture for the process of reform of theological interpretative technology and community practices to set in. These kinds of social

critiques reveal Islamic interpretative and social domain to be a contested one as opposed to the conservative frames that present a reified version of Islam or a monolithic Muslim community.

Engagements with the Secularism–Communalism Dichotomy

As we know, the Indian variant of secularism, as opposed to the Western artic-ulations, was creatively defined not in terms of opposition to religion *per se*, but as symmetrical treatment of all religions by the state and public policy. In this sense, secularism referred to toleration or plural coexistence and was concep-tualized in opposition to communalism which alluded to segmentary demands or violence based on religious identity. Consequently, secular nationalism was imagined to be antithetical to the forces of Hindu or Muslim nationalisms/communalisms by the Indian elite. However, this entrenched secular–com-munal dichotomy has been vigorously critiqued of late, both in academic and Dalit–Bahujan circles. Broadly, in these discussions communal violence is seen as a restorative instrument employed by the Hindu caste elite to suppress the democratic aspirations of the subaltern communities (Basu, 1997). Also, the secular–communal binary model is critiqued for being dominated by the high castes and having "de-legitimized all other aspirations that were now coming to the fore, including that of the Dalits" (Nigam, 2006: 233).

In pasmanda discourse, while secularism is embraced as a desirable norm, there is also a realization that the actually existing secular politics is dominated by powerful caste groups. The inaugural issue of the Mahaz's journal Pasmanda Awaaz proclaims: "secularism is not only our motto but rather it's an article of faith for us" (AIPMM, 2004: 2). However, this initial enthusiasm subsides in other writings: "Now to keep on reiterating secularism day in and day out won't do. One will also have to be democratic. Some people only know how to get our votes. Now they will have to learn to give us votes" (Anwar, 2005b: 4). In another instance, during the run-up to one of the elections, the Mahaz asked the pasmanda voters not to be hoodwinked by secularism, and that they should look at the qualities of individual candidates and not just vote on the basis of claims of secularism. Moreover, it asked the pasmanda voters to check the attempts made towards vote bank politics on the basis of "Muslim" identity (*Pluralism.in*, 2004). However, on the issue of communal ideology, while the Dalit–Bahujan articulations have taken serious issues with the forces of "Hindu nationalism", there seems to be little engagement with "Muslim nationalism" as such. The symbiotic and co-constitutive nature of these two contending communalisms appears to be under-discussed. The pasmanda discourse tries to cover this gap by foregrounding the complicity of the upper-caste Muslim elite in sustaining and reproducing the communal discourse that is often instru-mental in legitimizing episodes of communal violence. In fact, there is a stress on the dialectical relationship between majority and minority fundamentalisms and the pasmanda movement proposes to contest minoritarian fundamentalism from within in order to wage a decisive battle against majoritarian fundamentalism at the national level (A. Alam, 2003).

There is also a realization that, in instances of communal violence or false framing of Muslim youth in cases related to terror, it is the pasmanda Muslims who are the key victims (Pasmanda, 2013: 11). It was only recently that the caste breakup of victims of communal violence has received some academic/media attention. At least two recent papers on the Muzaffarnagar riots have employed the caste category in their analysis due to the influence of the pasmanda discourse. For instance, Hilal Ahmed says:

> The questions of Muslim caste-diversity and public presence are equally important aspects to understand the victimhood of Muslims in these riots (*though this point has been almost entirely ignored in most of the discussions*).
> [...]
> As per an unofficial estimate, most of those Muslims who died in the present violence were backwards [...] the marginalised, poor and backward sections of Muslims are the soft targets of communal violence.
> (Ahmed, 2013: 11; my emphasis)

And Singh: "The victims of the riot by and large belong to the poorer class of Pasmanda Muslims, generally engaged in non-agricultural occupations" (Singh, 2016: 94). Also, in some recent communal episodes in Dadri, Bijnor and Jharkhand and elsewhere, sections of the media have emphasized the lower-caste locations of Muslim victims (Naqvi, 2016; Sajjad, 2016).

Recognition and Redistributive Demands

In the last few decades there were various ways in which "cultural" (recognition) and "economic" (redistribution) rights of the marginalized sections have been theorized. Most of these works have critiqued difference-blind approaches to citizenship and have argued in favour of substantive equality in contrast to formal equality (Markell, 2006). In India, apart from the cultural protection to religious and linguistic minorities (recognition) or reservations/quotas for the subordinated (representation), the state also undertook general welfare measures (distribution) intended for different targeted populations (subsidized housing, public distribution system, agrarian and small-scale sector policies, scholarships for poor students, etc.).[12] In this context, the pasmanda movement has preferred to work within a framework of social justice rather than that of minority rights. In its pursuit of democratization, it has concentrated on intra-group inequality which often gets elided due to the focus on inter-group inequality in a minority rights frame. There is a sense that, in political institutions and public employment, while the ashrafs are over-represented, the pasmanda are grossly under-represented.

The Mandal Commission Report, by listing 82 Muslim lower-caste groups as "backward", unleashed the long-suppressed debate regarding whether reservations in government jobs should be articulated on the lines of religion or caste among Indian Muslims. Those arguing the former, mostly upper-caste Muslims, underlined the egalitarian ethic of Islam and dubbed caste-based reservations to be divisive and disruptive of the unity of Muslims as a "community". They argued for reservations for Muslims as a whole, or "total Muslim reservations" as it came to be called in pasmanda political discourse. Those arguing the latter, mostly lower-caste Muslims, highlighted that the social reality of Indian Muslims was caste-informed and reservations should legitimately be on the basis of caste. They argued that "total Muslim reservations" was a ploy of the advanced *ashraf* sections—constituting only 15 per cent of the Muslim population and already over-represented in state and community structures—to corner the benefits of reservations. The ashraf attempt to press for a quota on religious lines was dubbed as a "communal quota" and the danger of religious polarization that may result from it was emphasized (Anwar, 2004: 3). This battle between these two positions has writ large in the subsequent debates that have ensued over various government reports following the Mandal Moment.[13]

Moreover, a significantly large number of pasmanda Muslims work in the "unorganized sector" of the Indian economy as skilled or manual labour and share an ambivalent, or rather at most times hostile, relation with the process of globalization. The critical steps to globalize and privatize the Indian economy since the onset of the economic reforms of 1991 have witnessed massive erosion of traditional employment and disruption in cottage industries without actually creating commensurable new opportunities or avenues for the retraining of skilled labour in modern (or post-modern) sectors of the "new economy".

Towards a Post-Minority Condition

In the preceding section we have seen how, by employing caste analytics, the pasmanda discourse has attempted to rupture the key elements of mainstream Muslim or minority discourse. By taking recourse to a symbolic inversion it has trumped caste *vis-à-vis* religion and strived to displace the latter as the overarching determinant of the notion of community. In addition, it has engaged with other identifications within the minority space like gender, language or sect and has reconfigured their relationality through critical revaluations. In the pasmanda narratives, the "majority–minority" and "secular–communal" dichotomies are framed as upper-caste constructs that play a key role in invisibilizing the injuries and marginal status of the subordinated caste collectivities across religions. The attempt by the subordinated Muslim castes to enact a new identity and thereby qualify the mainstream Muslim (minority) identity may be grasped as an instance of what Connolly dubs as "the bumpy politics of becoming by which new movements jostle and disturb an established pattern of diversity as they seek a place on a modified register of legitimacy and justice" (Connolly, 2011: 652). From the vantage point of the pasmanda experience, the majority–minority (or secularism) framework has neither been able to contain inter-religious violence nor ensure justice for the vast majority of marginalized castes. Once the caste principle is employed the distinction of majority–minority informed primarily by religion cracks, and what emerges is a *minority* of dominant caste elite across religions lording over the *majority* of suppressed castes. Since caste movements are decentring entrenched categories which work for the interests of caste elite, the persistence of communal violence and fundamentalist trajectories in faith traditions may also be interpreted as restorative violence to arrest the democratic assertion of socially excluded caste groups. If such is the case, and some recent evidence points out at the large-scale casualties of mostly pasmanda Muslims in communal riots and other forms of Islamophobic violence, then we may have underplayed the role of Muslim caste as a factor in inter-religious violence as well. From the emerging evidence there are indications that the politics arranged around the category minority has resulted in the gross under-representation of pasmanda Muslims in power, on the one hand, and over-representation in catalogues of riot victims on the other.

However, while the deepening of democracy has clearly interrogated the extant minority framework and elements of mainstream Muslim discourse in India, it resonates with the experience elsewhere as well. Wilkinson, speaking from an Afro-American perspective, asks for a "systematic questioning of ingrained seductive words and value-based constructions like minority" and radically suggests that "researchers, clinicians, and teachers must seek ways to incorporate race and ethnicity in all relevant contexts and omit entirely the 'minority' concept" (Wilkinson, 2000: 124–25). A widely discussed volume has used the term "minorities within minorities" to refer to the situation where "efforts to develop reasons why political relations between mainstream majorities and minorities ought to be renegotiated tend to present contending interests as though they are uncontroversial within the groups that hold them" (Eisenberg and Spinner-Halev, 2005: 3). The volume outlines the difficulties in reconciling inter-group with that of intra-group inequalities.

Mahajan points out that out of the three broad suggestions that have been offered to address the concerns of internal minorities; that is, "(i) prescribing the limits of permissible diversity by invoking a historically or politically shared universal; (ii) providing exit options for community members; and (iii) seeking a deliberative consensus within the community" (Mahajan, 2005: 95), it is the last one that has found favour amongst most Indian commentators. Partha Chatterjee, for instance, is one of the key exponents of the "reforms from within" approach. Chatterjee argues against the state-led reforms of the Muslim community and advances a "strategic politics of toleration" which works on the principle that "if the struggle is for progressive change in social practices sanctioned by religion, then that struggle must be launched and won within the religious communities themselves" (Chatterjee, 1998b: 377). In other words, he rests his hope on *internal reform* carried by community institutions themselves that "must satisfy the same criteria of publicity and representativeness that members of the group demand of all public institutions having regulatory functions" (Chatterjee,1998b: 376). Moreover, the representativeness of the community institutions "could only achieve their actual form through a *political process* carried out primarily within each minority group" (Chatterjee, 1998b: 376). One may fairly posit that this formula of "a twofold struggle–resist homogenization from the outside, and push for democratization inside" (Chatterjee, 1998b: 378), and other key articulations on minorities in the Indian context confine themselves to minority accommodation and the dominant consensus on a majority–minority framework.

I see this as a closure primarily because the extant minority space may not be rendering justice to the sheer scale and radical diversity of new identifications and spaces of social transformation in India. Arguing from the vantage point of the post-colonial South African experience, Jean Comaroff and John Comaroff take cognizance of the hyper-politicization and fragmentation of identities and suggest that "the term 'multicultural(ism)' is insufficient to describe the fractious heterogeneity of postcolonies" (Comaroff and Comaroff, 2003: 456). They propose the terms "ID-ology" and "policulturalism" as post-colonial substitutes for the terms ideology and multiculturalism. While ID-ology refers to "the quest for a collective good, and sometimes goods, sanctioned by, and in the name of, a shared identity", "the prefix, spelled 'poli-'" in policulturalism "marks two things at once: plurality and its politicisation" (Comaroff and Comaroff, 2003: 456). For instance, in the case of caste, while its *politicization* has been much discussed, the recent evidence suggests its increasing *culturalization* as well (Natrajan, 2012). More and more subordinated caste units across religions are now developing their own mythologies of origin, replacing symbolisms of humiliation with pride, tracing their own heroes/icons and reconfiguring community norms/ practices. Here caste is reinvented as a cherished identity, indeed a community in its own right with all its implied holistic meanings, and ceases to be a marker that in the main implied injury. As stated earlier, Muslims have about 705 caste-based groupings which are increasingly undergoing the process of politicization and culturalization. Is the minority space capable enough of accommodating the symbolic and material aspirations of such a large number of groups? Is a single window transaction around religion the best way to address the emerging concerns around cultural difference? Is there a need to rethink the dominant consensus on religion as difference and caste as inequality in the face of increasing culturalization of caste?

While the discursive articulation of the pasmanda movement needs to be tested empirically for a more grounded appraisal of the movement or the efficacy of the minority space in accommodating the claims of pasmanda communities judiciously, one is tempted to say that the minority category probably invisibilizes more than it reveals as far as modes of misrecognition and systematic exclusion are concerned. Since the "demographic question is central to minority politics" (Robinson, 2012: 32) and pasmanda are basically a *majority within minority*, one feels that the term "minority within minority" may not be adequate in capturing the pasmanda experience of injury and disadvantage. I therefore suggest that the extant social and political conditions that circumscribe the democratic aspirations of pasmanda Muslims have probably exceeded the context that legitimated the earlier imagination of the minority space, and therefore the ensemble of emerging contestations around recognition/social justice, majority–minority and secular–communal duopolies, or reform may be provisionally termed as "post-minority". It does not necessarily mean the negation of earlier concerns around religious communalism or majority assimilationalism that quintessentially defined the minority space, but rather an appreciation for the dynamic nature of social space and the democratic possibilities opened by recent normative/symbolic inversions inaugurated by subaltern movements.

Notes

1 For an overview, see Kymlicka and Norman (1994).

2 For an overview, see Robinson (2012).

3 For instance, Pandey: "The all-India 'Hindu community' (and to a large extent, the all-India 'Muslim community' too) was a colonial creation for […] the social and economic changes brought by colonialism, Indian efforts to defend the indigenous religions and culture against western missionary attacks, the 'unifying' drive of the colonial state […]. In spite of a widely felt sense of 'Hinduness' and 'Muslimness', I would suggest that until the nineteenth century at any rate, people always had to work through caste, sect and so on to arrive at the unities implied in the conception of the 'Hindu community' and the 'Muslim community'" (Pandey, 1997: 316). And, Mushirul Hasan: "the act of 1909 (Indian Councils Act) was a calculated master-stroke. Separate electorates, along with reservations and weightages, gave birth to a sense of Muslims being a religio-political entity in the colonial image—of being unified, cohesive and segregated from the Hindus. They were homogenized" (M. Hasan, 1998: 15).

4 Broadly, the population of India is divided, in terms of religion, into the majority Hindu community (about 80%) and the religious minorities like Muslims, Sikhs, Christians, Jains, Buddhists, etc., which constitute the remainder. In the context of minorities the Muslims, which constitute around 14% of present India's population of about 1.21 billion, are the most significant minority in terms of numerical weight. However, the Hindu community follows a caste-based system of social stratification and is internally fragmented into five normative status-based caste groups or *varnas*—the *Brahmins* (priests), *Kshatriyas* (warriors), *Vaishyas* (merchants), *Shudras* (labourers/artisans) and a group of outcastes—the *Dalits* (formerly untouchables). The *varnas* are arranged in the form of a hierarchy based on the notions of purity-pollution with Brahmins at the top and the Dalits at the bottom. These *varnas* are further subdivided into a few thousand sub-castes or *jatis*, which are ranked, endogamous occupational groups. In practice, *jatis* are probably the more functional and easily identifiable units, even when their textual hierarchy is often complicated, subverted and redefined in the daily political (for a good introduction, see Jodhka [2012]). In fact, The 'People of India Project' has identified about 4,635 communities in India (K. S. Singh, 1995) (Singh, 1995) (Singh, 1995).

5 The Constitution upholds the rights of religious and linguistic minorities through Article 25 (freedom to practice and propagate one's religion), Article 26 (right to

maintain religious institutions), 29(1) (cultural preservation), 29(2) (educational right), Article 30(1) (right to establish and administer educational institutions) and Article 30(2) (right to state aid for educational institutions).

6 See Graff and Galonnier (2013).

7 By "caste analytics" I refer to the conceptual resources developed by anti-caste radicals like Jotiba Phule, EV Ramasamy Periyar and Dr. B. R. Ambedkar and so on, which are broadly labelled as the "Dalit-Bahujan" discourse (Rodrigues, 2008).

8 For caste movements in Sikhism and Christianity, see Jodhka (2004), Japhet and Moses (2011).

9 The reference is to Dr. B. R. Ambedkar's conceptualization of the caste system as a unique Indian institution which entailed "an official gradation laid down, fixed and permanent, *with an ascending scale of reverence and a descending scale of contempt*" (cited in Jaffrelot, 2003: 20). He articulated the principle of "graded inequality" where each caste had certain caste groups simultaneously arranged above and below it so that caste system was not a mere division of labour but *a division of labourers* (Rodrigues, 2002: 263).

10 For a very rich sociological account of this phenomenon see (Anwar, 2001: 37–70).

11 "Do you want me to stitch a jute patch on muslin cloth?" (The coarseness of jute signifying the pasmanda Muslims and the fineness of muslin allude to the upper-caste Muslims).

12 See Jayal (2013).

13 For an overview, see K. Ansari (2016).

References

Ahmad, Imtiaz (1978), "Introduction", in Imtiaz Ahmad (ed.), *Caste and Social Stratification among Muslims in India*. New Delhi: Manohar, xvii–xxxii.

Ahmed, Hilal (2013), "Muzaffarnagar 2013: Meanings of Violence", *Economic & Political Weekly*, 48(40), 10–13.

AIPMM—All India Pasmanda Muslim Mahaz (2004), "Pasmanda Awaaz Kyon?" *Pasmanda Awaaz*, December.

Alam, Anwar (2003), "Democratisation of Indian Muslims: Some Reflections", *Economic and Political Weekly*, 38(46), 4881–4885. Available at http://www.epw.in/journal/2003/46/s pecial-articles/democratisation-indian-muslims.html

Alam, M. (2005), "Roti-Beti ka Mamla: Shaitani Zehan Aaj Bhi Qayam", *Pasmanda Awaaz*, March, 10–12.

Aloysius, G. (1997), *Nationalism without a Nation in India*. New Delhi: Oxford University Press.

Anderson, Perry (2012), *The Indian Ideology*. New Delhi: Three Essays Collective.

Ansari, Ghaus (1960), *Muslim Caste in Uttar Pradesh: A Study of Culture Contact*. Lucknow: Ethnographic and Folk Culture Society.

Ansari, Khalid Anis (2009), "A Tale of Two Mosques", *Himal Southasian*, January.

Ansari, Khalid Anis (2013), "Muslims that 'Minority Politics' Left Behind", *The Hindu*, June 17. Retrieved from http://www.thehindu.com/opinion/lead/muslims-that-minority-p olitics-left-behind/article4820565.ece

Ansari, Khalid Anis (2016), "The Muslim Affirmative Action Debate: Post-Sachar Reflections", in Murzban Jal and Zaheer Ali (eds.), *What Ails Indian Muslims?* New Delhi: Aakar, 147–166.

Anwar, Ali (2001), *Masawaat ki Jung* [The Battle for Equality]. New Delhi: Vani Prakashan.

Anwar, Ali (2003), "Kabristaan Mein bhi Zaat-Paat" [Casteism even in the Graveyards], *Prabhat Khabar*, March 3.

Anwar, Ali (2004), "Muslim Arakshan Ghate ka Sauda", *Pasmanda Awaaz*, December.

Anwar, Ali (2005a), *Masawat Ki Jung*. New Delhi: Indian Social Institute.

Anwar, Ali (2005b), "Mahapanchayat ke Baad ab Chunawi Jung", *Pasmanda Awaaz*, January.

Azad, Mohd. Noor Hasan; Ansari, Khalid Anis (2011), "'Backward Muslims Are Not Creating Any New Caste Divisions': Pasmanda Muslim Mahaz", *Countercurrents.org*, 3 January. Retrieved 19.11.2016, from http://www.countercurrents.org/ansari030111.htm

Azmi, S. (2005), "Phir Zamana Humein Sarahega", *Pasmanda Awaaz*, January.

Bano, J. (2005), "Talaaq par Siyasi Tikram: Tab Pasmanda Muslim Personal Law Board bhi Banega", *Pasmanda Awaaz*, March.

Basu, Amrita (1997), "Reflections on Community Conflicts and the State in India", *The Journal of Asian Studies*, 56(2), 391–397.

Bhargava, Rajeev (2000), "Democratic Vision of a New Republic: India, 1950", in Francine R. Frankel, Zoya Hasan, Rajeev Bhargava and Balveer Arora (eds.), *Transforming India: Social and Political Dynamics of Democracy*. New Delhi: Oxford University Press, 26–59.

Chatterjee, Partha (1998a), "Community in the East", *Economic and Political Weekly*, 33(6), 277–282.

Chatterjee, Partha (1998b), "Secularism and Tolerance", in Rajeev Bhargava (ed.), *Secularism and Its Critics*. New Delhi: Oxford University Press, 345–379.

Cohn, Bernard (2009), "The Census, Social Structure and Objectification in South Asia", in *The Bernard Cohn Omnibus*. New Delhi: Oxford University Press, 224–254.

Comaroff, Jean; Comaroff, John (2003), "Reflections on Liberalism, Policulturalism, and ID-ology: Citizenship and Difference in South Africa", *Social Identities*, 9(4), 445–473.

Connolly, William E. (1996), "Pluralism, Multiculturalism and the Nation-State: Rethinking the Connections", *Journal of Political Ideologies*, 1(1), 53–73.

Connolly, William E. (2011), "Some Theses on Secularism", *Cultural Anthropology*, 26(4), 648–656.

de Zwart, Frank (2000), "The Logic of Affirmative Action: Caste, Class and Quotas in India", *Acta Sociologica*, 43(3), 235–249.

Deshpande, Satish; Bapna, Geetika (2008), *Dalits in the Muslim and Christian Communities: A Status Report on Current Social Scientific Knowledge*. New Delhi: National Commission for Minorities Government of India. Available at http://ncm.nic.in/pdf/report%20dalit%20%20reservation.pdf

Dirks, N. B. (2001), *Castes of Mind: Colonialism and the Making of Modern India*. Delhi: Permanent Black.

Eisenberg, Avigail; Spinner-Halev, Jeff (eds.). (2005), *Minorities within Minorities: Equality, Rights and Diversity*. Cambridge: Cambridge University Press.

Falahi, Masood Alam (2007), *Hindustan Mein Zaat Paat aur Musalman* [Caste and Muslims in India]. Delhi: Al Qazi Publishers.

Fuller, Christopher J. (1996), *Caste Today*. New Delhi: Oxford University Press.

Ghosh, Papiya (2007), "Pasmanda Politics in Bihar", *Khuda Bakhsh Library Journal*, 49, 129–144

Ghosh, Papiya (2010), "Contesting the Sharif: The Momin Conference", in Papiya Ghosh (ed.), *Muhajirs and the Nation: Bihar in the 1940s*. New Delhi: Routledge, 89–109.

Gilroy, Paul (1987), *There Ain't No Black in the Union Jack*. London: Hutchinson.

Giroux, Henry A. (1992), *Border Crossings*. London: Routledge.

Graff, Violette; Galonnier, Juliette (2013), "Hindu-Muslim Communal Riots in India I (1947–1986)", *Online Encyclopedia of Mass Violence*, 15 July. Retrieved from http://www .sciencespo.fr/mass-violence-war-massacre-resistance/en/document/hindu-muslim-co mmunal-riots-india-i-1947-1986

Guru, Gopal (2009), "Introduction: Theorizing Humiliation", in Gopal Guru (ed.), *Humiliation: Claims and Context*. New Delhi: Oxford University Press, 1–19.

Halalkhor, M. U. (2004), "Makhmal par Taat ki Paiband", *Pasmanda Awaaz*, December.

Hall, Stuart (1992), "The Questions of Cultural Identity", in Stuart Hall, David Held and Tony McGrew (eds.), *Modernity and Its Futures*. Cambridge: Polity Press, 274–316.

Hasan, Mushirul (1998), "Introduction", in Mushirul Hasan (ed.), *Islam, Communities and the Nation: Muslim Identities in South Asia & Beyond*. Delhi: Manohar, 7–24.

Hasan, Zoya (2009), *Politics of Inclusion: Castes, Minorities, and Affirmative Action*. New Delhi: Oxford University Press.

Hashmi, Shabnam (ed.) (2011), *What it Means to Be a Muslim in India Today*. New Delhi: Anhad.

Hawari, K. A. (2004), "Kahan Woh Sheikh, Kahan Tum Dhobi", *Pasmanda Awaaz*, December: 20.

Jaffrelot, Christophe (2003), *India's Silent Revolution: The Rise of Low Castes in North Indian Politics*. Delhi: Permanent Black.

Jairath, Vinod K. (2011), "Introduction: Towards a Framework", in Vinod K. Jairath (ed.), *Frontiers of Embedded Muslim Communities in India*. New Delhi: Routledge, 1–25.

Japhet, S.; Moses, Y. (2011), "The Unending Struggle of Dalit Christians and Dalit Muslims for Equality", *Kafila.org*, July 28. Retrieved 22.01.2012, from http://kafila.org/2011/07 /28/the-unending-struggle-of-dalit-christians-and-dalit-muslims-for-equality-s-japhet -and-y-moses/

Jayal, Niraja Gopal (2013), *Citizenship and Its Discontents: An Indian History*. New Delhi: Permanent Black.

Jodhka, Surinder S. (2004), "Sikhism and the Caste Question: Dalits and Their Politics in Contemporary Punjab", in Dipankar Gupta (ed.), *Caste in Question: Identity or Hierarchy?* New Delhi: SAGE, 165–192.

Jodhka, Surinder S. (2010), "Caste and Politics", in Niraja Gopal Jayal and Pratap Bhanu Mehta (eds.), *The Oxford Companion to Politics in India*. New Delhi: Oxford University Press, 154–167.

Jodhka, Surinder S. (2012), *Caste: Oxford India Short Introductions*. New Delhi: Oxford University Press.

Kaviraj, Sudipta (2010), *The Trajectories of the Indian State: Politics and Ideas*. Ranikhet, India: Permanent Black.

Kothari, Rajni (1997), "Caste and Modern Politics", in Sudipta Kaviraj (ed.), *Politics in India*. New Delhi: Oxford University Press, 57–70.

Kymlicka, Will; Norman, Wayne (1994), "Return of the Citizen: A Survey of Recent Work on Citizenship Theory", *Ethics*, 104(2), 352–381.

Mahajan, Gurpreet (2002), *The Multicultural Path: Issues of Diversity and Discrimination in Democracy*. New Delhi: SAGE.

Mahajan, Gurpreet (2005), "Can Intra-Group Equality Co-exist with Cultural Diversity? Re-examining Multicultural Frameworks of Accommodation", in A. Eisenberg and J. Spinner-Halev (eds.), *Minorities within Minorities: Equality, Rights and Diversity*. Cambridge: Cambridge University Press, 90–112.

Markell, Patchen (2006), "Recognition and Redistribution", in John S. Dryzek, Bonnie Honig and Anne Phillips (eds.), *The Oxford Handbook of Political Theory*. Oxford: Oxford University Press, 450–469.

May, Stephen, Modood, Tariq; Squires, Judith (2004), "Ethnicity, Nationalism, and Minority Rights: Charting the Disciplinary Debates", in Stephen May, Tariq Modood and Judith Squires (eds.), *Ethnicity, Nationalism, and Minority Rights*. New York: Cambridge University Press, 1–24.

Menon, Nivedita; Nigam, Aditya (2007), *Power and Contestation: India since 1989*. Halifax; London: Fernwood Publishing; Zed Books.

Mouffe, Chantal (2013), *Agonistics: Thinking the World Politically*. London: Verso.

Nadwi, A. K. (2005), "Ashraf Muslim Personal Law Board Se Nijaat Zaroori", *Pasmanda Awaaz*, June.

Naqvi, Saeed (2016), "Why Bijnor Communal Villainy Did not Spread", *The Citizen*, September 24. Retrieved 15.11.2016, from http://www.thecitizen.in/index.php/OldNewsPage/?Id=8802&Why/Bijnor/Communal/Villainy/Did/Not/Spread

Natrajan, B. (2012), *The Culturalization of Caste in India: Identity and Inequality in a Multicultural Age*. London: Routledge.

Nigam, Aditya (2006), *The Insurrection of Little Selves: The Crisis of Secular-Nationalism in India*. New Delhi: Oxford University Press.

Pandey, Gyanendra (1997), "Communalism as Construction", in Sudipta Kaviraj (ed.), *Politics in India*. New Delhi: Oxford University Press, 305–317.

Pasmanda Kranti Abhiyan (2013), "Pasmanda Kranti Abhiyan Pamphlet (Hindi): First Phase (Uttar Pradesh)", *Pasmanda Kranti Abhiyan* (Campaign for Pasmanda Revolution).

Pluralism.in (2004), "Pasmanda Dharmnirpekshta ke Jhaanse mein Nahin Ayein", *Pluralism.in*.

Robinson, Rowena. (2012), "Introduction", in Rowena Robinson (ed.), *Minority studies*. New Delhi: Oxford University Press, 1–48.

Rodrigues, Valerian (ed.). (2002), *The Essential Writings of B. R. Ambedkar*. New Delhi: Oxford University Press.

Rodrigues, Valerian (2008), *Dalit-Bahujan Discourse in Modern India*. New Delhi: Critical Quest.

Sajjad, Mohammad (2016), "The Communal Mood in UP is Turning Ugly", *Rediff News*, October 13. Retrieved 15.11.2016, from http://www.rediff.com/news/column/the-communal-mood-in-up-is-turning-ugly/20161013.htm

Sarkar, Sumit (2005), *Modern India: 1885–1947*. New Delhi: Macmillan.

Shah, Ghanshyam (2002), "Social Backwardness and the Politics of Reservations", in Ghanshyam Shah (ed.), *Caste and Democratic Politics in India*. New Delhi: Permanent Black, 388–412.

Sharma, Ursula (1999), *Caste*. New Delhi: Viva Books.

Singh, Jagpal (2016), "Communal Violence in Muzaffarnagar: Agrarian Transformation and Politics", *Economic & Political Weekly*, 51(31), 94–101. Available at http://www.epw.in/journal/2016/31/special-articles/communal-violence-muzaffarnagar.html

Singh, Kumar Suresh (ed.). (1995), *People of India*. Calcutta: Anthropological Survey of India.

Sultana, M. (2005), "Model Nikahnama Banam Teen Talaq: Personal Law Board Ka Irada, Jod Kam Ghatao Zyadah", *Pasmanda Awaaz*, April, 9–10.

Sultana, Shaheen (2005, February), Maslaqi Jhagda: Bach Ke Rehna Re Baba. *Pasmanda Awaaz*, (2), 14–15.

Upadhyay, R. (2012), "Mandalisation of Muslim Politics in India: A Shift from Religious Identity to Caste Identity?", *Eurasia Review*. Retrieved from http://www.eurasiareview.

com/28032012-mandalisation-of-muslim-politics-in-india-a-shift-from-religious-identi
ty-to-caste-identity-oped/

Upadhyaya, Prakash Chandra (1992), "The Politics of Indian Secularism", *Modern Asian Studies*, 26(4), 815–853.

Viswanathan, Gauri (1998), *Outside the Fold: Conversion, Modernity and Belief.* New Delhi: Oxford University Press.

Waheed, S. (2005), "Musalmanon mein Oonch-Neech", *Pasmanda Awaaz*, February.

Wilkinson, D. (2000), "Rethinking the Concept of 'Minority': A Task for Social Scientists and Practioners", *Journal of Sociology and Social Welfare*, 27(1), 115–132. Available at http://scholarworks.wmich.edu/jssw/vol27/iss1/7

Witsoe, Jeffrey (2011), "Rethinking Postcolonial Democracy: An Examination of the Politics of Lower-Caste Empowerment in North India", *American Anthropologist*, 113(4), 619–631.

Chapter 6

Picturing Law, Reform and Sexual Violence

Notes on the Delhi Protests of 2012–2013

Pratiksha Baxi

Introduction

In 2012–2013, unprecedented and sustained protests followed the brutal gang rape and subsequent death of a 23-year-old woman on a bus in Delhi on 16 December 2012. The protests transformed the discursive and juridical landscape by pointing to the need to do justice to those who reveal the public secret of rape. As Taussig has argued, a public secret is "that which is generally known, but cannot be articulated" (1999: 6). Public secrecy however finds specific revelation in rape trials in India, which does not bring justice to a rape survivor but addresses and reinforces deeply entrenched phallocentric notions of "justice" (P. Baxi, 2014). In this chapter, I highlight specific moments, alliances and conversations during the 2012–2013 protests to describe the terse relationship between publicity, public secrecy and the law. I underscore that feminist entanglement with the law as a form of critique is not limited to countering the cunning of law reform. This partial account of the protests woven around narration of different voices and temporalities offers a specific reading of how affective publics were constituted, carceral energies gathered and the violence of the law conserved in the phallocentric conversations between the masculine state and its subjects. At the same time, the chapter engages with how feminist interventions interrupted different kinds of phallocentric dialogues staged and performed at manifold sites of protests and reform, and in prolific modalities of witnessing and testifying. Finally, the discontents, reflexivity and improvisations within feminist politics offer a complicated picture of how feminists engage or disengage with the law.

Scripts of Panic and Difference

As the details of the brutality hit the media, it seemed as if the threshold of toleration of sexual violence had broken down. Brutal gang rape, mutilation of body parts and intolerable sexual humiliation, in the national capital; it could no longer be confined to "zones of emergency" inscribed on bodies of Dalit, tribal, religious or sexual minorities, some place out there that did not really hurt. The awareness that this *exception* ran through the capillaries of the city produced an unparalleled circulation and outpouring of public emotion. As the world consumed spectacularized images of the protests (Roychowdhury, 2013; Belair-Gagnon, 2014), Western media "isolated and differentiated India as a crucible for sexual violence, exacerbating global hierarchical power structures" (Durham, 2015: 185). These global representations remained disconnected with the histories of the anti-rape protests within the feminist and queer movements in India. The trance-like global obsession with the mass protests that unfolded in Delhi during the winter of 2012–2013 had created a global desire to "understand" rape culture in India, and how best to transform it (U. Baxi, 2012; Dutta and Sircar, 2013; Sen, 2013; Lodhia, 2015).

This period was marked by an intriguingly high number of hits on articles written by scholars and activists on rape, a frenetic search for experts who would speak authoritatively on the rape law and its discontents, a palpable excitement to experience the protests, and the need for expertise at home and abroad to understand "rape culture" in India. The intensification of the circulation of research on sexual violence, however, was not always accompanied by the creation of a demand for feminist reflection on sexual violence as a response to the crisis of law and governance. Law reform also created new objects of criminalization, censorship and regulation that demanded research. Rape became researchable in order to "understand" mind-sets, traits, culture, judicial behaviour and crime statistics (Verma et al., 2013).

The global publicity looped back to a nationalist rhetoric decrying the tarnishing of the image of the country abroad (Misri, 2014). Indian politicians responded by blaming the media, feminists and the protests for sensationalizing rape, and producing the crisis now posed to the image of a globalizing economy. The Delhi protests also became a potent resource for a certain kind of racialized sexual politics. At a protest I participated in, a white reporter appealed to a co-protester: "we are filming Indian women of all kinds. You look modern. Please, can you say—I am India's daughter". Unfazed by her angry refusal, the reporter found someone else to mime this script for the camera. Affirming that sexual violence is a marked category in the context of the "other cultures", whereas sexual violence, which operates as an unmarked category in the West is not seen as cultural violence (Kapur, 2005; Basu, 2011). Techniques of *othering*—be these about cultures, civilizations or nations—posit rape as a defining *trait* of the inferior other (Shalhoub-Kevorkian, 1999, 2009).

As the protest against sexual violence found newer forms of publicity, feminist critique of sexual violence was simultaneously folded into the creation of what Kapur (2013) characterizes as the "sexual security regime". Feminists have since debated whether or not this moment marked the emergence of "governance feminism", "carceral feminism" or "sexual security apparatus"; or excluded the voices of Dalits or sexual minorities (Halley et al., 2006; Bernstein, 2007; Xalxo, 2012; Kapur, 2013; Teltumbde, 2013; Agnes, 2015; Misri, 2014). While there were debates on the politics of location of the Harvard-based feminists who set themselves as experts,[1] there were intense contestations within the women's and queer movements on how best to reform the rape law (Puri, 2011; Menon, 2014).

The culture of silence and silencing found the radical challenge such that sexist responses to rape were viscerally challenged and a context was created enabling rape survivors to testify to their experiences in public. However, the most trenchant critique of the re-organization of public secrecy came from Dalit feminists and groups who argued that this publicity continued to relegate sexual violence on Dalit women to zones of sexual exceptionalism. The debates on gender neutrality pointed out towards the public secrets of rape on adult men and sexual minorities—highlighting the need to go beyond the very problematic binary inherent to the categories of "man" and "woman".

World over, anti-rape protests are often appropriated to *fit* into stabilized political scripts that acknowledge certain kinds of sexual violence and silence other voices. For instance, Srila Roy (2012) argues that the revolutionary Naxalbari movement in Bengal politicized rape as the signature of state repression, but it did not construct rape within the movement as a product of its militarized political culture. The framing and memorialization of insurrectionary or revolutionary violence in popular culture erases records of sexual violence by those celebrated as the "liberators" or "heroes" of armed struggles (Mark, 2005; S. Roy, 2012).

Right-wing political parties respond to sexual violence by demanding capital punishment since rape is perceived as worse than death; by policing sexuality or framing rape through the ideology of the honour of the Hindu nation state. Public secrecy is used to normalize the toleration of targeted forms of sexual violence against certain kinds of women, whilst rape is condemned as if it produces horror equally irrespective of the subject position of the survivor. This kind of politics produces an optics of horror that uses rape to produce moral panic. This moral panic is productive of lynch mentalities, sexual repression and censorship, which energizes and unleashes the masculinist fantasy of the Hindu nation state.

Identification and Misrecognition

The Delhi protests in 2012–2013 addressed different kinds of publics—retributive, reformative and pornographic. Equally it made visible different kinds of male bodies—rapacious, castrating, raped and castrated. For the first time, many progressive male friends talked about how hurt they were by what had happened. They marched against sexual violence, wrote about affect and biography, and spoke publically about what it meant to be a man. Now, the Delhi gang rape hurt many *progressive* men friends, teachers and colleagues. Yet, the same men did not walk with us then in our protests against sexual violence. The complicated story of identification and misrecognition that followed offers many provocations.

It was argued that an identification was forged with the victim and her friend, Awindra Pandey—and there seemed shock that such exceptional violence could follow a perfectly routine affair of going to see a film and using public transport in the evening. There was an articulation of a collective sense of shock regarding that brutal gang rape; mutilation of body parts and intolerable sexual humiliation in public spaces was no longer confined to zones of emergency inscribed on bodies of Dalit, tribal, religious or sexual minorities. Dutta and Sircar wondered:

> whether this sense of collective mourning and outrage would have emerged had she been tortured and killed by other means and not penetrated by the penis; that is, if the incident was just as brutal but the violence not sexual in nature. The outrage signals the continuing primacy that is placed on sexual violence generally, and on penile-vaginal penetration in particular, as the ultimate form of violation.
>
> (Dutta and Sircar, 2013: 300)

This collective mourning and outrage was gendered. The Delhi gang rape, however, Rahul Roy (2012) argued, did not signal a "crisis of masculinity", as some argued,[2] "but indexed a spectacle of the very nature of masculinity". To quote him:

> Rape is the memorialising of what can be achieved through the practice of masculinities. The inability of the phallus to live up to all its myth making capabilities requires then the use of phallic replacements, harder metallic instruments that are more capable of performing feats that masculinities pushes men to achieve through their phallus. The use of metal rods, guns shoved inside mouths, stones inserted into the rectum, knives used to carve the skin are all expressions that have rather erroneously being analysed as emanating from a crisis of masculinity. It is in the nature of masculinity.
>
> (R. Roy, 2012)

Public opinion relegated rapacious masculinities to the working-class body, confined to states of mind and degeneration of bodies inhabiting particular geographies of poverty and criminality. As if this transaction of violence was never between men—or not about what it means to use sexual violence to "teach a lesson". As Mehta argues, "public violence provides one of the most powerful registers of the intimacies between male friends, so much so that it prohibits the democratization of the social body" (2013: 4).

From this followed the muted presence of the experiences of Awindra Pandey—the victim's friend—other than his eyewitness account, speculations of the nature of his friendship with the victim or his role as a witness in the trial that commenced. Roychowdhury argues that this illustrates the ongoing resilience and appeal of Gayatri Chakravorty Spivak's "white men saving brown women from brown men". Spivak's theory illuminates why Pandey's male friend, Awindra Pandey, disappeared from the pages of international media while Pandey and her assailants took pride of place in the discussion. Commentators seemed to forget that Awindra was even on the bus and was also physically assaulted, stripped naked, and dumped on the side of the road. He disappeared, firstly, because his body stood outside the economy of international care: white men are not in the business of saving brown men from other brown men. He also had to disappear because brown men are not typically viewed as allies of brown women. Specific acts of violence continue to become international causes because they index the inferiority of non-Western cultures.

(Roychowdhury, 2013: 284)

If we move attention from the predictable obsessions of the international media, Pandey's experience of violence remained muted amidst men too. Awindra too had been assaulted and stripped—yet his experience was not cited in thinking through sexual violence and the discontent with the rape law reform discourse.

On Awindra's Facebook page[3] there were posts of solidarity—primarily characterizing him as the icon of friendship—admiring of his loyalty that he stuck around to save his dying friend. There were also telling posts that saw Pandey as a *failure*—a man who was not able to protect *his* woman. Class also played a role here—as Jyoti Singh Pandey posted:

> It was unfortunate but had she chosen another guy like me who has a car and a motorcycle to take her out and drop her back then she would not have met this fate, but instead she chose to go out with that guy who does not have a car, bike or even a scooter and takes her out in a public bus or auto, LOL!! :D.[4]

Others were more offensive[5] when they called him emasculated—stigmatized as a *Chka, hijra* or a *na-mard*—despised categories for *real* men.

Narratives in the media suggested that a haunted Pandey felt the need to repeat that he did his best to save his friend, fought the assailants in the bus and saved her from being run over.[6] His guilt at surviving to testify to something that could have been avoided in the first place was emphasized in the media. As a survivor and a witness, his trauma was made to speak to the restless retributive public—eliciting from him an affirmation of death penalty. Further, the structure of the trial constituted the way his story was told in the media. It was significant that the fact that he was stripped naked was not framed as a form of sexual humiliation: nor was the abduction to witness unimaginable sexual violence named as trauma. Pandey was also a victim of such pedagogy of violence—encoded in the violent expression "teaching a lesson". Yet this experience of sexual humiliation remained a public secret.

The Many Sites of Retribution

Feminists who were opposed to the death penalty also could not align Pandey easily to their politics against masculine retribution. During the protests, there were many speeches and writings against the emergence of a retributive public, where the cry for the death penalty or castration became a vocabulary of protest most shrilly framed by the 24/7 news channels. The camera acted as a phallo-centric substitute that sought to restore the now-broken promise between the male-defined state and its male subjects—state violence had to be secured to avenge male subjects (*read*: upper caste, middle class, upwardly mobile) unable to protect *their* women.

The spontaneous protests focused on the idea of retribution. Kavita Krishnan (2014) recalls in response to the retributive public,

> The first thing we did was try and find a slogan that would resonate with people that would take things away from the single minded focus on the death penalty.
>
> Because we noticed that while there were many thousands of people out with these death penalty placards, there were also many thousands of first time protesters with no exposure whatsoever to the women's movement or the left movement who had placards against victim blaming.
>
> They were saying "don't tell women what kind of clothes to wear, tell men not to rape".
>
> There were persuasive and angry placards and posters, including some by men. We saw one boy painting a poster on his own, which said: "We men can wear shirts that show off our biceps, and nobody is going to tell us we're in danger of being raped".
>
> (Krishnan, 2014)

In this sense there were many protests under the sign of one event.

It seemed that a discursive space was created for men to respond to sexual violence through the confessional, through guilt, through anger and with pleasure. Each entails distinct forms of identification and misrecognition. The confessional admitted publically to flashes of recognition expressing tortured doubts about whether each sexual act entailed full and voluntary consent over the man's life. The response of guilt narrated complicity in witnessing acts of sexual violence or harassment without doing anything about it. The response to sexual violence as anger by men was directed against the accused for the manner in which the public secrecy of rape was exposed. The response of pleasure was manifest in the formation of the pornographic public where the everyday conversations about rape became a resource for pleasure.

From this moment, let us move forward to the angry debates in the media over the complaint of sexual assault against a well-known journalist—where the newly amended sexual violence law was now implemented. Noting the "ferocity" of the critique of sexual harassment that followed this case, Rahul Roy (2013) argued that the mediatized debates did not index a "zero tolerance to sexual assault and harassment of women". Rather, "men seem to be getting some kind of a pleasure out of abusing" the accused journalist (R. Roy, 2013, see also Menon, 2014). Indeed, if one read the comments, it was apparent that men used this case as a way to learn how to seek pleasure and expressions of anger that were deeply personalized against the accused. What then propelled men to protest so ferociously or identify with the accused so instantly? About this case, Roy hazards:

> Is it that in some strange way the Tehelka case is turning the mirror to many men and the reflection they see is so frightening, so close and so familiar that this anger is a desperate attempt to purge themselves of the shadow of Tarun Tejpal? He is the twin that needs to be punished for revealing himself through the cracked mirror.
>
> (R. Roy, 2013)

In contrast, during the Delhi protests, as Mehta (2013: 4) argues, the rapist was constructed as "a type of man, a body, a case history, an almost alien form of life". The construction of the rapist as an alien form of life—a move mirrored in judicial discourse that stereotypes rapists as pathological beasts—informed the men who claim the monopoly over the legal profession through the male-defined Bar Associations. Various Bar Associations (the Saket Bar and Delhi Associations in particular)[7] decided to boycott those accused of rape and even threatened the lawyers who decided to represent the accused. The boycott became part of the logic of retribution, however, when executed by lawyers—mostly male—it hollowed the law of its constitutional meaning. Not only was there no evidence that any feminist challenge had been posed by male lawyers to the Bar whom we petitioned in the wake of the Delhi protests, but they also sought to stage a mock trial for the accused by staging a boycott in the glare of publicity. The boycott became the only technique of performing horror—directing attention away from how lawyers manage and produce the public secrets of rape trials (P. Baxi, 2014). Horror, publicity and retribution produced through the boycott intensified the actualization of the violence that followed.

Carceral desires flowed through the prison bringing death and humiliation to the accused in the Delhi gang rape case, as Roychowdhury notes:

> The retributive dimensions of Pandey's case surfaced early on in activists' demands for castration and capital punishment, but they took a concrete and visceral form when Pandey's assailants were arrested and awaiting trial in Tihar jail. One of the accused, Mukesh Singh, was beaten and forced to consume human excrement by fellow prisoners on December 20, 2012. A few months later, his brother, Ram Singh, the reported ring leader of Pandey's assault and the driver of the bus, allegedly committed suicide on March 11, 2013.
>
> (Roychowdhury, 2013: 287)

In 2013, 35 inmates were reported to have died in Tihar—2 suicides (including Ram Singh) and 2 murders, whilst 31 inmate deaths were attributed to medical negligence and lack of supervision.[8] Amidst discussions on whether this was suicide or murder,[9] Ram Singh was ultimately reduced to a statistic in the doubling of custodial deaths in Tihar in 2013. Thus normalizing prison deaths, most recently reported from Cherlapalli Central Prison in Hyderabad, where six inmates died in 15 days.[10]

Ram Singh's death was significant in affirming the retributive public conjoining the secrecy of punishment with the spectacle of the trial. The failure of the criminal legal system was in service of the collective cry for putting the rapists to death immediately. Ram Singh's death routinized by a magisterial inquiry was celebrated whilst noting the scepticism of the government's will to avenge. On a Facebook page called *I Support Damini, I want to kill the Rapists*,[11] the news of Ram Singh's death was posted. The following comments to this post register the retributive effect.

\#   Doesn't really a matter [...] the poor girl was brutally raped and murdered and yet these clowns were under trial [...] if I had the access, probably I would have killed all of them.

\#   good riddance

\#   Whatever friends, ramsingh death rdy [...] Very good news for Nirbhaya Damiani murder or suicide [...] good riddance!! [...] wel at least nw his family will feel d same pain too [...] wt damini's family must be going through [...] and a death which makes d whole nation glad cant be treated as bad news [...] its gud news

The headline about the dead accused barely produced horror at the crisis facing the criminal legal apparatus—rather, it gave to the retributive public the closure it sought immediately—after all, the trial delayed the "gud news".

A group, *16 December Kranti*, which had named a site of memorialization after the survivor *Damini Chowk* in Janpath, demanded the *Damini Law*.[12] This included the death penalty for rapists, including for juveniles, a demand to criminalize marital rape, fast-track courts, compulsory filing of First Information Report (FIR) and punishment for women who levy false cases of rape.[13] The group enacted the hanging of the accused in the Delhi gang rape case outside the Saket trial court when the verdict was to be pronounced.[14] The mock execution outside the court mirrored the sentence of death pronounced inside the court.

The Castrating Public

Retribution rests on the mobilizing effect that the pornography of violence generates. The nature of forensic reporting of what was done to the victim's body also created a pornographic public—where reporting not only directed male desire to geographies of sexual colonization but also produced pedagogies of sexual violence. There was a dark side to the reporting of sexual violence, which functioned as a pedagogy of rape, reproducing the pornography of rape.

The retributive public demanded castration as punishment for rape. The grammar of violence underlying the demand for the death penalty and castration essentializes the penis as a primordial weapon, negating the material and symbolic realities of sexual violence. It erases how sexualized violence is used to communicate a message to all women and some men—violently coded in the expression "teaching a lesson". Deepak Mehta argues that the call for castration

> rests on a misrecognition or at the very least, the failure to recognize. One dominant fiction of our public life calls upon the male subject to see himself, and the female subject to recognize and desire him only through the images of an unimpaired masculinity. It urges male and female subjects to believe in the absolute identity of penis with phallus so much so that one would not be complete without the other. It is almost as if classic male subjectivity rests upon the denial of castration, beyond the vicissitudes of ideology and history.
>
> (Mehta, 2013: 4)

It is then significant that castration acquired a retributive currency not witnessed in earlier protests against rape. How do we trace the emergence of castration as an alternative to the death penalty or a life sentence without parole or remission? Some may argue that such imagination is framed as if by cinematic courts of justice, to use Lawrence Liang's (2010) characterization, which imagines that pathological expression of patriarchal power is destroyed by cutting off the rapacious penis—since castration is understood as the paradigmatic state of mutilated masculinity. Indeed, posters of a bloody penis, cut off as an act of vengeance, populated the early days of the Delhi protests.[15]

Speaking of the political unconscious, Sophy Joseph (2013) reminds us of yet another genealogy by pointing out that castration as a tool of humiliation and punishment "has a stigmatized and inegalitarian historical legacy".

> According to *Dharma Shastras* and *Dharma Sutras*, castration was imposed as punishment for crimes such as adultery and rape. The *Gautama Dharmasutra* (12.2) and *Manusmriti* (8.374) accords punishment of castration on a Sudra who has intercourse with a woman of a higher *varna*. The *Narada Smriti* (12.72–74) goes to the extent of prescribing castration as the punishment of rape for any one belonging to non-Brahmin caste for polluting woman of Brahmin caste. While *Sudras* were punished with forcible castration by law, the Brahmin was allowed voluntary castration, that too only if he has intercourse with the wife of his guru or an elderly woman.
>
> (Joseph, 2013)

If we trace the genealogy of the debate on castration to these texts, we find a clear articulation of what castration meant for a phallocentric and caste-based response to sexual violence. For Brahmanical patriarchy, to use Uma Chakravarti's (2003) term, the regulation of sexuality is central.[16] The political unconscious of castration as a form of punishment in a caste-based patriarchy finds life in texts which uphold and celebrate a phallocentric caste order.

Although the demand for castration was rejected during the 2013 law reform, we saw the actualization of a castrating public that used a cleaver from a butcher's shop to castrate a man found assaulting a young girl in Rajasthan in October 2014.[17] The circulation of the graphic pictures of the castrated body on cyber space publicized the replacement of the noose with the cleaver,[18] and the replacement of a physical death with a sexual death. The victim of the castrating public doubly subjugated, once by the cleaver and then by the camera, now provided a contemporary picture of castration in the series of images produced earlier. During the Delhi protests, the juxtaposition of different kinds of images to construct an imagery of castration drew both on historical images of castration machines in the medieval West as well as other kinds of images belonging to punishment prescribed in the *Puranas*.[19]

The *Dainik Bhaskar* carried an image from the Delhi protests[20] of a woman holding a placard saying "chop off their raping tool"—thus juxtaposing two different moments of a demand and its actualization as coeval. The images of the castrating public that sit side by side with the demand for castration during the Delhi protests are framed by cinematic representation of rape and revenge where spectacular violence in surplus of the horror of rape is staged: only the protagonist is not the survivor but a male crowd angered by the modes by which the public secrecy of rape is revealed. The act of castration then produces the body of the rapist as alien and damaged. In this sense, the violence of the castrating mob is political—inscribing what Mehta (2013) calls a politics of misrecognition of both the penis and the phallus simultaneously.

Producing Discomfort[21]

How did the symbolic find challenge during the protests? The slogan of *bekhauf azadi* (fearless freedom) replaced the vocabulary of retribution in Delhi (P. Baxi 2016). Moving away from patriarchal languages of shame and honour, protective frameworks of "rescue", or carceral politics of retributive justice, we heard the powerful slogan for *azadi* (freedom). The protesters included loud voices of dissent, which named rape as an act of power, not sex. As a form of gendered and sexualized violence, rape and other forms of sexual assault found powerful critique. The victim-blaming discourse that says women provoke men to rape found visceral challenge—leading to a series of images, art and performances—which sought to create alternate imaginations of what it may feel like to inhabit life without the fear of rape. The protesters emphasized prevention and awareness, gender budgeting and city planning, safety audits and smart technology to prevent violence.

This was a protest, which drew attention to the continuum of violence from the everyday forms of sexual harassment to the aggravated forms of sexual assault. Slogans of *azadi* from the patriarchal control of the father, brother, husband, state repression, and enforced sexuality resounded during the protests (Prakash, 2014). The call for *azadi* was semantically rich, able to incorporate within it a critique of different forms of patriarchal violence, control, humiliation and censorship. The protesters addressed the humiliation enforced by section 377 of the IPC (the colonial law that criminalizes "unnatural sex"), the criminalization and medicalization of Lesbian, Gay, Bisexual, Transgender, Queer, Questioning and Intersex (LGBTQI) sexualities; critiqued marital rape; demanded the repeal of emergency laws such as Armed Forces (Special Powers) Acts (AFSPA) and insisted on respecting the sexual choices made by consenting adults. In other words, the call for *azadi* both memorialized narratives of resistance against sexual violence as well as offered an alternate imagination of a gender-just world.

The critique of heteronormative feminism, heightened during the intense debate on the question of gender neutrality of the rape law, was folded into the call for freedom from compulsory heterosexuality during the protests (Narrain, 2014; Prakash, 2014). The decision to replace the language of retribution that was based on a series of identifications and misrecognitions by the language of *bekhauf azadi* (fearless freedom) was deliberate (P. Baxi 2016). In her reflections on the Delhi protests, Krishnan (2013) talks about how the politics of producing discomfort interrupted the symbolic and political capital that rested in the retributive public. And the slogan for *azadi* marked a movement away from *suraksha* (protection), from rescue (paternalism), from policing (sexual regulation), from pathologizing (medicalizing sexualities) and, most importantly, from a juridical notion of retributive justice (see also Krishnan, 2014). Not only did it challenge the public–private divide, it made visible all kinds of bodies— children, men, women, gay, lesbian, inter-sex, transgender and queer. It made visible the everyday and the extraordinary, the custodial and the public, the structural and the collective. It was especially by the participation of those men who did not adopt the protectionist approach by proffering to regulate women presence's public space, but insisted on women's freedom and autonomy as a condition for equality (see Prakash, 2014). The protests then spoke directly to law reform in proliferate ways.

Epistemologies of Solidarity

The 2013 protests not only produced satirical performances that mocked the idea of men sourcing pleasure or power through rape, but simultaneously there was an important interrogation of protests as epistemologies of solidarity. I recall here the reflections of Stella James, who was interning with a judge during the protests in December 2012:

> Last December was momentous for the feminist movement in the country—almost an entire population seemed to rise up spontaneously against the violence on women, and the injustices of a seemingly apathetic government. In the strange irony of situations that our world is replete with, the protests were the backdrop of my own experience. In Delhi at that time, interning during the winter vacations of my final year in University, I dodged police barricades and fatigue to go to the assistance of a highly reputed, recently retired Supreme Court judge whom I was working under during my penultimate semester. For my supposed diligence, I was rewarded with sexual assault (not physically injurious, but nevertheless violating) from a man old enough to be my grandfather. I won't go into the gory details, but suffice it to say that long after I'd left the room, the memory remained, in fact, still remains, with me.[22]

The protests placed a specific kind of demand on women to speak out in anger and indignation, at a time when institutions and hierarchies remained unchanged, especially in the dark chambers of courts. James further said:

> While the incident affected me deeply, I felt little anger and almost no rancour towards the man; instead I was shocked and hurt that someone I respected so much would do something like this. My strongest reaction, really, was overwhelming sadness.
>
> This emotional response was also completely at odds with the powerful feelings of righteous anger that the protesters in Delhi displayed. I am not trying to say that anger at the violence that women face is not a just or true response, but the polarization of women's rights debates in India, along with their intense emotionality, left me feeling that my only options were to either strongly condemn the judge or to betray my feminist principles. [...] If the shared experiences of women cannot be easily understood through a feminist lens, then clearly there is a cognitive vacuum that feminism fails to fill.

This is a powerful critique of the "cognitive vacuum" of feminist discourses since protests could not translate into an epistemology of solidarity. Identifying the burden on survivors of violence to speak out by complaining to the police or the workplace, irrespective of whether or not they wish to choose to speak out in this way.

> The incident is now a while behind me, and they say time heals all wounds. But during the most difficult emotional times, what helped me most was

the "insensitivity" of a close friend whose light-hearted mocking allowed me to laugh at an incident (and a man) that had caused me so much pain. Allowing myself to feel more than just anger at a man who violated me, something that I had never done before, is liberating! So, I want to ask you to think of one thing alone—when dealing with sexual violence, can we allow ourselves to embrace feelings beyond or besides anger, and to accept the complexity of emotions that we face when dealing with any traumatic experience?

While her testimony ultimately travelled to the court to fix accountability and raised the issue of sexual harassment in law schools, James also raised important questions about how women defined feminism. She insisted that laughter and parody as a form of self-reflexive mode of being is as feminist as marching and shouting slogans in anger (P. Baxi 2016). The images of feminist protest that script anger as the appropriate response to sexual violence and the criminal complaint as the privileged act of resistance find powerful displacement in this narrative. The context then is what the spectacle of protest communicated to women who dodged barricades to go to work in 2013.

During the protests, a number of women protesters experienced sexual harassment by co-protesters and the police. Those working in the media would narrate how their workplace was sexualized—where salacious and titillating interest in sexual violence stories also extended to inappropriate comments and gestures to women reporters. And there were other cases where writing, talking and protesting against rape figured as the background for sexual harassment or rape. Retribution after all rests on the mobilizing effect that the pornography of violence generates. The nature of forensic reporting of what was done to the victim's body also created a pornographic public—where reporting not only directed male desire to geographies of sexual colonization, but also produced pedagogies of sexual violence (P. Baxi 2016).

Udwin and the Ban: Concluding Remarks

During the coverage of the protests, the camera acted as a phallocentric substitute that sought to restore the now-broken promise between the male-defined state and its male subjects—state violence had to avenge male subjects (*read*: upper caste, middle class, upwardly mobile) unable to protect *their* women. The camera became our "prosthetic eye" (Pinney, 2008) framing how and what must be consumed. This coverage brought Leslee Udwin to India to make a documentary film for the BBC on the events in 2012.

At the heart of the controversy surrounding the telecast of the BBC film by Leslee Udwin, *India's Daughter* on New Delhi Television (NDTV) was the interview with one of the 2012 Delhi accused, Mukesh Singh and his lawyers. After outrage hit the media and later the parliament, the telecast of the film was banned.[23] The political reasoning of the ban that found vehement articulation in the parliament congealed in the argument that the film defamed not only the victim but was also a "conspiracy" to defame India. This political rhetoric instantiated right-wing political discourse of national pride that uses sovereign power to stifle critique, dissent or dissension on the grounds that it is defamatory to expose state impunity. The voices asking for revoking the ban (and the accompanying insidious culture of censorship) opposed the caricaturing of dissent, satire or critique as *anti-national*. While feminists opposed the ban, a few prominent voices within the movement disagreed on two broad issues. The first question concerned the rights of the convicted rapist and a fair trial; and second, the regulation of the speech of the convicted rapist in the *public* interest, for his interview was seen as an incitement to violence. While the former was addressed through the law on contempt, the latter was addressed through the law on hate speech as an actualization of reasonable restriction on freedom of speech and expression.

Did Mukesh Singh, the accused rapist, instruct the viewers in the pedagogy of rape (see Jaising, 2015), or was this an expose of his *mind-set* (see Agnes, 2015)? Both positions in favour of or against the ban constitute the interview *as if* "no further eyewitnessing is necessary to establish the veracity of the image itself" (Pinney, 2008: 5). The viewer is now the eyewitness and the interview is consumed as the *truth* of a rapist's mind-set. In the film, we hear that rape was used to *teach a lesson*—a practice of domination which then is reduced to a "mentality" or a "mind-set". Should *practices* of sexualized domination be psychologized as an individual *trait*? While the accused justifies the violence as a method of *teaching a lesson*, vocabulary at the heart of the atrocity, the gang rape was reduced to the mentality of one rapist. As if each mind-set is identical and gang rape as an act of collective violence is the sum of individual mentalities. Rather than engage with this framework further here, I return to the question of how the protests were represented in the film.

In Leslie Udwin's film, we consume a powerful visual narrative of what it *looks* like to resist a state that tolerates rape. The protests are produced as a "critical event" (A. Roy, 2014) through a spectacularization that constitutes such moments of identification in deeply affective and subjective ways. Yet the identification mediated by these visual narratives remains disconnected from precedents of injustice, as the viewer's eyes glaze over the placards displaying the names of the icons of the women's movement. As the world consumed these images, a prolific response followed: some around narratives of rescue and others around narratives of longing. There were those who wanted to educate and transform; and there were those who wanted to participate and testify.

"India was leading the world by example", said Udwin, whose narrative began with a recollection of feeling inspired by the 2012/13 anti-rape protests. Udwin's narrative operated within a dual framework: reading the 2013 protests as constitutive of a *global* protest where affect, empathy and solidarity were instantiated in hyperreal time resulting in moments of identification and misrecognition. The latter was not only a claim to authenticity based in Udwin's experience as a rape survivor, it equally appeared to be a route to working out the *self* by engaging with the *other*. The desire to transform is equated with confronting alterity in embodied and affectual ways. And such encounters that seek to reveal the mind of the rapist to furnish evidence of truth to power could not escape being mesmerized by the frozen frame that enacts the violence graphically from the point of view of the perpetrator.

Here I evoke *Nirbhaya, the play*, enacted by survivors of sexual violence who perform their own stories inspired by Nirbhaya. Yet, each rendition of violence worked within the frozen frame of violence without the *before* or the *after*. The mimetic enactment of the Delhi gang rape performed mediatized, frame-by-frame accounts of what was done to the body. The hyperreal connection with the 16th December events seemed to create a context that allowed survivors to testify to their own experiences of sexual violence. As if this were a moment of collective testimony to sexual violence framed in a context of history and critique—yet here the context is provided by the spectacularization of protests that empties the event of history (Dutta and Sircar, 2013). It was lacerating that what this moment of identification and misrecognition means was disparaged in the media—dramatized fully in the actress-turned-politician Jaya Bacchan's interview on the 24/7 television channel *Times Now*, which caricatured Udwin's narrative of her life after being raped.[24]

Imagining what it would mean to blink when the camera looks into the eye of the accused, Aeysha Kidwai makes a powerfully poignant intervention:

> In my film, I would not let him escape into his narrative—I wouldn't let him just assert his innocence. I would not be so transfixed by his violence that I wouldn't dare ask him or his lawyers even one question that would unravel the script being played out for me. In my film, I would not be so respectful to the Great Indian Protests either. I would not be so in awe of this mass uprising that they would just be great visuals, I would ask them—young men and women—what had changed? What did social change mean for them, who was Soni Sori, who was Manorama Devi, why did she speak to all of them. […] And why did they all go home after a while? Did they leave because they were scared? Or were they sent away? Have they indeed gone home, or are they still there, kissing in front of Jhandewalan?[25]

Udwin, however, was not worried about where the young protesters have gone—she was transfixed by another kind of optic of power. As she left the country, Udwin looked into the camera, directly addressing Prime Minister Modi, urging him to see her film.[26] Udwin said, "I have turned to camera on so many interviews I cannot begin to tell you, and I have appealed to him. And I can only hope that he has seen one of those appeals".[27] In the same interview, Udwin said:

> There is not a day that passes and there's not a night that I lie here trying to fall asleep that I do not think these very thoughts that I'm about to express

to you now—this film is an absolute reflection of all the admirable, the eloquent and the welcome things that we've heard from Prime Minister Modi since he took office. He has talked about resetting the moral compass, he has got a *Beti Bachao, Beti Padhao* campaign. This film is an absolute mirror held up to his views, to his convictions in this regard and here was the perfect opportunity for him, along with other world leaders and prominent people around the world, to embrace this film.

The film is positioned as a mirror to the rape culture in India; and simultaneously it is positioned as an "absolute" mirror of the views held by Prime Minister Modi.

When film-maker Sheena Sumaria at a screening and discussion in a law firm in London asked Udwin

about the basis of Udwin's optimism, given that there were dozens of cases of rape and violence against Muslim women in 2002, when Modi was the chief minister there, Udwin shut her eyes, shook her head and said: "Darling, that was a long time ago. The past is past; we should think about the future. I can't do anything about what had happened".[28]

And to Salil Tripathi's question, "why she was relying on Modi, whose record of protecting freedom of expression was highly questionable", Udwin responded:

'Then what do you suppose I should do?' she asked. I said she should rely on Indian civil society as her ally. She shook her head and dismissed our concerns—'You are a pessimist, I am an optimist', she said.

The optimistic gaze of the film-maker is emptied of history when invited to look back at the past. Yet this contrast between "optimism" and "pessimism" stands differently when thought of by victims and those violated, whose nightmares of the ghoulish violence now may enjoin with the ban.

In her thoughts, as she tries to sleep, Udwin urges Prime Minister Modi to watch her film to see for himself and she tells him that she identifies with him— or his promise of the future that would not repeat the past. Surely, she reasons, the *Ban* of her film does not belong to the *ban* of the films, those who refuse to forget the past. Her film is *different* since it exposes an a-historical *mind-set*—a mind-set that Prime Minister Modi sought to change when he said that "every parent has a responsibility to teach their sons the difference between right and wrong".[29] Udwin seems to suggest that her script was as much his script—a speech and a film about reforming mind-sets in a shared idea about the future.

The nervous energy of the Ban occupies Udwin's soul every night since she fails to recognize that those who script the wilful forgetting do not themselves forget the past. Rather, the platform where the release of the film sensationalizes the "interview" provides the political pretext to entrench the politics of national pride, making it unnecessary to view the film to ban it. This is consistent with the political strategy of placing the responsibility to reform perverted *mind-sets* on individuals (parents, criminologists and educators). If such a *reform* fails, in the death penalty lies the cure. This debate seemingly produces a crisis. This crisis lies in recognizing that the flash of the prosthetic eye blinds us to the ocular split between development and violence—seeing this optic of power is productive of a crisis, which is then folded back into the present premised on forgetting and secrecy.

Notes

1 Dear Sisters (and brothers?) at Harvard, Letter from Indian feminists Vrinda Grover, Mary E. John, Kavita Panjabi, Shilpa Phadke, Shweta Vachani, Urvashi Butalia and others, to their siblings at Harvard, *Kafila*, 20 February 2013: <http://kafila.org/2013/02/20/dear-sisters-and-brothers-at-harvard/>.
2 See Ratna Kapur "Rape and the crisis of Indian masculinity", *The Hindu*, 19 December 2012. Available at: <www.thehindu.com/opinion/op-ed/rape-and-the-crisis-of-indian-masculinity/article4214267.ece>. A discussion may be found here: <www.jgu.edu.in/sites/default/files/article/policing.pdf>.
3 <www.facebook.com/AwindraPandey>, accessed on 16 November 2014.
4 <www.facebook.com/msjyotisinghpandey>, accessed on 16 November 2014, posted on 29 September at 21.30.
5 <www.facebook.com/AwindraPandey>, accessed on 16 November 2014.
6 <www.spiegel.de/international/world/exploring-the-lives-of-the-rape-victim-and-suspects-in-india-a-879187-2.html>, accessed on 16 November 2014. There was silence on whether region or caste contributed to the public response to the violence (see also Dutta and Sirkar 2013).
7 <www.hindustantimes.com/india/lawyers-boycott-can-help-accused/story-ewO6mUiXO4QiX5t1iTykhK.html>.
8 As compared to 18 deaths—2 suicides and 16 unexplained deaths of inmates in 2012. See <www.thehindu.com/todays-paper/deaths-double-inside-tihar-poor-healthcare-to-blame/article5711908.ece>, accessed on 17 November 2014.
9 See also Menon (2013).
10 <http://timesofindia.indiatimes.com/city/hyderabad/Prisoner-deaths-on-the-rise-in-Cherlapalli/articleshow/45028597.cms>, accessed on 17 November 2014.
11 <www.facebook.com/woman.in.india/posts/490686230978909>, accessed on 17 November 2014.
12 In India, section 228(a) of the Indian Penal Code (IPC) mandates that the rape survivor's real name cannot be published unless she gives written consent and, in case of a dead victim, consent may be given by the next of kin to the use of her real name only to a social welfare organization recognized by the government. The rape victim was given cinematic pseudonyms such as Damini (after one such character of a rape survivor in a Hindi film) and Nirbhaya (which means fearless in Hindi).
13 See <www.facebook.com/pages/16-December-Kranti-Official/336117143158590>.
14 See <www.tehelka.com/four-accused-held-guilty-of-rape-murder-in-delhi-gangrape-case-sentencing-tomorrow/>.
15 Yet this demand to castrate men accused of sexual violence did not emerge only during the protests. In State v. Dinesh Yadav, Judge Lau held: "My conscious [sic] however tells me that this is a crime which is required to be addressed differently and a full public debate with regard to imposition of Castration (both Surgical and Chemical) as

an alternative punishment for the offence of rape and molestation is the crying need of the hour" (at FIR No. 138/2009, PS Swaroop Nagar decided on 30.4.2011, page 58). Also see State v. Nandan Sessions Case No. 42/2011, Rohini Court, Delhi, 24 January 2012.

16 Chakravarti argues that "brahmanical patriarchy" describes "a set of rules and institutions [...] where women are crucial in maintaining the boundaries between castes. Patriarchal codes in this structure can ensure that the caste system can be reproduced without violating the hierarchical order of closed endogamous circles" (2003: 21).

17 <http://daily.bhaskar.com/news/RAJ-OTC-rajasthan-mans-genitals-castrated-by-angry-mob-for-rape-attempt-4772232-NOR.html>.

18 <www.youtube.com/watch?v=h19PMZuH7LE>.

19 This image is borrowed from images of the Garuda Paruna depicting Krimibhojana (described as "selfish survival"/"eating other's work" where the punishment is "being eaten by insects") that circulate on the internet; and made to re-signify as in the series of imagery of castration as a form of punishment. See <www.infomedicblogspot.com /2012/06/garuda-puranas-list-of-punishments.html>.

20 <http://flubby9.weebly.com/a-picture-tells-1000-words.html>.

21 See Krishnan (2013).

22 <https://jilsblognujs.wordpress.com/2013/11/06/through-my-looking-glass/>, accessed on 29 February 2016.

23 <www.independent.co.uk/news/world/asia/indias-daughter-how-india-tried-to-su ppress-the-bbc-delhi-gangrape-documentary-10088890.html>.

24 <www.timesnow.tv/Rapist-made-a-celebrity-Jaya-Bachchan/videoshow/4474050 .cms>.

25 Facebook, 5 March 2015: < www.facebook.com/ayesha.kidwai.9/posts/78370648171 9739?fref=nf&pnref=story>.

26 <www.deccanherald.com/content/463553/leslee-udwin-seeks-modis-intervention.h tml>.

27 <www.asianage.com/interview-week/avanindra-wanted-money-give-his-interview-a nd-i-refused-point-blank-579>.

28 Tripathi, Salil. 2015. The naïveté behind 'India's Daughter', 13 March, <www.livemi nt.com/Leisure/bsOJmK1ifPoJU2Vos3kbyJ/The-navet-behind-Indias-Daughter.html ?utm_source=copy>.

29 www.ndtv.com/india-news/pm-modi-on-rape-cases-correct-sons-dont-question-da ughters-649181>.

References

Agnes, Flavia (2015), "Inside the Minds of Rapists", *Asian Age*, 8 March. Available at http:/ /www.asianage.com/columnists/inside-minds-rapists-043

Basu, Srimati (2011), "Sexual Property: Staging Rape and Marriage in Indian Law and Feminist Theory", *Feminist Studies*, 37(1), 185–211. Available at http://www.jstor.org /stable/23069892

Baxi, Pratiksha (2014), *Public Secrets of Law: Rape Trials in India*. Delhi: Oxford University Press.

Baxi, Pratiksha (2016), "Impractical Topics, Practical Fields: Notes on Researching Sexual Violence in India", *Economic and Political Weekly*, 51(18), 80–88.

Baxi, Upendra (2012), "Because Women's Rights Are Human Rights", *Indian Express*, 27 December. Available at http://archive.indianexpress.com/news/because-women-s-r ights-are-human-rights/1051053/

Belair-Gagnon, Valerie; Mishra, Smeeta; Agur, Colin (2014), "Reconstructing the Indian Public Sphere: Newswork and Social Media in the Delhi Gang Rape Case", *Journalism*, 15(8), 1059–1075. doi: 10.1177/1464884913513430

Bernstein, Elizabeth (2007), "The Sexual Politics of the 'New Abolitionism'", *Differences: A Journal of Feminist Cultural Studies*, 18(3), 128–151. doi: 10.1215/10407391-2007-013

Chakravarti, Uma (2003), *Gendering Caste: Through a Feminist Lens*. Calcutta: Stree.

Durham, Meenakshi Gigi (2015), "Scene of the Crime", *Feminist Media Studies*, 15(2), 175–191. doi: 10.1080/14680777.2014.930061

Dutta, Debolina; Sircar, Oishik (2013), "India's Winter of Discontent: Some Feminist Dilemmas in the Wake of a Rape", *Feminist Studies*, 39(1), 293.

Halley, Janet; Kotiswaran, Prabha; Shamir, Hila; Thomas, Chantal (2006), "From the International to the Local in Feminist Legal Responses to Rape, Prostitution/Sex Work and Sex Trafficking: Four Studies in Governance Feminism", *Harvard Journal of Law and Gender*, 29, 335–423. Available at http://www.law.harvard.edu/students/orgs/jlg/vol29 2/halley.pdf

Jaising, Indira (2015), "Documentary Violates the Law, Does Nothing for 'Awareness', *The Huffington Post India*, 14 March. Available at http://www.huffingtonpost.in/indira-jais ing-/documentary-violates-the-_b_6862010.html

Joseph, Sophy (2013), "'Castration' as a Hegemonic Form of Punishment: A Legal History Point of View", *Savari*, 24 January. Available at http://www.dalitweb.org/?p=1578

Kapur, Ratna (2005), *Law and the New Erotic Justice: Politics of Postcolonialism*. New Delhi: Permanent Black.

Kapur, Ratna (2013), "Gender, Sovereignty and the Rise of a Sexual Security Regime in International Law and Postcolonial India", *Melbourne Journal of International Law*, 14(2), 317–345. Available at http://www.austlii.edu.au/au/journals/MelbJIL/2013/12.html

Krishnan, Kavita (2013), "India's Anti-Rape Movement—Experiences, Reflection and Strategies for the Future", *Freedom without Fear*, 7 December. Available at http://fre edomwithoutfearplatformuk.blogspot.in/2013/12/indias-anti-rape-movement-experien ces.html

Krishnan, Kavita (2014), "Women's Liberation, Everyone's Liberation", *Green Left Weekly*, 4 July. Available at https://www.greenleft.org.au/node/56790

Lodhia, Sharmila (2015), "From 'Living Corpse' to India's Daughter: Exploring the Social, Political and Legal Landscape of the 2012 Delhi Gang Rape", *Women's Studies International Forum*, 50, 89–101. doi: 10.1016/j.wsif.2015.03.007

Liang, Lawrence (2010), "Juridical Affect and the Cinematic Courtroom", paper presented at a workshop on *The Image of Justice in French and Indian Films*, organized by Antoine Garapon, Maison des Sciences de la Communication, Paris. Available at http://www.just -india.net/?q=node/171

Mark, J. (2005), "Remembering Rape: Divided Social Memory and the Red Army in Hungary 1944–1945", *Past Present*, 188(1), 133–161. doi: 10.1093/pastj/gti020

Mehta, Deepak (2013), "Crowd, Cop, Camera: Notes on a Pathological Public Space", paper presented at an international conference, *Law by Other Means*, International Conference, Centre for the Study of Law and Governance, Jawaharlal Nehru University, New Delhi, 21–22 February.

Menon, Nivedita (2013), "Why Was Ram Singh Killed in Tihar Jail", *Kafila*, 12 March. Available at http://kafila.org/2013/03/12/why-was-ram-singh-killed-in-tihar-jail/

Menon, Nivedita (2014), "The Conundrum of Agency", *Seminar*, January. Available at http: //india-seminar.com/2014/653/653_nivedita_menon.htm

Misri, Deepti (2014), *Beyond Partition: Gender, Violence, and Representation in Postcolonial India*. Champaign, IL: University of Illinois Press.

Narrain, Arvind (2014), "Sexual Violence and the Death Penalty", *Economic & Political Weekly*, 49, 3, 38–42. Available at http://www.epw.in/journal/2014/3/perspectives/sexual-violence-and-death-penalty.html

Pinney, Christopher (2008), "The Prosthetic Eye: Photography as Cure and Poison", *Journal of the Royal Anthropological Institute*, 14, S33–S46. doi: 10.1111/j.1467-9655.2008.00491.x

Prakash, Anant Narayan (2014), *Politics of Anti-Rape Law Reform: A Socio-Legal Analysis of the Criminal Law Amendment Act, 2013*, Unpublished MPhil dissertation, Centre for the Study of Law and Governance, Jawaharlal Nehru University, New Delhi.

Puri, J. (2011), "GenderQueer Perspectives", in Arvind Narrain and Alok Gupta (eds.), *Law like Love: Queer Perspectives on Law*. Delhi: Yoda Press, 203–227.

Roy, Anupama (2014), "Critical Events, Incremental Memories and Gendered Violence", *Australian Feminist Studies*, 29(81), 238–254. doi: 10.1080/08164649.2014.959161

Roy, Rahul (2012), "What Do Men Have to Do With It?" *Kafila*, 28 December. Available at https://kafila.online/2012/12/28/what-do-men-have-to-do-with-it/

Roy, Rahul (2013), "A Hunt, the Aftermath, Angry Indian Men and a Tragedy", *Kafila*, 4 December. Available at https://kafila.online/2013/12/04/a-hunt-the-aftermath-angry-indian-men-and-a-tragedy-rahul-roy/

Roy, Srila (2012), *Remembering Revolution: Gender, Violence and Subjectivity in India's Naxalbari Movement*. Delhi: Oxford University Press.

Roychowdhury, Poulami (2013), "'The Delhi Gang Rape': The Making of International Causes", *Feminist Studies*, 39(1), 282–292. Available at http://www.jstor.org/stable/23719317

Sen, Rukmini (2013), "The Need for an Everyday Culture of Protest", *Economic and Political Weekly*, 48(2), 12 January. Available at http://www.epw.in/journal/2013/02/web-exclusives/need-everyday-culture-protest.html

Shalhoub-Kevorkian, Nadera (1999), "Towards a Cultural Definition of Rape: Dilemmas in Dealing with Rape Victims in Palestinian Society", *Women's Studies International Forum*, 22(2), 157–173. doi: 10.1016/S0277-5395(99)00004-7

Shalhoub-Kevorkian, Nadera (2009), *Militarization and Violence against Women in Conflict Zones in the Middle East: A Palestinian Case Study*. Cambridge: Cambridge University Press.

Taussig, Michael (1999), *Defacement: Public Secrecy and the Labor of the Negative*. Stanford, CA: Stanford University Press.

Teltumbde, Anand (2013), "Delhi Gang Rape Case: Some Uncomfortable Questions", *Economic and Political Weekly*, 48(6), 9 February. Available at http://www.epw.in/journal/2013/06/margin-speak-columns/delhi-gang-rape-case.html

Verma, J.S.; Seth, L.; Subramanium, G. (2013), *Report of the Committee on Amendments to Criminal Law*, January 23. http://www.prsindia.org/uploads/media/Justice%20verma%20committee/js%20verma%20committe%20report.pdf

Xalxo, Madhuri (2012), "Delhi Protests and the Caste Hindu Paradigm: Of Sacred and Paraded Bodies", *Round Table India*, 27 December. Available at http://roundtableindia.co.in/index.php?option=com_content&view=article&id=6120:delhi-protests-and-the-caste-hindu-paradigm-of-sacred-and-paraded-bodies&catid=119:feature&Itemid=132

Chapter 7

Women and Mass Violence in Mozambique during the Late Colonial Period*

Maria Paula Meneses

Silencing Gender Agency against Mass Violence

Colonialism is about violence, is about war. War mistreats bodies and feelings; war shatters societies, physically, emotionally and mentally. In this chapter I examine the widespread violence against African women whose experiences invoke the question raised in the introduction of this book: "why does so much unjust human suffering exist that is not considered a violation of human rights?" Thus, I aim to "vocalize" women's experiences and memories of war within a broader discussion of mass violence under European colonial rule in Africa, taking Mozambique as a case study. Culture of evidence suggests that such violence was indeed either a norm or a simmering threat to a norm starting from the onset of modern colonialism, with pacification campaigns, which led to millions demised in Congo, Namibia/South West Africa, Kenya, Mozambique or Algeria. While this is true epistemically, the truth from below is that women's voices about their experience of oppression, violence and resistance remain buried by layers or degrees of silence. Mozambican women's roles in the nationalist struggles were unique in many ways, as I will discuss in this chapter, yet their experiences share commonalities with women in other nationalist struggles in southern Africa.

The right for self-determination was, since the late 1950s, the claim of a growing number of Mozambicans, men and women (Liesegang and Tembe, 2005). The use of armed struggle as a revolutionary solution was vindicated because the African majority was not regarded as a legitimate political actor. In 1964, at the outbreak of the liberation war, FRELIMO,[1] the main nationalist movement, explained its positions stating, "the Mozambican revolution is an immense movement—as irreversible as a force of nature—with roots in the wills and aspirations of each Mozambican" (FRELIMO, 1977a: 79).

* This chapter is based on various research projects. I am thankful to the financial support of the Foundation for Science and Technology (FCT/MEC) Portugal (with national funds and co-funded by ERDF through the Programa Operacional Competitividade e Inovação COMPETE 2020) whose fellowship PTDC/CVI-ANT/6100/2014—POCI-01-0145-FEDER-016859 funded part of the research. It also benefited from a European research project funded by ERC and coordinated by Boaventura de Sousa Santos (FP/2007–2013/ERC Grant Agreement no. [269807]).

However, the perverse association of colonial authority with the "local" male authorities (embodying the corpus of "traditional power structures") in colonial Mozambique has produced a power/knowledge nexus filled with the silence of exclusions, erasures, distortions and arbitrary fictions about women in contemporary struggles for rights and dignity. This nexus has been actively silencing women's presence in the frontline, concealing a variety of tensions and antagonisms that permeated (and still permeate) Mozambique's recent history, a period that needs to be explored, to expose the multiple dimensions of African women's involvement in the nationalist struggle, and how their participation became crucial for its success. In Mozambique, as in other African contexts, the nationalist project included gendered identities (McClintock, 1995: 355). Yet, how women have claimed their participation in the nationalist struggles illustrates both their importance and participation, and helps to understand the construction of the silence about their presence in the frontline.[2]

The liberation armed struggle in Mozambique was fought until September 1974.[3] This struggle was longer and more intense in northern Mozambique,[4] where a fundamental part of the liberation war burden fell upon women. Shaping knowledges and silencing realities are elements that express power. Portuguese military and history books seldom publicly document the strategic targeting of women and children, even though frontline realities show how frequently these strategies were used (Meneses, 2013). A fundamental point relates to the methodological procedures used to question women whose testimonies are part of the oral history about the violence of war. As my experience shows, in order to ask questions and to be understood by women, the way one speaks has to be decipherable to all involved in each conversation. More often than wanted, the concepts used to decode the experiences transmitted by testimonies limit their reading because of the power/knowledge nexus associated with them. The alternative is to explore testifying as performative, a position that requires unequivocally the construction of the meanings as a process (Dhada, 2015). This process entails pre-existing knowledges born out of experiences and struggles (Santos, 2006: 14–15), and is simultaneously shaped by the encounter and the engagement when the testimony is given.

Patriarchal colonialism, engendered by Portuguese administration, guaranteed the impossibility of women giving testimony, reproducing silences around women's colonial experiences. This translated itself in the lack of credibility of women's testimony about their role in the nationalist struggles. When I decided to initiate a study on women's experiences about their life in the northern Mozambique war zone, as well as their later memories, I found very little recorded in archives and libraries. At the core of this chapter is the methodological proposal advanced by Boaventura de Sousa Santos—the *sociology of absences* (2006: 15–17)—as I sought to give visibility to facts and actors that have been actively produced as non-existent by dominant historical approaches; that is, as a non-credible alternative to the dominant narrative about the nationalist struggles. This line of inquiry aims to subvert the production of absences—in this case, the role of women in the liberation struggle—by turning them into present subjects. To overcome the silences concerning gendered violence, I sought to document in more detail the women's understanding of their role in the struggle for freedom, combining oral history,[5] archival research and media analysis (newspaper and audio-visual research).

As I will analyze in this paper, from early on, women understood that their liberation was essential for the liberation of the country, and that it was fundamental to "take the struggle for liberation in our hands" (Paulina Mateus, quoted in Mussanhane, 2012: 641). However, as in Guinea Bissau (Urdang, 1979: 17), in Angola (Paredes, 2015) or in Zimbabwe (Lyons, 2002), women's liberation was not given. Women were able to free themselves in the struggle, fighting for human rights. It was a right that was conquered with struggle, so that the liberation was theirs too.

In the Mozambican media, right from independence, the national political historical project includes a much reduced number of heroines, all of them protagonists of the armed struggle. In contrast, the available materials disclosed a hard reality—it is not the women themselves, but the institutions and structures present, out of women's control, that regulate their voices, forcing them to remain silent about their experiences and memories of struggle for freedom, a silencing that continued with independence.

This reality is linked with the debates on historical objectivity in Mozambique, debates that materialized in a context where the liberation struggles are intimately associated with a political environment where the oral and written narratives of the struggle led by FRELIMO are seen as the single source of authority in the production of knowledge about Mozambique's recent past. The alliance between politics and history generated an official historical narrative about the nationalist struggle, a narrative that became an instrument to legitimize the party's hegemonic authority, rendering it unquestionable (Coelho, 2014: 21). This strategy has promoted the glorification mostly of male warriors and silenced the other voices involved in the struggle for independence: thousands of women and girls that took active part in the struggle (Meneses, 2015).

Over the last decades, public and scholarly interdisciplinary studies have addressed how Mozambican women experienced and lived through the colonial war, particularly by exploring the participation of women in the national liberation struggle (West, 2000; Zimba, 2012; Saide, 2014). Hence, the current historiography on the liberation war (the "other" Mozambican side of the colonial war) is primarily focused on the investigation and discussion of fights between FRELIMO and the Portuguese army (and their allies).[6]

Against this backdrop, oral historical narratives represent a precious element to deepen our understanding on the recent violent past. These stories are about war crimes, atrocities, outrages to human dignity, human rights abuses committed by military and security forces; they represent "untold stories" of people whose voices and experiences have been excluded from a broader debate about the past and have to be analyzed in context, as no one interpretation can be seen as a neutral instrument to interpret the past. Knowing, seeing, witnessing, attesting and speaking always flows from a particular body, located in a particular time and space, both literally and relationally. From the point of view of historiography, it is impossible to capture the diversity of perspectives about a single event. Any event is filled with constitutive absences, an integrative part of the construction process of the historical event itself. Ominous, however, in these power games, is the reduction of huge pieces of history to silence, to invisibility.

Mozambican women's role in the clandestine struggle and as political militants against oppression and exploitation remains a lesser-studied topic (Casimiro, 1986) and the presence of civil women in the frontline is a forgotten topic. As a result, women's experiences and memories of the war are rendered invisible in the official history. Listening to some of these "little voices" allowed me to grasp the multivocity of the nationalist struggle in Mozambique, a double-questioning path towards challenging the hegemony of "national" discourse and reintroducing the question of agency and instrumentality back into the narrative.

The Everyday Violence in the Late Colonial Period Stage

The Wiriyamu Massacre, one of the gruesome episodes that ultimately presaged the end of the Portuguese Empire in Africa, captured world public awareness in July 1973.[7] However, this episode was not an abnormality; rather, it was a symbol of excessive, indiscriminate use of military force; of gender-based violence to which women were exposed; psychological torture and arbitrary arrests to enforce obedience that took place in the frontline regions, a clear sign of the securitization and militarization of Mozambique during the late colonial period (IDAF, 1973).

The reports available for the northern, heavily militarized regions of the country, such as Tete,[8] present a civil population hostage to this violence, divided between those who were "kept under Portuguese control" and those "with the enemy". As a result, the foundations of communities' livelihoods were destroyed and groups violently resettled and split. An arbitrarily abyssal line separated two political projects, embodied in the mined fields surrounding *aldeamentos* (resettlement villages).[9]

With the spreading out of war southwards, the Portuguese administration forced the African population to move into *aldeamentos*, resettlement villages, trying to "win their bodies and souls" and thus preventing them from joining or supporting guerrilla forces. Early in 1974, over 40 per cent of the African population in the war provinces was living in resettlements (Jundanian, 1974: 524), where land was short and where youths grew up in squalid conditions. However, resettlements did not stop the progression of the war, as many authors underline. And the support of women in the frontline regions was fundamental to overcome the growing repression.

The full involvement of women in the nationalist struggle as guerrillas gained international visibility since the late 1960s, challenging the "traditional" subordinate position that was reserved for women. To FRELIMO leadership, the emancipation of women was seen as "a *fundamental* necessity for the revolution, the guarantee of its continuity and the precondition for its victory" (Machel,

1982: 24). This ideological proposal influenced the way women saw their participation in the struggle, precisely because this liberation project empowered them to claim political power beyond the limits of their "traditional" roles; in parallel, the testimony of women during the nationalist struggle extends the possibility of interpreting the violence of war beyond the political proposals advanced by the movement leadership (Arthur et al., 1992).

The rural communities that did not join *aldeamentos* were normally perceived as being under FRELIMO's influence and were raided frequently. A report from PIDE-DGS, the Portuguese secret political police, from 1972 referred: "our forces detected a significant enemy stronghold with the banner of FRELIMO. The heli-cannon bombed the site and the surrounding areas where there were many agricultural fields, fatally killing 17 individuals who are supposed to be the enemy farmers".[10]

Women participated directly in the struggle, but especially supporting the guerrillas with food, accommodation and clothing. They also played a significant role in propaganda activity and with contacts and, whenever possible, collecting information (Zimba, 2012: 32–37). As several testimonies reported, younger and attractive women would approach the Portuguese soldiers in order to gather information to be passed on to guerrilla forces. But the work in the *schambas*—a predominately female activity—achieved greater importance, as famine became a phantom killer. On the one hand, the work in the fields was fundamental to (re)establish relationships and to mobilize the communities; on the other hand, it strengthened women's contribution to the struggle. To avoid being detected by the Portuguese "enemy", women opened small individual fields trying to produce enough to support themselves, their family and the guerrilla groups, and tried to withstand the burden of attacks and robberies by the enemy:

> the *schambas* we had in our communities were not collective, they were individual. This way we were able to cope with our need to support the struggle and not to starve when the whites [Portuguese] came and burned our fields. This is why we kept our *schambas* small and scattered.[11]

For the Portuguese government, the "final solution" became growingly the answer to the nationalist voice, defined as the terrorist enemy. The strategy of total destruction was vehemently denounced by the nationalist movements, and rebuffed by Portugal.[12] However, a careful analysis of archived military reports substantiates this claim. In addition to the dead and wounded enemies, the weapons destroyed or captured, the third dimension of this war was the destruction of bases, burning of fields and the destruction of crops and granaries. The reports repeat how this task was accomplished: "Several tons of foodstuffs and livelihoods destroyed [...] and destroyed 66 granaries";[13] "Destroyed many livelihoods (300 kg) and miscellaneous equipment [...] and destroyed supply equipment and clothing;"[14] "Destroyed about 40 to 50 huts and 4 granaries

[…]; destroyed 95 huts and 50 granaries; […] destroyed about 50 huts, 10 granaries and various means of life […]; destroyed 11 granaries full of corn";[15] "160 huts destroyed; substantial quantities of cassava flour, rice, salt, eggs, poultry and household items destroyed or rendered unusable;"[16] "Enemy livelihoods destroyed: flour, clothes, utensils, significant number of cattle […]; destruction of two corn fields by aerial spraying".[17]

These brief quotations, examples of many references present in the reports of Portuguese military actions, illustrate that the colonial administration (civil and military), faced with the advance of the nationalist war, had opted, insidiously, for the total solution. And at the centre of this "attack" to the people of Mozambique were women, those guaranteeing agricultural production and social reproduction (Meneses, 2013). The result was a famine that took the lives of many people and put the local economy in shambles.

In December 1972, 300 Makonde women[18] organized a demonstration in front of the Mueda administration, where another massacre had taken place in 1960. Women were very affected by colonialism, as the vast majority worked on small-scale agriculture. Colonial policies restructured the economy and introduced forced agricultural labour. As the colonial-capitalist economy progressed, women's essential work in production was systematically undervalued and they lost access to land.

In a war context, these women dared to organize a manifestation to protest the constant arrests made by the secret political police of their husbands and relatives. The women demanded the prisoners be brought from Ibo jail back to Mueda, as well as the restitution of the money and clothing that had been taken away from them. They dare to denounce that the "confessions had been extracted under duress". And the group threatened not to return to the fields to work the land if their husbands would not come back.[19] As this protest reveals, colonialism is about violence, physical, spiritual and epistemic; it is about the non-recognition of the Africans as human beings.[20]

The colonial state demanded sovereignty without any guarantee of citizenship rights to the vast majority of the African population; on the contrary, the inhabitants of colonial space were subjected to the colonial power, unprotected by the laws of the state. In the context of war, Africans had become the "enemy" to the colonial power in their own territory. And the double exclusion that targeted women reinforced their subordinate status. Fighting for their freedom in the face of traditional society and the colonial system, women in Mozambique fought alongside men in different, but no less important, fronts. These positions signal women's agency, their position to decide about their own life and their engagement with the struggle, a topic that needs further study.

Women and the Massacre of Mueda

One stellar example of the colonial pathological violence occurred at Mueda, in Cabo Delgado's province, when, in June 1960, the Portuguese administration indulged in a spectacular massacre of villagers, unarmed women and men, who were demonstrating in unison against sorely needed reforms to undergird fare wages for labour and fair prices for goods. This massacre ultimately propelled the formation of FRELIMO, which in turn was said to have laid the groundwork for armed insurrection against Portuguese colonialism (Coelho, 1993: 129).

Portuguese colonial power established itself in northern Mozambique territories from the late 19th century through a set of coercive practices, transforming Africans from citizens into native subjects, with obligations, but little or no rights. Among the vicissitudes brought in was the reconceptualization of labour, a reconceptualization that revealed the foundational contradictions of the modern colonial state. Most notably, it clearly exposes the dark side of the civilizational project proposed by Portugal, revealed by the antagonism opposing the right to freedom and the right to work—at the core of modern idea of citizenship—and the forced labour regime as a path to transform the native into a citizen in the colonial space. Among the various forms of coercion were prison labour, contract labour and forced work for the colonial administration and for mega-plantations (Sheldon, 1994: 38). Forced labour included the mandatory cultivation of rice, sisal and cotton, the latter to be exported to Portugal's textile industry (CEA, 1981).

In northern Mozambique, from the end of World War I, many Makonde people and others had opted to migrate to Tanganyika, Zanzibar, Kenya, escaping the regime of forced labour. In neighbouring colonies, although life was not easy, Africans were allowed to open small stores, obtain a drivers' license, etc. In the late 1950s, these migrants were already organized in various nationalist organizations, societies and clubs, in which both men and women participated (Cahen, 1999: 32). African women were less mobile, because they had to care for their families. Therefore, the burden of forced labour fell upon them, having to grow cotton compulsorily; in order to meet their quotas, they neglected their own food production (Casimiro, 1986: 26–32). In this context, the women's agency in the struggle against colonial oppression took different forms, including a mutual support network of labour for women—*ligwilanilo*, and the work in small plots of land to feed their families, among others.

In the late 1950s, Mozambicans living in the Makonde highlands organized an agricultural cooperative that was soon banned by Portuguese officials, with the excuse that it had become a focus of subversive activities. However short-lived, this cooperative played a significant political role in the history of Mozambique. Among its goals, it sought to protect its members from labour abuses inherent to the system of forced cotton production in the region. The research carried out in the region shows this cooperative, a grassroots movement, to be firmly implanted among local peasants, providing a hospitable terrain for covert anti-colonial activities (Isaacman et al., 1980). Two women interviewed confirmed that, from the late 1950s to the early 1960s, while working on the plantations, the elders would mobilize the youngsters to join the struggle against exploitation and for self-determination (*uhuru*[21]).

From the late 1950 to the early 1960s, several of these migrants in Tanganyika travelled back to Mozambique, seeking to expand the African organizations, and thought to help manage the return of the peasant migrants to Mozambique. This process was coordinated by various Makonde people, including a woman, Modesta Neva[22] (Coelho, 1993). Between February and early March 1960, several meetings were organized with the population, until the Portuguese administration in Mueda decided to arrest several of them. This arrest provoked some agitation and several claims for *uhuru* were heard.

On 16 June 1960, in the village of Mueda, a demonstration requesting the release of the representatives arrested turned violent and ended in a massacre, after the police appeared to lose control of the situation, panicked and opened fire on the crowd.[23] In the words of one of the participants:

> I went to Mueda to attend the talks between the colonial government and Faustino.[24] When I got there, people were already concentrated. There were men, women and some children. Many people were very well dressed. There were people of different races: Indian, white and black. Moments later the colonialists hoisted the banners. The Portuguese administrator urged people to take part in the flag raising. But people refused to rise up [to salute the flag], saying they had gone there to hear the words of Faustino and Kibiriti.[25] Kibiriti and Faustino were standing handcuffed under a mango tree. [...] Then, the governor called them individually inside. However, they could not kill him [Kibiriti]; then they called Faustino and it was repeated, because he did not die. They left the administration building tied and sat in the back of the car. But we circled the car and said that "this car will not move". They had done the same with the first group where Modesta was, but now it would not happen again, we said. It was then that people started throwing stones. The governor called the cipaios[26] and ordered the army to open fire. [...] I run away. When I got back later, I noticed about 17 people killed.[27]

The excerpts and testimonies of this event show women at the centre of the resistance against colonialism, a political stance silenced by thick masculine mantles of epistemic silence. For the great majority of women, the demands of day-to-day family survival took precedence over any form of strategic organizing. As the actions and testimonies of women living in the frontline, the changes occurred because of the burden of colonialism and the war it had generated. According to witnesses of the Mueda events, during the meeting with the administrator, Modesta Neva stood firm in her protest, asking for freedom to be given to Mozambicans:

> Modesta was carrying a cassava stake and waved it as she spoke with Governor Garcia Soares. It was the especially upfront attitude manifested by Modesta that left the [Portuguese] administrator very embarrassed; at

the same time, it encouraged the people nearby to engage in the revolt against colonialism. Modesta Neva even stated that Mr. Garcia Soares, the administrator, should get ready to definitely leave Mozambique to Portugal, and she was handling him the cassava, as a memento to remember Mozambique.

(Pachinuapa and Manguedye, 2009: 28–29)

Together with the other arrested, Modesta was sentenced to prison and was banished to the south of Mozambique—an unfamiliar environment to her, being a Makonde woman—where she ended her days (Coelho, 1993: 137).

As the massacre occurred in remote northern Mozambique, the news about the event only reached the media a couple of days later.[28] The news insisted on ascribing the authorship of the event to "foreign" agitators, an interpretation that also found echo in PIDE's version, denying the capacity of Mozambicans (especially women) to self-organize themselves in the search for self-determination:

> It is estimated that about 5,000 blacks besieged the administration in Mueda [...]. The aero-transported troops, the first to arrive, soon secured the situation with the first burst of gunfire. Those who did not fall ran away, as there were more than 2,000 bikes left, whose owners did not appear. In a thorough search that followed this operation, in the jungle, only women and children were found, plus a considerable amount of small modern arms, whose origin remains a secret, but it is said to be of Russian manufacture.[29]

The Mueda Massacre remains an example of a political and military operation of the colonial system, exposing its internal contradictions: the use of force to shoot a peaceful manifestation of several thousand peasants claiming space to carry out their economic activities with more autonomy. In parallel, this massacre exposed the violent nature of the colonial state (Adam and Duty, 1993: 118). For over two years, the colonial authorities sought laboriously to carry out the punishment of the ringleaders of the events that took place in Mueda on 16 June 1960; in parallel, the Portuguese administration intensified the repression, hitting hard both men and women.

> Both my parents had been arrested during the war. My father was arrested accused of being part of the unrest that followed Mueda events. He was part of the local authorities and did not stand for the Portuguese. [...] My mother was arrested latter [1968], accused of selling FRELIMO cards (*chamas*). We had to stay with my grandmother because my mother went to jail in Ibo, in Cabo Delgado.[30]

A couple of years later, by mid-1962, when the Mueda case seemed settled, FRELIMO was formed, with a strong basis in what was then Tanganyika. The resistance re-emerged in the region, although with a very different nature, now organized under the leadership of a modern nationalism movement (Liesegang and Tembe, 2005). The eruption of the armed struggle in 1964 put more tension upon women, as it brought an increasing devastation of social and economic infrastructures, causing immense suffering to the inhabitants of the regions where the war became a reality, with massacres being reported at a ghastly rhythm.

In the last week of September 1964, as retaliation against the first military attacks by FRELIMO, a series of massacres were reported around Chai and also in Cabo Delgado. One of the few survivors, who lost her husband and a child, testified to the violence of this massacre:[31]

> The Portuguese soldiers began to arrive in our village a little after midday; they came with a *cipaio* named Victor. They brought with them more people from other small villages that existed along the main road [...]. There was a lot of people, 100 or 120 people. In our village there were 9 houses with two rooms and balconies, thatched and covered. The soldiers began to push everyone into three houses that lay across the road. They filled the rooms with us, as if we were cobs. Those who did not fit inside anymore were left on the balcony. Then the soldiers started firing with machine guns, and throwing grenades to burn the house.

The cost in human suffering was caused by more than the destruction of goods. The Portuguese army used rape and other forms of sexual violence as weapons of terror and intimidation, especially in *aldeamentos* close to the frontline. Murder, rape and mutilation were perpetrated on a massive scale. Homes were plundered, land and crops were burnt and livestock butchered.

> I was raped during the war. It was a shame to us. It happened when we were forced to come to Mueda, to the *aldeamento*. Trucks came and brought us here. In the beginning there were even no houses. Many people did not want to stay, but we had no option, as my part of my family had been arrested. They [Portuguese military] had guns and the *aldeamento* soon was all surrounded with barbed wire and mines. It was almost impossible to leave the place; and people would point at us as if we had enjoyed being raped. I seldom talk about it, but here people kept talking about it even after the war was over. Some even accused us of being prostitutes. After they raped me several times, they laughed. I was working for the army, I used to wash the clothing for the Portuguese military. I needed the money, as it was difficult to cross to the field to plant due to the war, mines.[32]

The terror that was instilled in ordinary people and the wholesale destruction of homes and land disrupted the functioning of families and entire communities, prompting many to find refuge in Tanzania or Malawi.

> When the Mueda massacre happened, I was a child. As a consequence, lots of people left the area to take refuge in Tanzania, as part of my family did. We fled and became refugees in Rutamba camp. People got really scared with the violence.[33]

Women were at the core of the resistance struggle. However, having been involved in research on the liberation struggle in Mozambique (Meneses and Martins, 2013; Meneses, 2015), an interrogation haunted me: what were the women's reasons, their goals, while being part of the struggle? For some years I have been listening to stories, their memories and unachieved dreams. As one of the interviewees emphasized,

> I am thankful to the liberation struggle because it made so much for viewing us as human beings, for listening and trying to take into account our positions, our goals. In the past, we were seen both by our men and the Portuguese as brainless, submissive to our husbands or fathers. The struggle made me recognize that we, women, are human beings with dreams. We fought, we suffered, but we dreamed to be free [...] we fought for you to be here today, asking about colonialism. This is why we also fought, to make exploitation and oppression history, but we are still fighting.[34]

Mozambique won its long struggle for independence in June 1975. The participation of women in the war was crucial for its success. In the rural areas, where most of the guerrilla activity took place, women were the backbone of the struggle, providing food, shelter and clothing to the guerrilla, supporting the mobilization, often risking their lives for it:

> In the war, we were there on the side of those fighting for the independence. We carried guns on our heads, we supported with food, we helped with information about the enemy [...] Our situation as women since independence, with the end of the war of national liberation, cannot say it has not improved; but we still have to fight for our rights, for men to respect us. The war is over, then? Then we were important, but after, only the female guerrillas got to be recognized; we went back to be just women [...] After all, we fought, but are we respected?[35]

Women and the Nationalist Struggle after Mueda

If the end of the subaltern condition of Mozambican women under colonialism became, from the 1960s, a fundamental element of the nationalist struggle, this awareness was the product of struggles within the various nationalist movements and organizations involved in the struggle.[36] Right from the beginning, FRELIMO expressed the importance of the support of women to the cause of liberation.

> Our mothers, sisters, daughters are exploited, oppressed, raped with impunity by the colonialists. The dignity of the Mozambican women is downtrodden. [...] In the liberated areas, FRELIMO lays the foundations for a progressive Mozambique, prosperous and democratic [...] conducting political, social, economic and cultural emancipation of Mozambican women, realizing the equal rights of men and woman in Mozambique, supporting the growing participation of women in the national liberation struggle.
>
> (FRELIMO, 1977b: 17).

In the early 1960s, women living outside Mozambique, many of which had relatives in FRELIMO, decided to create an association, LIFEMO (Feminine League of Mozambique), to support social causes.[37] Most of them had long ago left Mozambique, being far from the war reality experienced with the developing of the struggle inside the country. Although the statute of LIFEMO referred that the main goal of the organization was to implicate all women in the national liberation struggle, this translated itself primarily in support to those living abroad, including caring for widows, refugees, supporting the organization of women abroad and the social work with orphans. The constitutive conference of LIFEMO took place in 1966 in Mbeya, Tanzania. Speaking during the conference, its first president, Celina Simango[38] stated: "As I am speaking, hundreds of women in Mozambique with arms in their hands are facing the enemy, and defending the populations. [...] The Mozambican woman is devoting her full participation to the struggle, the liberation of Mozambique."[39] However, many women involved in the armed struggle stressed the LIFEMO did not have among its priorities the work inside the liberated areas of Mozambique.

The beginning of the liberation war marked the beginning of the participation of women in the warfront in Mozambique, both as guerrillas and as mobilizers of the struggle.

> Filipe Samuel Magaia [leading commander of FRELIMO] was visiting the bases to check the work in the interior and to understand the evolution of the fight. It was in September 1965. It was then that he learned that there were women who were fighting as guerrilla. But this was a big secret in FRELIMO, in relation to women in war. So we were still wearing male names. [In 1966] after the Central Committee decided that we could undergo political-military training, the problems continued. Part of FRELIMO leadership disagreed with the presence of women with guns struggling against colonialism.[40] They said that it was against our traditions in Mozambique, because for them the women's place was the kitchen.[41]

The Female Detachment (DF),[42] part of FRELIMO, was only formally created in 1967 (Zimba, 2012: 26–28). From then on, the presence of female guerrillas in FRELIMO gained international visibility, challenging the "traditional" subordinate position which was reserved for them. Nevertheless, the two main female organizations—DF and LIFEMO continued functioning in parallel, claiming to represent all the women of Mozambique. As described by Paulina Mateus,

> the Central Committee of FRELIMO called Celina Simango, head of LIFEMO, to inform her of the existence of a group women freedom fighters inside Mozambique. Given the good work the freedom fighters were doing, it was important to link the struggles. But the head of LIFEMO did not agree.[43]

In order to bridge this split, various meetings were held between LIFEMO and DF members, making it possible to identify the problems separating the two female organizations: the guerrilla women claimed they could not marry, while those who militated in LIFEMO were allowed; women inside Mozambique felt that the burden of war fell over them—the tasks of mobilization; the transport of war material; the agricultural work in the fields—while LIFEMO's women lived abroad, supporting orphans, widows and refugees and participating in congresses and conferences, contributing very little to the war effort. The contradiction between the political refugees and the guerrilla positions built up rapidly. The participation of women in armed struggle was one of the reasons for the deep political crisis that affected FRELIMO in 1968–1969, as their active involvement challenged the system of oppression and exploitation that affected not only women but all Mozambicans (Casimiro, 1986: 130–131).

In 1969, in the aftermath of the political crisis inside FRELIMO, the movement decided to merge the Female Detachment with LIFEMO, resulting in the consolidation of the overpowering position of the guerrilla women. The next stage of merging came in 1973 with the formation of the Organization of Mozambican Women,[44] following a decision taken in 1972 by FRELIMO's Central Committee. Throughout the last years of the armed liberation struggle,[45] FRELIMO's position on women's contribution to the struggle would accentuate their role in mobilizing and organizing the people, although the goals of this mobilization remain uncertain.

> When we, women, began to participate, there was strong opposition to us, because it was contrary to our tradition. Then we started a large campaign, explaining [...] that the struggle was indeed a popular struggle in which all the people should participate and that we, women, we were even more oppressed than men, but we had the same rights and the same determination to fight for them.[46]

This testimony, together with many others, accentuates that for women the importance of mobilization translated into a fight for their dignity, for equality, against "traditional values" that insisted in maintaining a subordinate position for women in the public and private spheres. Whereas for FRELIMO, the struggle for women's emancipation was considered secondary, as the main goal was the struggle against colonial and imperialist oppression and exploitation (Meneses, 2015). This differentiation is crucial as it reveals a tension between mobilizing as women or mobilizing as FRELIMO revolutionaries (Disney, 2008: 51), because the agendas of the two struggles were not identical. With FRELIMO committed to capitalize on the gains of the advances in the armed struggle, one witnesses the growing centrality of the guerrilla women in the nationalist narrative, while other contributions and forms of participation were silenced.

The personal trajectories of women (shaped by elements such as age, class, ethnicity, race) defined their responses to the war, their survival strategies and their achievements. Not surprisingly, there was a perplexing and contradictory gender struggle characterized by a provocative combination of radicalism and conservatism. With husbands and other male relatives away, women were gradually taking on more and more responsibilities; simultaneously, their political education, based upon their experience in the struggle, signalled unlimited possibilities of participation to "the defeat of oppression and exploitation" (Liberation Support Movement, 1974: 5). With the advancement of the struggle, women found new opportunities to negotiate their traditional roles, especially in war zones in northern Mozambique. However, although Samora Machel, the president of FRELIMO, would argue that "the liberation of women is a fundamental necessity of the revolution, the guarantee of its continuity and the precondition for its victory" (1982: 20), promises of equality are hollow in the face of failed attempts to challenge traditional practices and sexist attitudes, a clear demonstration of the absence of a real commitment to women's liberation and with the construction of a new national history.

Conclusion: The Troubles with a Single Liberation Narrative

This chapter aimed to emphasize the possibility of an alternative retelling of the events and history of violence endured by women along the struggle for liberation, and to demand radical changes of the national history. The Mueda Massacre clearly signalled that only by the force of arms could Mozambicans aspire to independence; Wiriyamu symbolizes the end of the regime, which disintegrated itself in the aftermath of the April 25th 1974 coup d'état. Massacres (Mueda, Chai, Mutanga, Mucumbura, Chiuaio, Wiryamu, Inhaminga, just to name a few), together with the various elements of violence that are part of war—torture, rape, among others—have shaped the experience of the colonial war in Mozambique, episodes of extreme violence that are widely recognized as military atrocities and acts of mass murder committed on civilians and non-combatants (General Assembly of the United Nations, 1974). The voices of the survivors of these moments of mass atrocities can still be heard, expressing their private thoughts and an almost unbearable pain. At the core of this chapter are several of their testimonies and rescued memories. Their voices signal the challenges they have been confronting while also creating visions of a positive future, using their voice to document their participation in struggles, to bear witness to oppressions and to share successful experiences of resistance.

The debate over gender and women's emancipation inside FRELIMO throughout the war highlighted the political contradictions about women's roles. For example, the experience of armed struggle depended on women transporting arms, provisioning FRELIMO's forces and ensuring the support of local communities through their grassroots health and education campaigns. On the other side, the role of women in the frontline regions has been underestimated, assuming that their peasant's activities could be interpreted as traditional "support roles". However, women's voices reveal another picture. By listening to oral episodes of history, it becomes possible to uncover the dense texture of war and societal relations, with far-reaching effects, particularly in the realm of gender. A more nuanced portrait of women and war emerges, showing the persistent invisibility of women's participation in the war effort, their very unacknowledged, behind the lines contributions towards independence. In northern Mozambique, women's presence in the war front cannot be subsumed to their participation in FRELIMO's DF.

The war changed women's lives radically, not only because of the death and destruction it brought, but also because it provided a possibility and an opportunity for transforming the stagnant social structures in which rural women lived. Many women found themselves heading their households, acquiring new roles and responsibilities (Thurshen, 1998: 20). Political and military violence was exercised in different forms, including the torture of hunger and total destruction (housing, food, water) as a way of doing politics (Meneses, 2013), affecting especially women, the key family providers. On the other side, the new political and economic contexts and the relationships they brought about, associated with increasing male migration,[47] meant a growing burden and centrality of women's work in maintaining and reproducing their extended families.

The colonial war, as this article sought to expose, operated without rules; worse, women were not considered collateral victims of this war. Thus, universal concepts of human rights were not applied in Mozambican war zones. On the opposite, the use of systematic torture, detention without trial, collective punishment, villagization and omnipresent violence against women became the norm, in a context were Portugal insisted on justifying these policies against Mozambicans as a reaction against internal disturbances and, thus, not a war that was subject to the regulations on human rights laid down by international conventions.

For Mozambican women, the possibility of freeing themselves from a subaltern condition under colonialism became, from the 1950–1960s, a fundamental element of the nationalist struggle. The armed struggle altered profoundly the geography of power and the position of women in society, introduced long-lasting changes to social relationships. A good example is the undermining of the elders' control over many young women in the rural communities of northern Mozambique that decided to join the nationalists (Pachinuapa and Manguedye, 2009).

At the core of modern nations one can find elements of extreme violence through the definition of the elements that define the official historical narrative. Here, what women did in frontline regions is constructed as an extension of their feminine functions—supporting the family and the community. Thus, women's contribution to the nationalist struggle is portrayed as secondary to the main event—the war. As this chapter seeks to reveal, Mozambican women fought the very triad of oppression and violence: colonialism, capitalism and patriarchy. The persistent silence about the African women's contribution to dignity and freedom evidences the heritage of a broader conflict that disrupted utterly the rights of all Africans—the latencies of the violent colonial encounter—a conflict that remains to be addressed in all its complexity.

FRELIMO held, until 1982, a series of "Truth Commissions" meeting to deal with the "wrongs" of the war (Meneses, 2015). However, nowhere in these meetings were the gender discriminations and the harms, discriminations and violence performed by all military forces against women and children addressed.[48] This violence takes many forms and is an indicator that the aspired transformations have not been achieved. As Tanya Lyons analyses for Zimbabwe, "promises of equality rang hollow in the face of failed attempts to challenge traditional practices [… and] simultaneously demonstrated a lack of real commitment to women's liberation" (2002: 319). Deeply entrenched patriarchal beliefs regarding the identity and role of women in Mozambique constituted and still constitute a strong barrier to the full participation and transformation of gender relations.

To unravel peace and gender equality from its androcentric moorings, one needs to learn from the subtle but complex political experiences of subaltern groups, from the sotto voce voices of women that tell another part of the liberation narrative. By drawing attention to the still marginalized and deinstitutionalized subaltern women, this analysis aims to bring to the forefront the silenced but inescapable achievements of ordinary women on the powerful and prolonged, but largely atomized, participation in local actions, with larger episodes of collective action. Fundamental to my understanding of what is happening today are Okot p'Bitek's perspectives. This author explores in detail how oral tradition shapes moral agents' formations and understandings of their place in society (p'Bitek, 1986). His work on oral tradition as social action provides insights into everyday micro-social processes, and, like contemporary articulations of the epistemologies of the South (Santos, 2006) and approaches to performativity, valorizing community and place-based methods of recovering after violence and/or conflict. If the struggle for human rights and dignity is studied through decontextualized, monocultural lenses imbued of a linear triumphalism, many unjust sufferings are not considered a violation of human rights, as Boaventura de Sousa Santos has maintained (2013: 17). As

Santos argues, it is fundamental to develop a counter-hegemonic conception of human rights that could subvert the hegemonic vision and resonate with the needs of those who have been dispossessed of power and marginalized. If one does not understand women's active participation through their own voice, it becomes very hard to understand why so many women insist, in Mozambique, that the "struggles continue", a clear sign that the liberation and dignity were not fully achieved by women with independence.

Notes

1 FRELIMO (Mozambique Liberation Front) initiated the armed struggle against Portuguese colonialism in 1964, gaining access to power on independence, in June 1975. It transformed itself into a political party in 1977, remaining the dominant political force in contemporary Mozambique.

2 In guerrilla-war contexts, all villages and communities got involved in the conflict, often without choice. Because the war is very mobile and decentralized, it is rather difficult to distinguish between the "frontline" and the rear.

3 Two main movements were involved: FRELIMO and, in a minor scale, COREMO (Mozambique Revolutionary Committee), which carried out military actions mainly in the northern Tete region.

4 Mozambique's northern neighbouring countries—Tanzania and Zambia—supported the armed struggle until 1974, becoming fundamental (for their support included the presence of training bases) for its successful outcome.

5 Several of the interviewees whose testimonies integrate this chapter have asked to remain anonymous. In order to protect their identities, I have opted to hide the surnames.

6 From 1970 onwards, FRELIMO (and, to a lesser extent, COREMO) became more active in central Mozambique, fighting against the Portuguese army and the supporting forces of the white regimes of southern Africa. On this topic, see Meneses and Martins (2013).

7 Adrian Hastings, "Portuguese massacre reported by priests", *The Times*, 10 July 1973.

8 See Hastings (1974) and Dhada (2015).

9 Arquivo Nacional da Torre do Tombo—PIDE, "Situação no distrito de Tete no período de 1–15 de Janeiro de 1972", AN/TT Processo SC-CI(2) GU, box 5; PIDE, "Situação no período de 16–29 de Fevereiro de 1972", AN/TT Processo SC-CI(2) GU, box 6; PIDE, "Relatório de Situação n.º 22/72, 16–30 de Novembro de 1972", AN/TT Processo SC-CI(2) GU, box 13.

10 AN/TT—PIDE, "Relatório de Situação n.º 23/72, de 1–15 de Dezembro de 1972", AN/TT Processo SC-CI(2) GU, box 13.

11 Saquina B., interviewed in Pemba in 2012.

12 See, for example, COREMO's *O Combatente*, vol. 1(2), 1967.

13 Arquivo Histórico-Militar (AHM), Fundo da 2.ª Divisão, 7.ª Secção, box 62, n.º 4, about Tete, 1972.

14 AHM, Fundo da 2.ª Divisão, 7.ª Secção, box 89, n.º 7, 5.ª Companhia de Comandos de Moçambique, 1973.

15 AHM, Fundo da 2.ª Divisão, 7.ª Secção, box 62, n.º 2, 3.ª Companhia de Comandos de Moçambique, 1971.

16 AHM, Fundo da 2.ª Divisão, 7.ª Secção, box 132, n.º 1, Grupos Especiais—1973.

17 AHM, Fundo da 2.ª Divisão, 7.ª Secção, box 133, n.º 1, Grupos Especiais—1972.

18 An ethno-linguistic group split between Tanzania and Mozambique, comprising the majority of the population of the Mueda region.
19 AN/TT—PIDE, "Manifestação de Protesto de Mulheres Macondes", 6 December 1972, AN/TT Processo SC-CI(2) GU, box 13.
20 So far, no credible number of civilian victims of this conflict is available, as civilians only recently became part of the war fatalities as "collateral damages".
21 Freedom for the land, in Kiswahili.
22 Also referred as Modesta Yssufo. Besides the participation in the demonstration in Mueda, Modesta was also involved in the distribution of membership cards of one of the movements that gave rise to FRELIMO, MANU (Mozambique African National Union, created in Tanganyika in 1959 by migrants of Mozambique). See Casimiro (1986: 137).
23 The number of casualties is contested, ranging from between 30–40 up to over 600 casualties.
24 Reference to Faustino Vanomba, one of the arrested and a leader of the process.
25 Reference to Kibiriti Diwane, another Makonde arrested.
26 African policemen attached to local administration.
27 Testimony of Daniel Muilundo quoted in Adam and Duty (1993: 118–119).
28 "Agitadores estrangeiros nos macondes", Notícias (Lourenço Marques), 19 June, 1960; "Reunião de indígenas perturbada por agitadores estrangeiros que foram repelidos", O Século (Lisbon), 19 June 1960.
29 AN/TT-PIDE, "Informação n.° 340/60-GU, 12 August 1972, AN/TT Processo AOS/CO/UL-32 A1.
30 Rabia M., interviewed in Pemba in 2012.
31 "Chai: o massacre que os colonialistas esconderam", Revista Tempo, no. 364, 25 September 1977, pp. 34–37.
32 Rabia M., interviewed in Pemba, in 2012.
33 Bibiana F., interviewed in Maputo in 2002.
34 Maria L., interviewed in Pemba in 2012.
35 Interview carried out in Maputo in 2012.
36 Regarding COREMO, the available documents are silent about the role of women in the nationalist cause. Although this organization would appeal to the "sons and daughters" of Mozambique to support the struggle, women's emancipation and gender equality were not in its political agenda.
37 LIFEMO subsisted as an autonomous group until it was banned in late 1974.
38 Celina Simango was the wife of the then vice-president of FRELIMO, Uria Simango, who was later discharged from this position in the sequence of events following the political crisis of 1968–1969 in the movement. Uria Simango later joined COREMO and, together with other parties and organizations, attempted to constitute a front against the hegemony of FRELIMO in the transition period towards independence. He was arrested, accused of treason and, together with other "traitors", sent to a "reeducation camp", where he and his wife were executed.
39 "Discurso de abertura da Sra. Selina Simango, Presidente da LIFEMO", A Voz da Revolução (FRELIMO), September 6, 1966.
40 As several women revealed, several guerrilla men would be harder on women; to prove their inability they sought to transform guerrilla women into their lovers and, when they did not accept, attributed them very heavy tasks. See also Casimiro (1986).
41 Paulina Mateus quoted in Mussanhane (2012: 641–42).
42 Destacamento Feminino, in portuguese.
43 Paulina Mateus quoted in Saide (2014: 595).
44 In Portuguese: Organização da Mulher Moçambicana (OMM).
45 The war ended in September 1974, when several agreements were signed between the Portuguese government and FRELIMO.

46 Filomena C. interviewed in Maputo in 1994.
47 Including to be part of military/security groups, on both sides of the war.
48 Both on the Portuguese side and among the nationalist forces.

References

Adam, Yussuf; Duty, Hilário A. (1993), "O massacre de Mueda: falam testemunhas", *Arquivo*, 14, 117–128.

Arthur, Maria José et al. (1992), *O Estatuto da Mulher na Luta Armada (relatório)*. Maputo: ARPAC—Arquivos do Património Cultural.

Cahen, Michel (1999), "The Mueda Case and Maconde Political Ethnicity", *Africana Studia*, 2, 29–46.

Casimiro, Isabel (1986), *Transformação nas relações homem-mulher em Moçambique, 1960–1974*. Graduate dissertation, Eduardo Mondlane University, Maputo.

CEA (1981), *Cotton Production in Mozambique: A Survey (1936–1979)*. Maputo: CEA/UEM.

Coelho, João Paulo Borges (1993), "O Estado Colonial e o massacre de Mueda: processo de Quibirite Divane e Faustino Vanombe", *Arquivo*, 14, 129–154.

Coelho, João Paulo Borges (2014), "Politics and Contemporary History of Mozambique: A Set of Epistemological Notes", *Kronos*, 39, 20–31.

Dhada, Mustafah (2015), *The 1972 Wiriyamu Massacre of Mozambique*. London: Bloomsbury Academic Press.

Disney, Jennifer Leigh (2008), *Women's Activism and Feminist Agency in Mozambique and Nicaragua*. Philadelphia, PA: Temple University Press.

FRELIMO (1977a), "Proclamação ao povo moçambicano", in FRELIMO (ed.), *O Processo Revolucionário da Guerra Popular de Libertação*. Maputo: DTI FRELIMO, 75–78.

FRELIMO (1977b), "Iº Congresso da FRELIMO", in FRELIMO (ed.) *Declaração Geral - Documentos Base da FRELIMO*, 1. Maputo: Tempo, 15–18.

General Assembly of the United Nations (1974), *Report of the Commission of Inquiry on the Reported Massacres in Mozambique*. New York: UN Official Records—Twenty-Ninth Session Supplement No. 21 (A/9621).

Hastings, Adrian (1974), *Wiriyamu: My Lai in Mozambique*. London: Search Press.

IDAF—International Defence and Aid Fund (1973), *Terror in Tete: A Documentary Report of Portuguese Atrocities in Tete District, Mozambique, 1971–72*. London: IDAF.

Isaacman, Allen et al. (1980), "Cotton is the Mother of Poverty: Peasant Resistance against Forced Cotton Production in Mozambique, 1938–1961," *International Journal of African Historical Studies*, 13(4), 581–615. doi: 10.2307/218197

Jundanian, Brendan F. (1974), "Resettlement Programs: Counterinsurgency in Mozambique", *Comparative Politics*, 6(4), 519–540. doi: 10.2307/421336

Liberation Support Mouvement (1974), *Mozambican Woman in the Revolution*. Oakland, CA: LSM Information Center.

Liesegang, Gerhard; Tembe, Joel das Neves (2005), *Subsídios para a Historia da UDENAMO e FRELIMO*, 1–27. www.academia.edu/9800597/Da_Udenamo_a_Frelimo

Lyons, Tanya (2002), "Guerrilla Girls and Women", in Jean Allman, Susan Geiger and Nakanyike Musisi (eds.), *Women in African Colonial Wars*. Bloomighton, IN: Indiana University Press, 305–326.

Machel, Samora (1982), *Mozambique: Sowing the Seeds of Revolution*. Harare: Zimbabwe Publishing House.

McClintock, Anne (1995), *Imperial Leather: Race, Gender and Sexuality in the Colonial Contest.* New York: Routledge.

Meneses, Maria Paula (2013), "Para ampliar as Epistemologias do Sul: verbalizando sabores e revelando lutas", *Configurações*, 12, 13–27. doi: 10.4000/configuracoes.1948

Meneses, Maria Paula (2015), "'Xiconhoca, o inimigo': Narrativas de violência sobre a construção da nação em Moçambique", *Revista Crítica de Ciências Sociais*, 106, 9–52. doi: 10.4000/rccs.5869

Meneses, Maria Paula; Martins, Bruno Sena (eds.) (2013), *As Guerras de Libertação e os Sonhos Coloniais.* Coimbra: CES/Almedina.

Mussanhane, Ana Bouene (2012), "Paulina Mateus Nkunda", in Ana Bouene Mussanhane (ed.), *Protagonistas da Luta de Libertação Nacional.* Maputo: Marimbique, 631–648.

P'bitek, Okot (1986), *Artist, the Ruler: Essays on Art, Culture and Values.* Nairobi: East African Educational Publishers.

Pachinuapa, Raimundo; Manguedye, Marina (2009), *A vida do casal Pachinuapa.* Maputo: JV Editores.

Paredes, Margarida (2015), *Combater Duas Vezes. Mulheres na Luta Armada em Angola.* Lisboa: Verso da História.

Saide, Alda Saúte (2014), "As mulheres e a luta de libertação nacional", in Joel das Neves Tembe (ed.), *História da Luta de Libertação Nacional* (vol. 1). Maputo: Ministérios dos Combatentes, 553–601.

Santos, Boaventura de Sousa (2006), *The Rise of the Global Left. The World Social Forum and Beyond.* London: Zed Books.

Santos, Boaventura de Sousa (2013), "Human Rights: A Fragile Hegemony", in François Crépeau and Colleen Sheppard (eds.), *Human Rights and Diverse Societies: Challenges and Possibilities.* Cambridge: Cambridge Scholars Publishing, 17–25.

Sheldon, Kathleen (1994), "Women and Revolution in Mozambique: A Luta Continua!", in Mary Ann Tetreault (ed.), *Women and Revolution in Africa, Asia, and the New World.* Columbia, SC: University of South Carolina Press, 33–61.

Thurshen, Meredith (1998), "Women's War Stories", in Meredith Thurshen and Clotilde Twagiramariya (eds.), *What Women Do in Wartime.* London: Zed Books, 1–26.

Urdang, Stephanie (1979), *Fighting Two Colonialisms: Women in Guinea Bissau.* New York: Monthly Review Press.

West, Harry G. (2000), "Girls with Guns: Narrating the Experience of War of Frelimo's 'Female Detachment'", *Anthropological Quarterly*, 73(4), 180–194. doi: 10.1353/anq.2000.0015

Zimba, Benigna (ed.) (2012), *A Mulher Moçambicana na luta de Libertação Nacional: Memórias do Destacamento Feminino.* Maputo: CPHLLN.

Chapter 8

Women's Human Rights, Legal Mobilization and Epistemologies of the South

Cecília MacDowell Santos

Introduction

In 2012, I made a presentation at the grassroots feminist organization União de Mulheres de São Paulo (hereafter, União de Mulheres), based in the downtown area of São Paulo. My talk drew on research that I was conducting on transnational legal mobilization and women's human rights in Brazil for the ALICE Project.[1] I then showed a PowerPoint slide including all cases of violence and discrimination against women presented against the Brazilian state to the Inter-American Commission on Human Rights (IACHR). I had identified these cases based on the reports published in the website of the IACHR and by contacting human rights and feminist non-governmental organizations (NGOs). At the end of my presentation, Deise Leopoldi, a member of União de Mulheres, corrected my table and pointed out that the petition to initiate the case of Márcia Leopoldi should be dated 1996, not 1998. Deise is the only sister of Márcia Lepoldi, who was assassinated by her ex-boyfriend in the early 1980s. Due to impunity, the case of Márcia Leopoldi was sent to the IACHR by União de Mulheres and three regional NGOs: Center for Justice and International Law (CEJIL), Human Rights Watch/Americas and the Latin American and Caribbean Committee for the Defense of Women's Rights (CLADEM/Brazil). This was the first case of violence against women presented to the IACHR against the Brazilian state!

Yet, until 2012, there was no information on the case of Márcia Leopoldi in the website of the IACHR. I was able to find out about it because I knew the feminist activist Maria Amélia de Almeida Teles (known as Amelinha), a founding member and leader of União de Mulheres. Amelinha had told me that the IACHR had assigned a number to their petition in 1998. Amelinha did not have a copy of the petition and was unclear on its date. CLADEM/Brazil did not have a copy of the petition either. Human Rights Watch had closed its office in Brazil and abandoned the case. CEJIL was the only organization that had a copy of this petition. But its representative in Brazil did not want to share it with me, claiming that disclosing this information could harm the litigation process. Because it would be very difficult to trace all petitions initiated by NGOs against the Brazilian state, I decided to focus only on the cases that were made public in the website of the IACHR. Thus, I did not pay much attention to the case of Márcia Leopoldi and assumed that it had been initiated in the same year as the well-known case of Maria da Penha, which I had selected for analysis.

Besides correcting my slide, Deise gave me a pen drive with copies of all documents relating to the case of Márcia Leopoldi, including the petition sent to the IACHR in 1996. She also made herself available for an interview and encouraged me to write about this case. This would help to show that the case existed. Deise hoped that my research would also give visibility to the difficulties facing women's human rights struggles for justice both nationally and internationally. Some difficulties related to the lack of, and unequal, access to the IACHR. CEJIL and CLADEM/Brazil were important allies for their knowledge of international human rights law. However, the delay of international justice became a critical issue. Moreover, despite these NGOs' position to give up on the case pending in the IACHR when the murderer of Márcia Leopoldi was arrested in 2005, União de Mulheres and Deise had a different vision of legal mobilization and continued to demand a response from the IACHR with the goal of shaming the Brazilian state for the inefficiency of its justice system.

The case of Márcia Leopoldi provides an example of what I have dubbed as "transnational legal activism"; that is, an activism carried out transnationally by human rights NGOs and social movement actors who use international human rights law not only to seek individual remedies for the victims, but to pressure states to make legal and policy changes, to promote human rights ideas and cultures, as well as to strengthen the demands of social movements (C. M. Santos, 2007). In addition to professionalized human rights NGOs, diverse feminist and women's NGOs have engaged in transnational legal activism as a strategy to reconstruct and promote women's human rights discourses and norms. This type of legal mobilization clearly illustrates what Keck and Sikkink (1998) call "transnational advocacy networks" (TANs). Indeed, the human rights and feminist NGOs involved in transnational legal activism create networks to communicate and exchange legal and other kinds of knowledge, forming transnational alliances to "plead the causes of others or defend a cause or proposition" (Keck and Sikkink, 1998: 8).

Yet, contrary to Keck and Sikkink's original conceptualization of TANs as "forms of organization characterized by voluntary, reciprocal, and horizontal patterns of communication and exchange" (1998: 8), the case of Márcia Leopoldi indicates that the relationship between actors involved in transnational activism is often contentious and asymmetrical, as researchers have pointed out (e.g., Mendez, 2002; Farrell and McDermott, 2005; Thayer, 2010; Rodríguez-Garavito, 2014). The emerging scholarship on transnational legal mobilization tends, however, to overlook the relationship between NGOs centred on different issue areas (human rights and feminist advocacy networks, for example), or between NGOs and the victims (or family victims) whose knowledge and experience serve as the basis for transnational legal mobilization practices. Thus, an examination of the ways in which human rights and feminist NGOs, as well as victims of women's rights abuses, interact with one another might reveal who is considered a legitimate actor in the international human (and women's) rights field, and whose strategic visions on human rights, transnational legal mobilization and transnational justice become hegemonic within this field.

Drawing from research on the cases of women's human rights presented to the IACHR against Brazil, this chapter shows that the practice of transnational legal mobilization is contentious and involves unequal knowledge/power relations.[2] International and domestic human rights NGOs that specialize in transnational human rights litigation, feminist advocacy NGOs, grassroots feminist NGOs and victims (or family victims) alike engage in transnational legal mobilization and exchange different types of knowledge. However, the work of translating their knowledge through transnational legal mobilization can both build and break alliances. Most importantly, the legalistic view on human rights held by the more professionalized NGOs tends to prevail over other perspectives. In what follows, I will draw on two cases of domestic violence against women—*Márcia Leopoldi v. Brazil* and *Maria da Penha v. Brazil*—to illustrate these points. Before examining these cases, I briefly explain the approaches to transnational legal mobilization and human rights that inform my analysis.

Transnational Legal Mobilization as Translation of Human Rights Grammars

The literature on transnational legal mobilization has expanded in the last decade. It builds on studies of legal mobilization, transnational advocacy networks, and counter-hegemonic uses of law in the context of globalization. McCann (2008) broadly defines legal mobilization as a practice of translating a perceived harm, a desire or a want into a demand expressed as an assertion of rights. Litigation is one specific dimension of legal mobilization and refers to the translation of a harm into a "complaint" (of a norm violation) presented to a court. In addition to litigation, legal mobilization can include other actions, such as raising legal consciousness, rights talk, legal campaigns to change or create laws and policies and so on.

Going beyond the limits of the nation-state and of individualistic uses of law, Boaventura de Sousa Santos and Cesar Rodríguez-Garavito (2005) propose an approach that they call "subaltern cosmopolitan legality" to refer to the transnational, counter-hegemonic mobilization of law by social movement actors. "Subaltern cosmopolitan legality" is characterized by four expansions of the conception of law and of the politics of legality. First, there must be a combination of political and legal mobilization. In fact, subaltern cosmopolitan legality is a form of political mobilization of law. It presupposes the politicization of the use of law and courts. Legal mobilization, in turn, may involve legal, illegal and non-legal actions. Second, the politics of legal mobilization needs to be conceived of at three different scales—the local, the national and the global, so that the struggles are linked across borders. Third, there must be an expansion of professional legal knowledge, of the nation-state law, and of the legal canon that privileges individual rights. This does not mean that individual rights are abandoned by subaltern cosmopolitan politics and legality, even though there is an emphasis on collective rights. Finally, the time frame of the legal struggle must be expanded to include the time frame of the social struggle that serves to politicize the legal dispute. This means that the social conflicts are conceived of as structural problems related to capitalism, colonialism, patriarchy, authoritarian political regimes and so on (B. S. Santos, 2005: 30).

The legal defence of leaders and causes of social movements by "popular advocacy" in Brazil is an example of the political mobilization of law. This can be illustrated by the struggles for agrarian reform and counter-hegemonic globalization waged by the Movement of Landless Rural Workers (B. S. Santos and Carlet, 2010). The so-called "strategic litigation" (litígio estratégico), carried out in Latin America by human rights NGOs that specialize in litigation to defend a cause, is also an example of the political mobilization of law that can go beyond the limits of the nation-state (Rodríguez-Garavito, 2011; Cardoso, 2012). The "transnational legal activism" practices by NGOs and social movement actors that use the Inter-American system of human rights to pressure states to promote legal and policy changes at the domestic level might also serve as an example of subaltern cosmopolitan legality (C. M. Santos, 2007).

The transnational legal mobilization of human rights can be viewed as a "politics of reading human rights" (Baxi, 2006); that is, a discursive practice of translation that both includes and excludes the representation of varying forms of human rights violations, as well as different ideas and conceptions of human rights and justice. In her approach to the "vernacularization" or translation of global women's human rights ideas and frameworks into local settings, Merry (2006) refers to transnational activists as "translators/negotiators" embedded in power relations between the global and the local. Thayer (2010) also examines the transnational process of translating gender discourses as practices embedded in power relationships, but she goes beyond a global–local dichotomy, showing that "local" actors, such as women rural workers in Northeast Brazil, are not simply receivers of a global feminist or gender discourse; they are already embedded in global feminist discourses. Building on Thayer's perspective, I would add that the victims of human rights abuses are not isolated "local" actors either. While the "local" actors' legal and political strategies to achieve justice may differ from those of legal experts and professionalized human rights NGOs, they also embrace aspects of legalistic views on human rights and justice. Moreover, as noted by Hernández Castillo (2016), the victims can become "human rights defenders" in the process of international litigation.

The "epistemologies of the South" (Santos, 2014) framework provides further analytical insights to conceive of transnational legal mobilization as a practice of translation of diverse human rights grammars beyond the global–local divide. The "South" is understood in both geopolitical and epistemic senses.

It corresponds to diverse types of knowledge produced by marginalized groups both in the global South and the North (Santos, 2014). This framework starts with the premise that ecologies of knowledge, including diverse human rights grammars, exist in different locales all over the world. Acknowledging the existence of this ecology of knowledge and learning from all kinds of human rights knowledge and practices (e.g., liberal legal knowledge and litigation practices, feminist practices of human rights, indigenous cosmovisions on environmental and collective rights) can contribute to global social justice. In this perspective, transnational justice work depends on and includes epistemic justice.

In addition to acknowledging the existence of ecologies of knowledge, the "epistemologies of the South" framework considers that intercultural translation is necessary to overcome hierarchical epistemic relationships (Santos, 2014). Implicit in this perspective is the idea that intercultural and multidirectional translation will help to build cross-national solidarities between different groups fighting for global/local justice. Thus, it is important to ask what kinds of transnational legal mobilization practices correspond to an "epistemology of the South". As the following cases of domestic violence presented against Brazil to the IACHR will illustrate, not all actors involved in transnational legal mobilization are viewed as legitimate "transnational legal activists" and equal producers of "women's human rights" grammars. The legal knowledge of professionalized human rights and feminist NGOs tends to prevail over the popular feminist knowledge and practices of grassroots organizations and victims of human rights violations.

Mobilizing Women's Human Rights in the IACHR: Who Can Cross the Gate?

The Inter-American system of human rights within the Organization of American States (OAS) includes one judicial organ, the Inter-American Court of Human Rights (IACtHR), and a quasi-judicial organ, the Inter-American Commission on Human Rights (IACHR). Only the IACHR or a state party to the OAS can send a case to the IACtHR. NGOs and the victims of human rights violations can send petitions directly to the IACHR. Since the early 1990s, international and domestic human rights NGOs have increasingly engaged in transnational legal mobilization in the IACHR. The national adoption of regional human rights norms in most countries in Latin America has created legal opportunities for transnational "strategic litigation" (Cardoso, 2012). The petitions denounce violations of the human rights norms adopted by the OAS and ratified by the state parties.

Similarly to the practices of human rights mobilization in other countries in Latin America, international and domestic human rights NGOs have sent a number of petitions against the Brazilian state to the IACHR. Brazil ratified the American Convention on Human Rights in 1992. Three years later, Brazil ratified the Inter-American Convention on the Prevention, Punishment and

Eradication of Violence against Women (known as the Convention of Belém do Pará, adopted by the OAS in 1994 in the city of Belém, capital of the Brazilian Pará state). In 1998, Brazil recognized the jurisdiction of the IACtHR.

Types of Cases

The NGOs select "paradigmatic cases" to show that the human rights violations are endemic and require both individual remedies and domestic policy changes. International and domestic human rights NGOs form transnational alliances to advocate for the rights of various groups and individuals who are marginalized and subjected to abuses, including children in situations of vulnerability, prisoners, indigenous peoples, Blacks, women and so on. Their engagement with the IACHR is a clear example of transnational legal activism (C. M. Santos, 2007). Among more than 300 cases against the Brazilian state in the period from 1996 to 2012, the IACHR's annual reports show that only 7 cases concerned women's human rights, focusing particularly on violence and/or discrimination against women (see Table 8.1). The petitioners include international and domestic NGOs, as well as victims. Various types of NGOs are part of the legal mobilization process, including international and domestic human rights and feminist NGOs, Blacks' rights NGOs and grassroots feminist and social movement organizations. Given the small number of cases and the year of the first petition (1996), it is clear that the IACHR is a new terrain for all of these actors' engagement with transnational litigation on women's human rights.

Based on the types of complaints and the norms invoked by the litigants, I classified the seven cases on women's human rights as follows: cases of **gender-based violence** (four cases); cases of **racial discrimination against Black women** (two cases); and cases of **class-based violence against rural women workers** (one case). Among the cases of gender-based violence, three related to domestic (intimate partner) violence against women and one referred to sexual violence perpetrated by a medical doctor against a female teenager who was his patient. The table below summarizes each case by year of the initial petition, names of petitioners and the norms used to frame the complaints.

The IACHR reports do not tell us how litigators have developed and negotiated their legal strategies. What role does each actor play in the process of mobilizing women's human rights? Are all types of NGOs and the victims viewed as legitimate actors in the transnational practice of mobilizing women's human rights? Can they all knock on the door of the IACHR? Two cases of domestic violence—*Márcia Leopoldi v. Brazil* and *Maria da Penha v. Brazil*—help to shed light on these questions.

Knowledge Mobilized and Strategies of Legal Mobilization

The case of Márcia Leopoldi, a young woman who was assassinated by her ex-boyfriend, was sent to IACHR in 1996. This is the first case on women's

Table 8.1 Cases of women's human rights presented to the IACHR against Brazil (1996–2012)

Type of Case	Year of Petition	Petitioners	Complaint	Norms
Márcia Leopoldi Case (domestic violence)	1996	CEJIL, CLADEM, União de Mulheres de São Paulo	Homicide of Márcia by ex-boyfriend	American Convention on Human Rights; and Belém do Pará Convention
Simone Diniz Case (racial discrimination)	1997	Simone Diniz, CEJIL, Sub-Committee of Human Rights of Blacks at São Paulo Bar Association, and Father Batista Institute of Blacks	Racial discrimination in the hiring of a domestic worker	Am Conv on Human Rights; Additional Protocol to Am Conv on HR in the area of Econ, Social and Cultural Rights; Int Conv on the Elimination of All Forms of Racial Discrimination; and Conv 111 of the ILO
Maria da Penha Case (domestic violence)	1998	Maria da Penha, CEJIL, and CLADEM	Attempted murder by former husband, victim became paraplegic as a result	Am Conv on HR; and Belém do Pará Convention
Márcia Barbosa de Sousa Case (domestic violence)	2000	CEJIL and National Movement of Human Rights	Homicide of Márcia, perpetrated by ex-lover, a Congressman	Am Conv on HR; and Belém do Pará Convention
Margarida Maria Alves Case (class-based violence against rural women workers)	2000	GAJOP-Cabinet for Popular Legal Assistance, CEJIL, National Movement of Human Rights-MNDH, Land Pastoral Commission-CPT, Margarida Maria Alves Foundation for the Defense of Human Rights	Homicide of Margarida, union leader of rural workers	American Convention on Human Rights

Samanta Nunes da Silva Case (sexual violence)	2003	Themis	Sexual violence perpetrated by a medical doctor	Am Conv on HR; and **Belém do Pará Convention**
Neusa dos Santos e Gisele Ana Ferreira Case (racial discrimination)	2003	Geledés-Institute of Black Women	Racial discrimination in the hiring of a domestic worker	Am Conv on Human Rights; Additional Protocol to Am Conv on HR in the area of Econ, Social and Cultural Rights; Int Conv on the Elimination of All Forms of Racial Discrimination; and Conv 111 of the ILO

human rights presented against Brazil, as noted in the beginning of this chapter. The petition was signed by the CEJIL, Human Rights Watch/Americas, the Latin American and Caribbean Committee for the Defense of Women's Rights (CLADEM/Brazil) and União de Mulheres de São Paulo. The case of Maria da Penha, a woman who survived attempted murder perpetrated by her former husband and became paraplegic as a result of this aggression, is the second case on domestic violence and was sent to the IACHR in 1998. The petition was signed by Maria da Penha Maia Fernandes, CEJIL and CLADEM/Brazil. Both petitions alleged violations of the American Convention on Human Rights and the Convention of Belém do Pará.

Drawing on interviews with the NGO representatives and the victims, I identified the following types of knowledge mobilized by the petitioners: (1) human rights legal knowledge; (2) feminist legal advocacy knowledge; (3) feminist popular knowledge; (3) corporeal knowledge.[3] I should note that these are "ideal types" of knowledge, in the Weberian sense of the term. The knowledge and practices of actors involved in transnational legal mobilization are not clearly separated. But it is possible to identify some forms of knowledge that stem from their experience and inform their legal practices and strategies of legal mobilization.

Human rights legal knowledge relies on a legalistic framework of human rights. It is used by professionalized NGOs engaged in strategic litigation within and across borders. CEJIL embodies this type of legal mobilization, specializing in litigation in the Inter-American system of human rights. Founded in 1991 by a group of human rights defenders, CEJIL works with the system to strengthen it and to promote human rights and democracy in the state parties of the OAS.[4] CEJIL has consultative status before the OAS, the United Nations, and the African Commission on Human and Peoples' Rights. Its headquarters are located in Washington D.C., where the IACHR is also located. But CEJIL has offices in different countries throughout the Americas. In Brazil, CEJIL's office is located in the city of Rio de Janeiro. The office includes one director, who is an experienced human rights defender, and one administrative assistant. CEJIL is a major legal actor in the cases presented against Brazil in the IACHR. As the table above indicates, CEJIL is one of the petitioners in five of the seven cases on women's human rights brought to the IACHR. CEJIL selects and mobilizes its cases in partnership with local NGOs. The victims are also involved in the selection and preparation of the cases. One of the criteria used by CEJIL to select a case includes the victims' authorization to file a complaint and their willingness to cooperate with the legal action, providing all needed information to support the case. It is also necessary to count on local NGOs and/or attorneys to follow up on the legal case in the domestic court system and to help with the mobilization of the case outside of courts. These are important conditions to guarantee the "success" of the case. A "good case" is one that exemplifies a pattern of human rights violations and that can be used to establish a judicial precedent and promote domestic policy and/

or legal changes. A successful case does not necessarily mean that the IACHR will publish a report on the merits of the case and hold the state accountable for the alleged violations. An agreement between the petitioners and the state can be settled in the course of the legal dispute. But it is necessary that the case be admitted, so it can be used as a weapon to pressure the state in question.[5] Thus, CEJIL is concerned with framing the cases according to the procedural and material normative requirements for admissibility. CEJIL's strategic legal use of international human rights norms is counter-hegemonic as it confronts state and non-state anti-human rights discourses and practices. Yet, the legalistic perspective of CEJIL may also be viewed as hegemonic vis-à-vis non-legal, subaltern cosmopolitan mobilization practices.

Feminist legal advocacy also relies on a legalistic framework of human rights. It is used by both domestic and international professionalized feminist NGOs engaged in legal advocacy to change national and international women's human rights policies and laws, and/or to disseminate and implement international women's human rights norms at the domestic level. CLADEM, a regional network of feminist legal experts established in 1987, carries out this type of transnational feminist advocacy work. Like CEJIL, CLADEM has offices in different countries in Latin America. In Brazil, CLADEM has been alternating offices based in different cities over the years, and has been represented by established feminist law professors, feminist attorneys, and/or feminist activists. In contrast with CEJIL, CLADEM focuses only on women's human rights and seeks to promote legal and policy changes from a gender perspective. Moreover, CLADEM does not specialize in transnational litigation and does not centre exclusively on the use of the Inter-American system, although CLADEM has begun to develop a "global legal program" dedicated to transnational strategic litigation both in the Inter-American system and in the Convention on the Elimination of All Forms of Discrimination against Women (CEDAW) bodies.[6] Like CEJIL, CLADEM also mobilizes on the cases in partnership with local NGOs. In addition to the two cases of domestic violence presented to the IACHR, CLADEM/Brazil has presented one case of women's human rights violation against the Brazilian state to the CEDAW Committee. Similarly to CEJIL, the legal feminist perspective embraced by CLADEM, based on advocacy work and litigation, can be viewed as counter-hegemonic since it challenges sexist practices and ideologies promoted by both state and civil society actors. Yet, this feminist legal perspective can also be viewed as hegemonic in relation to grassroots and marginalized forms of feminist activism.

Feminist popular knowledge is mobilized by grassroots organizations like União de Mulheres de São Paulo. These are voluntary associations working to educate women about their rights, using women's human rights discourse and laws to empower women. They also seek to change cultural norms and stereotypes about gender, and to change state institutions and political cultures. They use human rights norms as a legal and political tool to strengthen their causes and promote women's rights. They work both against and with the legal system, organizing campaigns against impunity and protests to have domestic violence policies and legislation established and implemented. Created in 1981, União de Mulheres is one of the oldest and most active feminist grassroots organizations in the city of São Paulo.[7] Since 1994, União de Mulheres has offered courses on feminist popular legal education (*promotoras legais populares*).[8] Feminist law professors and legal professionals give classes in these courses. Members of CLADEM/Brazil and other feminist NGOs have also contributed to these courses. Even though União de Mulheres has provided legal advice and emotional support to battered women, this organization does not initiate legal cases either locally or internationally. The case of Márcia Leopoldi is an exception. While União de Mulheres shares CEJIL's and CLADEM's goals to promote human rights, justice and policy changes through transnational legal mobilization, its approach to the state and to domestic and international legal systems is not legalistic. União de Mulheres approaches legal mobilization from a critical, oppositional perspective. Legal mobilization is an additional weapon that must serve social and political struggles. The objective is not to strengthen the Inter-American system of human rights, but rather to use it to strengthen the demands of the women's movements. Thus, the engagement of União de Mulheres with legal mobilization, both locally and internationally, can be viewed as a practice of subaltern cosmopolitan legality. And its approach to women's human rights illustrates an epistemology of the South.

Finally, the victims of human rights violations bring in to transnational legal mobilization a distinct experience and type of knowledge that I dub **corporeal knowledge**. Not all victims may gain consciousness of their rights and fight for justice. But the victims or family victims engaged in legal mobilization share a common knowledge rooted in their bodily experience of physical, psychological and emotional harm. The search for justice is sparked by a distinct experience of indignation that starts with the act of violence and is then transformed into a type of corporeal knowledge that might drive a reaction or a struggle for some kind of justice. The survivors of domestic violence, such as the sister of Márcia Leopoldi and Maria da Penha, have gained consciousness of their rights and have learned about the legal system in the process of fighting for justice, which started before they met their NGO allies. Their corporeal knowledge, their personal experience learning about law and facing an unjust legal system, their representation of the double act of violence (interpersonal and institutional) through the oral and written narration of their stories, all of these accumulated types of corporeal and legal knowledge were crucial for the transnational legal actions that they initiated in alliance with the human rights and feminist NGOs that crossed their paths in search for justice. These victims became subjects of rights, they gained consciousness of their human rights as women, they taught and learned from the NGOs, they became activists and actors in the field of women's human rights and transnational legal mobilization, even if temporary legal mobilization actors and not necessarily joining a human rights and/or feminist NGO.

In this perspective, the cases of Márcia Leopoldi and Maria da Penha illustrate that cosmopolitan and local actors learn from each other's knowledge of harm, rights violations, collective and individual histories, as well as legal and political repertoires of action, resources and strategies. These actors' subjectivities and identities may be transformed in the process of transnational legal mobilization. However, this process is charged with not only alliances, but also tensions and conflicts. The actors may produce what I dub a "convergent translation" of their knowledge, building alliances and a common strategy to pursue justice. Yet, a "divergent translation" and conflicting views on the use of law may also lead to breaking alliances in the process of legal mobilization.

Convergent and Divergent Translations, Building and Breaking Alliances

Márcia Leopoldi was assassinated in 1984 by her ex-boyfriend, José Antônio Brandão Lago, in the city of Santos, near the city of São Paulo. Deise Leopoldi, the only sister of Márcia, began then to struggle for justice. Coming from an upper-class family, Deise was able to hire well-known attorneys to assist the public prosecutors in charge of the case. In the second trial that took place in the early 1990s, the jury found Lago guilty. He was sentenced to 15 years in prison. However, he ran away and was not arrested by the police until 2005. This arrest was made possible thanks to Deise's appearance in the popular TV show *Mais Você*, broadcasted every morning by the network *Rede Globo*. Deise was interviewed in this show to talk about domestic violence and then took the opportunity to show Lago's picture on national television.

At that time, Deise had become a feminist activist and was member of União de Mulheres. She had heard about this organization through one of the lawyers who assisted her.[9] In 1992, she contacted União de Mulheres in search of support. In the same year she joined the organization. She actively participated in the campaign "Impunity Is Accomplice to Violence" that was then created by União de Mulheres. The case of Márcia Leopoldi served well for the purpose of this campaign. União de Mulheres actively mobilized on this case, organized a protest in front of the court when the second trial was held, made a poster with Lago's picture, and even publicized the case and took this poster to the Fourth World Conference on Women, held in Beijing in 1995.

In 1994, the feminist organizations CLADEM/Brazil and União de Mulheres began to discuss the idea of sending this case to the IACHR. This discussion took place when União de Mulheres offered the first course on popular legal education for women. The following year Brazil ratified the Convention of Belém do Pará, as noted. CLADEM/Brazil members thought then that the case of Márcia Leopoldi was ideal for testing the application of the Convention and for pressuring the Brazilian state to establish domestic violence laws and policies. During that time, Brazil had created over 200 separate women's police stations throughout the country. But there was no comprehensive legislation and national policy to effectively confront the problem of domestic violence against women. Feminist members of CLADEM/Brazil had drafted a proposal for a domestic violence bill, but their allies in Congress were unable to introduce this bill (C. M. Santos, 2010). CLADEM/Brazil and União de Mulheres then looked for the support of CEJIL to take the case of Márcia Leopoldi to the IACHR. CEJIL had not yet mobilized on a case of women's rights, so this was an opportunity to expand its issue areas, using the Convention of Belém do Pará to provoke a "boomerang effect" (Keck and Sikkink, 1998) while setting a judicial precedent on gender-based violence for the whole Latin American region. Thus, all actors learned and benefited from this alliance around the case of Márcia Leopoldi. Deise was hopeful that justice was going to be finally achieved.

However, the IACHR did not open the case immediately. It took two years to assign a number to the petition (Petition no. 11,996). There was no "case" number and no decision on this case until 16 years after the petition was filed. In March 2012, the IACHR finally published its report on the case, considering it inadmissible (Report no. 9/12). The IACHR considered that the case had been resolved and lost its object because Lago was arrested in 2005.

CEJIL and CLADEM/Brazil agreed with the IACHR's position. In fact, after Lago's arrest, their representatives in Brazil had a discussion and disagreement with Deise Leopoldi and União de Mulheres over whether they should continue to pressure and request that the IACHR admit the case. Deise and other members of União de Mulheres considered that Lago had been arrested thanks to their mobilizing efforts, not the Brazilian state's. They wanted to use the case to show that the Brazilian state was negligent and did not protect women from violence. Representatives of CEJIL were concerned about losing the case, because the very object of the complaint—to arrest Lago—had been accomplished, and they did not have any legal precedents to support a demand for the continuation of the case.[10] Representatives of CLADEM/Brazil were also concerned about the legal chance of the case, although they recognized Deise's work and understood how important it was to continue fighting for an admissibility report in the IACHR.[11]

Yet, this disagreement was not resolved and culminated in the breaking of their alliance. In 2007, Deise and other leaders of União de Mulheres published a book on the case of Márcia Leopoldi (Leopoldi et al., 2007). This book provides a detailed history of Deise's and União de Mulheres' struggle for justice. The book also recounts the NGOs' conflicting strategies to pursue justice in the IACHR (Leopoldi et al., 2007: 117). Bypassing CEJIL and its assigned role as the primary interlocutor with the IACHR, Deise and União de Mulheres sent a copy of this book to the IACHR in 2010 and requested that the case be admitted. This was a final move to break their alliance with CEJIL and CLADEM/Brazil. União de Mulheres continued to work in collaboration with these NGOs in other mobilization practices. But the transnational alliance that had been forged with the family victim was broken by the time the IACHR published the inadmissibility report in 2012.

Despite the IACHR's dismissal of the case, the subjectivity and the identity of the victim—in this case, a family victim—were clearly transformed in the process of transnational legal mobilization. Deise moved to the city of São Paulo, joined a feminist grassroots organization, and became a feminist activist fighting to change the legal system and to end domestic violence against women. CEJIL and CLADEM/Brazil members, however, do not consider this to be a "successful" case. Although this case is cited in the website of CLADEM, both CLADEM/Brazil and CEJIL did not make efforts to bring it to public attention. CEJIL omits the case of Márcia Leopoldi from its website.

The case of Maria da Penha, on the other hand, is easily found in the websites of both CLADEM/BRAZIL and CEJIL. In the website of CEJIL, the case of Maria da Penha is an example of successful litigation with an "impact". Indeed, the legal mobilization on this case contributed to promote domestic legal change, legal consciousness of women's human rights, and public awareness about the issue of domestic violence against women in Brazil. In addition, this case illustrates a "convergent translation" of different types of knowledge and a process of building alliances among all actors involved from beginning to the end of the legal mobilization process. It also contributed to empowering the victim, who became an activist and joined an organization, though at first she did not join a feminist or human rights NGO.

Maria da Penha is a white, middle-class, well-educated, disabled woman who lives in the city of Fortaleza, in the northeast of Brazil. She was victim of attempted murder committed in 1983 by her then husband, Marco Antonio Heredia Viveros. He was found guilty by a second jury and sentenced to ten years in prison. However, he appealed. And, until 2001, the case was pending in the Superior Tribunal of Justice. As noted above, the case of Maria da Penha was sent to the IACHR in 1998, two years after the case of Márcia Leopoldi. The petition was signed by Maria da Penha, CEJIL, and CLADEM/Brazil. As in the case of Márcia Leopoldi, I interviewed all petitioners.[12] A sign of CEJIL's role as gatekeeper to the IACHR was that only CEJIL had a copy of the petition. A representative from CEJIL visited Fortaleza in 1998 in search of paradigmatic cases on violence against women. She learned about the Maria Penha case through the State Council on Women's Rights of Ceará. In 1994, the Council had published the first edition of Maria da Penha's book, *Sobrevivi … Posso Contar* (I Survived … I Can Tell My Story) (Fernandes, 1994). The book narrates Maria da Penha's corporeal and legal knowledge of violence and injustice. It shows how she became a survivor of domestic violence, describing her search for justice and denouncing the inefficiency of the legal system and the impunity of the perpetrator.

When I visited Fortaleza in 2008 to interview Maria da Penha, I was very impressed with her involvement with different activities relating to domestic violence against women. She was then the president of the NGO Associação de Parentes de Vítimas de Violência—APAVV (Association of Relatives of Victims of Violence). She was also a member of the State Council on Women's

Rights. She had then just received reparations from the Ceará State, as recommended by the IACHR report on the merits of her case published in 2001. She knew all of the institutional agents working for the network of services that had been created in the city of Fortaleza, as mandated by the then newly-created domestic violence statute, Law no. 11340/2006, also known as Maria da Penha Law. This law was named after Maria da Penha by then President Luiz Inácio Lula da Silva as a result of her successful case. The president invited Maria da Penha to the ceremony held on August 6, 2006, in Brasília, the nation's capital, for the signing of this law. This ceremony was largely publicized in the media.

Even though the case of Maria da Penha is not the only factor that contributed to the creation of the Maria da Penha Law and to increasing public awareness of domestic violence, it is evident that transnational legal mobilization on this case produced positive material and symbolic effects. In addition to illustrating the alliances between feminist and human rights NGOs, Maria da Penha's story and her persistent struggle for justice also served as inspiration for Deise Leopoldi. Deise contacted Maria da Penha in the mid-2000s to seek advice on how to approach the IACHR. In the footsteps of Maria da Penha, Deise wrote a book about her struggle for justice. Yet, from a legal perspective, the case of Márcia Leopoldi did not have a chance to produce the same legal effects as the Maria da Penha case did.

Nevertheless, these cases illustrate that transnational legal mobilization involves a work of translation of different human rights grammars. Even though international human rights NGOs based in the global North tend to have more knowledge of the norms regulating transnational litigation and operate like gatekeepers to access the IACHR, they also share this legal knowledge with domestic human rights NGOs in the process of transnational legal mobilization. Human rights NGOs have also expanded their issue areas and have made alliances with international and domestic feminist NGOs. However, "local" grassroots NGOs and especially victims are not necessarily perceived as legitimate legal mobilization actors and members of transnational human rights advocacy networks.

Concluding Remarks on Human Rights Mobilization and Epistemologies of the South

Transnational legal mobilization has the potential to produce not only material and direct effects on the adoption and implementation of domestic laws and policies. As noted by Holzmeyer (2009), increasing the organizational capacity of transnational advocacy networks and promoting diverse actors' rights consciousness are some of the indirect effects that deserve further attention from transnational legal mobilization practice and theory. In addition, as this chapter has shown, victims are important actors in transnational legal mobilization and can become activists. Thus, research and legal advocacy on human rights and women's human rights must pay attention not only to material impacts of legal mobilization, but to the interactions between the actors involved and to their subjective experiences, broadening the generally accepted view on who counts as human rights advocates.

Ignoring and devaluing certain forms of knowledge in the mobilizing practices of human rights endangers the very work of promoting global justice. The languages and cultures of human rights need to go beyond a legalist perspective on the needs and rights of individuals and groups. Otherwise, epistemic justice will not be achieved and this will hinder the work for global justice. Mobilizing women's human rights through transnational legal mobilization can make invisible the practices and knowledge of actors who are also fighting for justice. The cases of Márcia Leopoldi and Maria da Penha illustrate that the history of struggles carried out by grassroots organizations such as União de Mulheres and victims (and family victims) of domestic violence, such as Deise Leopoldi and Maria da Penha, are essential for promoting global justice. They have not only learned from the more professionalized human rights defenders, but also taught their knowledge from their bodily experience and from a long history of individual and collective struggles that can be truly viewed as "epistemologies of the South". Recognizing the knowledge and the contributions of these actors to the making of ecologies of women's human rights grammars is also part of the global justice work that human rights defenders shall seek to promote.

Notes

1 My research project, titled "What Counts as 'Women's Human Rights'? How Brazilian Black Women's and Feminist NGOs Mobilize International Human Rights Law", is part of the larger research project "ALICE—Strange Mirrors, Unsuspected Lessons: Leading Europe to a new way of sharing the world experiences", coordinated by Boaventura de Sousa Santos at the Center for Social Studies at the University of Coimbra.

2 An extended version of this text has been published in the *Journal of Human Rights Practice* in 2018. Preliminary versions were presented at the International Colloquium "Epistemologies of the South: South–South, South–North and North–South Global Learning", at the University of Coimbra, July 2014, and at the Workshop "Transnational Advocacy Networks: Reflecting on 15 Years of Evolving Theory and Practice", at the Watson Institute for International Studies, Brown University, 30 April 2015–2 May 2015. The chapter draws on field research that counted on the support of the Faculty Development Fund at the University of San Francisco. I am grateful for the comments from Boaventura de Sousa Santos and other members of the ALICE Project. I also thank Peter Evans and Cesar Rodríguez-Garavito for their comments on a shorter version of this text. I am thankful to the human rights activists who gave me interviews, information and documents on their legal practices. My special thanks are due to Deise Leopoldi and Maria da Penha Maia Fernandes for their generosity in sharing with me their knowledge and the documents relating to their respective legal cases.

3 The interviews were conducted over the past ten years for a research program that I have developed on transnational legal activism and cases presented against Brazil to the Inter-American Commission on Human Rights. This research has benefited from multiple grants awarded by the Faculty Development Fund at the University

of San Francisco. Besides interviews with Deise Leopoldi and Maria da Penha Maia Fernandes, this chapter draws on interviews conducted with representatives of the following NGOs: União de Mulheres de São Paulo, CLADEM/Brazil and CEJIL.

4 Further details on the history and work carried out by CEJIL can be found in their website: <https://cejil.org/en/what-we-do> (accessed 2 June 2016).

5 Other human rights NGOs based in Brazil, such as Justiça Global and GAJOP, which engage in transnational litigation in the Inter-American system of human rights, use the same criteria to select their cases. In fact, GAJOP, a local human rights NGO with an office in the northeast of Brazil, learned from CEJIL and established a program on transnational litigation in the early 2000s.

6 See more details on this program in the website of CLADEM, at: <www.cladem.org/en/our-programs/litigation> (accessed 15 June 2016).

7 For more details on the history of this organization, see União de Mulheres de São Paulo (2011).

8 Details on this project carried out by União de Mulheres can be found at: <http://promotoraslegaispopulares.org.br> (accessed 10 June 2016).

9 The information on Deise Leopoldi's struggle for justice is based on an interview that I conducted with her in São Paulo on 20 May 2013. The history of this struggle and of Márcia Leopoldi case is also narrated in the book by Leopoldi, Teles, and Gonzaga (2007). My recounting of the legal mobilization trajectory of the Márcia Leopoldi case is also based on the following interviews conducted in the early stages of my research on transnational legal activism: Beatriz Affonso, representative of CEJIL in Brazil in the past 11 years (interviewed in Rio de Janeiro, 17 August 2006); and Valéria Pandjarjian, former member of CLADEM/Brazil who participated in most of the litigation efforts relating to both the Márcia Leopoldi and the Maria da Penha cases (interviewed in São Paulo, 31 August 2006).

10 Interview with Beatriz Affonso, Rio de Janeiro, 17 August 2006.

11 Interview with Valéria Pandjarjian, São Paulo, 31 August 2006.

12 Besides the interviews with representatives of CEJIL and CLADEM/Brazil, cited above in Footnotes 10 and 11, I interviewed Maria da Penha twice: the first interview was conducted over the phone on 3 April 2007; the second interview was conducted in Fortaleza, 19 February 2008. I also interviewed Maria da Penha's attorney in Fortaleza, on 21 February 2008.

References

Baxi, Upendra (2006), "Politics of Reading Human Rights: Inclusion and Exclusion within the Production of Human Rights", in S. Meckled-García and B. Çali (eds.), *The Legalization of Human Rights: Multidisciplinary Perspectives on Human Rights and Human Rights Law*. New York: Routledge, 182–200.

Cardoso, Evorah L. C. (2012), *Litígio Estratégico e Sistema Interamericano de Direitos Humanos*. Belo Horizonte: Editora Fórum.

Farrell, Amy; McDermott, Patrice (2005), "Claiming Afghan Women: The Challenge of Human Rights Discourse for Transnational Feminism", in Wendy S. Hesford and Wendy Kozol (eds.), *Just Advocacy?: Women's Human Rights, Transnational Feminisms, and the Politics of Representation*. New Brunswick, NJ: Rutgers University Press, 33–55.

Fernandes, Maria da Penha Maia (1994), *Sobrevivi… Posso Contar*. Fortaleza: Conselho Cearense dos Direitos da Mulher (1st ed.).

Hernández Castillo, R. Aída (2016), "From Victims to Human Rights Defenders: International Litigation and the Struggle for Justice of Indigenous Women", in R. Aída

Hernández Castillo (ed.), *Multiple Injustices: Indigenous Women, Law, and Political Struggle in Latin America*. Tucson, AZ: University of Arizona Press, 163–189.

Holzmeyer, Cheryl (2009), "Human Rights in an Era of Neoliberal Globalization: The Alien Tort Claims Act and Grassroots Mobilization in Doe v. Unocal", *Law and Society Review*, 43(2), 271–304. doi: 10.1111/j.1540-5893.2009.00373.x

Keck, Margaret; Sikkink, Kathryn (1998), *Activists beyond Borders: Advocacy Networks in International Politics*. Ithaca, NY: Cornell University Press.

Leopoldi, Deise; Teles, M. Amélia; Gonzaga, Terezinha de Oliveira (2007), *Do Silêncio ao Grito contra a Impunidade: O Caso Márcia Leopoldi*. São Paulo: União de Mulheres de São Paulo.

McCann, Michael (2008), "Litigation and Legal Mobilization", in K. E. Whittington, R. D. Kelemen, and G. A. Caldeira (eds.), *The Oxford Handbook of Law and Politics*. New York: Oxford University Press, 522–540.

Mendez, Jennifer Bickham (2002), "Creating Alternatives from a Gender Perspective: Transnational Organizing for Maquila Workers' Rights in Central America", in Nancy A. Naples and Manisha Desai (eds.), *Women's Activism and Globalization: Linking Local Struggles and Transnational Politics*. New York: Routledge, 121–141.

Merry, Sally Engle (2006), *Human Rights and Gender Violence: Translating International Law into Local Justice*. Chicago, IL: University of Chicago Press.

Rodríguez-Garavito, Cesar (2011), "Beyond the Courtroom: The Impact of Judicial Activism on Socioeconomic Rights in Latin America", *Texas Law Review*, 89, 1669–1698.

Rodríguez-Garavito, Cesar (2014), "The Future of Human Rights: From Gatekeeping to Symbiosis", *Sur—International Journal of Human Rights*, 11(20), 499–509. Available at https://sur.conectas.org/en/home/issue-20

Santos, Boaventura de Sousa (2005), "Beyond Neoliberal Governance: The World Social Forum as Subaltern Cosmopolitan Politics and Legality", in Boaventura de Sousa Santos and Cesar Rodríguez-Garavito (eds.), *Law and Globalization from Below: Towards a Cosmopolitan Legality*. Cambridge: Cambridge University Press, 29–63.

Santos, Boaventura de Sousa (2014), *Epistemologies of the South: Justice against Epistemicide*. Boulder, CO: Paradigm Publications.

Santos, Boaventura de Sousa; Carlet, Flávia (2010), "Movement of Landless Rural Workers in Brazil and Their Struggles for Access to Law and Justice", in Yash Ghai and Jill Cottrell (eds.), *Marginalized Communities and Access to Justice*. Abingdon: Routledge, 60–82.

Santos, Boaventura de Sousa; Rodríguez-Garavito, César A. (2005), "Law, Politics, and the Subaltern in Counter-Hegemonic Globalization", in Boaventura de Sousa Santos and César A. Rodríguez-Garavito (eds.), *Law and Globalization from Below: Towards a Cosmopolitan Legality*. Cambridge: Cambridge University Press, 1–26.

Santos, Cecília MacDowell (2007), "Transnational Legal Activism and the State: Reflections on Cases against Brazil in the Inter-American Commission on Human Rights", *Sur—International Journal of Human Rights*, 4(7), 29–60. Available at https://sur.conectas.org/en/home/issue-07/

Santos, Cecília MacDowell (2010), "Da Delegacia da Mulher à Lei Maria da Penha: Absorção/Tradução de Demandas Feministas pelo Estado", *Revista Crítica de Ciências Sociais*, 89, 153–170. doi: 10.4000/rccs.3759

Thayer, Millie (2010), *Making Transnational Feminism: Rural Women, NGO Activists, and Northern Donors in Brazil*. New York: Routledge.

União de Mulheres de São Paulo (2011), *União de Mulheres de São Paulo, 30 Anos, 1981–2011*. São Paulo: União de Mulheres de São Paulo.

Chapter 9

The Power of Racism in Academia
Knowledge Production and Political Disputes

Marta Araújo and Silvia R. Maeso

Introduction

In Europe the issue of racism has been increasingly addressed in public debates in recent years, particularly in the media, and usually in connection with complaints of cases of segregation, situations of police violence and questions of cultural representation. However, these debates tend to draw attention to the tip of the iceberg, supporting and being supported by a Eurocentric approach to racism that explains it as the result of prejudice on the part of individuals with less acceptance of difference (in urban planning, the police force or the culture industry). The prejudice paradigm (Henriques, 1998)—which resists questioning how difference is produced—makes other understandings of racism invisible. Its hegemony reproduces the absence of debate not only on the diverse conceptualizations of racism underlying the discussion, but also on their implicit political solutions: it is an absence that has been naturalized and legitimized in various contexts.[1] As formulated by Boaventura de Sousa Santos, with regard to the "sociology of absences",

> what does not exist is, in fact, actively produced as such, as a non-credible alternative to what exists. Its empirical object is considered impossible from the perspective of the conventional social sciences, so that its simple formulation already amounts to a rupture with them.
>
> (Santos, 2002: 246)

The aim of this chapter is therefore to contribute towards questioning a conceptualization of racism circulating in both academic and political spheres and which enshrines specific power relations. We consider it vital to understand how proposals for an in-depth, systematic analysis of racism as the legacy of the racial governmentalities of European imperial projects, institutionalized in contemporary democracies, have been delegitimized (Hesse, 2004).

We argue that the lack of debate on the production of knowledge on racism and the different political projects associated with it should be understood as the result of the consensus on race constructed in the West from the inter-war period onwards, and particularly in the 1950s. In *The Silent War: Imperialism and the Changing Perception of Race* (1998), Frank Füredi noted a shift from racial confidence and superiority to racial anxiety and fear in the context of the perceived decline of the West following the moral crisis associated with the acknowledgement of the Holocaust. The emerging "racial etiquette" (illustrated by the founding of UNESCO in 1945) demanded that racism should be formally condemned, as a means of discouraging international mobilization around race against a background of national liberation struggles, the Cold War, the civil rights movement in the USA and the anti-apartheid campaign in South Africa. In other words, this "silent protocol on race" aimed to contain the "reaction" to racism, rather than combat this historical and political phenomenon. As such, the formal condemnation of racism was not accompanied by a commitment to changing the socio-political structures that had generated the existing racial inequalities (Füredi, 1998).

This context is particularly relevant to our understanding of racism in contemporary times, given that its hegemonic conceptualization is closely connected to political and academic concerns over fascism and anti-Semitism. Racism was linked to the Holocaust as "the paradigmatic experience underwriting the abstraction" (Hesse, 2004: 15), thus erasing the routine forms of racial governmentality developed by the various European colonial projects. This gave rise to the idea of "racial prejudice"—the product of specific ideologies which shape a set of beliefs (Ibid.: 11)—which has become prevalent in academic approaches and political debates ever since (notably, in the various statements issued by UNESCO on race and racial prejudice since the 1950s [Barker, 2002: 476; Hesse, 2004]).

The analysis presented in this chapter aims to highlight the way in which the hegemony of a specific conceptualization of racism (and the silences and absences it upholds) safeguards and reproduces racial privilege in academia, considering international processes and debates in relation to the Portuguese context. We therefore examine the theoretical-methodological framework for the prejudice studies paradigm and its centrality in contemporary research on racism, observing the Portuguese context in the first decade of the 21st century in closer detail.[2] The depoliticizing effect of the prejudice paradigm is then contrasted with critical and decolonial approaches to modernity/coloniality and Eurocentrism in the production of knowledge, ending with a proposal for a "political anti-racism" to combat "institutional racism". We focus in particular on political denunciations and debates that have taken place in different universities, including the University of Coimbra and University of Warwick.

The Prejudice Paradigm and the Depoliticization of Racism in the Production of Knowledge[3]

The "racial etiquette" that emerged during the inter-war period would be consolidated in the second half of the century with the proliferation of quantitative approaches to the study of racism—particularly in the field of social psychology in the United States, in its search for scientific status. The prejudice studies paradigm is broadly characterized by methodological individualism (Cohen, 1992: 77), the assumption of a society–individual dichotomy (Henriques, 1998: 60) and a "clinical approach" to social attitudes in order to identify tolerant and racist individuals in a given society (Bonilla-Silva, 2003: 64). Stressing the cognitive and interpersonal processes of the "racist individual", this paradigm has since become hegemonic in academia and in politics, influencing legal and institutional responses to racism which focus on the individual (such as aware-ness campaigns and educational initiatives) and revealing an unrelenting faith in legislation as the guarantor of equality, dignity and human rights.

In this "clinical approach", stereotypes are understood as a deviation from the correct representation, as "transgressions of the rational limits of category use, that is, as irrational categories" (Goldberg, 1990: 321). This results from differentiating between "rational and objective information processing that produces a perfect representation" (in this case, of the "immigrant/minority group") (Henriques, 1998: 75) and "erroneous generalization" (Ibid.: 73), based on prejudice. In this paradigm it is possible to detect, on the one hand, a belief in rationality as the ideal for democratic societies and, on the other hand, a concept of the individual as the *locus* for the breakdown of this rationality (Ibid.: 66). Thus, society is exonerated and understood as the site for democracy, tol-erance and human rights (Goldberg, 2006, 2009), which is only occasionally contaminated by a few "rotten apples" (Henriques, 1998: 62). Moreover, the "racist subject" is seen as "socially sick" and therefore not morally accountable (Goldberg, 1990: 318). This is reflected in the use of metaphors of disease to refer to racism (see also, Hesse, 2004), with the metaphor of cancer, in par-ticular, used frequently, suggesting that racism is abnormal and external, i.e. an intruder in an otherwise healthy body, namely democratic society. Also implicit in this definition of racism as irrational bias is the notion that prejudice is a problem associated with uneducated people who have not been given the "cor-rect" information. This is a very common assumption in academic literature on racism, including studies produced in Portugal: without a conceptualization of racial domination, the prejudice paradigm promotes an understanding of rac-ism as "cognitive bias"—justified by ignorance and fear (particularly in times of "crisis")—which can be "cured" by information and knowledge (Henriques, 1998; Goldberg, 1990; Sarup, 1991).[4] The following citations are illustrative:

> A report by the European Monitoring Centre on Racism and Xenophobia presented in March 2005 stated that most Portuguese feel there is an exces-sive number of foreigners in the country. [...] This position is sometimes interpreted in the press as "resistance to immigrants" or even xenophobia. However, this is not necessarily the case. It is important to note that the Portuguese are in favour of equal civic rights and a multicultural soci-ety. Moreover, this general feeling about the "excessive" number of for-eigners should also be understood in the context of the present economic

environment, which is defined by a shrinking labour market and increasing unemployment. Finally, there has been a lack of information about the economic and social benefits of immigration.

(Fonseca, Malheiros and Silva, 2005: 4–5)

This perception [which views immigrants as consumers of collective resources] is facilitated by the fact that there is no information in the media that immigrants do not compete with citizens in host countries in the same areas of employment, nor about how they contribute to economic growth.

(Vala, Pereira and Ramos, 2006: 223)

From this perspective, prejudice (which results in immigrants being seen as "consumers of collective resources") is explained by a lack of correct information to counter this myth,[5] implying the prescription of education and awareness campaigns in order to cure this evil. This approach disregards the fact that "'ignorance' is an effect of particular knowledge, not an absence of knowledge" (Lesko and Bloom, 1998: 380), thus marginalizing any consideration of ideology and structure.

Within the prejudice paradigm, when research collectively frames such individuals ("racists"), it tends to do so by concentrating on those who are considered deviant groups, such as extremist organizations. This helps to situate racism on the margins of social and political culture, as Paul Gilroy has argued with reference to the British context:

The price of over-identifying the struggle against racism with the activities of these extremist groups and grouplets is that however much of a problem they may be in a particular area (and I am not denying the need to combat their organizing), they are exceptional. They exist on the fringes. [...] A more productive starting point is provided by focusing on racism in the mainstream and seeing "race" and racism not as fringe questions but as a volatile presence at the very centre of British politics.

(Gilroy, 1992: 51)

In contrast, most academic work in this field promotes a narrow understanding of racism—reducing the political to the activities of far-right organizations and absolving the more "moderate" parties—meaning that only the most obvious manifestations are recognized (namely the "politicisation of anti-immigrant discourses" [Marques, 2007: 33]):

It may be said that that not only is there no open racism in Portugal, but also that cases of militant racism are extremely rare.*

*Both public opinion and the authorities have always firmly condemned any racist incidents that have taken place in the past decade.

(Baganha and Marques, 2001: 70)

Portugal is one of the European Union countries in which there are practically no social, party political or broader political expressions of the acceptance and promotion of racist or xenophobic ideologies.

(Machado, 2001: 53)

This frequently resulted in eliminating the issue of power from academic concerns regarding racism, dispensing with the need to investigate its "well-meant" or "moderate" expressions within political centrism or the higher echelons of democratic institutions, thus protecting the racial privilege of the elites (van Dijk, 1993).

Consequently, a great deal of academic work within this paradigm continues to separate racism from the routine forms of racialized governmentality which determine what is identified as racist, making racism dependent on motivation and intent (for example, Machado, 2001: 60–61). This effectively constructs racism as an externality, "an aberrant ideological affront to the enduring ideals of the Enlightenment and the values of the Judeo-Christian tradition" (Hesse, 2004: 22), rather than considering it as a political practice inherent to the founding of the nation state in the history of Europe. The following examples are illustrative of the prevalence of this idea of racism as external to Europe and notions of Europeanness:

In modern societies, racism in fact represents a betrayal of the proclaimed values, a significant departure from the norm of equality.

In a young democracy based on the principle of universal citizenship and built on the ashes of a fascist-inspired regime, expressions of racism effectively constitute a serious distancing from the values of civic, political and legal equality.

(Marques, 2007: 15)

The fight against racism is carried out in several ways, ranging from the exemplary punishment of violent racist crimes to the assertion of the civilizational values of equality and respect for the dignity of human beings.

(Amâncio, 2007: 9–10)

This externalization of racism—on the fringes of "democratic society"—involves both the naturalization of prejudice itself and the reification of difference.

The European Social Survey—an academic transnational survey conducted in 24 countries—would appear to be central to consolidating the approach to racism as prejudiced social attitudes, particularly since the beginning of the 2000s. In these studies, prejudice is identified as occurring within an "endogroup" and directed towards an "exogroup" (Vala, Brito and Lopes, 1999), or in relations between the minority and the majority, thus problematically assuming the rigidity of such groups. The following citations demonstrate how this approach contributes, on the one hand, to reducing racism to ethnocentrism

and heterophobia—by naturalizing them—and, on the other hand, to essential-
izing "ethnic minorities" and delegitimizing the "perception" of racism:

> At the level of individual psychological differences, our model included
> the following variables: *ethnocentrism*, a tendency to reject exogroups, a
> variable emerging from the studies of Adorno (1950), according to which
> discrimination against one exogroup is merely a symptom of a more gen-
> eral tendency to discriminate against any exogroup.
>
> (Vala, Brito and Lopes, 1999: 182–183)

> It is known that Guineans of ethnic Muslim origin live in spatially more
> concentrated areas than average and have strong intra-ethnic and weak
> inter-ethnic social relations and the greatest contrasts with the society
> which surrounds them, in terms of language and religion (Machado, 1999).
> If we add to this the fact that they are the most visible in their difference
> due to their particular clothing, which distinguishes them from all others, it
> is not wrong to think that they may, due to these accumulated differences,
> more often be the target of actions which they take to be racist, and that
> this is precisely what their perceptions reflect.
>
> (Machado, 2001: 69)

With this reification of difference, race is transformed into "the force of prejudice exercised against newcomers [...] an irrational excess" (Goldberg, 2009:
162). The focus is no longer on racism, but "other" "cultures" and "life-
styles"—which are seen as separate, clearly identifiable categories, essentialized
and approached as pathological. This paves the way for an understanding of
racism as a fear of the unknown and hostility towards those seen as a threat "to
our way of life" or, in other words, a natural response to the "other", invoking
what Teun van Dijk has termed "the "ubiquity" argument [...], which says
that prejudice and discrimination are universal, human properties" (1993: 169;
see also Goldberg, 1990: 320–322). This approach therefore explains "racist
attitudes" as a matter of "social and cultural contrasts", reifying the "divide"
between "nationals", who are seen as homogeneous, and "immigrants/minori-
ties" (for example, Machado, 2001: 71; see also Marques, 2007: 50).

The naturalization of hostility (Barker, 1981) effectively transforms the
problem of discrimination into a problem of "integration"—dependent on the
so-called level of social and cultural contrast—and its victims into "potential
objects of tolerance" (Brown, 2006: 3):

> In the case of Portugal, [...] anti-Gypsy racism is stronger than anti-Afri-
> can racism which is, in turn, stronger than anti-Indian racism, which is
> relatively uncommon. The Gypsy minority is precisely the group which
> contains the most social and cultural contrasts, the various African popu-
> lations have marked social contrasts but significant continuities in terms

of sociability, language or religion, while the Indian minorities combine cultural contrasts with social continuities.

(Machado, 2001: 71–72)

Unlike the situation in countries with a longer history of immigration, immigrants have not, so far, been targeted by differentialist racism, which may be due to various different factors. Firstly, the existence of significant cultural continuities between immigrants of African origin and the Portuguese with whom they are in closest contact should be emphasised. In other words, unlike the northern European countries, there are no truly significant cultural contrasts – in terms of language, religion and even family structures—between the majority of the immigrant populations and the autochthonous population.

(Marques, 2007: 50–51)

This approach, based on a view of prejudice as biased knowledge about the "other", ends up by shifting "the object of the study from the prejudiced person onto the stimulus object" (Sarup, 1991: 56), blaming the victims of racism—constructed as the "unknown object"—rather than addressing the "unknowing" subject (Ibid.) and how this lack of knowledge is produced. As a result, the problem under debate is no longer discrimination, but difference. "Proof" of willingness to integrate is the solution:

Individuals from Eastern Europe frequently have (or claim to have) higher qualifications […] although, for many of these immigrants, the jobs they initially get require considerably fewer qualifications than they actually possess, it is expected that when they have acquired a reasonable command of Portuguese and provided proof of their ability to work in more qualified or specialised jobs, they will gradually gain entry to these positions.

(Rocha-Trindade, 2003: 177)

In fact, this inverted rationale reflects the idea that it is racial and cultural diversity—and not its political management or underlying racist logics—which has created tensions and conflict, as the following extract demonstrates:

The ethnic or "racial" conflict observable in the suburbs of the main cities has its roots in the problems of social mobility, fear of exclusion and uneasiness regarding the[ir] equation to the social status of the "immigrant". Racism is therefore expressed by transferring the existing difficulties of autochthonous people to the close presence of immigrant populations.

(Marques, 2007: 41)

Consequently, most empirical studies on racism in Portugal have been undertaken in the Lisbon metropolitan area where "immigrants" and "ethnic minorities" tend to be based—the area defined as their *empirical concentration* (Machado, 2001; Ferreira, 2003). This assumes and reproduces the idea of hostility or fear as a natural reaction to "contact" with the "presence" of "immigrants" or "minorities", most of whom live in "disadvantaged neighbourhoods". This reading of racism as the result of direct contact with the "other" is explained as the contrast between the "exoticism" of the immigrant and the "modernity" of the host society (Sayyid, 2004; Hesse and Sayyid, 2006).

Significantly, the approach to racism which we have attempted to define grounded on the Portuguese case is also hegemonic in other contexts. We will now examine this, on the basis of various cases of political disputes in universities.

(Anti-)Racism as Political Dispute, the University as an Arena of Struggle

In March 2016, an episode of the discussion programme *Ce soir (ou jamais!)*— broadcast by one of the main French state television channels—was dedicated to the anti-racist struggle and its internal divisions: it opened by asking "What's the current situation of the anti-racist movement? Has it failed?". Frédéric Taddeï, the journalist who moderated the debate, began by asking the guests: "What has changed in the anti-racist movement?" The different replies mirrored the political map of the dispute over (anti-)racism in Europe, beyond France's specific historico-political reality: the photographer Oliviero Toscani[6] considered that racism was not relevant since the main gap was between the rich and the poor and argued that, if we declare ourselves as anti-racist, we are accepting racism; Emmanuel Debono, a historian, stated that the anti-racist movement had always been deeply divided but that there had been a transition from universalism to a more communitarian form of activism; Nadia Remadna, a mediator in suburban neighbourhoods and the founder of the association *La brigade des mères*, noted that nowadays there is an intercommunity racism in neighbourhoods where people were trapped in self-victimization; Maboula Soumahoro, a teacher of Afro-American studies and the organizer of the *Journées Africana*, stressed that the racialized had taken up the debate today and that racism was not a question of feelings, but a system of oppression, exclusion and marginalization; Houria Bouteldja, a spokesperson for the *Parti des indigènes de la République*, stressed the need to point out that he will address state racism rather than intercommunity racism, and therefore political anti-racism; that is, the fight against structural racism in a context of dominated by moral anti-racism; finally, the political scientist Thomas Guénolé claimed that what has changed is the fact that nowadays the majority of anti-racist movements were racist (i.e. the configuration of "anti-white racism") and gave the example of the political and intellectual work of Houria Bouteldja.[7] On the basis of this mapping, we can identify three cleavages within the political debate that reveal the legacies of the process of depoliticizing (anti-)racism analyzed in the previous section. Firstly, in opposition to an understanding of racism as a system of oppression historically rooted in modernity/coloniality (Quijano, 2000; Hesse, 2004; Goldberg, 2006; Dussel, 2008;), the dominant conceptualization focuses on the ubiquity of prejudice in most forms of social relation; secondly, the fight against political processes which protect/reproduce white privilege (for example: legislation, public policies and international politics) is marginalized by a moralizing anti-racism whose mission is to educate and correct racist individuals (Cox, 1970 [1948]: 519–538; Henriques, 1998[1984]); finally, the "political existence" of those who are racialized (Khiari, 2009: 9–18; Bouteldja, 2016: 111–118) is delegitimized by this moral anti-racism, which considers that race "consciousness" itself (i.e. political struggles that assume that the hierarchization of races is the product of historico-political processes) reproduces racism.

It is therefore crucial to stress that anti-racism is a political field that encompasses fundamental differences, both in the production of knowledge on racism itself and in the proposals for political change. In the current European context, since the mid-1990s, the contours of these differences have been shaped by the incorporation of anti-discrimination legislation and discourses of "diversity" and "interculturality" in the public policies implemented by various states. Jointly with hegemonic anti-racist organizations and the diverse "academic industries" in this area (ranging from studies on migration and minorities to studies on prejudice and attitudes), there has been a strengthening of the denial of structural racism and bringing discredit on political anti-racism (see Lentin, 2004, 2008; Essed and Nimako, 2006; Araújo, 2013; Maeso and Araújo, 2014).

Although marginal, decolonial approaches and critical studies on race produced by academics and anti-racist organizations are challenging the conventional Eurocentric approach to the problem of racism within the broader Euro-American context. They provide continuity with the political struggles which, since at least the 1940s, have developed a radical critique of prejudice and policies focusing on "integration" or moral reform. These struggles have brought about a subversive appropriation of the concept of racism, as analyzed by Barnor Hesse in the North American context. For Hesse, the emergence of "black analytics"—or a "black sociology" within academia—has confronted the conceptualization of racism (*qua* Nazi regime) as an illiberal aberration, and the protection and silencing of "white normativity" in the colonial governmentality over the non-West (Hesse, 2014: 148–156). Within this context, the sociologist Oliver Cox wrote, in 1948, an in-depth critique of abstract approaches to racism in the form of general theories on ethnocentrism and conflict, or as a set of ideas and philosophies. Cox proposed to situate the historical understanding of race within modernity and the colonial domination of Europeans over non-Europeans (1970 [1948]: 477–484. He was equally critical of Gunnar Myrdal's construction of the "Negro problem" and, in particular, his confidence in white people's moral reform. Cox considered that, amongst other aspects, he evaded the question of the "struggle for power" (Ibid.: 534) and framed racial prejudice as a "moral dilemma", for ultimately trusting in "time" as "the great corrector of all evil" (Ibid.: 538). In 1967, Stokely Carmichael (later known as Kwame Ture) and Charles Hamilton published the book *Black Power: The Politics of Liberation in America,* that also contested the mainstream approach to "racial prejudice" and the question of "intentionality", which currently underlies the moral approach to (anti-)racism. They denounced racism as the result of "inaction" by "established and respected" individuals, which was contributing towards keeping blacks in a subordinate position in the USA, in a situation of internal colonialism—in housing, education and the economy, for example (1971: 19–22). Thus, "institutional racism" was conceived of as "maintained deliberately by the power structure and through indifference, inertia and lack of courage on the part of the white masses as well as petty officials" (Ibid.: 38). The work of Cox, Carmichael/Ture and Hamilton illustrates how the struggle for the politicization of anti-racism since the 1940s has made the question of power a key issue, unlike the hegemonic approaches constructed around the demystification of stereotypes.

In recent years, the political debate on (anti-)racism in the university, both in terms of everyday social relationships and the production of knowledge, has re-emerged in the Euro-American context and within this process we can acknowledge the continuities with the abovementioned divergences. Universities, like states, present themselves as institutional spaces in which "racism is not permitted", an affirmation that, however, ends up translated into the idea that "racism is not a problem".

We will now analyze two cases of denunciations of racism at the University of Coimbra and the University of Warwick that exemplify the lack of any effective anti-racist policy in universities, a situation which is closely linked to the enduring Eurocentric approach to racism.

In January 2014, a group of students of the University of Coimbra (UC) launched a campaign to denounce several situations where they had been subjected to racist, sexist and homophobic treatment by colleagues and lecturers.[8] The campaign followed the model used in other universities around the world in recent years, particularly in the United States, whereby students (usually appearing anonymously) displayed placards bearing the offensive words that had been addressed to them. The news of the discriminatory acts was first reported by the Brazilian media,[9] since most of the students who made public these denunciations were from Brazil. In addition to a social media campaign, a small demonstration was also held at the beginning of 2014 and an open letter was sent to the University requesting an official inquiry and the creation of a system for reporting and combatting discrimination.[10]

The UC was reluctant to accept the complains and did not open an official inquiry. It presented its official position on the university website on 17 February 2014 (UC, 2014), in a text that ended up encouraging a "victim-blaming" discourse by portraying the students who had been harassed as "suspicious" (publicly affirming that they were "raising suspicions of xenophobic behaviour", somehow implying that the students that were "spreading suspicions" had acted irresponsibly by providing "extremely vague" reports of "alleged cases" [UC, 2014]). The UC, the university with the greatest international profile in the country,[11] also reacted by launching and circulating videos containing statements by other Brazilian students testifying to how well-integrated they felt in Coimbra and at the university[12]—thus contributing even more to constructing those who had reported cases of discrimination as politically biased and tendentious and, consequently, protecting racial privilege. Thus, the UC reaffirmed its "ivory tower" position, evoking its past history of intellectual struggle for freedom:

> The centuries-long productive conviviality between students from count-less different places is one of the hallmarks of the University of Coimbra. As a university, freedom, debating ideas and sharing different perspectives constitute a legacy that we greatly value. […] Naturally, the University of Coimbra is not immune to the problems raised by the existing prejudices and stereotypes in this society. In a context of more than 30,000 individuals there will always be occasional disagreements and misunderstandings provoked by a wide range of reasons, either between Portuguese nationals, or between citizens from other countries or involving people of different nationalities. None of this should be mistaken for an atmosphere of xenophobia at the University of Coimbra.
>
> (UC, 2014)

We would like to highlight the Eurocentric concept of racism (Hesse, 2004) invoked in this excerpt—within the prejudice paradigm—as a model which evades the routine practices of the racialized governmentality inherited from colonialism and, therefore, institutional racism. We will focus on three aspects: firstly, the presentation of the university as historically free of racism and defined by "a centuries-long conviviality"; secondly, the naturalization of the "[alleged] atmosphere of xenophobia", considered to be created by a series of random events resulting from an "ordinary" problem of interpersonal relations; thirdly, the levelling out of a historically asymmetrical power relationship. In emphasizing the tradition of freedom and "debate" at the UC, the verbal offences are reinterpreted as merely an "exchange of opinions" amongst people of the same or different nationalities.

In April 2014, two students and a researcher had a meeting with the Student Ombudsman (*Provedor do Estudante*) at the UC, who stated that he agreed with the official position of the university and stressed that the lack of any formal complaint prevented him from intervening. Although the students pointed out that focusing on individual formal complaints places the issue as a matter of the victim's responsibility and their behaviour becomes the subject of discussion, the Ombudsman was sceptical of the possibility of the Principal's cabinet agreeing to adopt an intervention protocol. The students eventually returned to Brazil without any official inquiry having been opened and the case no longer received any public attention, like many similar situations which have not been reported due to the lack of any safe system that would enable students to denounce cases of racism.[13] The message conveyed by the UC, albeit inadvertently, was that there was no need to make provisions for reporting and discussing racism. The institutional mechanisms of the university ensured that the case did not receive due attention, thus transforming racist behaviour into a series of isolated incidents lacking evidence: the phenomenon disappeared when the (politicized) students returned to Brazil.

On 5 April 2016, Faramade Ifaturoti, a first-year student at the University of Warwick, posted a photograph via her Twitter account—taken in the kitchen of her residence hall on the university campus—showing a bunch of bananas with the words "monkey!" and "n***a!" written on them. "Just entered my kitchen and look at what one of my flatmates has done. I am extremely disgusted @ WarwickAccomm", Ifaturoti wrote, including the user name of the university accommodation service provider, *Warwick Accommodation*, so that they would be aware of the episode. On the same day, the Warwick student newspaper, *The Boar*, published a report on the incident, noting that the tweet was being widely shared—a hashtag (#WeStandWithFara) had been created to show solidarity with the student—and the university was investigating the incident. The *Warwick Anti-Racism Society* (WARSoc), a student association founded in 2013, told the newspaper: "The Warwick Accommodation handbook has absolutely nothing regarding racism, yet the institution will happily shout about diversity and champion signing the Race Equality Charter" (Pickard, 2016).

WARSoc created a public petition[14] asking for the university to be held accountable for racism within its walls. The text contained three demands: a thorough review of its policy on racial discrimination at the university; the transformation of the curriculum that perpetuates Eurocentric knowledge[15] and ignores both the ideas of non-white intellectuals and academics and the experiences of black and ethnic minority students; and greater representation of black and ethnic minority students in the different areas of the university.

Articles and posts published over the next few days in the student newspaper and on social media revealed, on the one hand, discrepancies in the efforts made by the university, and specifically the accommodation service, to respond to the situation affecting the student (Barker and Pickard, 2016); and, on the other, the recurrence of students' experiences of racism at the university.[16] *The Boar* published various testimonies from students which exposed the lack of any adequate institutional response:[17]

> I've felt the university cares little for the wellbeing of minorities on campus. In my first year, I was called a n****r for two terms by a flatmate, another flatmate labelled [me] a terrorist and called [me] a "dirty, brown, Tamil girl". I had someone tell me they didn't think I was intelligent because I was black. I had flatmates tell me they'd never date black women, employing derogatory terms and using to [*sic*] racist stereotypes to justify their disgusting attitudes. Reporting it was futile because there were no

dire consequences for the perpetrators and the residence tutor would say there was "no evidence" so they "couldn't intervene".

(Anonymous Writer, 2016)

These two cases are not exceptions. In Britain, the debate on racism and Eurocentrism in the curriculum has been addressed, since 2014, by the campaign and film "*Why is my curriculum white?*" led by the Black & Minority Ethnic Students' Network at London University.[18]

In the Netherlands, the international meeting "Decolonizing the University" was jointly organized by the organizations New Urban Collective and University of Colour, and held at the University of Amsterdam in October 2015.[19] This event gathered mainly political activists, students and researchers, and brought about international struggles, aiming to analyze racism and Eurocentrism at the university and explore proposals for its transformation.

In South Africa, the *Rhodes Must Fall* movement, organized by students, teachers and employees of the University of Cape Town, started a debate, in March 2015, on institutional racism at the university and the decolonization of knowledge. One of its initiatives was the campaign to remove the statue of the British imperialist Cecil Rhodes from the university campus—inaugurated in 1934 to honour him and the fact that he had "donated" the land where the university was built. The statue was removed on 9 April 2015.[20]

In the United States, movements dedicated to debating the nation's racist legacy exist in various universities. In 2015, for example, the *Black Justice League* at Princeton University initiated a debate on the central role of Woodrow Wilson in the university's identity and drew up a list of demands which included recognition of the racist legacy that Wilson represents—they demanded the university to remove a mural painted in his honour and Wilson's name from buildings on the campus—and a public debate on freedom of expression and anti-black racism. [21]

These cases show how universities protect racist structures and practices and how racism is a key issue in the functioning of these institutions as a whole (Law, Philips and Turney, 2004). However, they also show how the political argument surrounding anti-racism will install itself in its midst, despite resistance in the different spheres of institutional life. It is a dispute that is reviving and reinscribing longstanding demands for the transformation of the curriculum and the effective fight against racism in everyday academic life. In different contexts, this debate is already challenging the actual history of universities—in terms of their relationship to colonialism and its legacies—and the benevolent images of "coexistence" and "diversity".

Conclusions

Anti-racism must repoliticise the origins and the stakes of racism and, for this, its allies shall be few.

(Lentin, 2004: 317)

Our aim in this chapter has been to show how—in academic production and everyday university life—the discussion on racism effectively evades the issue of its institutionalization. This absence in the debate is constantly produced by the workings of certain structures, processes and routine practices (Essed, 1991) which enshrine a Eurocentric understanding of racism (Hesse, 2004). It is therefore seen as a set of "wrong" or "biased" ideas about people who are viewed as "different", leading to "natural" feelings of "fear" and "hostility" when faced with the "unknown". Consequently, two interrelated processes emerge: on the one hand, the establishment of the "us/others" boundary and the reification of difference; on the other hand, suspicion and the blaming of victims who denounce incidences of racial discrimination. Institutional racism thus ends up being reproduced through its denial, including via specific initiatives launched in the name of "fostering equality", "integration of minorities" or "cultural diversity", which disconnect racism from white privilege and, therefore, from its history.

In contrast, and in line with both the proposals produced by grassroots anti-racist and decolonial movements, and critical theories of race, we consider racism a historically configured political phenomenon and the notion of institutional racism crucial to understanding prejudices and attitudes as merely the tip of the iceberg, reflecting socio-political structures which are significant generators and reproducers of inequality. This reveals how identifying the racist or prejudiced subject—and demanding that "proof" must be found—is a fallacy. As Philomena Essed argues, "the term 'individual racism' is a contradiction in itself because racism is, by definition, the expression or activation of group power" (1991: 37). Thus, she proposes a more productive approach, which involves identifying the ways in which racism is routinely reproduced and renewed through discriminatory ideologies, processes and structures. This explains the inadequacy of any diagnosis of the problem that merely leads to identifying and morally punishing individuals or racist acts. Sara Ahmed, reflecting on the basis of her research, experience and pedagogical work on race and diversity in universities, argues that the institution constructs an insurmountable "brick wall" when confronted with accusations of racism:

> To speak about racism would hurt not just the organisation, reimagined as a subject with feelings, but also those subjects who identify with the organisation. They would be hurt by what is heard as a charge, such that the charge becomes *about their* hurt. There is an implicit injunction not to speak about racism, to protect whiteness from being hurt. Speaking about racism is thus heard as an injury, not to those who speak but to those who are spoken about
>
> (Ahmed, 2012: 147; italics in original).

A conceptual framework that included race/power, its history and contemporary legacies within the different areas analyzed here would therefore allow for the discussion of diverse notions of racism as a political phenomenon which permeate the production of knowledge on the "problem". This is crucial to pursue political solutions that have the genuine capacity to challenge structures and canons, abandoning the banalizing discourses on diversity in favour of an in-depth discussion on decolonizing the university. This discussion, although marginal, is nowadays a reality. As we have seen in this chapter, universities, like other institutional domains, are on the defensive over their "wounded pride". In this context, white privilege is at stake and therefore "allies" in the anti-racist struggle "shall be few".

Notes

1 See also Araújo (2013).
2 Studies on racism have been relatively scarce in Portugal and the subject can only be considered an academic research field since the late 1990s. From an early stage, it was an area defined by studies in social psychology, the sociology of inequality and migration, and urban geography. Although research within the sociology of inequality and migration and urban geography does not focus as specifically on the problem of racism, the work published in these areas has produced interpretations of this phenomenon which should be considered here.
3 This section draws on a literature review undertaken for the project *TOLERACE—The semantics of tolerance and (anti-)racism in Europe: Public bodies and civil society in comparative perspective* (2010–2013, EC, ref. 244633). The project was coordinated by a research team based at the Centre for Social Studies led by Boaventura de Sousa Santos, Silvia Maeso and Marta Araújo. For further information, see <www.ces.uc.pt/projectos/tolerace>.
4 Most contemporary approaches share this assumption, proposing liberal political initiatives to deal with racism which tend to evade the dynamics of power and focus on understanding the "other".
5 For an analysis of this rationale in political-academic discourse in Portugal from the 2000s onwards, see Maeso and Araújo (2013, 2014).
6 Responsible for advertising campaigns for the Italian company *United Colors of Benetton* in the 1990s.
7 Debate broadcast on 18 March. Sabrina Goldman, a representative from the International League against Racism and Anti-Semitism (LICRA), and the political scientist Anastasia Colosimo also participated in the debate. Consulted on 11 April 2016, available at <www.youtube.com/watch?v=eNl7G90aaFk&nohtml5=False>. The debate had major repercussions on social networks and both left-wing and right-wing political discussion forums. On 28 March Houria Bouteldja and Maboula Soumahoro organized a debate at *La Java* in Paris, moderated by Nacira Guénif-Souilamas, a sociologist and member of *Marche des femmes pour la dignité* (Madef), to discuss the significance of the television debate and its political consequences. Consulted on 11 May 2016, available at <www.reperes-antiracistes.org/2016/04/ce-soir-ou-jamais-sur-l-antiracisme-decryptage-par-h-bouteldja-m-soumahoro-n-guenif.html>.
8 This campaign was supported by *Lista R*, one of the lists of candidates for the elections for the Directorate-General of the *Associação Académica de Coimbra*, the students' union. See <http://resetaaac.wix.com/lista-r#!/c1iqw>, consulted on 16 October 2015.
9 See <http://oglobo.globo.com/sociedade/educacao/alunos-denunciam-preconceito-na-universidade-de-coimbra-11263679>, consulted on 16 October 2015.

10 We were involved in this process of reporting and mobilization, via *Coimbra Contra a Opressão*, a network of students and activists.
11 *Jornal i*, 13 November 2015, consulted on 31 January 2016, available at <www.ionline .pt/480104>.
12 See, for example, <www.youtube.com/watch?v=5tvDawkL7Jg&list=PLXU1zPdSn JEEd9cexi-zW9AoFPqlCqjou>, consulted on 16 October 2015.
13 Although the students could have submitted a complain to the justice system, it should be noted that they were in a vulnerable situation, since the denunciations referred to teachers as well as colleagues, and they were also grant-holders.
14 Consulted on 10 April 2016, available at <www.change.org/p/warwick-university -the-university-of-warwick-must-be-held-accountable-for-racism-within-its-walls? recruiter=522348992&utm_source=share_petition&utm_medium=copylink>.
15 WARSoc has organized numerous debates on racism in the university, as well as on the organization of black and ethnic minority students, and the fight against Eurocentrism and the reproduction of colonial knowledge in the curriculum. In March 2016, the first conference was held on the theme *Decolonising our university*, attended by teachers and students from Warwick University and other British institutions. Consulted on 13 April 2016, available at <www.warwicksu.com/events/4000/13586>.
16 *The Boar*, together with other student newspapers, set up an anonymous online survey on racism in British universities. Consulted on 14 April 2016, available at <https://docs .google.com/forms/d/1f92fTWumsqZ3tieP5K8QyEC5G76UjZGNpGhEI7ORGHk /viewform>.
17 This situation was also reported in numerous comments by individuals who signed the WARSoc public petition.
18 Consulted on 13 April 2016, available at <https://blogs.ucl.ac.uk/events/2014/11/21 /ucl-faces-race-why-is-my-curriculum-white>.
19 Consulted on 26 January 2016, available at <http://nucnet.nl/decolonizing-the-univer sity-conference-october-24th-2015-vu-university-amsterdam>.
20 Consulted on 26 January 2016, available at http://rhodesmustfall.co.za/
21 Consulted on 23 February 2016, available at www.change.org/p/princeton-universi ty-administration-occupynassau-meet-black-student-s-demands. In April 2016, the University Board of Trustees decided to keep the mural and Wilson's name on the buildings. Christopher L. Eisgruber, the University President, stated that they had made the right decision, since "the best way to pursue diversity and inclusion is not by tearing down names from the past but rather being more honest about our history, including the bad parts of our history" (Markovich, 2016).

References

Adorno, Theodor W. (1950), *The Authoritarian personality*. New York: Harper.
Ahmed, Sara (2012), *On Being Included: Racism and Institutional Life*. Durham, NC: Duke University Press.
Amâncio, Lígia (2007), "Prefácio", in Rosa Cabecinhas (ed.), *Preto e branco: A naturalisation da discriminação racial*. Porto: Campo das Letras, 7–10.
Anonymous Writer (2016), "Testimonials of Racism on Campus: It Affects Us All", *The Boar*, 12 April. Accessed 13.04.2016, at https://theboar.org/2016/04/testimonials-raci sm-campus
Araújo, Marta (2013), "Challenging Narratives on Diversity and Immigration in Portugal: The (De)politicization of Colonialism and Racism", in Jorge Capetillo, Glenn Jacobs

and Philip Kretsedemas (eds.), *Migrant Marginality: A Transnational Perspective*. New York: Routledge, 27–46.

Baganha, Maria Ioannis; Marques, José Carlos (2001), *Imigração e política: O caso português*. Lisbon: Fundação Luso-Americana para o Desenvolvimento.

Barker, Martin (1981), *The New Racism*. London: Junction Books.

Barker, Martin (2002), "Reflections on 'The Problems with Racism'", in Philomena Essed and David Goldberg (eds.), *Race Critical Theories. Text and Context*. Malden, MA: Blackwell Publishing, 471–480.

Barker, Matt; Pickard, Lily (2016), "Four Hours, 'No Response': Warwick Reaction to Racist Incident under Fire", *The Boar*, 7 April. Accessed 12.04.2016 at https://theboar.org/2016/04/four-hours-no-response-warwick-act-quickly-enough

Bonilla-Silva, Eduardo (2003), "Racial Attitudes or Racial Ideology? An Alternative Paradigm for Examining Actors' Racial Views", *Journal of Political Ideologies*, 8(1), 63–82. doi: 10.1080/13569310306082

Bouteldja, Houria (2016), *Les Blancs, les Juifs et nous. Vers une politique de l'amour révolutionnaire*. Paris: La Fabrique.

Brown, Wendy (2006), *Regulating Aversion. Tolerance in the Age of Identity and Empire*. Princeton, NJ: Princeton University Press.

Carmichael, Stokely (Ture, Kwame); Hamilton, Charles V. (1971), *Black Power: The Politics of Liberation in America*. New York: Vintage [reprint; orig. 1967].

Cohen, Phil (1992), "It's Racism What Dunnit! Hidden Narratives in Theories of Racism", in Ali Rattansi and James Donald (eds.), *'Race', Culture and Difference*. London: SAGE/Open University, 62–103.

Cox, Oliver C. (1970 [1948]), *Caste, Class and Race. A Study in Social Dynamics*. New York: Monthly Review.

Dussel, Enrique (2008), *1492. El encubrimiento del Otro. Hacia el origen del "Mito de la modernidad"*. La Paz: Biblioteca Indígena.

Essed, Philomena (1991), *Understanding Everyday Racism*. London: SAGE.

Essed, Philomena; Nimako, Kwame (2006), "Designs and (Co)incidents. Cultures of Scholarship and Public Policy on Immigrants/Minorities in the Netherlands", *International Journal of Comparative Sociology*, 47(3/4), 281–312. doi: 10.1177/0020715206065784

Ferreira, Vítor Sérgio (2003), "Uma Polaroid Sociográfica", in Vítor Sérgio, Ferreira, Marcus Eugêneo Lima, Diniz Lopes and Jorge Vala (eds.), *Simetrias e identidades: Jovens negros em Portugal*. Oeiras: Celta, 23–50.

Fonseca, Maria Lucinda; Malheiros, Jorge Macaísta; Silva, Sandra (2005), "Portugal", in Jan Niessen, Yongmi Schibel and Cressida Thompson (eds.), *Current Immigration Debates in Europe: A Publication of the European Migration Dialogue*. Brussels: MPG. Accessed 18.09.2016 at http://citeseerx.ist.psu.edu/viewdoc/summary?doi=10.1.1.506.1428

Füredi, Frank (1998), *The Silent War: Imperialism and the Changing Perception of Race*. New Brunswick, NJ: Rutgers University Press.

Gilroy, Paul (1992), "The End of Anti-Racism", in James Donald and Ali Rattansi (eds.), *'Race', Culture, and Difference*. London: SAGE, 49–61.

Goldberg, David Theo (1990), "Racism and Rationality: The Need for a New Critique", *Philosophy of the Social Sciences*, 20(3), 317–350. doi: 10.1177/004839319002000303

Goldberg, David Theo (2006), "Racial Europeanization", *Ethnic and Racial Studies*, 29(2), 331–364. doi: 10.1080/01419870500465611

Goldberg, David Theo (2009), *The Threat of Race. Reflections on Racial Neoliberalism*. Malden, MA: Wiley-Blackwell.

Henriques, Julian (1998[1984]), "Social Psychology and the Politics of Racism", in Julian Henriques, Wendy Hollway, Cathy Urwin, Couze Venn and Valerie Walkerdine (eds.), *Changing the Subject: Psychology, Social Regulation and Subjectivity*. London: Routledge, 60–90.

Hesse, Barnor (2004), "Im/plausible Deniability: Racism's Conceptual Double Bind", *Social Identities*, 10(1), 9–29. doi: 10.1080/1350463042000190976

Hesse, Barnor (2014), "Racism's Alterity. The After-Life of Black Sociology", in Wulf D. Hund and Alana Lentin (ed.), *Racism and Sociology—Racism Analysis | Yearbook 5*. Berlin: LIT, 141–174.

Hesse, Barnor; Sayyid, Salman (2006), "Narrating the Postcolonial Political and the Immigrant Imaginary", in Nasreen Ali; Virinder S. Kalra; Salman Sayyid (eds.), *A Postcolonial People: South Asians in Britain*. London: Hurst, 13–31.

Khiari, Sadri (2009), *La contre-révolution coloniale en France. De Gaulle à Sarkozy*. Paris: La Fabrique.

Law, Ian; Philips, Deborah; Turney, Laura (eds.), (2004), *Institutional racism in higher education*. Stoke-on-Trent: Trentham Books.

Lentin, Alana (2004), *Racism and Anti-racism in Europe*. London: Pluto.

Lentin, Alana (2008), "After Anti-racism?", *European Journal of Cultural Studies*, 11(3), 311–331. doi: 10.1177/1367549408091846

Lesko, Nancy; Bloom, Leslie (1998), "Close Encounters: Truth, Experience and Interpretation in Multicultural Teacher Education", *Journal of Curriculum Studies*, 30(4), 375–395. doi: 10.1080/002202798183530

Machado, Fernando Luís (1999), "Imigrantes e estrutura social", *Sociologia—Problemas e Práticas*, 36, 51–76.

Machado, Fernando Luís (2001), "Contextos e percepções de racismo no quotidiano", *Sociologia—Problemas e Práticas*, 36, 53–80. Available at http://www.scielo.mec.pt/pdf/spp/n36/n36a03.pdf

Maeso, Silvia Rodríguez; Araújo, Marta (2013), "A quadratura do círculo: (Anti)racismo, imigração e a(s) política(s) da integração em Portugal nos anos 2000", *Oficina do CES*, 407. Available at http://www.ces.uc.pt/projectos/tolerace/pages/pt/dissemination-materials-activities/publications.html

Maeso, Silvia Rodríguez; Araújo, Marta (2014), "The Politics of (Anti-)racism. Academic Research and Policy Discourse in Europe", in Wulf D. Hund and Alana Lentin (eds.), *Racism and Sociology—Racism Analysis | Yearbook 5*. Berlin: LIT, 207–237.

Markovich, Alexandra (2016), "Princeton Board Votes to Keep Woodrow Wilson's Name on Campus Buildings", *The New York Times*, 4 April. Accessed 12.04.2016 at http://www.nytimes.com/2016/04/05/nyregion/princeton-board-votes-to-keep-woodrow-wilsons-name-on-campus-buildings.html

Marques, João Filipe (2007), *Do "não racismo" dos portugueses aos dois racismos dos portugueses*. Lisbon: ACIDI.

Pickard, Lily (2016), "BREAKING: Racist Incident Reported in Warwick Halls of Residence", *The Boar*, 5 April. Accessed 10.04.2016 at http://theboar.org/2016/04/breaking-racist-incident-reported-warwick-halls-residence

Quijano, Aníbal (2000), "Coloniality of Power, Eurocentrism and Latin America", *Nepantla: Views from South*, 1(3), 533–580. Available at https://muse.jhu.edu/article/23906/summary

Rocha-Trindade, Maria Beatriz (2003), "A realidade da imigração em Portugal", in *do Actas I congresso imigração em Portugal: Diversidade, cidadania, integração*. Lisbon: ACIME, 172–183.

Available at http://www.museu-emigrantes.org/docs/conhecimento/actas_Icongresso%20imigracao%20em%20portugal.pdf

Santos, Boaventura de Sousa (2002), "Para uma sociologia das ausências e uma sociologia das emergências", *Revista Crítica de Ciências Sociais*, 63, 237–280. doi: 10.4000/rccs.1285

Sarup, Madan (1991), *Education and the ideologies of racism*. Stoke-on-Trent: Trentham Books.

Sayyid, Salman (2004), "Slippery People: The Immigrant Imaginary and the Grammar of Colours", in Ian Law; Deborah Phillips; Laura Turney (eds.), *Institutional Racism in Higher Education*. Stoke on Trent: Trentham Books, 149–159.

UC—Universidade de Coimbra (2014), *Posição oficial sobre alegados casos de xenofobia na UC*, 17 February. Accessed 16.10.2015, at http://www.uc.pt/tomenota/2014/022014/17022014_2

Vala, Jorge; Brito, Rodrigo; Lopes, Diniz (1999), *Expressões dos racismos em Portugal*. Oeiras: Celta.

Vala, Jorge; Pereira, Cícero; Ramos, Alice (2006), "Preconceito racial, percepção de ameaça e oposição à imigração", in Jorge Vala and Anália Torres (eds.), *Contextos e atitudes sociais na Europa*. Lisbon: Imprensa de Ciências Sociais, 221–250.

van Dijk, Teun (1993), *Elite Discourse and Racism*. Newbury Park, CA: SAGE. Available at http://discourses.org/download/books

The Roma Collective Memory and the Epistemological Limits of Western Historiography

Cayetano Fernández

> From this cell of history this mute grave, we birth our rage.
>
> Janice Mirikitani, *"Prisons of Silence"*

Introduction

From the emergence of the first generation of Roma scholars to the current debates, confronting the hegemonic conception of "Roma history" has been a constant struggle. History, together with linguistics, is one of the fields to which Roma authors have contributed the most and have devoted more effort to challenging the hegemonic narrative created about us, without us. This is, in fact, understandable, given that looking for answers in history is never a neutral process for us, but something embedded in us. In one way or another we are looking for ourselves within this history, for links with our ancestors and, through them, with the very foundations of the identity that defines us as individuals and as a human collective. However, this drive is always frustrated, since what we find in this history is not our history, but a white creation about us and our ancestors, a Gadji[1] view of us that amounts to nothing more than an ontological search for white identity and legitimation.

Different authors have dealt with this imbalance in different ways, ranging from Ian Hancock's (1987) approach in his masterful *"The pariah syndrome"* which attempts to shed some light on one of the darkest periods hidden in the prevailing historiography on the Roma, namely the enslavement of Roma in Moldavia and Wallachia until 1856, to Marcel Courthiade's (2016) critique of the biased and prejudiced argument for the historical origins of the Roma, or Sarah Carmona's (2013) efforts, based on archival research, to produce reliable data to support statements made by other Roma scholars. This list of efforts by Roma intellectuals could certainly be enlarged: an entire trend of thought is attempting to confront the hegemonic framing of "Roma history" by "re-writing", or somehow striving to "re-right" history, either by producing knowledge on the hidden aspects of our collective memories or criticizing certain methodologies. This approach assumes that this is actually a possibility, as if the aporia within this discipline is just a minor technical problem that needs to be located, isolated and fixed.

Since the value, relevance and commitment of these contributions are downplayed, when these critical approaches emerge in academia they seem destined to experience the same frustrations previously noted or, at best, are consigned to the margins of academic debates and considered secondary literature, as has been the case since the very foundation of the so-called Romani Studies.

This highlights a prior, deeper problematic: the question of the limitations of the epistemological foundations of history as a discipline traversed by a system of racist domination based on European modernity and its civilizing pretensions. It is a debate which should address the issue of a "Roma history" produced by such a deep-rooted and partisan perspective on the fluctuating alterity embedded in the memory of our ancestors, and the credibility—or even the possibility—of continuing to struggle to rectify "Roma history" without questioning the epistemological grounds of this discipline or, alternatively, whether these efforts should be redirected towards developing a "counter-history" which displaces the modern logic that claims self-legitimation by turning us into the inner barbarian within European societies. It should also examine how this depiction of the Roma-other configured by history is affecting the present power relations that condition the materiality of our life in contemporary Europe and the political implications this has for the Roma as a collective subject.

How Important Should History Be for Us?

Before moving on to discuss the limitations and conflicts that "Roma history" as a modern discipline presents, it is worth reflecting on the importance for us of facing this issue as Roma. Hence, it is necessary to pay attention firstly to our own collective experience of this matter, but also to the experience of other peoples who, like us, have been historically, politically and spatially placed below the line of humanity denounced by Frantz Fanon (1952 [1986], 1961 [1983]). In the late 1990s, the Maori scholar Linda Tuhiwai Smith had already raised the key question: "Is history in its modernist construction important or not important for indigenous peoples?" (L. Smith, 1999: 34). It is a relevant question for the Roma as well, since there is a kind of veiled hope of justice which is very strong in some cases and easily detected in many pages written by Roma authors on our history, together with the will to overcome the atrocities suffered by our people by identifying them, shedding light on the darkest corners of history and, as a result, achieving some justice. However, no matter how frustrating this is, we must accept the reality described by Linda Smith, that this entire idea of transforming history into justice is not just a matter of will or moral commitment, but a question of power:

> It is because of this relationship with power that we have been excluded, marginalized and "Othered". In this sense history is not important for

indigenous peoples because a thousand accounts of the "truth" will not alter the "fact" that indigenous peoples are still marginal and do not possess the power to transform history into justice.

(L. Smith, 1999: 34)

We must agree with the author that history, as a discipline, is embedded in power. "In fact, history is mostly about power" she states, meaning that what should be stressed in relations between two racialized peoples such as the Roma and the Gadje is the urgent need to re-read and re-codify "Roma history" in terms of the status attributed to it by the power relations in which these narratives are rooted and which sustain them. It is important to foreground the system that upholds this unequal power relationship, based on the racial differentiation between the Roma and non-Roma populations, which began with the arrival of our ancestors in Early Modern Europe and has been fuelled and maintained up to the present day. In other words, we need to identify the "anti-gypsyism" embedded in the very essence of "Roma history", since both anti-gypsyism and the discipline of history derive from the same source: the civilizing project of European modernity.

Understood in this way, "Roma history" as a discipline clearly became a weapon of domination, a code used to manage our collective memory and usurp our own identity with a plot that plays against us. Moreover, for exactly the same reasons, this discipline is also a key field in which to identify and analyze the silences, resistances and tensions that accompany the creation of the "Roma-Other", as an operational narrative that still has a powerful presence in both academic and political spheres.

The Modern Roots of an Old History

This section will discuss the main points of contention that collapse when the dominant approaches used in Western historiography attempt to address the history of the Roma. This confrontation is mainly an expression of the epistemological limitations that create the frustrating situation whereby we, as Roma, cannot find ourselves within "Roma history".

The first issue that needs to be addressed is the methodological problem concerning the definition of the "object of Roma history". Like any other discipline, "Roma history" should be required to define its object of study. However, as S. Seth (2011) claims, one of the key factors that characterizes the particularity of history as a "Western code" is the creation of the illusion that history, unlike other disciplines, "has no need to think its object, because its object simply is. History-as-facts simply happens, and history-as-discipline is an attempt to recreate that happening to the degree that documents allow us to do so" (Seth, 2011: 3), stressing that this is an expression of "epistemological naïveté". The issue has a deeper epistemological dimension when it intersects with the forces that contextualize this process and therefore, due to the importance of this concern, it will be discussed separately in the next section. For the moment, what is essential to note is the fact that when it comes to "Roma history", the structural ingenuousness identified by Seth is, as in the entire field of Romani Studies, anything but innocent, precisely because there is a direct connection between the production of "Roma history", supposedly based on "facts" alone, and the mainstream understanding of Gadje Western academia with regard to "objectivism" as a scientific criterion. The constant, resounding claim for "objectivism" in Romani Studies debates in recent years can only be understood as the reaction of white privilege and its obsession with hermetically sealing off academia from the questions and kind of research which we, as Roma, feel the need to address, and the questioning of where our interests lie. This mainstream interpretation of "objectivism" in "Roma history" is understood as a pure, neutral approach to our collective past with no ideological and/or epistemological conditioning of the hermeneutics required to recall the events and protagonists of this past. The real meaning for us of this regulatory insulation of scholarship only becomes clear when it is seen as a product of the coloniality of power and knowledge. The sacred criterion of "objectivism" is then unveiled as a weapon of domination deployed to legitimize certain kinds of knowledge and categorically exclude others. As Maldonado-Torres states:

> Driven by anxiety and fear, "objectivity," along with other presumably lofty ideals such as excellence, are used to keep or increase the boundaries between those who claim to be in the zone of being human and those condemned to the zone of dehumanization.
>
> (Maldonado-Torres, 2016: 14)

At this point it is sufficiently clear that the issue addressed by well-known scholars in Romani Studies, such as Yaron Matras (2016) or Michael Stewarts (2017) among others, regarding the supposed lack of "objectivity" of critical Roma contributions to Romani Studies is indeed a major political matter masked by the appearance of scholarship deliberately designed to justify and legitimize the particular kind of governance and supervision directed towards the Roma on an academic level.[2]

One of the particular forms adopted by this "disinterested objectivity" to discredit Roma scholars' contributions to academia is the accusation that they are "intoxicated" by the activist approach of the Roma movement. This critique has sometimes been voiced explicitly but is often implicit or veiled in subtle ways. It has mainly been associated with "Roma history" as a discipline, although it can be found in other fields as well. One of the most explicit examples concerns the influential and respected linguist Yaron Matras (2004) who—when discussing our ancestors' connections with certain wars, armies and military affairs prior to their arrival in Europe in his paper *The role of language in mystifying and demystifying Gypsy identity*—makes the following statement:

The warrior origin theory is gaining ground because Romani activists and others sympathetic to their cause wish to see the Rom they sympathize with in a consistent, smooth and indisputable victim role throughout history. They want, in a sense, a package-Gypsies which will sell better on the human rights market. [...] Having accepted this viewpoint, the only way they can protect themselves from the supposedly shameful image is to replace it by a proud ancestry: to postulate, namely, that they have been turned into what they are reluctantly, having held a prestigious and honourable social position before being victimized.

(Matras, 2004: 73)

What Matras is directly attacking is the theory of the military connections associated with the origins of the Roma people, first presented by Ian Hancock (2000, 2010), one of the pioneer Roma intellectuals in academia, and subsequently supported by other Roma scholars. However, what is of interest for the subject under discussion here is an analysis of the discourse and the implications of his reaction. Matras's criticism is based on the dubious assumption that the contribution made by Roma scholars to their own history is a kind of activist manipulation whose main intention is to produce knowledge that will "sell better on the human rights market". This is just one example, among many others, which reveals the stigma that every Roma willing to engage critically in the academic debate on so-called Romani Studies has to be prepared to deal with. In one way or another, both Western academia and "Roma history" as a discipline "read" us as an impurity that has invaded their domain, a stain caused by militant ethnic commitment that manipulates and interferes in "*their*" business.

In the Western historiographical approach in general, and in the discipline of "Roma history" as a by-product of the same epistemological orientation, the issue of "purity" is heavily stressed: it feels like a stronghold built to avoid any "alien" contributions based on our political or activist experiences. This is why the theoretical framework of the decolonial approach and the concept of scholar-activism and "situated knowledge" are becoming vital to the struggle for Roma scholarship nowadays (Brooks, 2015; Mirga-Kruszelnicka, 2015; Fernández, 2016). Ultimately, the ideological justification which Sanjay Seth refers to as the "assumed epistemological superiority of historiography" lies in this concept of the purity of history (Seth, 2011: 71): it has been present from the very moment that the discipline was formalized and institutionalized in the nineteenth century. In the case of "Roma history" as the enforced administration of our collective memories, the assumed superiority of Gadje historiography takes many forms, ranging from the privileged, dominant role attributed to the white view of us and its legitimation as universal science, to the Gadjo-centrism that pervades the entire field of Romani Studies and even there usurps our role, excluding our oral memory as unworthy material that is not considered legitimate knowledge. In fact, the constant marginalization of the oral history of the Roma, as is the case with many other peoples, is a permanent feature of the dominant Western scientific approach, since it is a way of emphasizing our imposed "sub-humanization", "lack of civilization" and "inability" to produce proper knowledge.

> Writing has been viewed as the mark of a superior civilization and other societies have been judged, by this view, to be incapable of thinking critically and objectively, or having distance from ideas and emotions. Writing is part of theorizing and writing is part of history.
>
> (L. Smith, 1999: 29)

This hierarchical assumption denounced by Linda Smith essentially provides the same support for the prevailing "Roma history", which privileges a particular fictitious white perspective on the Roma whilst belittling any other methods used by the Roma to relate to our past, such as the collective connection with our ancestral memory, which is mainly preserved orally. The entire notion of written history is nothing more than an imposition of the Western discipline of history which limits any full understanding of the non-West past (Seth, 2011). It is also evidence of an inability to understand its own European history, since the epistemological imperialism of the modern historiographical approach is unable to represent and rememorize the Roma past as part of European history, whilst also failing to tell the history of the Gadje.

The Historiographical Construction of an Anti-Modern Object

At this point in the discussion it is relevant to reflect on the epistemological implications of the construction of the "object" of "Roma history". Questioning an "object" of history necessarily takes us to the other side of the question, the crucial issue of entitlement to be considered a "subject" of history. In this regard, Linda Smith refers to the philosopher who established the modern concept of history: "Hegel conceived of the fully human subject as someone capable of 'creating (his) own history'" (L. Smith, 1999: 32). The obvious consequence of this rigid statement is that history, in its modern sense, can be only understood as a narrative related to those conceived of as "fully human". This epistemological assumption is evidently not unconnected with the "zeitgeist" underlying this historical momentum and gives rise to what Nelson Maldonado-Torres defines as a "metaphysical catastrophe", referring to "the production of zones of being human and zones of not-being human or not being human enough" (Maldonado-Torres, 2016: 14). As Enrique Dussel (1994) and Anibal Quijano (2000), among others, have pointed out, this sequence of events corresponds to the modern model for power and knowledge in which the Western invention of "race" is rooted.

Elaborating on these notions in terms of their relationship to "Roma history" and the ways in which our presence, bodies, ancestry and memories are, and have been, read—from an academic and political point of view—clearly brings all the tensions, domination and resistance present in the very epistemological foundations of this discipline to the surface. Consequently, the violence that breaks through the entire construction of a European white identity from the "Roma-Otherness" cannot be disregarded if the nature and far-ranging implications of this semantic process of resignification are to be understood. In this sense, this is when history becomes significant and meaningful for us. Thus, Tuhiwai's observations on the implications of the categories functioning at the bottom of this sense of history are highly significant:

> It should also be self-evident that many of these ideas are predicated on a sense of Otherness. They are views which invite a comparison with "something/ someone else" which exists on the outside, such as the oriental, the "Negro", the "Jew", the "Indian", the "Aborigine". Views about the Other had already existed for centuries in Europe, but during the Enlightenment these views became more formalized through science, philosophy and imperialism, into explicit systems of classification and "regimes of truth".
>
> (Tuhiwai, 1999: 32)

Reflecting on the discourse produced in the specific legislation against Roma in Spain from early modernity up to the current constitution, adopted in 1978, the Roma scholar Isaac Motos (2009) proposes a conceptual distinction between what he calls "lo gitano" and "los gitanos":

> "Lo gitano" no lo identifico sin más con "los gitanos" porque ambos términos tienen contenidos distintos. Con este segundo término hago referencia al modo en que los propios gitanos se miran y ven a sí mismos y a los mecanismos sociales que sustentan tal cosmovisión, mientas que con el primer término quiero señalar, no ya tanto el modo en que han sido interpretados, sino más bien el entramado de condiciones epistemológicas, técnicas y morales que han posibilitado una determinada recepción del hecho gitano. O si se prefiere, con "lo gitano" quiero indicar el horizonte semántico que hace que una determinada interpretación del hecho gitano sea inteligible.
>
> (Motos, 2009: 62)

Due to the fact that the word "gitano" is itself an exonym (González, 2009), a white creation to define us and thus exercise power over us, I consider it more appropriate and coherent to define the two approaches as the dissimilarity between being "Roma" and being defined as "Gypsy"[3]. Leaving nomenclature aside, this epistemological distinction between, on the one hand, the meaning of "Roma" or "Kale" or any other endo-ethnonym used by us and by our ancestors to define ourselves, our heritage and our cosmovision and, on the other hand, the meaning of "Gypsy" as a fictitious white concept is vital to constructing an accurate framework for the semantic content of the "object" of "Roma history".

The structural division between the Roma people and "the Gypsy" is constitutive of European modernity and it entraps us in its own logic, notably when it comes to confronting academic discourses constructed about (and against) us and political rhetoric and practice since, to some extent, they both share the same epistemological ground. Moreover, as Helios F. Garcés (2016) points out, this dichotomy is the key to understanding the process of building the modern European nation state. The division can also be understood in the light of the concept of "abyssal thinking" proposed by Boaventura de Sousa Santos (2007) in the framework for the *Epistemologies of the South*:

> The same abyssal cartography is constitutive of modern knowledge. Again, the colonial zone is, par excellence, the realm of incomprehensible beliefs and behaviours which in no way can be considered knowledge, whether true or false. The other side of the line harbours only incomprehensible magical or idolatrous practices. The utter strangeness of such practices led to denying the very human nature of the agents of such practices. On the basis of their refined conceptions of humanity and human dignity, the humanists reached the conclusion that the savages were sub-human. Do the Indians have a soul? was the question.
>
> (Santos, 2007: 48)

One expression of this "abyssal line" referred to by Santos in the process of building and universalizing modern Western knowledge of the Roma is, in essence, rooted in the very separation between the Roma and "the Gypsy". Given that our culture, social practices and beliefs cannot be encapsulated within, or are not even compatible with, the logic of modernity, we were not allowed to be considered human. For the Roma, the event corresponding to the discussion between Bartolomé de las Casas and Ginés de Sepúlveda cited by Boaventura de Sousa took place in Germany when the philosopher, jurist and theologian Jacobus Thomasius (1622–1684) came to the conclusion that "these black-looking heathen foreigners speaking a strange tongue, were not fully human" (cited by Lewy, 2000: 2).

bell hooks (1989) draws on the Afro-American experience to develop the political/academic exercise of "*talking back*", reflecting on the objectification of "the Other" practised in the field of history. She defines the relational distinction between "subjects" and "objects" in the sense that the former "have the right to define their own reality, establish their own identities, name their history" (hooks, 1989: 42), and hence the history of the "Other", our history, is merely defined in relation to the white identity, the Gadje identity. This is why it is imperative for us to distance ourselves from the logics violently imposed by the civilizing project of modernity in order to write a history of the Roma in which we, our ancestors and our collective memories are not a footnote to the white Western history of Europe, but a history that looks in the other direction, essentially a history that *"talks back"* in our own name.

In the first half of the nineteenth century, George Borrow, one of the fathers of the so-called Romani Studies, was already claiming that "the Romas have no history" (Borrow, 1841: 159), based both on the assumption that there is no history of oral-based memories and on his exoticizing approach to depicting the Roma as a nomadic people with no territorial roots. From the outset, "Roma History" became a mechanism for managing and controlling the collective memory of our people: from the moment it was established as a discipline to the recent historiographical studies on the Roma, we find an exclusionary machinery being deployed, created to justify the racial system of domination which confronts Roma people. This was made possible by eliminating our ancestry from history, eradicating Roma agency and subjectivity and replacing it with an imaginary "object" and extreme "other" that embedded all the frustrations, fears and anguish of white/Gadje society. The creation of an "enemy within" in European society was based on the semantic creation of "the Gypsy" as the perfect incarnation of barbarism, immorality, maladjustment and inhumanity that enabled the Gadje to see themselves and be seen as the inverse image of what they had created.

Following this modern operation, the words "gypsy", *"gitano"*, *"zigani"*, *"cigano"*, *"zigeuner"*, "Egyptian" and many other names we have been called became very ambiguous words whose meanings fluctuate between ethnic, social, moral or even legal terms, according to the needs of the dominant identity (Fernández and Cortés, 2015: 509–514). The ultimate objective of this conceptual operation was to create a narrative about the Roma as an anti-modern collective, a people anchored in tradition, uninterested in the gifts of modernity, isolated from progress and incapable of achieving such glories by themselves: in essence, a people trapped in their pre-modern status. The next step in this semantic operation would be the reverse manoeuvre of closing the circle with the notion of the need to save these "barbarians" for their own good: it marks the beginning of the current ideology of integration.

Conclusion

In these pages I have discussed the relevance of questions about how the object of "Roma history" has been constructed and the epistemological background from which this process has been built up, as well as the semantic implications of why and for whom this past is evoked. As shown above, in order not to fail into the trap of the ingenuousness highlighted by Seth, it is necessary to ask these questions within the context of the power relations in which knowledge of "Roma history" is produced. In effect, the specific power relations defined as anti-gypsyism or romanophobia, a system of racist domination historically grounded in the enshrinement and universalization of modern European values, are still very much alive and widespread today. Moreover, the knowledge produced within the field of "Roma history", like any other academic product about us, is not immune to this phenomenon. As the Maori scholar Cherry Smith claims, "colonialism, racism and cultural imperialism do not occur only in society, outside of the gates of universities" (C. Smith, 1994: 13) or, as I have stated in a previous work with regard to the knowledge produced in the field of so-called Romani Studies:

> Beneath its veneer of neutrality, we often find that scholars and experts harbor familiar prejudices against Roma. Moreover, scholars researching Roma often see them as an object to be studied, rather than a collective living, breathing subject.
>
> (Fernández, 2016)

I argue that this is not just a methodological problematic that can be solved by redirecting the perspective to the "object", but rather that, as a direct consequence of the combined forces embedded in the nature of this discipline itself, such projections and tensions between Gadje and Roma, and between researcher and "object" are inevitable in a discipline such as "Roma history", given that this discipline is not only created by the epistemological principles of Western modernity but is also an indispensable weapon in the civilizing project that accompanies this ideology at every step. However, what is specific to the case of "Roma history" is that the discipline does not identify the collective and engage in research in order to narrate its past, but this "object" is instead semantically created independently of the reality faced by the human collective that is supposed to the central figure in this history.

Moreover, I have argued for the need to create a Roma history that takes us into account as the subject and agent of our own history. This not only implies "talking back", in the sense that bell hooks (1989) uses the expression, but also the need to examine the tensions and violence produced in the historical events in which our ancestors played a leading role, as well as in the historical production of the modern construction of the concept of anti-gypsyism, as a semantic framework of interpretation. Such history, namely a Roma-centred history, is needed, above all, to serve as a counter-history, an answer to modern Western mythology. Furthermore, such history cannot disregard the material and conceptual formation of the reality faced by our people nowadays: by examining the tensions, violence, and biases in our past it should represent an exercise in historical reparation. It is an exercise that will entail the need to redirect our view to the past to provide us with specific answers to challenge the current political role that has been allocated to us. In short, Roma history becomes meaningful when it escapes the enforced depoliticization imposed by the criteria of white scholarship to become a conceptual weapon committed to our interests and, by analyzing the processes that have led from the past to the present faced by our people, challenges them and thus envisages the future roadmap that can overcome this reality.

As previously detailed, it is crucial to understand the implications of the epistemological construction of the "Gypsy object" within the current political understanding of the Roma in Europe. The process defined here is not unconnected with the pogroms and episodes of anti-gypsyism that all too often break out in Europe, and with the high level of tolerance towards this form of structural racism, frequently practiced and orchestrated by the "civilized" European states themselves. Furthermore, in deeper and more subtle ways, this epistemological construction of the Roma as "Gypsy" extends to the very essence of public policies for the Roma and their implementation. All of these policies, from local to international level, are conceptualized by a vast mechanism constructed from what may be termed the "ideology of integration". The aims of this ideology are basically inspired by a notion of "integration" understood as a forced process of transformation involving a "barbarian anti-modern community that needs to be saved from itself". The reasons underlying this ideology aim to control and discipline the "Gypsy other" and the kind of problematic they might create for Gadje society as the dominant social body: this is the real meaning of the words "development", "implementation", "empowerment" and other similar terms often used in the policies that target Roma people. This ideological agenda, hidden in the very core of the "ideology of integration", has dominated and perverted every possible notion of "Roma integration" and all the ways it in which is implemented on a political and social level. Therefore, for us "integration" represents nothing other than a constant reminder of the power exerted over us, whose only achievement has been to depoliticize the Roma struggle for self-emancipation, resulting in a complicit lack of interest in the impact of white privilege and a Gadje-centred interest in the construction of such policies, as well as the persistent rejection of the policy we need most urgently, namely a policy for the historical reparation of the Roma people.

Notes

1 "*Gadje*" in the plural, and "*gadjo*" and "*gadji*" as the masculine and feminine forms, are Romani words which refer to non-Roma or white people.

2 In the past years this debate has become increasingly relevant as Roma voices and institutions have been contributing greatly to the controversy. One clear example of what I call "white privilege in Romani Studies" can be seen in Matras (2016) and Stewart (2017), among others. For a detailed analysis of this issue, see my article "Our voices matter. A Roma decolonial approach to the white trauma in Romani Studies" presented at the Conference "*Critical Approaches to Romani Studies*" in 24–25th May, 2018 at Central European University of Budapest (Hungary).

3 The word "gypsy" and its translation in other languages derives from the word "Egyptian" because when the Roma first arrived in Europe, the Gadje population believed they had come from Egypt. This fact was proved as incorrect but the white terminology used to define us was maintained by the power relations established in

Europe between the Roma and non-Roma populations. However, our ancestors never identified themselves with this term. A detailed explanation of the historical "misunderstanding" can be found in Fraser (1995).

References

Borrow, George H. (1841), *The Zincali: An Account of the Gypsies of Spain* (Vol. 1). London: Journal Murray. Available at https://archive.org/details/zincaliaccountof00borruoft

Brooks, Ethel (2015), "The Importance of Feminists and 'Halfies' in Romani Studies: New Epistemological Possibilities", *Roma Rights: Journal of the European Roma Rights Centre*, 2, 57–62. Retrieved from http://www.errc.org/uploads/upload_en/file/roma-rights-2-2015-nothing-about-us-without-us.pdf

Carmona, Sarah (2013), "Nuevas perspectivas sobre la génesis de la historia gitana", *Quaderns de La Mediterrània*, 18–19, 321–327.

Courthiade, Marcel (2016), "Knowledge Based on Sources and Historical Data versus Knowledge Based on Clichés and Legends in the Indian Stage of Rromani History", *Analele Universității "Ovidius" din Constanța. Seria Filologie*, XXVII(2), 237–282. Retrieved from http://litere.univ-ovidius.ro/Anale/documente-z/articole-2016-2/20%20Courthiade_2_2016_art.pdf

Dussel, Enrique (1994), *1492: El encubrimiento del Otro: Hacia el origen del "mito de la modernidad"*. La Paz: Plural. Retrieved from http://biblioteca.clacso.edu.ar/clacso/otros/20111218114130/1942.pdf

Fanon, Frantz (1983 [1961]), *The Wretched of the Earth*. Harmondsworth: Penguin.

Fanon, Frantz (1986 [1952]), *Black Skin, White Masks*. London: Pluto.

Fernández, Cayetano (2016), "Two Milestones Put Romani Cultural Discourse in the Hands of Roma Themselves", *Open Society Foundations.org*, January 15. Retrieved 24.01.2018, from https://www.opensocietyfoundations.org/voices/two-milestones-put-romani-cultural-discourse-hands-roma-themselves

Fernández, Cayetano; Cortés, Ismael (2015), "El Nomadismo Romaní como resistencia refractaria frente al racismo de Estado en la Modernidad española", *Memorias del 5o Congreso de Filosofía Joven*, Horizontes de Compromiso: La Vida, La Zubia, Granada, 5–8 july, 498–517. Available at https://horizontesdecompromiso.wordpress.com/revista-libro-del-congreso

Fraser, Angus (1995), *The Gypsies*. Oxford: Blackwell (2nd ed.).

Garcés, Helios F. (2016), "El racismo antirom/antigitano y la opción decolonial", *Tabula Rasa*, 25, 225–251. Doi: https://doi.org/10.25058/20112742.82

González, Nicolás Jiménez (2009), "¿El romanó, el caló, el romanó-kaló o el gitañol? Cincuenta y tres notas sociolingüísticas en torno a los gitanos españoles", *Anales de Historia Contemporánea*, 25, 149–161.

Hancock, Ian (1987), *The Pariah Syndrome: An Account of Gypsy Slavery and Persecution*. Ann Arbor, MI: Karoma.

Hancock, Ian (2000), "The Emergence of Romani as a Koïne Outside of India", in Thomas Acton (ed.), *Scholarship and Gypsy Struggle: Commitment in Romani Studies*. Hatfield: University of Hertfordshire Press, 1–13.

Hancock, Ian (2010), "On Romani Origins and Identity", in Ian Hancock (ed.), *Danger! Educated Gypsy: Selected Essays*. Hatfield: University of Hertfordshire Press, 54–94.

hooks, bell (1989), *Talking Back: Thinking Feminist, Thinking Black*. Boston, MA: South End Press.

Lewy, Guenter (2000), *The Nazi Persecution of the Gypsies*. Oxford: Oxford University Press.

Maldonado-Torres, Nelson (2016), "Outline of Ten Theses on Coloniality and Decoloniality", Fondation Frantz Fanon.com, October 26. Retrieved from http://fra ntzfanonfoundation-fondationfrantzfanon.com/article2360.html

Matras, Yaron (2004), "The Role of Language in Mystifying and Demystifying Gypsy Identity", in Nicholas Saul and Susan Tebbutt (eds.), *The Role of the Romanies: Images and Counter-Images of 'Gypsies'/Romanies in European Cultures*. Liverpool: Liverpool University Press, 53–78. doi: 10.5949/liverpool/9780853236795.003.0005

Matras, Yaron (2016), "Do Roma Need Protection from Themselves? The Council of Europe Comes under Fire from Academics for Reinforcing Prejudice", *romea.cz*, March 24. Retrieved January 24, 2018, from http://www.romea.cz/en/features-and-comm entary/commentary/yaron-matras-do-roma-need-protection-from-themselves-the-council-of-europe-comes-under-fire-from-academics-for-reinforcing

Mirga-Kruszelnicka, Anna (2015), "Romani Studies and Emerging Romani Scholarship", *Roma Rights: Journal of the European Roma Rights Centre*, 2, 39–46. Retrieved from http:/ /www.errc.org/uploads/upload_en/file/roma-rights-2-2015-nothing-about-us-withou t-us.pdf

Motos, Isaac (2009), "Lo que no se olvida: 1499–1978". *Anales de Historia Contemporánea*, 25, 57–74. Retrieved from http://revistas.um.es/analeshc/article/view/71681

Quijano, Anibal (2000), "Colonialidad del poder, eurocentrismo y América Latina", in Edgardo Lander (comp.), *La colonialidad del saber: eurocentrismo y ciencias sociales. Perspectivas Latinoamericanas*. Buenos Aires: Clacso, 201–246. Retrieved from http://www.decolonia ltranslation.com/espanol/quijano-colonialidad-del-poder.pdf

Santos, Boaventura de Sousa (2007), "Beyond Abyssal Thinking: From Global Lines to Ecologies of Knowledges", *Review (Fernand Braudel Center)*, 30(1), 45–89. Available at https://www.jstor.org/stable/40241677

Seth, Sanjay (2011), "Historiography and Nonwestern Pasts", *Historein*, 10, 71–81. doi: 10.12681/historein.7

Smith, Cherryl (1994), *Kimihia Te Matauranga: Colonization and Iwi Development*, MA Thesis, University of Auckland, New Zealand. Retrieved from http://teatawhai.maori.nz/imag es/downloads/kimihia_te_maramatanga_intro.pdf

Smith, Linda Tuhiwai (1999), *Decolonizing Methodologies: Research and Indigenous Peoples*. London: Zed Books.

Stewart, Michael (2017), "Nothing about Us without Us, or the Dangers of a Closed-Society Research Paradigm", *Romani Studies*, 27(2), 125–146. doi: 10.3828/rs.2017.8

Chapter 11

Rights, Confinement and Liberation
Rearguard Theory and Freedom of Movements

Julia Suárez-Krabbe

Introduction

On the 26th of January 2016, as the Danish government was passing the so-called "migrant assets bill", Freedom of Movements—a political anti-racist organization based in Copenhagen composed of immigrants, asylum seekers, refugees, as well as people with citizenship—held a demonstration based on a call for solidarity from asylum seekers in the Sjælsmark Deportation Centre, north of Copenhagen. While the "migrant assets bill" is yet another effort to strengthen the systematic criminalization of asylum seekers and immigrants at the hands of the Danish state, Freedom of Movements forwarded the following 11 demands:

1. We demand not to be transferred by force to Ikast (a prison in Jylland).
2. We are not criminals. We demand that the Danish Prison and Probation Service (Kriminalforsorgen) will not be in charge of our lives.
3. We demand the end of forced deportations, whether secret or public. We are refugees, our countries are at war.
4. We demand the right to work.
5. We demand adequate housing. We don't even have hot water.
6. We demand the right to medicine and treatment that meets our needs.
7. We demand asylum in Denmark.
8. We demand accountability from authorities. Who can we ask about our cases? How long do we have to wait in Sjælsmark?
9. We demand an end to "motivationsfremmende foranstaltninger". The policies that aim to "motivate" us to leave through dehumanizing and humiliating us.
10. We demand freedom of movement and freedom to stay. We demand the right to have rights!
11. Finally, we demand the abolition of camps like Sjælsmark.

An "action of theoretical intervention woven inside forms of life", this chapter engages in rearguard theory (Santos, 2014: 13) with Freedom of Movements, and aims to contribute to our understanding of how racism localizes in

Denmark focusing on migration detention camps and deportation camps, specifically Sjælsmark. To this end, the chapter combines insights from the Prison Industrial Complex (PIC) approach with Boaventura de Sousa Santos' work on sociology of law and Achille Mbembe's *necropolitics*.

The core concern of the chapter is racism, a globalized system of oppression closely tied to capitalism. This globalized system produces dissimilar realities for different people, and it has distinct—yet interconnected—local expressions. However, in the dominant thinking expressed within academia, in the media and in everyday talk, globalization seems to be associated with connections and movement; cultural, technological, economic, political. How globalization is also concerned with forced displacement, confinement, restraint and exploitation tends to be conveniently ignored. Notwithstanding, the fact is that historically, hegemonic globalization has worked in both ways; it has allowed connections and movement among the global elites, while forcibly displacing, limiting and restricting racialized populations in order to control, exploit and/or eradicate them. The first example of this form of globalization is the transatlantic slave trade. Heralded by the elites of the time in order to increase production in the colonies (Cox, 1959: 332), the transatlantic slave trade involved the forced displacement, confinement and dehumanization of people in large numbers. This practice quickly became a global institution central to global capitalism (Davis, 2003; Gilmore, 2007). As trade with humans, and with the goods their forced labour helped produce, increased, so were the livelihoods of the elites and the social conditions in their societies significantly improved. These improvements required the detriment of the livelihoods and social conditions of the racialized populations. The transatlantic slave trade and the global institution of slavery were part and parcel of colonialism, which accompanied the practices of voluntary mobility, economic enhancement and increased living conditions for some based on the generalized oppression and dehumanization of the majority of the world's populations.

In its current form, hegemonic globalization arguably involves increased interconnections: economic through trade, cultural through communication technologies and travel, and political and legal through transnational institutions. However, as in colonial times, these interconnections pertain only to a small part of the world's population, whereas the majority continues to be forcibly displaced, confined, exploited and dehumanized. The production of the goods that the global elites consume, as well as our quality of life, depends directly upon this system. To maintain this system, large populations must remain wretched: only so can be guaranteed the cheap and uneducated labour force, plus the raw materials needed to keep the elites' quality of life intact. The continued existence of these practices is racism; that is, "the state-sanctioned and/or legal production and exploitation of group-differentiated vulnerabilities to premature death, in distinct yet densely interconnected political geographies" (Gilmore, 2007: 28). In other words, racism is central to capitalism; both function on a global scale. The primary actors responsible for upholding this system of oppression are the global elites; the people who have the power to define, defend and enforce national and international policies and legal frameworks used to make the system operational: the death project (Suárez-Krabbe, 2015: 3–4). In Europe, the death project materializes in relation to its immigrant populations, and takes some of its crudest forms in migration detention and deportation camps. In order to substantiate this claim, this chapter is organized as follows: the next section makes a brief presentation of the Sjælsmark Deportation Centre, including the most important legal frameworks that apply to the people subjected to life in that camp, and a general overview of how problems similar to Sjælsmark are addressed in scholarly work, and the insights these provide. Drawing on the sociology of law of Boaventura de Sousa Santos and Achille Mbembe's necropolitics, the chapter's next section then explains the relationship between rights and death using economic, social and cultural rights as a point of inception. The relationship between rights and death is then further explored and substantiated as it pertains to law, democracy and freedom vis-à-vis confinement (prisons and camps), drawing primarily upon the theory of Angela Davis. The final section concludes that, in the face of the problems with prisons and camps and the close relationship between law and exclusion, rights and death, struggles that aim to abolish prisons and camps offer strong alternatives as practices of freedom.

Prisons and Camps: Sjælsmark Deportation Centre

With Ruth Gilmore's definition of racism as "the state-sanctioned and/or legal production and exploitation of group-differentiated vulnerabilities to premature death, in distinct yet densely interconnected political geographies" (2007: 28), in the introduction, I made the claim that the policies and legal frameworks that allow this system to be put into practice—the death project—materialize in Europe in relation to its immigrant populations. This section approaches the relationship between prisons and camps in the face of the global system of racism, spelling out the ways in which this relationship is relevant in regard to the specific ways in which racism takes form in Denmark in relation to Sjælsmark Deportation Centre. Sjælsmark Deportation Centre lies in an isolated area approximately 25 km north of Copenhagen, close to military barracks in a military active area and 2 km from the asylum centre at Sandholm. Sjælsmark Deportation Centre (in Danish, *Udrejsecenter Sjælsmark*) was established in February 2015 as a special centre harbouring approximately 150 single men and women who have been denied asylum in Denmark. However, because of war, violence, terrorism, political beliefs, religion, skin colour or sexuality, many persons currently confined in the Centre cannot return to their countries of origin. They cannot leave Denmark and seek asylum elsewhere, either due to the rules of the Dublin Convention, which state that asylum seekers have their case decided in the country where they register first. In this sense, people are trapped; they cannot leave the country, and they cannot stay in Denmark. This results in a condition where they are in a nowhere place, a sort of permanent state of exception (cf. Agamben).

Adding to the severity of the problems faced by the people who are confined in this centre—as in general by people seeking asylum—is the uncertainty of how long they have to face these conditions. Indeed, a core characteristic of the conditions lived by people seeking asylum relates to temporal uncertainty, the lack of knowledge about, and answers to, the question of how long they will have to be subjected to specific dehumanizing conditions. As the first demand by Freedom of Movements states, people in Sjælsmark now face uncertainty in relation to whether or not they will be forcibly moved to a prison in an even more isolated area—Ikast. This prison has recently been emptied in order to make it operational as a deportation camp. At the time of writing, it is uncertain how the plans to increase the capacity of Sjælsmark from its current capacity of approximately 150 persons to 400 fit into this scheme, but it seems to work as part of the global expansion of the prison industrial complex (Ryan, 2010), where, in the Danish case, the definition of crime, which is closely tied to nationalism and its constitutive racism, works together with the defence of capitalism, specifically in terms of applying austerity measures on public services like education and health care, while at the same time encouraging and protecting transnational companies. Indeed, while Danish prisons are state-owned, the expansion of the prison industrial complex in the country would be unsurprising, insofar as the companies engaged are transnational and very powerful. Investment in the prison industrial complex, especially in private prisons, is highly attractive to the global elites. In Denmark, the specific localization of the PIC here involves companies that produce fences, building material, security know-how, catering companies, the NGOs and humanitarian industry and the like.

A recent study on the consequences of asylum centres for local communities in rural Denmark conducted by three Danish anthropologists (Larsen, Whyte and Olwig, 2015) additionally suggests that the asylum centres are improving conditions for the local communities where the centres lie: they provide new jobs, economic improvement and population influx to areas otherwise characterized by population decrease due to internal migration towards the cities. Interestingly, this study regards social reality from a one-sided, dominant perspective; "local communities" clearly do not really include the persons in the centres, and their realities are barely mentioned. Additionally, in its effort to highlight the positive economic aspects of the camps in the Danish rural areas, the report is complicit in defending the death project: the asylum camps are, in fact, one of the ways in which the Danish state exposes people to premature death. The study unwittingly confirms that the global expansion of the prison industrial complex is also taking place in Denmark, although it might find itself in an adaptation phase, and thus in fluctuation:

> While seven years ago there were only 7 asylum centers, at the beginning of 2015 there was a total of 67. Head of one of the centers of the Red

Cross told [us] she had personally participated in opening and closing more than 100 centers during her career. There are several reasons to this notable variability. The most basic cause is that the number of asylum seekers in Denmark varies enormously. This happens primarily in tandem with the number of refugees in the world, as well as it depends on how long the cases of the asylum seekers take in the Danish asylum system. On top of this, the Danish Immigration Service and the managing organizations of the asylum centers continuously seek to make the asylum system more effective – a process that implies closing and opening camps. The overall results are a generalized state of temporariness that has consequences for the asylum seekers, the center personnel and the involved local communities.

(Romme, Whyte and Olwig, 2015: 17)

Angela Davis has stated that "[the prison] relieves us of the responsibility of seriously engaging with the problems of our society, especially those produced by racism and, increasingly, global capitalism" (Davis, 2003: 16). As is the case with the report mentioned above, many studies on these matters tend to downplay or completely ignore racism and global capitalism (Black, 1998; Golash-Boza, 2009a, 2009b; Gill, Conlon and Moran, 2013; Moran, 2015). Recognizing the problems of racism and global capitalism, yet other scholars tend to dissolve responsibility in an overtly Agambean and/or Deleuze-Guattarian perspective, where racism seems to become a cloudy matter devoid of responsible actors and unequal power relations (Tesfahuney and Dahlstedt, 2008; Mirza, 2014; Rembis, 2014).[1] As such, most of these last mentioned contributions start with—and conclude—that refugee and/or migration detention camps are sites where the Agambean state of exception is in play, and that immigrants and refugees are *bare life*, *homo sacer*. Approaches from law to migration detention camps coming also abound. In this field, most studies emphasize different dimensions of the legal frameworks relating to asylum seekers in Europe, describing how international and national legal frameworks may clash. These studies alert that the use of detention in the context of immigration law enforcement has increased in all European member states, and the

institutionalized practice of immigration detention has become an inherent part of a policy package that has as its main aims to deter future migrants and to remove those already in national territory as rapidly and as effectively as possible.

(Cornelisse, 2010: 2)

Additionally, there is a generalized lack of transparency in the handling of the people in immigration detention—legally as well as in terms of the conditions to which they are subjected and what instances might bear responsibility (Cornelisse, 2010: 2). Adding to the lack of transparency is the fact that many of the facilities used in immigration detention, such as Sjælsmark and the prison in

Ikast, are located in remote or isolated areas and hence, in practice, are virtually invisible to the larger population; that there are blurred and/or complex lines in the legal terminology used in relation to detention;[2] and that immigrants and asylum seekers in Europe for the most part fall under administrative law, not civil law, which often trumps human rights law (Flynn, 2012: 44–45). As Flynn and Cannon assert in a working paper of the Global Detention Project on "The Privatization of Immigration Detention",

> detainees in immigration detention facilities [across Europe] are generally not convicted criminals, or even remand prisoners waiting for their day in court. Rather, they are administrative detainees, people who are not charged with a crime but whom the state has decided to detain in order to carry out administrative procedures, like deportations or decisions on asylum claims.
>
> (Flynn and Cannon. 2009: 3)

Due to the fuzziness pertaining to the legal frameworks that are applied in relation to asylum seekers and refugees, Michael Flynn proposes the following definition of immigration detention: "the deprivation of liberty of non-citizens because of their status" (2012: 42). His definition of deprivation of liberty in this understanding is "forcibly-imposed confinement within an enclosed space for any length of time" (2012: 45). According to Flynn's definition, the parallel that I am making in this chapter between prisons and camps would not be possible: according to his understanding, only facilities that "physically prevent people from leaving" can be considered migration detention facilities. Flynn operates from within legal thinking, and hence also within a limited framework of understanding freedom. We will return to this discussion in the section Law, Democracy and Freedom. For now, what is important to note is that, at least in the case of the persons in Sjælsmark Deportation Centre, law is the major element in the deprivation of their liberty. Indeed, as with any other asylum seekers in Denmark, the people in Sjælsmark are not allowed to work or study. But, in contrast to asylum seekers, the ones whose cases have been rejected by the Danish state do not get any pocket money, and they are not allowed to cook their own food. They get a bed in shared dormitories and food three times a day. The food which the refugees are served in Sjælsmark is of very poor quality, sometimes it is barely cooked and it does not cater for people who are ill (e.g. diabetes, allergies, etc.).

These are the dehumanizing living conditions addressed most explicitly in demands 4, 5 and 6 of Freedom of Movements, and they are to be understood as part of the legal measures taken by the Danish state known as "*motivationsfremmende foranstaltninger*" (literally: measures to enhance motivation) addressed in the 9th demand. The explicit objective of this policy is to "motivate" people who have been defined as unwanted, violent or uncooperative by the Danish state to leave Denmark. The motivation-enhancement measures were approved as changes in the Danish Alien Act in the summer of 1997 (Danish Alien Act §§ 34, 2 and 42a, 5 and 6—law no. 407, from 10 June 1997), and adjusted by law no. 473, from 1 July 1998 (by including § 42a, 7), including several changes and bills in the later years, the most recent of which was the so-called "migrant assets bill" mentioned in the introduction. Among the most serious measures, the bill states that an asylum seeker cannot apply for family reunion during his or her first three years in Denmark, and it gives the police and authorities the right to search clothes and luggage of asylum seekers at any time (also when in the asylum system), and to confiscate valuables and cash worth more than approximately 1,340 Euros (10,000 Danish Kroner). In regard to the valuables, these can be taken from the asylum seekers if they cannot tell a sentimental story which proves that they have not taken the valuable with them due to its market-value. Similar measures are already in play in Germany, the Netherlands and Switzerland. As to the motivation-enhancement measures, the most relevant parts of the Danish Alien Act are § 34, 2 and § 42a 4–11. These paragraphs state that the police can require that the person reports to them if they are deemed uncooperative, do not come to the meetings with the authorities concerning their case, have shown violent behaviour, do not stay where they have been assigned to stay by the Danish Immigration Service, or if the police is taking care of the deportation of the person and the latter does not collaborate.

Danish Alien Act states, in § 42a, 5, that the Danish Ministry of Foreign Affairs is responsible for handling the overall management of the centres, including accommodation, handover of pocket money (which does not apply in the case of the rejected asylum seekers—cf. § 42a 11 and 12) and money for living expenses, food, education, activities and health care. The Ministry can allocate these responsibilities to the Danish Immigration Service (which is under the Ministry of Foreign Affairs), to the Danish Red Cross, the Danish Emergency Management Agency, the Danish Refugee Council (NGO) and local governmental authorities. As the second demand of Freedom of Movements implies, in the case of Sjælsmark, responsibility has been allocated to the Danish Prison and Probation Service, revealing the government's systematic efforts to criminalize asylum seekers. Additionally, § 42a, 6 states that the Minister of Interior decides the rules for financial responsibility, including how institutions will cover the costs associated with the asylum centres, while 7 and 9 state that the asylum seeker or rejected asylum seeker who cannot "be returned", respectively, has to live where the Danish Immigration Service dictates, and that the asylum seeker must not lay violent or threatening hindrances to the work of the people in the place where she or he is lodged.[3]

Among other things included in the 11 demands, during the demonstration held on the 26th of January in Sjælsmark, the refugees highlighted that they were not criminals. As we have seen above, however, the Danish state is taking several concrete measures to criminalize the asylum seekers, and indeed one of the key points in the Prison Industrial Complex approach relates to how the system itself generates specific forms of crime and disregards others, most notably white-collar crimes, and crimes against humanity committed by prominent figures belonging to the global elites; for example, in their responsibility for the wars in Iraq and Afghanistan—the very same crimes that produced the forced displacement of many people, including those who right now find themselves confined in Sjælsmark. This fact alone makes it relevant to look at the connections between prisons and camps. The following section presents a more in-depth discussion of how law is part of the problem.

Rights and Death

The problem of the limits of human rights, and of law in general, is being debated with great force among diverse social movements and in certain research fields such as the decolonial perspective and sociology of law, especially in the work of Boaventura de Sousa Santos. According to Santos (1998: 198–214), sociology of law has shown interest in studying the ways in which the legal system itself is embedded in larger social contexts, and paid special attention to where the barriers that impede marginalized populations' access to the legal system lie. This field has established that there is an intrinsic link between people's social, cultural and economic conditions and their access to justice. In other words, the legal system is not democratic to people in disadvantageous social, cultural and economic circumstances. Two elements need to be highlighted in this context. First, the critical studies within sociology of law suggest a close relationship between Economic, Social and Cultural Rights (ESCR) and the legal system, or rather, the connection between economically, socially and culturally disadvantaged people and the undemocratic workings of the legal system. Second, one of the social conditions that brought the attention of sociology of law to the problems connected to the procedural, institutional and organizational dimensions of law were the social struggles led by those in disadvantageous social positions, among others in struggles for what we today refer to as ESCR, and the democratization of rights.

Concretely, the studies within sociology of law concluded the following relating to the economic, social and cultural obstructions to access the legal system (Santos, 1998: 202). The economic hindrances are connected to the costs attached to the access to justice in terms of making a denunciation or taking a case to a tribunal (1998: 202–203). The social and cultural barriers are connected to: a) lack of knowledge about rights; b) lack of social and emotional resources to carry out a legal action in court; c) lack of trust or resignation before the courts or the problems faced; d) fear of reprisals; and e) lack of social network—especially legal experts—that can help make the legal processes effective (1998: 204–205). On the basis of this, according to Santos (1998: 214), one of the most important research activities within sociology of law is concerned with the democratization of the dominant legal power. Indeed, the legal system is seen as a fundamental dimension to the democratization of social, economic and political life. This democratization has two strands: The first refers to the internal constitution of the [juridical] process and [the] second refers to the democratization of access to justice.

(Santos: 1998: 214)

However, Santos' point is that, while being an important measure, the democratization of justice can only reach the goal of "balancing the mechanisms of the reproduction of inequalities" (1998: 214). As a consequence,

the more detailed a law protects the popular and emergent interests, the greater is the probability that it is not applied. Being as it is, the democratic struggle for law has to be, in this context, a struggle for the application of existing law as much as a struggle to reform it.

(Santos: 1998: 215)

In other words, rights and law have significant limitations: being part of the system that produces inequality, law can at best work to balance some of the outcomes of that system. It can, however, not redress the very system. To do so, law needs to be reformed.

The question that interests Santos is how reforming the law can take place in a way that not only "adds rights" to an unjust system, but significantly contributes to dismantle that very unjust system. In his conceptualization of the "abyssal line" (Santos, 2014: 118–135), Santos has addressed elements constitutive of our current unjust system. These elements include Western rationality, temporality and political practice, which in fact raise themselves as "true" knowledge and "just" politics at the same time as they exclude all others—and legitimating such exclusion. Santos does not conceptualize these problems in terms of racism; however, seen through this lens, his analysis allows the displaying of some of the major traits of such a global system of oppression. In relation to law, his ideas about the abyssal line allow an understanding of how, while the above-mentioned economic, social and cultural hindrances can be harsh enough for the lower social classes, they are aggravated when we take into account the problems of racism.

For racialized subjects, the rule is not regulation and emancipation in the face of conflicts, but violence and appropriation (Santos, 2014: 118–135). As we saw in the case of Sjælsmark, for racialized subjects, "codes of law such as labor rights, human rights, or women's rights are suspended, and emancipation discourses such as equality, autonomy, liberty, individual or human dignity are not recognized" (Grosfoguel and Suárez-Krabbe, 2013: 82). In his analysis of necropolitics, Achille Mbembe (2010) forwards a similar—yet even more devastating—point, implying that racism manifests as a state of exception and state of siege. Notably, racism is not simply about sovereignty's dictates of who may live and who must die, as conceptualized in Foucault's biopower.

Instead, necropower manifests in the production of death-worlds: "new and unique forms of social existence in which vast populations are subjected to conditions of life conferring upon them the status of *living dead*" (Mbembe, 2010: 40). Among others, through the contemporary establishment of death-worlds—specific geographical sites and places where the living conditions are so bad that they, instead of fostering life, foster death—forced displacement is produced. Be it due to imperial wars, economic circumstances, environmental degradation or health issues—and often as the effect of several of them—forced displacement is a direct effect of the death project: the set of hegemonic practices, where racism, capitalism, patriarchy and predatory behaviours against nature are closely linked (Suárez-Krabbe, 2015: 4). In order to subject people to death-worlds, the death project combines military and economic power with political, legal and ideological power. While Mbembe captures the workings of racism in some of its crudest, yet state-sanctioned forms, Santos' work reminds us that thinking, rationality, is itself part of the problem. Indeed, in contrast to Mbembe, according to Santos, the exercise of power does not primarily occur outside of the law; instead, legality is used to make people lawfully, as well as politically, inexistent, being closely linked to the interests of past and present colonizers (Santos, 2014). As mentioned, then, an important part of the problem lies both in law and its institutions, as well as in dominant Western thinking and in its institutions.

How can we establish connections between physical confinement and the restriction of ideas in hegemonic globalization? And how is this connected to camps? Before bringing the thought of Angela Davis and Ruth Gilmore concerning the prison industrial complex to this discussion, it is important to go back to the barriers listed by sociology of law pertaining to peoples' access to law, complexifying them by including the considerations of racism as a global structure of oppression and as such:

- **(a)** Beyond the discussion of racialized subjects' lack of knowledge about rights, we must simply speak of the lack of rights and, in some cases, even of racialized subjects existence in and by itself being a violation of law, as in being "illegal" and "terrorist" (cf. Gordon, 1999). To lack rights or to be that which violates the law merely by insisting on having rights, being treated with dignity and respect, and having a political voice, is to be socially and politically dead. In this sense, when conceptualizing the problems of law, we must also direct attention away from the "victims" as lacking something, and towards the problems of the system that produces death-worlds.
- **(b, c and e)** The lack of social and emotional resources to carry out a legal action in a court, and the lack of trust or resignation before the courts or the problems faced must be seen in the light of the lack of rights mentioned above and, as such, as specific expressions of being socially and politically dead. The denial of racism throughout most of Europe

must also be taken into account, as well as the legal institutions that are supposed to assist racialized subjects in relation to the legal system, the systematic "otherization" of racialized subjects in the media and in political campaigns,[4] and the devastating socio-psychological effects that these structural processes have on racialized subjects (DuBois, 1903; Fanon, 1967; Gordon, 1999).

- **(d)** Instead of a fear of reprisals, we must speak of reprisals as a problem that needs to be addressed. Indeed, while reprisals might be an exception to people who are regarded as "native" or who are not otherized in Europe, to racialized subjects, reprisals are the rule. These reprisals can be of economic nature, they can be social and cultural (from accusing people of "playing the race-card" to marking them as "fundamentalists" or "terrorists"), and they can be physically violent (as in attacks from far-right movements, in police harassment, arbitrary detentions, confinement in asylum detention camps or deportation). In most of these cases, people are not subjects of rights. Instead, the legal system is used to keep them without rights.

Several questions emerge from these concerns. The first obvious question is: how can racialized subjects trust that the different European nations guarantee their basic human rights when the systematic otherization of communities continues to take place, despite diverse legal instruments that are supposed to protect marginalized populations from racism? The second concern is connected to the first: is it possible to guarantee marginalized populations' basic rights in contexts where the problem of racism as a systematic and historically constituted practice is either denied, or the legal instruments that exist to protect these populations more often than not are simply disregarded by those persons who are responsible for their implementation, or overruled by other legal measures doomed to be more pressing, such as anti-terror acts? As stated in the draft report entitled "Economic, Social and Cultural Rights of Migrant Children and Children Born to Migrant Parents":

> xenophobia and racism affect the ESCR of migrants in many ways, including: (i) the establishment of laws and public policies based in xenophobia that deny or arbitrarily restrict the human rights of migrants (documented or undocumented); (ii) the dissemination and perpetuation of the wrongful belief that irregular migrants are not entitled to social rights, such as education and health care; (iii) restrictions rooted in xenophobia on migrants' access to public services, including children's access to education; (iv) negative impacts of xenophobia on the educational performance of migrant children and adolescents and children and adolescents born to migrant parents, which may result in higher dropout rates; and (v) negative impacts of xenophobia on migrant adolescents' access to employment and vocational training. It is important to bear in mind that within the current context of

the economic crisis, xenophobia and discrimination have increased, as have the corresponding negative impacts on the economic and social rights of migrant workers and their families.

(UNICEF and National University of Lanos, 2010: 8)

Besides reflecting the problems connected to not always naming racism by its name by choosing to privilege the more cloudy term "xenophobia", the document however highlights some of the aspects that, seen together, provide a clear picture of how death-worlds are produced and kept alive, not necessarily in specific places (such as a typical state of exception or a state of siege), but as temporally unrestrained conditions with no specific location (see Mbembe, 2010), and manifested in daily practice. As we saw in the previous section, camps are restrictions of temporal as well as spatial nature. The above leads to a third concern: what are the possibilities of struggle of racialized subjects within this complex functioning of systematic racism? The work of Angela Davis and Ruth Gilmore provides important elements to approach an answer to this question.

Law, Democracy and Freedom

The work of activists and thinkers Angela Davis and Ruth Gilmore on the prison industrial complex allows a more in-depth understanding of the intersections between racism, capitalism and patriarchy, and how the juridical system and the prison industrial complex are fundamental to the global system of oppression. Angela Davis is among the founding members of the Critical Resistance movement, a long-term anti-racist abolitionist project that aims to generate a broad coalition against the prison industrial complex. Critical Resistance works to raise awareness on the emergence of an expanding and increasingly repressive prison industrial complex, and on the economic, political and ideological agendas of the punishment industry, which have generated similar relations to the military industrial complex (Davis, 2012: 55). Prisons are central to the maintenance of social inequalities and in the production of second-class citizens in the USA as well as on a global level. The production of second-class citizens, in turn, is what sustains the prison industrial complex; it is its *raison d'être*. To take prisons seriously forces us to think through the state of democracy in our societies (2012: 138). For instance, Davis has noted that the term

> "civil rights" refers to the rights of all the citizens, but because the very nature of citizenship in the US has always been troubled by the refusal to grant citizenship to subordinated groups—indigenous people, African slaves, women of all racial and an economic backgrounds—we tend to think of some people as "model" citizens, as archetypical citizens, those whose civil rights are never placed in question [...] and others as having to

wage struggles for the right to be regarded as citizens. And some—undocumented immigrants or "suspected" undocumented immigrants, along with ex-felons or "suspected" ex-felons, are beyond the reach of citizenship altogether.

(Davis, 2012: 181–182)

Davis' point is that imprisonment as a punishment assumes that people have rights and liberties that can be taken away from them (2012: 182). This is a core observation that is not solely concerned with the prison industrial complex, but with the ideas that underscore the juridical system and the laws mentioned in the previous section.

According to Davis, this way of thinking about punishment—as a removal of peoples' fundamental rights and liberties—is highly problematic. It is equivalent to the death punishment in the sense that it is a *de facto* application of civil and political death. Prisons are a death machinery (2012: 58), "totalitarian institutions, just as the death penalty is an obsolete and totalitarian form of punishment" (2012: 56). In her search for the meaning of freedom, Davis has formulated this question: "what does it mean to live in a democracy where there are closed institutions that engage in repressive and totalitarian practices?" (2012: 61). It means that democracy does not exist. It is an illusion that sustains a false sense of security promoted by the prison industrial complex (2012: 110–112). In practice, what happens is the following:

> [The] criminal justice system sends increasing numbers of people to prison by first robbing them of housing, health care, education, and welfare, and then punishing them when they participate in underground economies. What should we think of a system that will, on the one hand, sacrifice social services, human compassion, housing and decent schools, mental health care and jobs, while on the other hand developing an ever larger and ever more profitable prison system that subjects ever larger numbers of people to daily regimes of coercion and abuse?
>
> (Davis, 2012: 62)

That system, that society that could otherwise invest in services destined to democratize itself, to care for its citizens, uses the money to construct and operate prisons. That means that the prison industrial complex "reproduces the conditions of its own expansion, creating a syndrome of self-perpetuation" (Davis, 2012: 67).

As mentioned previously, the definition of crime is linked to the law. According to Davis, the fact that "the fundamental legal definition of crime is an action in violation of the law" (2012: 67) means that in any instance in which we disobey the law we have committed a crime. But what happens when the law itself only works to protect the interests and rights of the few because, among other reasons, the few depend on the prison industrial complex and its production of the social death of large segments of the population? And what happens to the very logic of the law—for example the laws that protect private property? Is this law not inherently ideological? (2012: 67–69). As has already been amply established through research, the idea of private property and the laws that sustain it are rooted in the efforts of early colonial powers to justify and legalize their exploitation of peoples and territories in the Americas, and they are also intimately linked to the idea that certain groups of people themselves can be other people's private property. And the idea that some people can be the private property of others is linked to racialization, more specifically to slavery.

Indeed, since slavery, racism has been associated with death (Davis, 2012: 175). Davis uses Ruth Gilmore's definition of racism that, as cited in the introduction to this chapter, involves "the state-sanctioned and/or legal production and exploitation of group-differentiated vulnerabilities to premature death, in distinct yet densely interconnected political geographies" (Gilmore, 2007: 28). According to Davis, "the death to which Gilmore refers is multidimensional, embracing corporeal death, social death, and civil death" (2012: 175). The point is that, since its inception, the institution of the prison has been linked to the political order of democracy because it demonstrates the centrality of the individual rights and liberties—in negative terms (2012: 175). The prison industrial complex reproduces those logics and continues those practices. In Mbembe's terms, the prison and the camps are death-worlds (2010). Let us return for a moment to the problem of social death. One of the most important aspects of slavery was the production of social death, which included civil and political death. That is, enslaved persons could not participate in political life, or in civil life. What does incarceration do? And what does non-citizenship do? The same: they prevent people from participating in political and civil life. By this, they are a *de facto* political and civil killing, especially in relation to racialized populations (Davis, 2012: 165–176).

One could perhaps argue that the idea of civil and political life is that it can be free from the participation of criminals. That we cannot have criminals participating in political and civil life. The problem is that if criminality—or lack of the same—is a standard that decides whether a person can or cannot participate in political and civil life, then this standard is not applied. In fact, many governments in the world include criminals—be they people who justify and carry out crimes against humanity, be they people who threaten, kill and kidnap in order to get to power or stay in power, be they people who profit from the drug trade, people who defend violence against women, etc.—yet all of them participate happily and in impunity in political and civil life. And then we have prisons and camps—prisons and camps restraining people who have organized politically against some of the above-mentioned problems: they have done what was in their power to change their situation of disadvantage and exclusion. While the first group—the elites—lives out its freedoms at the expense of the freedoms and wellbeing of the other groups, while they profit from the exploitation of people around the world carried out by transnational corporations, while they turn the health systems—including mental health systems—into systems that work against the health of the vast majorities, while they increase the numbers of impoverished people and divest children of a worthy future, it is the last, the wretched by the system, who will be the majorities inside the prison industrial complex, including the camps. And, as imprisoned people, the social death produced by not having access to health care, to quality education, to food, to a future with dignity—that very same social killing will be completed by a civil and political death. The lack of a future, the lack of *de facto* freedom outside and inside prison and camps, and the final civil and political killing off inside prison is equivalent to the social, civil and political death that we had during slavery.

Another important aspect in relation to the working of the prison industrial complex and immigration detention is security. The prison industrial complex sells an idea of false security; it presents itself as an institution that ultimately protects us from crime. However, crime, and with it law, protects the interests of the few at the expense of the freedom and dignity of the many. The idea of security is false because it is based on the idea that crime is something inherent to the human being—not in the fact that the social structures generate crime through the removal of people's dignity, their possibilities of life, of education, of health care. The generation of crime is part and parcel of the capitalist, racist and patriarchal system in which the prison industrial complex is central. The generation of crime is part of the system that produces second-class citizens, citizens who are candidates to incarceration, to being civilly and politically killed (Davis, 2012: 39–44). When the Critical Resistance movement speaks about the prison industrial complex—and not simply about the prison system—they do so because they are referring to an assemblage of economic and political relationships in which the penal system is rooted. That assemblage is global. The term "prison industrial complex" is used "to point out that there is a global proliferation of prisons and prisoners that is more clearly linked to economic and political structures and ideologies than to individual criminal conduct and efforts to curb crime" (2012: 147). They point to how the global expansion of the prison industrial complex corresponds with the global expansion of the transnational corporations (2012: 42–44). The so-called wars for democracy carried out by Western powers in the global South equate democracy with capitalism (2012: 145). To be more precise, it is a "democracy that uses capitalism as its model, that sees the free market as the paradigm for freedom and that sees competition as the paradigm for freedom" (2012: 145–146). This is intimately linked to the social killing mentioned earlier because the neoliberal idea of economic freedom requires that the state retract from all social services. In this logic, freedom emerges because the market determines the distribution of education, health and so on as if by divine providence (2012: 146). To Critical Resistance, that logic of freedom is inherently murderous, racist, anti-democratic and patriarchal.

Liberation and Freedom of Movements

As we have seen, the perspective on the prison industrial complex allows us to see several major problems related to the justice system, and it is useful to think through the conditions faced by people confined in migration detention camps, including Sjælsmark Deportation Centre. Firstly, the framework of thinking from which the justice system emerges excludes the majority of the population of the earth. Secondly, in practice, ideas like "freedom", "equality" and "dignity" protect the privileges of the few at the expense of the freedom, equality and dignity of the rest. They produce the civil, social and political death of the excluded majority. Thirdly, as an integral part of the juridical system, the prison industrial complex, including the camps, is built upon the legacy of slavery; it continues its racist logic and reproduces segregation. Finally, the prison industrial complex and the juridical system incarcerate the future. The prison industrial complex does so because it physically incarcerates large amounts of a population who could otherwise engage in political activism towards alternative and just futures. It is designed to crush dreams, to dismember communities, to depoliticize people. The juridical system goes hand in hand with the prison industrial complex, monopolizing the exercise of rights by, among other means, forcing social struggles to adapt to the dominant language and logic of rights. This means that the political projects, the futures that are dreamt and wished for by excluded social groups, do not have a space to be within the juridical system, but work, rather, as political imposition towards the struggles of the oppressed.

The work of Critical Resistance is an important contribution to understanding the complexity of the global injustice system. It points to the uni-versality of contemporary rights thinking: it verses around one logic, the one that underscores the racist, capitalist and patriarchal system. That uni-versality is intrinsic to the legal system, which, with the prison industrial complex, generates "crime" in order to be able to perpetuate itself. When Angela Davis affirms that some "futures are only possible through struggle" (2012: 36), she is speaking on the basis of the multidimensional analysis of the prison industrial complex. She is pointing at least to two fundamental concerns. On the one hand, she is referring to how the system as such works to close off the future of many people because it initially produces their social death. In the best of cases, people who have been socially killed—those who are deprived of access to health care, to food, to human compassion—will struggle against that very system that produces their death. Such is the case of the asylum seekers involved in the work of Freedom of Movements. In this case, the struggle itself is resistance to social death and it forges their right to participate in political and civil life. In the worst cases, people who have been socially killed will be imprisoned, or will suffer physical death before entering prison. The point here is that the very struggle against the racist, capitalist and patriarchal system is the very practice of freedom, it is an exercise of life. On this basis, Davis understands "the nature of freedom as forged by those who have had most at stake in the struggle for liberation" (2012: 196).

To Davis, the struggle of Critical Resistance against the prison industrial complex is a struggle for radical change that is not limited to the abolition of prisons, but that includes the construction of institutions that support the protection of health, education, social life and dignity of people—of everyone (20112: 115). The 11th demand of Freedom of Movement is, in line with this, concerned with the abolition of camps. The struggle against prisons and camps opens up the possibility to think of freedom as being something infinitely more fruitful and complex than the neoliberal freedom that is produced at the cost of the death of others. Struggle against these logics and against the system of oppression opens up fissures in the very system that allows us to think of rights not only through one sole logic and one sole lucrative interest, but in relation to the different realities generated by the very system in the first place. To think beyond those realities; that is, to think towards overcoming the racist, capitalist and patriarchal system of oppression, would imply the construction of institutions that support the construction of the fundamental conditions that we need in order to have different life projects, different futures, without one being at the cost of the other. They would be institutions that support freedom understood as Davis understands it: freedom as the collective search for real democracy, thus understanding freedom and the very practice of democratization of democracy. Freedom of Movements: social, political, economic and epistemological movements.

Notes

1 For a similar criticism of post-structuralist tendencies to de-materialize and de-politicize social problems, as well as to operate teleologically, see Flynn (2015). Flynn's analysis and argument could be significantly improved by taking into account Ruth Gilmore's seminal analysis of the prison industrial complex (2007).

2 For example, between "deprivation of liberty" and "restriction upon personal liberty". See Cornelisse (2010) for an in-depth discussion of these issues.

3 Information compiled through retsinformation.dk, a state-owned webpage where all the Danish legal texts are available. The relevant text in this case is: 'Bekendtgørelse af udlændingeloven': www.retsinformation.dk/forms/R0710.aspx?id=164258#Kap7, last visited on 27 January 2016.

4 All these problems have been covered thoroughly in the recent years through the European-wide research Project "TOLERACE: the Semantics of Tolerance and (Anti-)Racism in Europe" at: www.ces.uc.pt/tolerace.

References

Black, Richard (1998), "Putting Refugees in Camps", *Forced Migration Review*, 2, 4–7. Available at http://www.fmreview.org/camps.html

Cornelisse, Galina (2010), "Immigration Detention in Contemporary Europe", in Galina Cornelisse (ed.), *Immigration Detention and Human Rights: Rethinking Territorial Sovereignty*. Leiden: Martinus Nijhoff Publishers, 1–30.

Cox, Oliver Cromwell (1959), *Caste, Class and Race. A Study in Social Dynamics*. New York: Monthly Review Press.

Davis, Angela (2003), *Are Prisons Obsolete?* New York: Seven Stories Press.

Davis, Angela (2012), *The Meaning of Freedom and Other Difficult Dialogues*. San Francisco, CA: City Lights.

DuBois, W. E. B. (1903), *The Souls of Black Folk. Essays and Sketches*. Chicago, IL: A.C. McClurg & Co.

Fanon, Frantz (1967), *Black Skins White Masks*. London: Grove Press. Transl. by Charles Lam Markman.

Flynn, Matthew (2015), "Bureaucratic Capitalism and the Immigration Detention Complex", *Global Detention Project Working Paper No. 9*. Geneva: Global Detention Project. Available at http://www.globaldetentionproject.org/publications/bureaucratic -capitalism-and-immigration-detention-complex

Flynn, Michael (2012), "Who Must Be Detained? Proportionality as a Tool for Critiquing Immigration Detention Policy", *Refugee Survey Quarterly*, 31(3), 40–68. doi: 10.1093/ rsq/hds008

Flynn, Michael; Cannon, Cecilia (2009), "The Privatization of Immigration Detention: Towards a Global View", *Global Detention Project Working Paper*. Geneva: Global Detention Project. Available at http://www.globaldetentionproject.org/content/priv atization-immigration-detention-towards-global-view-0

Gill, Nick; Moran, Dominique; Conlon, Deirdre (2013), "Dialogues across Carceral Space. Migration, Mobility, Space and Agency", in Dominique Moran and Deirdre Conlon (eds.), *Carceral Spaces: Mobility and Agency in Imprisonment and Migrant Detention*. Farnham: Ashgate, 239–247.

Gilmore, Ruth (2007), *Golden Gulag. Prisons, Surplus, Crisis and Opposition in Globalizing California*. Los Angeles, CA: University of California Press.

Golash-Boza, Tanya (2009a), "A Confluence of Interests in Immigration Enforcement: How Politicians, the Media, and Corporations Profit from Immigration Policies Destined to Fail", *Sociology Compass*, 3(2), 283–294. doi: 10.1111/j.1751-9020.2008.00192.x

Golash-Boza, Tanya (2009b), "The Immigration Industrial Complex. Why We Enforce Immigration Policies Destined to Fail", *Sociology Compass*, 3(2), 295–309. doi: 10.1111/j.1751-9020.2008.00193.x

Gordon, Lewis (1999), *Bad Faith and Antiblack Racism*. New York: Humanity Books.

Grosfoguel, Ramón; Suárez-Krabbe, Julia (2013), "Letter to the European White Left", in *Alice Project & Popular University of Social Movements, Letters to the Europeans*. Coimbra: Alice Project and Popular University of Social Movements, 74–90. Available at http: //alice.ces.uc.pt/en/wp-content/uploads/2013/06/Letter-to-the-europeans-Book.pdf

Larsen, Birgitte Romme; Whyte, Zachary; Olwig, Karen Fogh (2015), *Den nye landbefolkning. Asylcentres betydning og konsekvens for lokale fællesskaber i danske landdistrikter*. København: Forfatterne og Institut for Antropologi, Københavns Universitet. Available at http://ant hropology.ku.dk/research/research-projects/current-projects/den-nye-landbefolkning/

Mbembe, Achille, (2010), "Necropolitics", *Public Culture*, 15(1), 11–40. doi: 10.1215/08992363-15-1-11

Mirza, Mansha (2014), "Refugee Camps, Asylum Detention, and the Geopolitics of Transnational Migration: Disability and Its Intersections with Humanitarian Confinement", in Liat Ben-Moshe, Chris Chapman and Allison Carey (eds.), *Disability Incarcerated: Imprisonment and Disability in the United States and Canada*. New York: Palgrave Macmillan, 217–236.

Moran, Dominique (2015), *Carceral Geography. Spaces and Practices of Incarceration*. Farnham: Ashgate.

Rembis, Michael (2014), "The New Asylums: Madness and Mass Incarceration in the Neoliberal Era", in Liat Ben-Moshe, Chris Chapman and Allison Carey (eds.), *Disability Incarcerated: Imprisonment and Disability in the United States and Canada*. New York: Palgrave Macmillan, 139–159.

Ryan, Mary K. (2010), "The Future of the Global Prison Industrial Complex", *Journal for the Study of Peace and Conflict, 2009–2010 Annual Edition*. Stevens Point, WI: Wisconsin Institute for Peace and Conflict Studies, 1–12. Available at http://www.uwsp.edu/cols-ap/WIPCS/Pages/journal.aspx

Santos, Boaventura de Sousa (1998), *De la mano de Alicia. Lo social y lo político en la postmodernidad*. Bogotá: Siglo del Hombre Editores y Uniandes Ediciones.

Santos, Boaventura de Sousa (2014), *Epistemologies of the South. Justice against Epistemicide*. London: Routledge.

Suárez-Krabbe, Julia (2015), *Race, Rights and Rebels. Alternatives to Human Rights and Development from the Global South*. London: Rowman & Littlefield.

Tesfahuney, Mekonnen; Dahlstedt, Magnus (2008), "Maze of Camps: (Im)mobilities, Racism and Spaces of Exception", in Maria Holmgren Troy and Elisabeth Wenö (eds.), *Space, Haunting, Discourse*. Newcastle, Cambridge Scholars Publishing, 172–201.

UNICEF & National University of Lanus (2010), *Economic, Social and Cultural Rights of Migrant Children and Children Born to Migrant Parents: Challenges, Good Practices and Recommendations*. United Nations Children's Fund (UNICEF) & National University of Lanus, Argentina. Accessed 15.11.13, at http://www.ohchr.org/Documents/Issues/MHR/Consultation2010/3a.UNICEF_ESCR_Migrants.pdf

Chapter 12

The Mediterranean as the EU Human Rights Boundary*

Angeles Castaño Madroñal

Inhuman Government

In the world of Marvel Comics, Triton was born a member of the Inhuman Royal Family. At the age of 18 he became an Inhuman explorer, watching over human maritime traffic around Attilan, the land of the Inhumans. According to the Marvel story, faced with undefined threats, Attilan was removed from the depths of the ocean to the Himalayas, relocated to the Island of Atlantis, then to the blue area of the Moon and from there was destined to float forever in space. It seems like a wonderful place to me, the only possible one for those who do not want to live with humans.

In the Mediterranean, traffic is patrolled by impersonal radars, trackers and inhumans, a fact incomprehensible to humanitarian humanity and therefore an insult to human intelligence. Known as "Triton", the Frontex maritime surveillance operation for the control and detention of immigrants in Italian waters, it came to life in the cold Olympian rooms of neoliberal post-modernity where EU policies are created. This is happening at the heart of an old Europe severely afflicted with senility and incapable of understanding or recognizing most of the grandchildren and great-grandchildren who are its heirs, the children of its colonization. It rejects them, locks them away and expels them beyond the perimeter where its eyes, half-blinded by cataracts, can still discern something of the disorder that has surrounded it throughout its lifetime.

Marvel is currently developing a big-screen version of its *Inhumans*, which is due to be launched on the global circuits of the culture industries in 2019. The EU creation has already been produced and has materialized as part of the political circuits and practices for border control, which are also global. This curious affinity could inspire an intriguing screenplay about parallel universes with universally identifiable codes for an exciting videogame to capture the attention of the new generations in the cybernetic interface (Manovich, 2005) in this urban existence immersed in the global screen-sphere of universal

* This chapter was developed through reflective scientific networks with the CES and working meetings and debates on global borders and the Mediterranean, in an enriching atmosphere of mutual collaboration with my companion and friend Paula Meneses in 2015 and 2016, shared with our companion and friend Juan Carlos Gimeno.

world-culture (Lipovetsky and Serroy, 2010): the consummate decoder of neo-mythologies reinvented within the aesthetics of a digital coloniality constructed from a radicalization of the inherited bases of modernity.[1] It is a symbolic parallelism that is more real than it seems at first glance. It is surprising how rarely fantasy is able to outperform reality or how often reality materializes in the most fantastic of human fantasies. Attracted by the plasticity of these parallels between the politics and the cultural products resulting from our modern-colonial imaginary, I have focussed on the situation in what I consider to be, in anthropological terms, "our shared Mediterranean", in an analysis which extends beyond the descriptive and genealogical nature of the politics that have led the Mediterranean peoples to this point. Given the very tragic nature of the horrors of political practices and their dramatic representation in the media, in these pages, I aim to show the context and the lingering coloniality which, in the twenty-first century, have consolidated division and separation in a Mediterranean that is both physical and symbolic, turning our coastlines into shocking mortuaries, our sea into a mass grave and plunging us into new shame before the world—a territory of new crimes against humanity to be inscribed in the history of genocidal violence in Europe.

It is curious how both the actions of *realpolitik* and the impulses of an imaginary that is socialized and shared amongst all consumers, naturally including EU technocrats, are aligned and confirm the endurance of a tradition learned from the way in which we, as Europeans, relate to the world (Said, 1991, 1996). These manifestations, which relate the practice of power in the global age to the hard, dichotomous outline of the totalitarian imaginary shown in the Marvel universe, reveal the persistence of a dual, opposed imaginary, a pragmatic reflection of abyssal thinking (Santos, 2010) and the cultural products of its imaginary, in which a few small chinks reveal other, unexplored possibilities. These are the many alternative possibilities that show us discomforting facts and deeply disturbed citizens, known as "activists" in *realmediatik* discourse, who launch themselves into the Aegean to rescue drifting humans—an action that cannot compete with the Aegean operation which carries out the same mission in Greek waters as Triton in the Italian seas.

By chance, or maybe not—I am inclined towards the latter—the world of Marvel and the world of the EU have constructed their inhumans, some adapted to the consumer styles of the culture industry and others to the consumption of the transnational policies of neoliberal post-modernity, both global in scope. If, in the fictitious cartoon world, Triton defends the Inhuman world of Attilan from humans, in terms of *realpolitik*, Frontex is the inexorable shield which defends "Fortress Europe" from insecurities on the Mediterranean coast caused by non-Europeans dehumanized in this new *weltpolitik* context. It is basically concerned with preventing non-Europeans from settling in the heart of "Fortress Europe": the fact that the colonizers think they are being colonized and/or invaded is a paradox. The totalitarian modernity of "comic" culture fuels this on a mass scale, more effectively than the national narratives of imagined communities (Anderson, 1993) found in boring history textbooks, the nationalist neo-fascisms of post-modernity. This thinking has left its mark on political practices in the twenty-first century, which continue to represent and reproduce a dichotomous world along the axes of the sterile abyssal thinking which addresses interculturality in this globalized world. Moreover, it draws on the legal and political reserves that construct the single European security area, "the abyssal global line that defines radical exclusion and legal nonexistence" in a "new abyssal colonial" context (Santos, 2009: 33–34).

"Triton" is both a fantasy creation and a surveillance operation serving a political fantasy. Fantasy is everything that has no real basis for its assumptions and is constructed from the imagination. The Eurocentric representation of migration and cultural diversity shares this characteristic, which is more typical of mythology than the real world. Both constructs are fictitious in the dual sense that both homonymous entities project: an individual with superpowers from a fantasy world, condemned in the Marvel comic saga to the cataclysm, and a prepotent, inappropriate political strategy for constructing the EU within the geopolitics of the economic blocs of globalization. Thus, Frontex is seen as a cornerstone of the Member States' coordinated management of their external borders, which includes security, control of flows and prevention of clandestine entry of individuals from the global South to the Mediterranean and to European territory.

Operation Triton has been operational since November 2014, when the Italian Prime Minister Renzi decided to abolish the maritime rescue system funded by the Italian budget, known as "Mare Nostrum"—a name which appealed to a shared past. However, following Renzi's requests for co-financing the rescue system, the EU ruled that its activities were not part of the Schengen area and therefore could not be co-funded. Clearly, this was how the migration pillar was structured within the shared "single area": Triton costs Italy only 38% of the operational expenses, with the remaining sum co-financed by the EU and contributions from the other Member States. After Mare Nostrum disappeared, deaths due to shipwrecks rose alarmingly,[2] but Lampedusa was very far away from Brussels and so small in the vast ocean that it was perfectly clear why it was invisible to the EU. Of course, since humans have a genetic survival instinct and a flexible capacity for adaptation, they eventually arrived, wretched bands of excluded human beings fleeing extinction. They have reached the external borders in their thousands, afflicting the media-focussed gaze of citizens. They arrive, by sea or by land, with almost all the possible frailties that can occur within the confines of the eastern zone and the fragmented maritime border: via the Aegean Sea to the Greek soil of Lesbos; via Idomeni to the border with Macedonia; from Röszke and Tomba to Hungary; via Ceuta to the Strait of Gibraltar; via Libya to Lampedusa. And by air, even though airport security checkpoints are deliberately invisible in the *realmediatik* of the global sphere-screen.

Analogue and digital borders (Lask and Winkin, 1995) construct contexts and spaces in which the renationalization of states clearly materializes within the paradoxes of economic and political transnationality. The technologization achieved within these territorial and symbolic transitional environments between boundaries reformulates and formats the legacies of modernity: they are the first to draw up the neocolonial map. The second to do so are the borders constructed for a privileged world and lifestyle which represents itself as shielded from the world's misery which, together with globalization, permeates the soil and the heart of its hegemonic centres. These borders provide an X-ray, from microcosms to mesocosms and macrocosms, of bodies in movement. Radars, satellites, millimetre wave and backscatter X-ray scanners track spaces and bodies. Nowadays, borders reveal systemic fragmentation in a way that no other construction can: even when they are liquid, Triton's radars can roam and navigate through them. Borders reveal privilege and exclusion, existence and non-existence, the circuits for communicating vessels and the watertight spaces, the exchange rate, the inputs and waste associated with all types of goods and bodies—whatever the nature of the body which passes through them. And, in addition, the calcified inconsistencies of the skeleton of the state, invested with modern anachronisms and spiritual hyperplasia.

Perhaps Schengen can hide the fact that the borders of globalization have broken the records for modernity. In this single area, new border topographies fragment our global cities, revealing the worlds which the many systemic expulsions (Sassen, 2015) are also constructing within the society we live in. It is hard, given the information overload from the media interface in which we are immersed, to perceive the breakdown of the failed Welfare State and the dismantling of the rule of law that has taken place in the past decade, more specifically since the financial crisis of 2008.

Thus, the dominant image communicates that the "Others" stay outside, lurking around the vigilant Triton. Humans on the lookout for a life do not disturb the virtual peace. Inhuman government aims to ensure a lunatic security—but security nevertheless, the cybermutants think or imagine. They will offer us, if need be, not the moon but the blue side at least.

The Construction of a Single Area

Attilan is a "comic" reflection of abyssal thinking and its cultural representations. This type of thinking is based on Eurocentric constructions of an imagined Europeanness in the face of the antagonistic Otherness of the rest of the world which does not share the new civilizational project. Attilan is a product of the dichotomous epistemology with which the West has constructed and absorbed a bipolar notion of the world inherited from modernity. It is a representation of a worn-out civilization which is feeling besieged, a world of inhuman Atlases with superpowers defending themselves from the destabilizing arbitrariness of the inferior humans who surround them. Is it not curious, this mirror image of an EU which conceives of itself as superior—in terms of civilization and technology—and protects itself from the migrant, displaced humanity, which it considers inferior and capable of destabilizing its cultural core, with an entire internal/external neocolonial political system based on political, economic and cultural relations designed for a new order within a world system in which it tries to preserve its hegemonies with minimum changes? How can we interpret the symbolic parallels between the ideas evoked by the Attilan of the Marvel Comics and the parallels in the technocratic minds of the EU, which has set Triton to patrol the twenty-first century Mediterranean? Why and how do these apparent anachronisms persist and reproduce themselves within contemporary political tools which are themselves the cultural products of the twentieth century, and how are they linked to the expulsion mechanisms of the global age?

When the Maastricht Treaty came into force in 1992, the US government began to proclaim the risks of "Fortress Europe syndrome", largely because of the obstacles and problems this could create in terms of the economic fluidity required for its specific state interests. The quarter of a century which followed laid the groundwork for eliminating these structural fears of neoliberalism but also revealed the very different meanings which "fortress" has acquired in the face of various types of expulsions on the edge of the system—peoples, economies and vital areas—as Sassen has analyzed, within the context of multidimensional crises in the current phase of predatory capitalism. It has been a phase marked by environmental extremes, economic violence, institutional and police violence, wars, changing values and a shift and reformulation of paradigms of thought. It is a period in which "the edge of the system is foundationally different from the geographic border in the interstate system" and is defined by a change from Keynesianism to globalism, characterized by "privatisations, deregulation and open borders for some", implying a change of phase—from one structured with the aim of attracting people into a consumer society to one which pushes them away and expels them (Sassen, 2015: 236). In my view, the "edge of the system" and the geographical and social borders share one analogous characteristic: they are places in which the entry–exit point for the actual context which creates them, creates and produces life in simultaneous presents. Although they are not acknowledged within the dominant scientific parameters, these presents exist and claim existence and conceptualization, to enable knowledge of other possible modes, which are increasing and are part of another globalization, to emerge (Santos, 2005; Gimeno and Castaño, 2014; Santos and Meneses, 2009; Meneses, 2016; Martins, 2016).

The Marvel content is implicit in this EU of cosmopolitan citizens who have the privilege of being able to move freely in the world in the imaginary of Europeanism which has emerged with the Schengen Agreement. The foundations of the ideological contents of imagined Europeanism can be found in Schengen, resting on a selective biopolitics which distinguishes between cultural natures, physically situated in people involved in the demographic movements produced within globalization. It is a foundation stone that cannot be separated from its base and historical roots, and one which constructs the meanings of Europeanism by setting the diversity of European nationals against the diversity of non-EU immigrants from the global South, who are seen as a destabilizing force. This foundational Agreement established a supranational "single area", which is unifying and exclusive from within and excluding and expulsive from the outside. In this sense, I consider the Schengen Agreement a marker of the change in the political nature of demographic movements in Europe.

I share with Arango the idea that the political nature of migration in Europe experienced an ideological turn in the second half of the 1970s when borders were closed during the Yom Kippur War and the Second Oil Crisis, with the emergence of the "zero immigration paradigm" and the notion of controlled admission of immigrants, in accordance with notions of sustainable limits for the host European Welfare States (Arango, 2005: 19–20). This context was constructed in the decade of change—the 1980s—and consolidated in operational terms from 1992 onwards when the Maastricht Treaty came into force. The template was created in 1995 with the policies for borders and internal/external EU circulation, materializing as a paradox: both the construction of a right and its negation. It has managed to establish a human right as a privilege exclusive to European citizens, and to deny a human right to people who, because they migrate, are inscribed in meanings associated with dehumanization. The privilege of freedom of movement is created for European citizens and the lack of this right is reserved for those from the global South who do not have citizenship credentials. However, the processes consolidate an order in which the free movement of this new *homo europaeus*, as produced by modernity, remains in the past and "the control and selection of people is the objective" (Arango, 2005: 18)—from now into the future, I would add. I will later attempt to explain the reasons which have led to this paradoxical situation for Europeans.

With the construction of the Schengen area, a semantic change is taking place which has a crucial influence on how migration is understood on the basis of modernity, given that it may be the most unavoidable activity to which the greater part of humanity is exposed within the environmental limits in which we find ourselves.

Refugees and Detention

Drawing on the Foucauldain notion of power present in the biopolitical content consumed under modernity, I find certain similarities between the systemic predatory surges in recent past history and the current imbalances. If we focus on Nazism and the other "isms" of European totalitarian regimes, the racial biopolitics which established the limits between the superior and inferior races was one of the axes of the systemic rationale for modernity at the heart of the colonial nation states. These ideologies constructed the idea of nation from the Hispanic national-Catholic master race in the case of Spain, or the Germanic Aryan master race in the case of Germany, to give two examples. I consider that what Sassen calls "the edges of the system", an "expulsion area" in the global era (2015: 248), is constructed on the basis of biopolitics—which remains structural in a system that expels people "to the other side of the line", beyond what is constructed as existing (Santos, 2010: 12)—and that some of the political instruments being used have parallels with these predatory and violent peaks. Borders and immigration policies reveal the endurance of the biopolitical content I have identified and their resemantization. Far from a return to including people within the line that defines existence, these policies package them up for indefinite periods of time in places defined by invisibility and non-existence. Although its discourse and semantics have been reformulated, biopolitics continues to act on the former colonial spaces through new forms of confinement, and also on the bodies which migrate to our cities from these places, using physical, mental and political incarceration mechanisms. The political limitations are enacted through "immigration laws" which impose obstacles to integration measures, and the mental and ideological limitations mean that the non-beings on the other side of the line remain associated with meanings constructed on the basis of colonial difference. Thus, the black African savage from the tribe and the hunter-gatherer subsistence economy camps in our cities, a new version of the semi-savage gathering a minimum wage by selling scarves by the traffic lights, at the entrance to the metro or around the parking lots, the transient non-places for beings in the urban jungles of the global cities. The crafty, swindling Moorish trader camps in his neighbourhood ghettos, moving within the available frameworks of an endogenous underground economy—whether in his own ethnic networks or the flows and exchanges of interests and resources involving impoverished local networks—in the niches of the precarious labour market which workers share in this brutal crisis. Schengen clearly establishes other supranational structural mechanisms to define the southern border of the Mediterranean in the form of EU migration control and internal security policies which particularly affect black African and/or Muslim African/oriental migration within the confines of its "single area". Within these limits, incarceration emerges, acting on bodies by using detention centres for foreigners and/or "humanitarian" camps.

In their extreme form, the Nazisms and fascisms of the twentieth century focussed on extermination and mass confinements in prisons or in the open air for reasons of race and/or ideological dissidence, deploying a logic—also extreme—of exploiting dehumanized people for the production of goods and the construction of infrastructures with minimum energy waste, until they were wiped out. They hunted and penned up groups of infra-humanized or dehumanized humans, cutting off their chances of escape through migration or exile.

In different parts of the world today we find people who, having exhausted the limits of the system, are held in sealed-off areas known as refugee camps or detention centres for immigrants. These are "humanitarian" closed areas, where they spend long stretches of their lives, sometimes years or generations.[3] The prevailing euphemism in these different types of produced and constructed non-existences considers them "humanitarian" places of confinement because they subsist between institutionalized humanitarian aid and informal economic transfers and activities, albeit in total invisibility and in environments in which access is controlled by "humanitarian" and "activist" operations. They are not exploited and are not needed as producers and consumers in the global age. They are completely irrelevant to the system: this is the difference.

Before the Second Wold War, the popular proverb "legs to take you anywhere you want" was a possible solution which worked for many people, since the mass identity and population registration system was weak and still not fully organized. Migrating was a form of social death—and therefore political death and consequently symbolic death—that could be used to pay off debts to society: there can be no non-existence in the collective present. Thus, migrating could be a transition to reincarnation in another place. Since 1492, America has been the great promised land for the socially or politically dead, but also for the citizen entrepreneur in search of glory and rewards. The Indians only remained the elite in the Spanish twentieth-century imaginary. These promising horizons were rapidly followed or completed by others within the colonial expansion of a Europe that had been outgrowing itself since the seventeenth century. Australia was first a prison on a continental scale for modern Anglo-Saxon social Darwinism before it was transformed into a promised land and its "conquest" continued. Africa, which was considered more indomitable and inaccessible, also received European adventurers, a process which lasted centuries although it accelerated from the eighteenth century onwards. However, whilst an imaginary of Asia was being constructed to position the Far East, civilizations that were thousands of years old remained cloistered in self-imposed isolation from the Western promise. The Asians really did not know what they were missing! Within this narrative, migration was, for 500 years, a possible solution for white men, or a great adventure for pioneers. It seemed that nothing could stop it.

At a certain phase in lives in movement, individuals could be seen as "foreigners", "outsiders" or "aliens", before eventually being recognized as "local", i.e. "from the area". Obviously, however, the semantics of proximity have always distinguished between colonial, "national" ancestry in the new independent states since the nineteenth century, and the (un)civilized associations of "native" and "indigenous" used to define the pre-Colombian peoples and their descendants. In Spanish, these terms exist alongside others filled with meanings that construct colonial difference and a whole range of physical and mental borders, which acquire their full multidimensional meaning within the hyper-contextual and situated sociohistorical framework. The connections established within the local context enable us to unravel the semantics of a densely charged language which has left its mark up to the present day. For example, there are the biologicist and essentialist meanings with which ethnogenetic limits and stigmas were established (Perceval, 1986, 2010; de Zayas, 2006) for those of Moorish, Gypsy and Marrano cultural origins in the dominated population, through a kind of biological determinism of the cultural or a particular racialization of culture in a historical sequence that has unfolded since the fifteenth century, following the end of the Western crusades in Al-Andalus and the subsequent Atlanticization of the Iberian empires.

As the European colonial empires entered a phase of full global expansion, with 85% of the Earth's surface already conquered (Said, 1991: 64), the First World War represented the first collapse of the Western colonial empires which, together with the mass movements of those displaced by war, gave rise to the notion of the "refugee"—via an agency created by the League of Nations which began functioning in 1921 as the High Commission for Refugees (Mariño, 1983). This notion was reformulated several times until the 1951 Geneva Convention on the Status of Refugees in the aftermath of the next great colonial collapse, namely the Second World War. However, we cannot ignore the fact that these formulations coexisted with other completely contradictory practices: these periods of progress in the rights of peoples in situations of extreme vulnerability resulting from the violence of modern nation states existed alongside crimes against humanity perpetrated by the same states. It is very similar to the present historical moment, in which the existing totalitarianism that can impose strategy in the global era implies that states violate human rights: civil rights and the Welfare State are eroded, while citizens rally to defend them.

Situations of war within colonial modernity led to the first mass roundups or confinements of populations in large walled spaces since the eighteenth century,[4] which were known as concentration or detention camps. This modern-colonial practice posits the first historical traces of the denial of the right to migrate and to mobility for vast civilian collectives identified as the enemies of public order and state security. They were considered infra-humans simply due to colonial difference, racial stigma, ethnicity or even psychological pathologies or disabilities which eugenics helped to construct as genetic defects, and this would eventually apply to those identified as ideological dissenters as well. The Second World War, in this sense, was the high point of totalitarianism, although not an exceptional conjuncture, despite the difference in the scale of its systemic dimensions. Hence, these practices were not uniquely localized but were used in many colonial states from the eighteenth century onwards. The historical records for the Nazi/fascist phase include the detention camps for over half a million Spanish Republican exiles in French beaches on the Mediterranean[5] and in the French Pyrenees, or the work camps for political prisoners in the Spanish protectorate in Morocco, and in different locations in Francoist Spain.

Yet, immediately after the second major systemic collapse, the urban, political, social and economic reconstruction of a Europe devastated by all these excesses led to the organized management and political promotion of migrations from the European colonial space in Africa, Asia and the European Mediterranean peripheries, such as Greece, Italy and Spain, and their Atlantic counterparts, such as Ireland and Portugal. Internal colonialism in different part of Europe and the colonies provided the framework for population movements and the migration policies and practices designed for the control, regulation, acquisition and mobilization of people viewed as resources.[6] These dynamics have turned modern migrations into a complex transnational system (Castles and Kosack, 1984; Castaño, 2003; Sassen, 2013) linked to the coloniality of the state policies (Castaño, 2016) and supranational policies of European nation states within globalization, subject to various factors within the political economy. Systemic relations between human displacement and migration within capitalism were therefore a reality in colonial slave empires, nineteenth-century modernity and the twentieth-century wartime and post-war periods, and a keynote from the 1950s and 1960s onwards until almost the mid-1970s. Thus, the method of treating and managing the population, whether predominantly national or foreign, within the major diachronic axes of history continues to reveal its role as an economic resource within the biopolitics of capitalism—a very different role from the one within which the ideals of human rights are framed.

The Schengen Agreement represents a further turn in the legal–political construction of people and non-people, which transforms and transmits the modern-colonial legacies to European space, altering the notion of citizenship from national to European and introducing profound changes to the relative freedom of movement observed during the Keynesian phase. The fact that in certain countries legislation has not been properly adapted to the laws which accommodate this new, binding space is illustrative of the endurance of this legacy, which lingers on in the historical sequel to their national, pre-EU tradition. This is the case in Spain with the *Organic Law 4/2000 of 11 January, on the rights and freedoms of foreign nationals living in Spain and their social integration*, to which must be added the amended version of 30 October 2015, which came into force on 1 January 2016—to cut short the long saga of almost yearly amendments—that has been known as the "law on foreigners" since the 1990s. However, in reality its negative aspects and applications do not affect foreigners in particular but the "new immigration" from countries in the South or, in other words, people who are not from the European and Western area established in Schengen. To be more precise, it was created for migrants who are not national citizens recognized and accredited by any EU state or its preferred partners, specifically those from any poor area of the global South. The language maintains features of the modern imaginary of the foreigner living in our land with the locals, but the current legal texts construct hierarchical categories, degrees of subalternity, obligations, rights and privileges that distinguish between people with various legal statuses resulting from the fact that they have chosen to live amongst us and not in their home country. The fundamental distinction is based on the notion of "immigrant"—conceptually elaborated for individuals who arrive in our cities due to "immigration" from the poor countries of the global South, a process that has nothing to do with "our" North. This immigration has become a complete social fact, in the Maussian conceptual sense, as defined in the legal texts: a phenomenon subject to intervention policies and a specific legal apparatus; a phenomenon conceived of as capable of altering *per se* the cultural nature of our European societies. In this way, thanks to the performativity of political discourse, the resulting "immigrant", a person who has moved here from their home country, loses their identity as a potential political and social subject and adopts the one created by this phenomenon: they become a subject for intervention.

This way of thinking is very different from the notion of "foreigner", which is etymologically different from "immigrant". The term "foreigner" was applied to outsiders arriving from distant lands and its semantics, filled with classical Graeco-Latin meanings and positive and negative potential, denoted subjects who had to construct their own future in European states which, in the aftermath of the Second World War, could not yet be considered Welfare States. This notion also supported the construction of national, as opposed to political, nature on the basis of *jus sanguinis* and/or *jus soli*, reflecting a clear, uniform sense of nation and nationality (de Lucas, 2001) embedded in the political tradition of the modern European nation state since the eighteenth century. The meanings applied to non-national foreigners also allowed for a certain freedom of movement for political exiles, due to the turbulent history of Europe in the twentieth century, with the emergence of the notion of the refugee. Spanish, Italian, Portuguese, East German, Russian and Polish refugees, amongst others, arrived in European metropolises such as Paris or Berlin, bringing new life to the most important projects being developed in the sciences and arts in the last century, which are nowadays symbolic of European progressiveness and its representation of freedom, democracy, justice and development. Nevertheless, I agree with Balibar (1994) on the fact that access to the legal status of citizen has, from the past to the present day, constituted an instrument for exclusion and has obstructed the complex process involved in constructing citizenship in the EU, associated with the modern legacies in the transnationality that has profoundly changed nation states.

The great change began in the 1980s and in 1995 Schengen produced a dizzying semantic volte-face, emerging as the new biopolitics of migration. Foreigners who were European citizens with freedom of movement and the power to choose to live in anywhere in the single area were rendered invisible by immigrants. Another (second) notion appeared, replete with the scientific heritage of Eurocentric rationality and contaminated with meanings that construct the object, which is assumed to be a phenomenon subject to the interventionist policies superimposed on the Agreement: immigration is a socioeconomic phenomenon and a political problem; it is not a matter of people with their own names, life experiences, knowledge and aspirations.

Dual Immobility

In its construction of borders, this policy also enables a new imaginary of the map of Europe to be outlined, a new idea of the single area, a reformulation of shared diversity and a new idea of transnational sovereignty. The Schengen

Agreement constructs the single area in the globalized word and its reformulated imaginary. The "People's Europe" aims to share its tradition in a new map which defines and draws up its external outlines as a sign of security in the face of the global South and denies the existence of internal divisions.

Within the social sciences, texts which, from different perspectives, address the policies within EU-ropeanization for analyzing various economic, education, migration and borders issues are already commonplace—this is inevitable. We are no longer simply nation states with a relative degree of sovereignty within a tightly knit territory. The process which has constructed the EU as a globalized and transnational political space culminated in the series of policies created in the 1980s following the stalemate of the 1979 Oil Crisis, whose effects between mid-1978 and 1981 created the shock of insecurity in the West. A strategic reordering therefore emerged, consolidating this new phase in the European nation states. In 1986 the Single European Act signalled a new political "waltz" in which the EEC would reinvent itself, get a makeover and be repositioned within the new geopolitics of the economic blocs, changing an entire political legacy and destined to produce an economic area without internal borders, which also required producing the "security state" envisaged in the Schengen Agreement. It is an imagined security area which is exploding in front of the media-influenced gaze of the Eurocentric (dis)information society. A space is being constructed which, in the last phase of expansion in 2011, resulted in a shared external border of 42,673 km of maritime borders and 7,721 km of land borders. A space for privilege and expulsion, it is ambivalent both internally and externally, and ambiguous in terms of its exclusive centres and exclusionist peripheries.

The Agreement has helped to construct a dual territory within the EU— superimposed onto the historical legacies of cultural diversity and the potential economic and political inequalities. A Mediterranean periphery is constructed as a southern border in the face of the migrations, flows and traffic crossing the globalized South while, thanks to this exterior belt, a central, northern Europe receives a more delayed form of immigration, the second experiential trajectory in the migration process of those who arrive in our states, already regularized and managed for several years in the Mediterranean periphery. Both territories are developing a different role in geopolitical terms: the Mediterranean countries are conditioned by their role as a border, controller and regulator of flows and "traffic"—a position assumed by these states and consolidated in the past two decades by dual state legislation that gives control priority over integration. This reality also constructs a dual policy of inequality and internal coloniality within the actual Mediterranean states themselves, where integration is not a priority and control has become a matter of borderlands. The EU borders establish the confines of the coloniality of the nation states in question. The creation of the "Mediterranean model" (Finotelli, 2007) for migration policies within the EU was defined by duality, both in terms of migration policies and the territorial representation of the border area occupied by the peripheries within the internal colonialism of the Euro-Mediterranean nation states, as is the case with Andalusia. One of the observable results of the imbalances in this model is the fact that, according to the dynamics of migration and political and economic convenience, a cyclical trend can be seen in media representations of immigrants and migration and in the discourse of power—wavering between cultural or even biological racism and authorized, institutionalized interculturality as the panacea for all the evils of immigrant multiculturalism (Castaño and Periáñez, 2012; Castaño, 2016).

The **authorized interculturality** has transferred an ideology genealogically situated in the axes of European multiculturalism to the Euro-Mediterranean peripheries, which then materializes in the empty discourse of integration policies. This interculturality emphasises the everyday social interactions established in public spaces and urban social areas, such as the points of contact involved in seeking and accessing state social services—a far cry from considerations of epistemological diversity and pluriversality presented in the epistemologies of the South and the value of translation (Santos and Meneses, 2009). Moreover, it supports the assimilationist meanings which revolve around notions of the cultural **adaptation** of minorities and their **normalization**. The transnationalization of this Eurocentric discourse on interculturality does not translate into a policy that has any impact on integration, since control of migration is the key political point, on the basis of which difference and inequality are constructed in these states. When Merkel announced in 2010, before the media, that multiculturalism had failed in Germany and that she was in favour of a review of Schengen, a diverging context for the abandonment of integration was firmly established, leaving a single policy centred on border control in the Mediterranean in the context of the financial crisis and austerity.

Like Martínez (2015), I believe that, 20 years after the Schengen area was first established, nothing has changed and that the dynamics of expulsion and the degrading treatment of immigrants are continuing or have worsened—the issues highlighted in the critical production of the social sciences at the end of the 1990s still exist and have intensified. The social sciences have been concerned with stressing the distorted link between the Schengen Agreement and the political framework for migration (Mestre, 2000; de Lucas, 2001; Gil, 2001, 2003; Álvarez, 2002; Castaño, 2003, amongst others), emphasizing that it was situated on the same axes as the illicit trafficking of certain goods, associated with organized crime and migration. The leap from scientific objectification to political objectification taken by the technocracy with regard to migration does not simply imply a form of denaturalization, but also contributes towards dehumanizing migrants, criminalizing their movements through the semantic transposition effected in terms of public and international (in)security—a process which I believe is similar to the one involved in transposing meanings within the sociological construction of race with "second-order Darwinism" from the end of the nineteenth century (Said, 1991). This was a transposition constructed from the imaginary, from which science, sociology, economics and politics were produced in accordance with the presuppositions of eugenics and which also spilled over into migration in the first half of the twentieth century (García and Álvarez, 2007). Two decades after it came into force, the earliest of the abovementioned studies which identified the Schengen Agreement as a framework for inequality and exclusion, have been proved correct. In my view, it is the supranational idea which shapes biopolitical meanings and the phenomenal and problematic nature of security contained in migrations from the South. It is a biased, reformulated framework, a mould which constructs meanings for migration and the single area, which penetrates via the specific legislation for the nation states of the Union.

This scientific production has noted that state policies derived from Schengen construct categories for immigrants according to their country of origin: EU citizens with the right to free movement, and non-EU migrants whose rights are restricted by migration policies that may or may not grant the right to live and work in its sovereign areas. Critiques of the notion of "illegals", which stigmatizes people who circulate without documents, makes the act of migrating a crime and turns migrants in this situation into delinquents, are still relevant two decades later, and it has become genocidal in nature when this illegality is applied to war refugees. These end-of-century policies establish a relationship between unregulated immigration and crime in a rhetorical synecdoche of unresolved linked concepts that involve migration—associated with people—international organized crime—drugs and arms trafficking—and international terrorism. Two decades after this protest, the exclusionist and totalitarian semantics have still not been reformulated.

Immigrants from non-EU countries in the global South form a specific category of stigmatized individuals who embody the part of the collective cultural whole positioned on the opposite side of the line by the legacies of the modern-colonial system and, as such, on the other side of the privilege of free movement reserved for European nationals. These immigrants bear cultural stigmas which add to the political legacies that have shaped the imaginary of the immigrant in Europe (Hesse and Sayyd, 2006), limiting the possibilities of integration and, in their extreme forms, circulating outside the established domains, whilst reinforcing them. This imaginary of the immigrant, dominated by Islamophobic distortion deposited and transmitted in European material and political culture (Said, 1991), is emerging with recurring virulence within the context of global terrorism, as could be observed during the Paris attacks in 2015: *Charlie Hebdo*, in January, and the 13 November attack. It is also part of the justifications—for reasons of security—for closing off the interstate borders of peripheral Member States facing the arrival of asylum seekers from war zones such as Syria, Afghanistan and Iraq. It is, in fact, a partial dismantling of Schengen: the sealing of internal national borders which ultranationalist governments consider too fluid in the face of the implosion of violence produced by global imbalances.

This rupture with ideas established as human rights and enshrined in the 1951 Geneva Convention is becoming increasingly unsustainable to the triumphalist teleology of human rights identified in the introduction of this book. In the initial stages when refugees arrived in Europe in the context of the war in Syria in 2014, the tendency within discursive representations was to establish a political distinction between the status of immigrants and that of refuges. The refugee drama mobilized a humanitarian discourse which took as its banner the historical memory of the Second World War, in order to demand a political response within the terms of the Convention. It seemed that two categories of people were being established, with different rights: those legitimized by the Convention and those demeaned by the institutional violation of human rights. According to the quantitative data, both types of flows were comparable throughout 2015 and a symbiosis was produced, involving the same political treatment for both. However, during the terrorist crisis, Islamophobia dominated in representations of refugees and the assimilation of immigrants. As when border states wavered over the possibility of "shock" expulsion that would ignore the remaining legal constraints, as was the case with the Spanish border in Ceuta, there came the "inevitable" shipwrecks in Lampedusa, followed by the export of barbed wire fences made in Murcia, which were installed on the borders of Macedonia and Hungary as "good practice"—given their success in Spain—and then the construction of concentration camps for refugees, such as the one in Idomeni on the Macedonian border, which was attacked by soldiers using tear gas. The distortions reach their peak in the political discourses which claim that the control operation in the Mediterranean is associated with "military humanitarianism", despite the contradiction in terms, considering that acting "selectively" against the mafias is a means of dissuading immigrants from using them and vice-versa. The "humanitarian war" is an innovation of neoliberal global totalitarianism that has been formulated repeatedly in recent times, ever since NATO, situated in the "axis of good", organized a war against the "axis of evil" to bring "democracy and freedom" to Iraq in 2003. Responsibility for the mythical use of mafias as people smugglers in militarized border zones has shifted to the refugees and has made a significant contribution towards sanitizing the state violence that protects the borders to humanity.

World traffic reveals the enormous violence of the contradictions contained in this phase of globalization: the liberalization of global flows of commodities and financial trading has put an end to national restrictions and sovereignties, consolidating vast transition economy regions and tax havens whilst also constructing the compartmentalization of (human) beings and non-beings, at state and regional level. Beings are confined to the secure regions of the North, since the implosion of chaos which produces systemic imbalances and socioeconomic polarization, on which neocolonial state interdependence is constructed, produces violence in multiple locations due to "global terrorism" in large regions of the South. Some of the targets of this violence have been tourist resorts, constructed as exotic paradises made accessible by the global development of cultural diversity for tourism. The impression of a world at war transcends the UNHCR reports: sunbathing on a hotel beach is now considered risk tourism in many areas in the South following the assassination of 39 tourists on the beaches of Tunisia—in a Spanish hotel—by a lone Islamic State gunman on 26 June 2015. We are therefore standing at a crossroads where it may be said that on this side of the line of being, a state of "involuntary immobility" (Carling, 2002) is produced due to the erosion of human rights, leading to white privilege in the global era.

Non-beings find themselves in sealed-off states, due to the solidification and shielding of external borders in the vast transition zones to the North, such as the Mediterranean and the Mexican border. Both Southern borders define geostrategic South–North transition zones, although they are not the only sealed borders. Non-beings have been excluded from the privilege of free movement to or from the North, which prevents them from moving beyond neighbouring interstate borders subject to other political and symbolic frameworks within the post-coloniality of the South. Therefore, it may also be said that the modern attack on freedom of movement constructs an age of involuntary immobility (Carling, 2002) and that systemic expulsions (Sassen, 2015) create human waste (Bauman, 2005) embodied in the internal nobodies (Galeano, 1993) and external infra-humans waiting for a chance for life on the other side of the many borders.

Notes

1 I understand modernity on the basis of the aspects described in the perspective on the modernity/coloniality of power/knowledge/existence developed in the work of Dussel (2000), Lander (2000), Quijano (2000) and Mignolo (2003), and also the importance of revealing its processes—to establish a starting point to determine the bases of a new political culture and the production of a sociology of absences and emergences—in order to understand and make contemporary processes visible, which Santos (2005) develops in his work.

2 The International Organisation for Migration (IOM) reported on 5 July 2016 that 222,316 migrants and refugees had arrived in the EU via the Mediterranean, on the Greek, Italian, Cypriot and Spanish coasts; 2,920 people died at sea, compared to a total of 1,828 in 2015; 2,499 of those who perished died in the Italian islands, 376 in the Aegean and 45 in the Strait of Gibraltar. Consulted on 9 July 2016 at: www.iom.int/es/node/76195.

3 According to the UNHCR, in 2014, over 59,500,000 million people were refugees. These cases, which are claimed to be exceptions, are increasing: the total number of refugee camps, many of them indefinite, is currently 25—although none of the examples mentioned in this report match the dimensions of Gaza as a walled-off zone (UNHCR, *Mundo en Guerra. Tendencias Globales. Desplazamiento Forzado en 2014*). In Spain, there are currently 8 refugee detention centres which can hold immigrants who have no documents for 18 months, according to the European "Return" Directive (2008/115/CE). The continual degradation in these centres and flagrant violation of rights have been denounced by the Working Party of the Southern Border and Human Rights civil movement, which has been campaigning for the state to close detention centres since 2015. Consulted on 3 June 2015 at: https://fronterasurderechoshumanos.wordpress.com

4 In the eighteenth century, the Russians had already rounded up Polish subjects for deportation to Siberia. In the final phase of the Boer War, the British in South Africa constructed 45 concentration camps for Boers and 65 for black Africans, in which more than 25% of the over 100,000 prisoners died. At the beginning of the First World War, Thalerhof went down in history as the first Austro-Hungarian concentration camp for non-combatant civilians, where 20,000 individuals were tortured and maltreated until they died. Mass imprisonment of civilians is a modern invention of the colonial empires.

5 The historical memory movement in Spain is emerging in the light of the lack of historiography for the Spanish nation state, which I believe has been buried in the geopolitical interests of the Spanish Transition, linked to the reconfiguration of Europe in the 1980s. The platform www.todoslosnombres.org is a useful tool, and one of the most important works on audio-visual Andalusian anthropology is the volume by Ángel del Río (2014).

6 Internal colonialism in Spain during the Franco period led to internal south–north migration in the direction of Catalonia, Madrid and the Basque Country. Certain state regulatory measures which were used reveal its systemic dimensions and the effects in Andalusia. I have adopted the term "internal colonialism" from the work of González Casanova (1965) and Stavenhagen (1968).

References

Álvarez, Ignasi (2002), "La construcción del inintegrable cultural", in Javier de Lucas and Francisco Torres (eds.), *Inmigrantes, ¿cómo los tenemos?: algunos desafíos y (malas) respuestas*. Madrid: Talasa, 168–195.

Anderson, Benedict (1993), *Comunidades imaginadas*. Cidade do México: Fondo de Cultura Económica.

Arango, Joaquín (2005), "Dificultades y dilemas de la política de inmigración", *Arbor*, 181(713), 17–25. doi: 10.3989/arbor.2005.i713.439

Balibar, Etienne (1994), "¿Es posible una ciudadanía europea?", *Revista internacional de filosofía política*, 4, 22–40. Available at https://dialnet.unirioja.es/servlet/articulo?codigo =2704649

Bauman, Zygmunt (2005), *Vidas desperdiciadas: la modernidad y sus parias*. Barcelona: Paidós Ibérica.

Carling, Jørgen (2002), "Migration in the Age of Involuntary Immobility: Theoretical Reflections and Cape Verdean Experiences", *Journal of Migration and Ethnic Studies*, 28(1), 5–42. doi: 10.1080/13691830120103912

Castaño, Ángeles (2003), "Inmigración y relaciones interétnicas. ¿particularidades locales o procesos globales?", in Sandra Gil and Mohammed Dahiri (eds.), *Movimientos migratorios en el Mediterráneo occidental, ¿un fenómeno o un problema?* Córdova: Ayuntamiento de Córdoba, 169–182.

Castaño, Ángeles (2016), "Colonialidad interna y europeidad en la política para la inmigración en Andalucía", *Revista Andaluza de Antropología*, 10, 192–222. Available at http://www .revistaandaluzadeantropologia.org/uploads/raa/n10/castano.pdf

Castaño, Ángeles; Periáñez, Iván (2012), "Digital Press Discourses and Representations on Immigration, Islam and Immigrant Students in Andalusia", *Working Paper n.º 5. Projeto TOLERACE, 7th EU Framework Programme*. Available at http://www.ces.uc.pt/proj ectos/tolerace/media/Working%20paper%205/Digital%20Press%20Discourses%20and

%20Representations%20on%20Immigration%20Islam%20and%20Immigrant%20Stud
ents%20in%20Andalusia.pdf

Castles, Stephen; Kosack, Godula (1984), *Los trabajadores inmigrantes y la estructura de clases en la Europa Occidental*. Cidade do México: Fondo de Cultura Económica.

De Lucas, Javier (2001), "Hacia una ciudadanía euopea inclusiva. Su extensión a los inmigrantes", *Revista Cidob d'Afers Internacionals*, 53, 63–75. Available at http://www .cidob.org/es/media2/publicacions/afers/53/lucas_53

De Zayas, Rodrigo (2006), *Los moriscos y el racismo de estado. Creación, persecución y deportación (14991612)*. Córdova: Almuzara.

Del Río, Ángel (2014), *Memoria de las cenizas: Andaluces en los campos nazis*. Sevilha: Aconcagua.

Dussel, Enrique (2000), "Europa, modernidad y eurocentrismo", in Edgardo Lander (ed.), *La colonialidad del saber: eurocentrismo y ciencias sociales. Perspectivas Latinoamericanas*. Buenos Aires: CLACSO, 24–33. Accessed 8.05.2014, at http://bibliotecavirtual.clacso.org.ar/c lacso/sur-sur/20100708034410/lander.pdf

Finotelli, Claudia (2007), "Italia, España y el modelo mediterráneo en el siglo XXI", *Demografía, Población y Migraciones Internacionales, ARI Nº 58*. Accessed 30.06.2014, at http://www.realinstitutoelcano.org/wps/portal/rielcano/contenido?WCM_GLOBAL _CONTEXT=/elcano/elcano_es/zonas_es/demografia+y+poblacion/ari+58-2007

Galeano, Eduardo (1993), *El libro de los abrazos*. Madrid: Siglo XXI.

García González, Armando; Álvarez, Raquel (2007), *Las trampas del poder. Sanidad, eugenesia y migración. Cuba y Estados Unidos (1900–1940)*. Madrid: CSIC.

Gil, Sandra (2001), "Políticas migratorias de la Unión Europea: desplazando las fronteras", *Revista Viento Sur*, 56, 81–88. Available at http://vientosur.info/spip.php?article2004

Gil, Sandra (2003), "Las migraciones en las políticas de la fortaleza. Sobre las múltiples fronteras de la Europa comunitaria", in Sandra Gil and Mohammed Dahiri (eds.), *Movimientos migratorios en el Mediterráneo occidental, ¿un fenómeno o un problema?* Córdova: Ayuntamiento de Córdoba, 31–58.

Gimeno, Juan Carlos; Castaño, Ángeles (2014), "Antropología y descolonialidad. Desafíos etnográficos y descolonización de las metodologías", *Periferias, Fronteras y diálogos. Actas del XIII Congreso de Antropología de la FAAEE*. Tarragona: Universitat Rovira i Virgili, 3432–3446. Available at http://digital.publicacionsurv.cat/index.php/purv/catalog/book/123

González Casanova, Pablo (1965), "Internal Colonialism and National Development", *Studies in Comparative International Development*, 1(4), 27–37. doi: 10.1007/BF02800542

Hesse, Barnor; Sayyid, Salman (2006), "Narrating the Postcolonial Political and the Inmigrant Imaginary", in Nasreen Ali, Virinder S. Karla and Salman Sayyid (eds.), *A Postcolonial People. South Asians in Britain*. London: Hurst, 13–31.

Lander, Edgardo (2000), "Ciencias sociales: saberes coloniales y eurocéntricos", in Edgardo Lander (ed.), *La colonialidad del saber: eurocentrismo y ciencias sociales—perspectivas latinoamericanas*. Buenos Aires: CLACSO, 4–23. Accessed 8.05.2014, at http://bibliote cavirtual.clacso.org.ar/clacso/sur-sur/20100708034410/lander.pdf

Lask, Tomke; Winkin, Yves (1995), "Avant-propos: frontières visibles/frontières invisibles", *Quaderni*, 27(1), 59–64. Available at http://www.persee.fr/doc/quad_0987-1381_1995_ num_27_1_1123

Lipovetsky, Gilles; Serroy, Jean (2010), *La cultura-mundo. Respuesta a una sociedad desorientada*. Barcelona: Anagrama.

Manovich, Lev (2005), *El lenguaje de los nuevos medios de comunicación*. Barcelona: Paidós.

Mariño, Fernando M. (1983), "El Concepto de refugiado en un context de derecho internacional general", *Revista Española de Derecho Internacional*, 35(2), 337–370.

Martínez, Ubaldo (2015), "La invasión de los inmigrantes y el racismo. El eterno retorno de lo igual", *Revista Estudios y Cultura*, 72, 24–31. Available at http://www.1mayo.cco o.es/nova/NPcd/GestorPublicacionesVis?cod_primaria=1442&cod_publicacion=3027

Martins, Bruno Sena (2016), "Antropología y poscolonialismo. La memoria postabismal", *Revista andaluza de antropología*, 10, 102–118. Available at http://www.revistaandaluz adeantropologia.org/uploads/raa/n10/sena.pdf

Meneses, Maria Paula (2016), "Ampliando las epistemologías del Sur a partir de los sabores: diálogos desde los saberes de las mujeres de Mozambique", *Revista Andaluza de Antropología*, 10, 10–28. Available at http://www.revistaandaluzadeantropologia.org/ uploads/raa/n10/meneses.pdf

Mestre, Ruth (2000), "Género y migración en el Estado español", *Revista Mugak*, 9/10, 11–16.

Mignolo, Walter D. (2003), *Historias Locales/diseños globales. Colonialidad, conocimientos subalternos y pensamiento fronterizo*. Madrid: Akal.

Perceval, José María (1986), "Algarabía: ¿lengua o alboroto callejero?" *Manuscrits: Revista d'història moderna*, 3, 117–127. Available at http://www.raco.cat/index.php/Manuscrits /article/view/56814

Perceval, José María (2010), "Repensar la expulsión 400 años después: del "todos no son uno" al estudio de la complejidad morisca", *AWRAQ*, 1, 119–136. Available at http:// www.awraq.es/indice/resumen-palabras-clave.aspx?a=43

Quijano, Aníbal (2000), "Colonialidad del poder, eurocentrismo y América Latina", in Edgardo Lander (ed.), *La colonialidad del saber: eurocentrismo y ciencias sociales—perspectivas Latinoamericanas*. Buenos Aires: CLACSO, 122–151. Accessed on 8.05.2014 at http://bib liotecavirtual.clacso.org.ar/clacso/sur-sur/20100708034410/lander.pdf

Said, Edward W. (1991), *Orientalismo*. Madrid: Libertarias.

Said, Edward W. (1996), *Cultura e imperialismo*. Barcelona: Anagrama.

Santos, Boaventura de Sousa (2005), *El milenio huérfano. Ensayos para una nueva cultura política*. Madrid: Trotta.

Santos, Boaventura de Sousa (2009), "Para além do pensamento abissal: Das linhas globais a uma ecología de saberes", in Boaventura de Sousa Santos and Maria Paula Meneses (eds.), *Epistemologias do Sul*. Coimbra: Almedina, 23–71.

Santos, Boaventura de Sousa (2010), *Para descolonizar Occidente. Más allá del pensamiento abismal*. Buenos Aires: Prometeo Libros.

Santos, Boaventura de Sousa; Meneses, Maria Paula (eds.) (2009), *Epistemologias do Sul*. Coimbra: Almedina.

Sassen, Saskia (2013), *Inmigrantes y ciudadanos. De las migraciones masivas a la Europa fortaleza*. Madrid: Siglo XXI.

Sassen, Saskia (2015), *Expulsiones. Brutalidad y complejidad en la economía global*. Madrid: Katz.

Stavenhagen, Rodolfo (1968), "Clases, colonialismo y aculturación. Ensayo sobre un sistema de relaciones interétnicas en Mesoamérica", *Cuadernos del Seminario de Integración Social Guatemalteca*, 19. Guatemala: Ministerio de Educación.

Conclusion

Boaventura de Sousa Santos and Bruno Sena Martins

The aim of this book has been to think critically about what human rights are, and could be, if recreated within the vast pluriverse of the countless languages of dignity mobilized throughout the world in struggles against unjust suffering caused by capitalist, colonialist and patriarchal oppression. In different ways, the research and theoretical reflections contained in this volume enable us to rethink the future of human rights in close connection with the epistemologies of the South. In this book, learning from the South involves recognizing that human rights are a part of, and a reflection of, the epistemological and political exhaustion which blights Eurocentric critical thinking. According to modern critical thinking—where the maximum possible awareness in Western modernity can be found—humanity was envisaged as a given fact, not an aspiration. It was believed that the whole of humanity could be emancipated using the same mechanisms and principles, by appealing to trustworthy institutions founded on the idea that all men and women are equal in the eyes of the law. At the heart of this modernist imagination there has always been the idea of humanity as a whole, based on a common project: universal human rights.

This book has sought to reveal the limitations of the modernist imagination by examining conventional human rights. For the epistemologies of the South, in order to avoid wasting experience, it is essential to critically examine human rights to identify its limits but, at the same time, mobilize it in intercultural dialogue with other narratives of dignity and concepts of humanity constructed in different regions of the world. This perspective calls on us to believe that human rights can be salvaged for fruitful dialogue that challenges hierarchical concepts of humanity, repositioning the renewed concept of social emancipation within political ontologies which express an insurgent humanity.

As a response to global learning directed towards the political meaning of being human, the "ecology of knowledges" and "intercultural translation" are the two most significant procedures within the epistemologies of the South which address the political and ontological post-abyssal sense of human dignity. The ecology of knowledges has proved fundamental in calling for dehumanizing and epistemicidal processes to be transformed into a validation of non-Eurocentric knowledge, which is then understood as a potential source of learning, shaped by the past and full of future potential. We are referring here to knowledge which, in the light of modern Western science and in the wake of colonialism, had been stripped of the dignity of possessing a voice that conveyed wisdom. Intercultural translation, in turn, plays a central role in this book due to the way in which it seeks to transform incommunicability and devastating violence into a difficult but challenging dialogue between different concepts of dignity. In this sense, intercultural translation has been crucial to an agenda which reconciles cognitive and historical justice. Essentially, intercultural translation aims to establish a conversation between worlds which have been invalidated and the world defined as the centre which validates: a world based on inherited privilege, exploitation of the other and an abyssal view of the human.

This book has placed particular emphasis on how human borders shape conventional human rights, clearly revealing the urgency of making visible the historical and political processes that produce the systematic disqualification of populations defined as less human or sub-human. The construction of the modern, Eurocentric idea of the human therefore emerges as situated in the abyssal lines of modernity from which it was created. The book also exposes the way in which conventional human rights naturalize these abysses through their proclamations of universality which, when allied to colonial and imperialist processes or unable to confront them in any radical sense, have been instrumental in extending the supremacy of a Eurocentric version of humanity throughout the world. The force with which the borders of the human restrict the possibilities for diversity in the world in which we live has been countered by the force with which these borders are denounced and displaced by those who refuse to accept a reality without hope. Hope, albeit emerging subtly in multiple ways, is nevertheless the most inspiring feature of this book. It is our conviction that these texts, drawing on countless struggles in a wide variety of places throughout the world, will contribute towards a post-abyssal reinvention of human rights.